# Congress at War

# CONGRESS at WAR

*How Republican Reformers*
*Fought the Civil War,*
*Defied Lincoln,*
*Ended Slavery,*
*and Remade America*

## Fergus M. Bordewich

Alfred A. Knopf   New York   2020

THIS IS A BORZOI BOOK
PUBLISHED BY ALFRED A. KNOPF

Copyright © 2020 by Fergus M. Bordewich
Maps copyright © 2020 by David Lindroth Inc.

www.aaknopf.com

Knopf, Borzoi Books, and the colophon are registered trademarks of
Penguin Random House LLC.

All photos are courtesy of Library of Congress except the following:
the profile of Sen. William Pitt Fessenden from Bowdoin College Library,
Special Collections and the "Scene in the Hall of Representatives"
from the Office of the United States Senate Curator.

Library of Congress Cataloging-in-Publication Data
Names: Bordewich, Fergus M., author.
Title: Congress at War : How Republican Reformers Fought the Civil War,
Defied Lincoln, Ended Slavery, and Remade America / by Fergus M. Bordewich.
Description: First edition. | New York : Alfred A. Knopf, 2020. |
"A Borzoi Book." | Includes bibliographical references and index.
Identifiers: LCCN 2019015354 (print) | ISBN 9780451494443 (hardcover) |
ISBN 9780451494450 (ebook)
Subjects: LCSH: Republican Party (U.S. : 1854–)—History—19th century. |
United States—Politics and government—1861–1865. | United States. Congress—
History—19th century. | United States—History—Civil War, 1861–1865. |
Social change—United States—History—19th century.
Classification: LCC E459 .B745 2020 (print) | LCC E459 (ebook) |
DDC 324.2734—dc23
LC record available at https://lccn.loc.gov/2019015354

Front-of-jacket image: North Wind Picture Archives / Alamy
Jacket background image: Lightix/Shutterstock
Jacket design by John Vorhees

Manufactured in the United States of America
First Edition

*In memory of my forebears*
*John Madigan, Patrick Madigan, and James Patrick Farrell,*
*volunteers for the Union, 1861 to 1865.*

I would not have perfect quiet always,
in a republic especially. You never find quiet
except under a tyranny.

—SEN. WILLIAM PITT FESSENDEN

The Angel of Liberty has one ear of the
nation and the demon of slavery the other.

—FREDERICK DOUGLASS

# CONTENTS

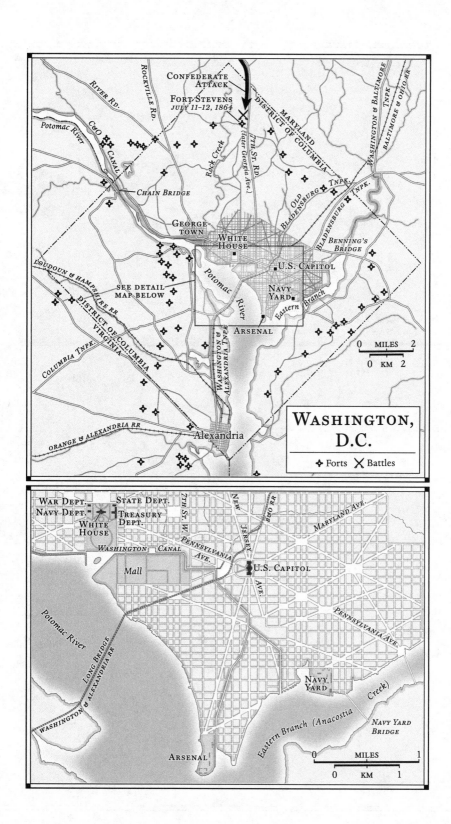

CONFEDERATE
ATTACK

FORT STEVENS
*JULY 11–12, 1864*

RIVER RD.

ROCKVILLE RD.

*Potomac River*

C&O CANAL

*Rock Creek*

7TH ST. RD.
*(later Georgia Ave.)*

MARYLAND

DISTRICT OF COLUMBIA

WASHINGTON & BALTIMORE TNPK.

BALTIMORE & OHIO RR

*Chain Bridge*

GEORGE-
TOWN

WHITE
HOUSE

OLD BLADENSBURG TNPK.

BLADENSBURG TNPK.

BENNING'S
BRIDGE

LOUDOUN & HAMPSHIRE RR

SEE DETAIL
MAP BELOW

*Potomac River*

U.S. CAPITOL

NAVY
YARD

*Eastern Branch*

DISTRICT OF COLUMBIA

VIRGINIA

COLUMBIA TNPK.

WASHINGTON & ALEXANDRIA TNPK.

ARSENAL

0    MILES    2
0    KM    2

ORANGE & ALEXANDRIA RR

Alexandria

# WASHINGTON,
# D.C.

✢ Forts   ✕ Battles

WAR DEPT.
NAVY DEPT.

STATE DEPT.

7TH ST. W.

NEW JERSEY

B&O RR

TREASURY
DEPT.

WHITE
HOUSE

MARYLAND AVE.

*Washington Canal*

PENNSYLVANIA AVE.

*Mall*

U.S. CAPITOL

PENNSYLVANIA AVE.

*Potomac River*

LONG BRIDGE

WASHINGTON & ALEXANDRIA RR

NAVY
YARD

*Eastern Branch (Anacostia Creek)*

NAVY YARD
BRIDGE

ARSENAL

0    MILES    1
0    KM    1

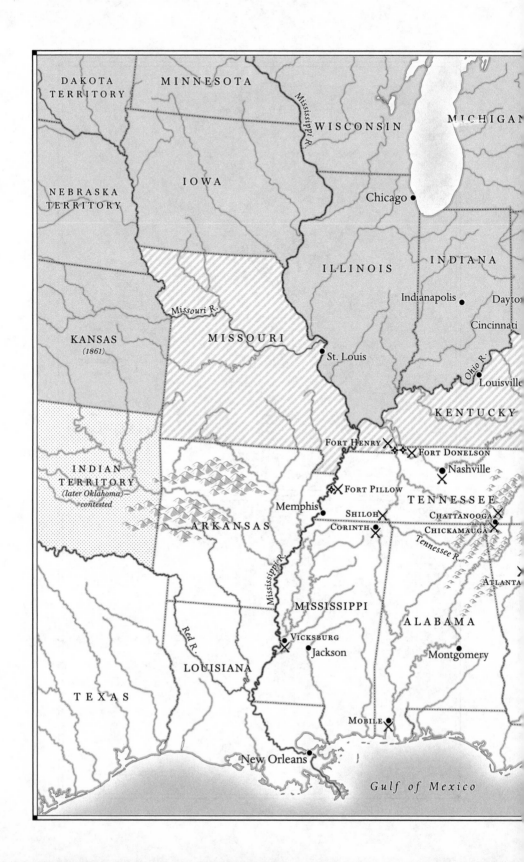

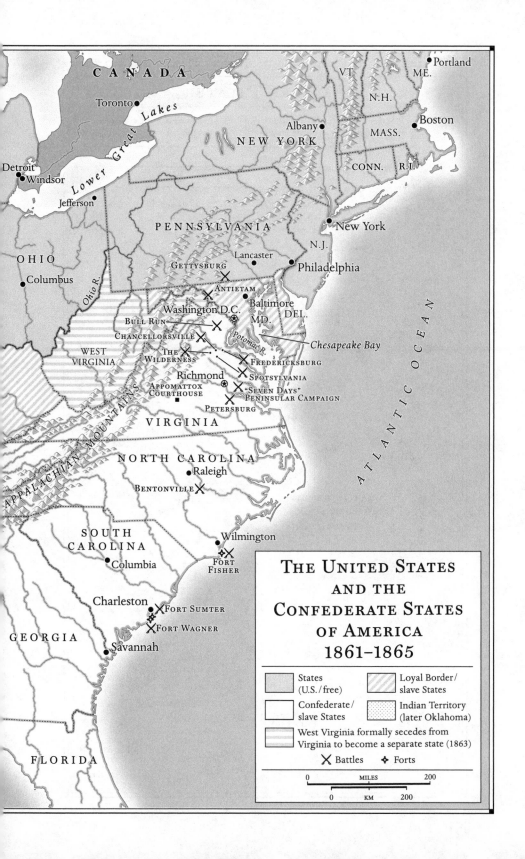

CANADA

Toronto

*Lower Great Lakes*

Detroit
Windsor
Jefferson

OHIO
Columbus

*Ohio R.*

WEST
VIRGINIA

Portland
ME.

VT.
N.H.

Albany
MASS.
Boston

NEW YORK
CONN.   R.I.

PENNSYLVANIA

Lancaster
GETTYSBURG ✕
ANTIETAM ✕
Washington D.C. ⊗
BULL RUN ✕
CHANCELLORSVILLE ✕
THE ✕
WILDERNESS
Richmond ⊗
APPOMATTOX
COURTHOUSE ■
PETERSBURG ✕

Philadelphia

N.J.

New York

Baltimore
MD.   DEL.

*Potomac R.*
FREDERICKSBURG ✕
SPOTSYLVANIA ✕
"SEVEN DAYS" ✕
PENINSULAR CAMPAIGN

*Chesapeake Bay*

VIRGINIA

*APPALACHIAN MOUNTAINS*

NORTH CAROLINA

Raleigh

BENTONVILLE ✕

Wilmington

FORT ✕✕
FISHER

SOUTH
CAROLINA
Columbia

Charleston ✕ FORT SUMTER
⊗✕ FORT WAGNER

GEORGIA
Savannah

FLORIDA

*ATLANTIC OCEAN*

## THE UNITED STATES
## AND THE
## CONFEDERATE STATES
## OF AMERICA
## 1861–1865

States
(U.S./free)

Loyal Border/
slave States

Confederate/
slave States

Indian Territory
(later Oklahoma)

West Virginia formally secedes from
Virginia to become a separate state (1863)

✕ Battles    ✦ Forts

0        MILES        200

0        KM        200

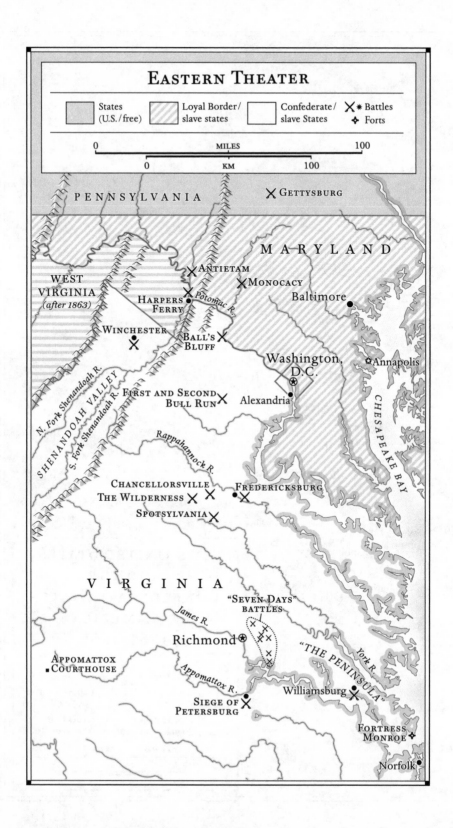

# EASTERN THEATER

States (U.S./free)
Loyal Border/slave states
Confederate/slave States
✖ ✱ Battles
✦ Forts

MILES
0          100

KM
0          100

PENNSYLVANIA

✖ GETTYSBURG

MARYLAND

WEST VIRGINIA (after 1863)

✖ ANTIETAM
✖ MONOCACY

HARPERS FERRY
Potomac R.

Baltimore ●

WINCHESTER
✖

BALL'S BLUFF ✖

Washington, D.C. ⊛

☆ Annapolis

N. Fork Shenandoah R.

SHENANDOAH VALLEY

S. Fork Shenandoah R.

FIRST AND SECOND BULL RUN ✖

Alexandria ●

CHESAPEAKE BAY

Rappahannock R.

CHANCELLORSVILLE
THE WILDERNESS ✖ ✖

FREDERICKSBURG ●

SPOTSYLVANIA ✖

VIRGINIA

"SEVEN DAYS" BATTLES

James R.

Richmond ⊛

APPOMATTOX COURTHOUSE ■

Appomattox R.

SIEGE OF PETERSBURG ✖

Williamsburg ✖

York R.

"THE PENINSULA"

FORTRESS MONROE ✦

Norfolk ●

# PREFACE

"Mr. Lincoln, his cabinet, and the 37th Congress were elected to do anything, everything, except what fell to them to do—fight the greatest civil war of history. It came upon them as an utter surprise." So wrote Rep. Albert Gallatin Riddle, a Republican Radical, in a late-life memoir. Few of the consequences of the coming war were foreseen in the blustery postelection autumn of 1860, and none were foreordained. Many Southerners thought secession could be accomplished peacefully, while many Northerners believed that a little saber-rattling would deflate the rebels. Of course, they were both wrong. As the nation hurtled toward war, Congress faced existential challenges greater than any that the nation had encountered: How could the North be mobilized for a war that as late as the spring of 1861 it never expected to fight? Was Congress or the president responsible for the waging of the war? Could the untried Republicans manage to govern? Should war be fought with respect for the sanctity of Southern property—including slaves—or with a ruthlessness that would bring the seceded states more quickly to their knees? Could the Constitution survive the suspension of fundamental civil rights in the name of national security? How would the war be paid for? Would its financial burden break the Northern economy? What should white Americans do about slavery? Could they prevent their party from splitting between antislavery Radicals and those who were willing to tolerate slavery as long as it was contained in the South? Should Negroes be recruited to serve in the army? Would white soldiers refuse to fight alongside them? After the war was won—assuming that the North triumphed—should the Southern states be broken up? Should ex-Confederates be prosecuted as war criminals?

No consensus existed on any of these questions and many others. The challenges were daunting. Suspicion of central government in general, distrust of a strong executive in particular, and embedded traditions of states' rights—in the North as well as the South—threatened to undermine the country's war-making ability. The nation's tiny sixteen-thousand-man army, scattered among Indian-fighting posts on the western frontier, was ill-prepared to suppress a rebellion that stretched from the Atlantic Coast to Texas. Deep-seated racism threatened any attempt to emancipate slaves. As James Bayard of Delaware told his Senate colleagues, "Antagonism between the races is a primary law of nature." Many, especially from the border states, also regarded any kind of tampering with slavery as a threat to basic property rights. "If you take from us today our right to hold slaves, how long will it be before you will take from us some other constitutional right," worried John W. Crisfield, a pro-slavery Unionist from Maryland.

Close allies often diverged sharply on some issues, and on others followed different trajectories toward a common goal, as many did on how to end slavery. Fear of failure—losing the war on the battlefield, financial collapse, weakness in the White House—stalked the halls of Congress virtually without respite. Idealism collided with ruthless pragmatism. Friends became enemies, and onetime enemies friends. Careers were made and ruined. Some men soared from obscurity to greatness. Others, famous in their day, sank beneath the quicksand of a changing political landscape.

With Southerners gone, the Republicans for the first time held decisive majorities in both houses of Congress, having won about three-fifths of the seats in each chamber in the 1860 elections, along with the presidency. By the spring of 1861, one-third of the seats in both chambers stood empty, abandoned by members who had defected to the Confederacy. Their absence opened the gates to one of the most dynamic eras of legislative activism in American history, one that would change American society beyond recognition. During the next four years Congress would help win the war, craft a peace, reinvent the nation's financial system, and enact a raft of forward-looking legislation that had long been blocked by Southern intransigence. In the course of doing so, Congress also laid the foundation for the strong activist central government that came fully into being in the twentieth century, permanently altered the relationship between the states and the federal government, and enshrined protection of civil rights as the responsibility of the federal government, initiating a racial and economic revolution that would overthrow the South's cotton economy and transform four million slaves from pieces of property into soldiers, free women and men, and eventually citizens. In short, as the historian Leonard P. Curry put it, "It was the members of this Congress—sometimes by accident and sometimes by design—who drew the blueprint for modern America."

It is sometimes popularly supposed that Abraham Lincoln alone led the Union war effort and freed the slaves, as if there were no more to the United States government than the gaunt and lonely man in the White House. Although the war drove Lincoln to attempt to govern more by executive order than had any of his predecessors, his ability to do so depended on the support of Republicans in Congress, many of whom vigorously insisted that the power to shape the course of the war resided on Capitol Hill, not in the White House. Congress enacted legislation that raised hundreds of thousands of troops for the Union, instituted the nation's first military draft when volunteers were no longer sufficient, and pushed consistently against an often reluctant Lincoln for more aggressive generals, a harsher strategy against the South, and the recruitment of African Americans. Congress also provided financing for the war, a herculean task, and in the process created the country's first national currency, the forerunner of the Internal Revenue Service, and the foundation of the Federal Reserve System. Long before Lincoln became willing to contemplate the emancipation of slaves, members of Congress demanded it, enacting an incremental series of laws that turned abolitionism from a fringe belief into public policy. The Homestead Act changed the face of the West. The Pacific Railway Act committed the government to linking the nation's heartland with California by rail, the largest and most expensive infrastructure project undertaken in the

United States up to that time. The Land-Grant College Act would lay the groundwork for public state university systems nationwide. Although these last three are not commonly recognized as war measures, it was the war that made them politically possible. Less happily, the widespread monitoring of antiwar dissidents created a precedent for the government surveillance of private communications and allegedly unpatriotic political activity that has become a feature of present-day life.

Although this book will sometimes venture onto the war's battlefields, it is primarily a political history of how Congress fought that war. The war did not take place in a political vacuum: politics sustained it, drove it to its revolutionary conclusion, and gave it lasting meaning. The story of how this was accomplished is often as gripping and fraught with uncertainty as anything that took place between the opposing armies. This is not a book about politics in the abstract, but about the men who practiced it in the chambers of the wartime Capitol. Like every Congress in American history, both the Senate and House of Representatives included the brilliant, the mediocre, and the incompetent. The great majority were imbued with a passionate patriotism that befitted a generation mostly born while the republic's Founders still lived, a few during Washington's presidency, and many more during John Adams's and Thomas Jefferson's. Virtually all could remember—and some had served with—Andrew Jackson, Henry Clay, Daniel Webster, and John C. Calhoun, the last three dead barely a decade. For the men of 1860, these were not demigods from a bygone Golden Age, but political men like themselves, whose conflicting traditions remained alive and vital. Most were professional politicians and lawyers, with a sprinkling of businessmen, farmers, and journalists. They were opinionated, often brilliantly eloquent, and colorfully combative. Of the House of Representatives, Rep. James G. Blaine later remarked, "There is no place where so little deference is paid to reputation previously acquired, or to eminence won outside; no place where so little consideration is shown for the feelings or the failures of beginners. What a man gains, he gains by sheer force of his own character, and if he loses and falls back he must expect no mercy and will receive no sympathy." Manners were only notionally better in the Senate.

Members of both houses enjoyed none of the resources that members of later Congresses would take for granted: no staffs, no private offices, no research facilities apart from the Library of Congress on the Capitol's second floor, where members might be seen poring over back copies of the *Congressional Globe,* old legal texts, or volumes of classical history to lend heft to their orations. When Congress met it was beneath the spectacularly aspirational but unfinished Capitol dome, an all too perfect symbol of the incomplete Union. Despite its grandiose interior decor, the atmosphere inside was democratic and informal, often rough in its manners, and perfumed with the aroma of cigars, whiskey, and, in the sweltering summer particularly, sweaty male bodies. Strangers wandered in and out of the chambers and sprawled at members' unoccupied desks. "Finding the coast clear, I gamboled up and down, from gallery to gallery, sat in Sumner's chair, examined Wilson's books, & pocketed a cast away autograph or two," one tourist gloated. Contractors and petitioners flooded the Rotunda, plucking at members' purse strings, begging an annuity for an aged veteran of the War of 1812, a subsidy for a proposed canal or railway spur, or a federal job. Visitors packed the galleries to witness the nation's gladiators of the spoken word in action, orating sometimes for hours on end without notes. Increasingly now, members were speaking not only to their colleagues, but also to the nation's newspapers, whose ravenous reporters peered down upon them from the press gallery, and to Americans across a nation newly wired for telegraphy which within hours of their delivery carried speeches to voters in the nation's parlors, churches, and taverns.

I have tried to capture the sound of their voices and the impassioned immediacy of their strife over issues that still stir our emotions and hopes. Of course, it is not possible to bring alive the human dimension of all the hundreds of men who served in Congress during those tumultuous years. So I have built my narrative mainly around four of them. Three of them were Republicans. Of these, two proudly embraced the label of Radicals, Rep. Thaddeus Stevens of Pennsylvania and Sen. Ben Wade of Ohio. One, Sen. William Pitt Fessenden of Maine, a conservative by nature, only belatedly and cautiously aligned himself with the Radicals. All three were critical leaders during the war. The fourth, Ohio representative Clement L. Vallandigham, was a Northern Democrat with Southern sympathies and the leading advocate of a negotiated peace. During his short, flaming career as spokesman for the antiwar opposition, he embodied the fate of the once impregnable Democratic Party, now splintered into factions of "War Democrats," and a rump of defiant skeptics like Vallandigham, whose views approached, and in the minds of many crossed, the line into treason. Although Vallandigham's racial attitudes are offensive to present-day values, he nonetheless was one of the most provocative dissenters in American history, and a self-described martyr to the administration's determination to squelch views that threatened the Union war effort. Throughout this book, I have tried to reflect the language that was in use at the time, for instance, generally opting for the word "Negro," a polite term in the 1860s, over the anachronistic "African American."

Measured by both the urgency of the problems they faced and by their dynamic productivity, the two wartime Congresses were among the most effective in American history. The many landmark laws they passed, Ohio senator John Sherman predicted, "will be a monument to good or evil. They cover such vast sums, delegate and regulate such vast powers, and are so far-reaching in their effects, that generations will be affected well or ill by them." But all this, as public men were fond of saying then, still lay in the womb of time.

History's lessons are often ambiguous. "The past," as the British novelist L. P. Hartley wrote, "is a foreign country. They do things differently there." Memory and truth alike may be distorted by our desire to enlist the past on behalf of our present concerns, by changing moral values, and by the difficulty of figuring out what our ancestors really meant even when we hear their literal words. That said, perhaps they have something to teach us about how our government can function at its best in challenging times, and how crisis may even make it stronger.

# Congress at War

# 1

# A Rope of Sand

They cannot expect to make us love slavery.

—REP. THADDEUS STEVENS

By any traditional measure, James Buchanan was one of the best qualified men ever to hold the presidency. Known fondly, if not altogether flatteringly as the "Old Public Functionary," beginning in the 1810s he had served in the Pennsylvania state legislature, in both the House of Representatives and the Senate, as ambassador to Russia under Andrew Jackson, secretary of state under James Polk, and ambassador to Britain under Franklin Pierce, before his election to the nation's highest office in 1856. Although Northern by birth, his support for Southern interests, including the protection of slavery, was staunch, lifelong, and untainted, at least in public, by any evidence of moral doubt. As president, he behaved like a sort of maiden aunt, a national mollifier who disliked confrontation, and felt genuinely distressed when states, like badly behaved children, were at each other's throats. Yet he had presided over one debilitating crisis after another: guerrilla warfare in Kansas, the inflammatory Dred Scott decision, the wildfire spread of Southern paranoia following John Brown's 1859 raid, and now the incendiary aftermath of Abraham Lincoln's election, which sent South Carolina hurtling toward secession. By December 1860, he was a lame duck facing the country's worst calamity ever.

Secession fever was sweeping South Carolina and percolating across the rest of the Deep South. Radical speakers were telling wildly cheering crowds that Lincoln's election would lead to a race war that could be forestalled only by a united South that was prepared to defend itself, and the slavery on which it depended, with rifle and bayonet if necessary. In Charleston, the Stars and Stripes was everywhere replaced by the state's palmetto flag. Young and old flocked to join the militia. Even children delivered secession speeches to their playmates and strutted the streets like soldiers.

At the direction of the pro-secession secretary of war, John Floyd, tens of thousands of weapons were shipped to the South from federal arsenals in the North. A new military committee in South Carolina was laying plans to fortify the coastline, and foreign consuls were said to be waiting for secession to open negotiations for recognition. The governor of Alabama called for the immediate secession of his state, as did Sen. Robert Toombs of Georgia. From Virginia to Texas, volunteer units were arming.

In his last State of the Union address, on December 3, Buchanan spoke as if lost in a political funk, retailing rhetorical bromides that swayed no one anymore. "The country has been eminently prosperous in all its material interests," he declared sunnily. "The general health has been excellent, our harvests have been abundant, and plenty smiles throughout the land." He then asked, "Why is it, then, that discontent so extensively prevails?" The answer was simple: it was all the abolitionists' fault. "Incessant and violent agitation" against slavery had wrought a "malign influence on the slaves, and inspired them with vague notions of freedom." As a result, white Southerners lived in terror of a servile insurrection. All that the slave states wanted, he asserted, was to be left alone to manage their "domestic institutions" in their own way. Instead, he claimed, "Many a matron throughout the South retires at night in dread of what may befall herself and her children before the morning."

In truth, if any whites in the South lived in real terror it was those few who dared to publicly imply, even inadvertently, that there was anything wrong with slavery. In the months since John Brown's raid, reports of lynchings, assaults, and the tar-and-feathering of hapless travelers, Yankee peddlers, and dissenters had steadily percolated northward. Vigilantes arrested white strangers for being seen in conversation with Negroes, drove out Northern-born schoolteachers, and tore open the U.S. mail in search of "subversive" literature. A South Carolina stonecutter was stripped naked, beaten, and covered with hot tar for having been heard to say that slavery caused white workers to be looked down upon; a Virginian was almost lynched in Alabama when he attempted to pass a banknote from Massachusetts; a daguerreotypist was beaten because one of his samples was a picture of Abraham Lincoln; a Mississippian was hanged for wearing a red sash, the supposed symbol of a nonexistent secret abolition society. Of such horrific events, Buchanan said nothing.

He waved away secession and its consequences. There was no constitutional basis for separation, he admitted. But the federal government was, sadly, a mere voluntary association, a "rope of sand" so fragile that any "adverse wave of public opinion" could wash it away. He was therefore helpless to stop the "demolition" of federal authority in South Carolina. There wasn't even a federal marshal left in the state to execute his orders, even if he issued any. He had no choice, he said, but to hand over responsibility for finding a solution to the crisis to Congress. Unfortunately, he added, in his opinion Congress had no more authority to compel a state to abide by federal law than the president did. But all was not lost. Fortunately, there was a solution at hand: a comprehensive compromise that would reassure the South that its interests and institutions would be protected.

Buchanan's complacency rested on an amendment to the Constitution that had just been proposed by Sen. John Crittenden, a slave-owning Kentucky Unionist, who was sometimes called "the Nestor of the Senate." Crittenden considered himself heir to the conciliatory spirit of his mentor and fellow Kentucky Whig, Henry Clay, dead since 1852, who had engineered several of the great sectional compromises of the past. Strictly speaking, Crittenden's proposal was hardly a compromise, since it required all its concessions from the North, and none from the South. Declaring that his amendment—it would be the thirteenth if it was ratified—would form "a permanent and unchangeable basis for peace and tranquility among the people," he proposed that Congress explicitly recognize the right to own slaves in the states where slavery already existed or might someday be established; that the right of slavery be guaranteed in every federal territory; that any state law which thwarted the recapture of fugitive slaves be automatically nullified; that the Constitution's three-fifths clause, guaranteeing extra representation for the South by counting that proportion of the enslaved population for the purpose of assigning representatives in Congress, be permanently fixed; that the Missouri Compromise line dividing slave states from free be carried west to the Pacific Ocean; that Congress be prohibited from interfering with the interstate slave trade, and pay compensation to the owners of slaves who escaped their masters with assistance from antislavery activists; and that Congress be empowered to sue any Northern county in which a fugitive slave was deliberately saved from recapture. The capstone of the amendment was draconian: it stipulated that no future amendment to the Constitution could ever repeal the Crittenden amendment's previous provisions.

Crittenden was racing against time. Seventeen days after Buchanan's State of the Union address, on December 20, South Carolina formally seceded, charging that the federal government had failed to enforce the Fugitive Slave Law, and that the states of the North had expressed an intolerable hostility to slavery by permitting the formation of abolition societies and inciting "servile insurrection." In December, complaining of the "wrongs" to which the South had allegedly been subjected by Northern "despotism," a secession convention meeting in Charleston's Hibernian Hall called on the slaveholding states to unite in "a great slaveholding Confederacy, stretching its arms over a territory larger than any power in Europe possesses." After the vote, the delegates flooded into the streets, shouting, "We are afloat!" as church bells rang, bonfires blazed, and fireworks shot through the sky. In breaking up the Union, the Carolinians claimed, they were but following in the footsteps of the Founding Fathers, who had established the United States as a "union of slaveholding States." State authorities quickly seized federal customs houses, armories, and forts, and deployed militiamen against a possible assault by national troops.

The only organized federal force remaining in South Carolina consisted of seventy-five soldiers commanded by Maj. Robert Anderson, based at Fort Moultrie on Sullivan's Island, a key link in the city's formidable shore defenses. The problem with Fort Moultrie was that its powerful guns pointed out to sea, whence any attack was expected to come. The fort was virtually defenseless on its landward side, an open invitation to capture by the Southern forces that were massing around the city. However, Anderson was a Kentuckian, a longtime friend of Jefferson Davis, and married to the daughter of a Georgia plantation owner. South Carolinians expected him to hand over the fort without resistance. But on the night of December 26, to the astonishment of the secessionists, Anderson proved his unwavering loyalty to the national government by leading his men under cover of darkness to the most defensible position available to him, a damp, gloomy brick fastness that rose upon an artificial island in the harbor: Fort Sumter.

Buchanan seemed oblivious to the deepening crisis. Public disgust with his passivity sank to new depths. "Old James Buchanan now stands lowest, I think, in the dirty catalogue of treasonable mischief-makers," fumed George Templeton Strong, a prominent New York businessman, in his diary. "Is there any way to take control of the affairs of government out of the hands of that old imbecilic president?" begged one Ohioan of Sen. Benjamin F. Wade. "Are the president and his secretaries and advisers traitors?" demanded another. Where were the party's leaders when they were so desperately needed? Where, most of all, was Lincoln? In Buchanan's hometown of Lancaster, Pennsylvania, Rep. Thaddeus Stevens worried that the president-elect, for whom he had vigorously campaigned, lacked spine enough to face off against the secessionists. Lincoln, he wrote to a friend, must "imitate [Andrew] Jackson and set vigorously about coercing obedience." If he failed to do so and instead sought "to purchase peace by concession," Stevens thought he would lose hope and give up completely on politics. So disgusted was Stevens at the spectacle of the government "crawling on its knees at the feet of traitors," that he refused to set foot in Washington for most of December: "I do not care to be present while the humiliation is going on."

Lincoln's election had climaxed a gradual shift of power from the

South to the more populous North. Although the slave states represented barely one-fourth of the free people of the United States, they had controlled the government for generations. But demographics ate away glacially at the slave states' grip. In the 1840s, they lost control of the House of Representatives, and after 1850 their dominance of the Senate, although with the support of Northern Democrats they continued to dominate government through the end of the decade. "You own the cabinet, you own the Senate, and you own the President of the United States as much as you own the servant on your own plantation," Ben Wade caustically remarked on the Senate floor in December 1860.

The elections of 1860 finally broke the slaveholders' grip. Although Lincoln triumphed decisively in the electoral college, he captured just under 40 percent of the popular vote, receiving no votes below the Mason-Dixon line in the four-way contest for the presidency. For the first time, a party professing opposition to the expansion of slavery had won control of the government. The Republican platform, while conceding the right of states to control their "domestic institutions," denounced as unconstitutional and revolutionary the "new dogma" that slavery could be carried into any of the territories. This was no embrace of general emancipation, but jubilant antislavery men believed that the long era of concessions and compromises with slavery was finally over. The Boston abolitionist Wendell Phillips effused, "For the first time in our history, the slave has chosen a president."

The Republicans had bolstered their antislavery posture by the nomination of the outspokenly abolitionist vice-president-elect Hannibal Hamlin of Maine, who had served in the House and then the Senate since the 1840s. Although Hamlin lacked Lincoln's verbal gift, he was capable and well-liked, and lent moral weight to the ticket in New England, where Lincoln was little known. He had stooping shoulders, a massive head, and deep-set eyes, and his clean-shaven face was so swarthy that enemies alleged, untruthfully, that he had Negro blood. He learned only after the fact that the convention had named him Lincoln's running mate, and the two men met for the first time two weeks after the election.

Southern nationalists reacted to the election's results with fear and fury. "Now that the black radical Republicans have the power, I suppose they will [John] Brown us all," the worried Charleston socialite Mary Boykin Chesnut confided to her diary. More menacingly, one of many anonymous letters to the president-elect shrieked: "God damn your goddamned old Hellfired soul to hell god damn you and goddamn your god damned family's god damned hellfired god damned soul to hell."

Lincoln, meanwhile, remained at his home in Springfield, blandly reassuring Americans that all would be well, and asserting that the crisis was merely an artificial one. Lincoln was still a near-cipher to most Easterners. Many hardly knew what to make of him. "He is lank and hard-featured, among the ugliest white men I have ever seen," remarked George Templeton Strong. "Decidedly plebian. Superficially vulgar and a snob. But not essentially. He seems to me clear-headed and sound-hearted, though his laugh is that of a yahoo; and his grammar is weak." Pressed for a clear statement of policy, the president-elect reiterated his campaign promise not to interfere with slavery. "It is now apparent to all that he was not the man for the emergency," reflected one discouraged Republican. "Though he might build a ship, he was not born to command." Southerners, when they were not attacking Lincoln as a menace to their institutions, were dismissive of him. Sen. Louis Wigfall of Texas, the most violent secessionist still in Congress, scoffed contemptuously in the Senate that nothing could be expected from a man "who is taken up because he is an ex-rail-splitter, an ex-grocery keeper, an ex-flatboat captain, and an ex-Abolition lecturer."

Yet few Americans could believe that Southerners would really abandon the Union and relinquish the outsized power they had exerted since the founding of the republic. Surely, they told each other, the rebels would eventually negotiate. Ben Wade, one of the most radical members of the Senate, scoffed that secession was a scare tactic designed to undermine support for the Republicans. Call the Southerners' bluff, he urged: impose a blockade on their ports "and they will soon beg to get back." Wade's Senate colleague William Pitt Fessenden of Maine cautioned their fellow Republicans to "coolly watch the enemy's game—for it is a game." Would-be secessionists had repeatedly threatened disunion—in 1790, in 1820, in the 1830s, in 1850—and some kind of compromise had always been found. Once Southerners realized that the Republicans didn't really intend to tamper with slavery they would surely settle down. Many Republicans, including Lincoln, also believed that a silent majority of Unionists existed in the South and would rise up to overthrow the secessionists once they realized that conciliatory Northerners were in earnest. As one Kentucky Unionist put it in a letter to Wade, "You cannot whip the South into the traces like a horse and govern her like conquered provinces. *Conciliate Conciliate Compromise.* If you break up the Union or involve the country in a civil war you will be cursed by both sections of the country."

Under pressure from the more forceful members of his cabinet, Buchanan finally roused himself to order the dispatch of a relief ship to Fort Sumter, carrying supplies and a meager detachment of 250 reinforcements. Typical of the president's endless havering, he failed to tell Major Anderson that relief was even on the way. Buchanan had also chartered a defenseless commercial steamer, *The Star of the West,* so as not to make the Carolinians feel threatened. On January 9, the ship hove to off Charleston. "The one flag we longed to see had come at last, in a timid, apologetic way, and not as a war power of the government," wrote the disappointed Capt. Abner Doubleday, Anderson's second in command, and one of the rare open abolitionists in the army's officer corps. "It was hard to believe the government would send us a mercantile steamer when it could have dispatched a man of war." Secessionist batteries opened fire from the barrier islands at the mouth of the harbor. One shot struck near *The Star of the West*'s rudder, another just above the waterline. The ship's captain quickly reversed course and fled out to sea. "I rejoiced at this insult to the flag of your country," Wigfall sneered to his fellow senators. "It ought to be fired at, and it should be torn down and trampled upon."

Meanwhile, the debate over the Crittenden amendment lurched stumblingly onward. On December 31, as Major Anderson's tiny command was hastening to strengthen its defenses, the committee empowered to write Crittenden's amendment into legislation gave up in defeat when its five Republican members and its two members from the Deep South—Jefferson Davis of Mississippi and Robert Toombs of Georgia—flatly rejected compromise. As the tide of secessionist passion spread across the Deep South, desperate members of both houses of Congress floated new compromise proposals. Most jettisoned at least some of Crittenden's provisions, but virtually all incorporated the guarantee that the federal government forever be barred from tampering with slavery. A few independent Southern Whigs, such as Emerson Etheridge, a slave owner from western Tennessee, argued that the Republicans posed no serious threat to either the South or slavery. Northern Democrats, whose strength as a party had depended for decades on Southern votes, appealed to the moral sense, the good faith, and the patriotism of the free states to repeal the personal liberty laws that protected fugitive slaves and gave offense to the South, while others bluntly rejected any action that might be taken to bring South Carolina to heel. Rep. Daniel Sickles, a swaggering Tammany blusterer from New York, for one, declared that anyone who imagined that the Union could or should be preserved by force was "hallucinating." And Rep. Clement L. Vallandigham of Ohio swore that he would never permit federal troops ordered south to suppress secession to march through his congressional district unless they marched over his corpse.

Vallandigham proposed the most extreme compromise formula of all. He was a paradoxical figure. Bright-eyed and animated, intellectual by temperament and an avid reader of the classics, he was a pro-Southern Negrophobe of the deepest hue, as well as an eloquent advocate for the immigrant working class, an opponent of capital punishment, and a critic of the brutal treatment suffered by seamen on American ships. The son of a Presbyterian minister, he was so stubborn in his opposition to alcohol that he was said to have once pulled a pistol on friends who tried to force him to drink at an otherwise convivial gathering. As a rising star in the Democratic Party, he had chaired the National Democratic Campaign Committee during the recent election and stumped the Midwest for the party's presidential candidate Stephen A. Douglas. Everywhere he went, he had attacked racial "amalgamation" and "negro equality," denounced Lincoln's views as subversive, and charged that a Republican victory would lead to the emancipation of millions of slaves who would flood north to steal white men's jobs. Vallandigham's mouthpiece, the *Dayton Daily Empire,* warned its readers that if Lincoln won, "stinking niggers" would soon be sitting next to them on workmen's benches, and their daughters would be forced to marry "black boys" who would impregnate them with "black babies." A few days before the election, he declared to an enthusiastic Democratic audience in New York that he "never would, as a Representative in Congress of the United States, vote one dollar of money whereby one drop of American blood should be shed in a civil war." Lincoln's election, he wrote to his wife, was "the saddest day I ever passed."

Vallandigham took particular pride in having no New England blood in his veins, and in being wholly of Southern ancestry "with a slight cross of Pennsylvania Scotch-Irish." He was utterly convinced that the abolition of slavery would be a national disaster that no one wanted except for a radical fringe of rabble-rousers who didn't even understand the consequences of their demands for emanci- pation. He was not a full-throated advocate for slavery per se. But he couldn't understand why so many Northerners who had noth- ing to do with slavery were so upset about it. He considered aboli- tionists hypocrites, who despite their professed care for the Negro would never dare to give him political or social equality. An apostle of small government in the Jacksonian tradition—"low, simple, and democratic"—he blamed the Union's troubles almost as much on the "continually increasing power and patronage of the federal govern- ment" as he did on agitation over slavery. He opposed public debt, protective tariffs, and public works, all of which, he charged, only benefited "the special interests of the moneyed classes." In both his populism and his racism, he was largely in tune with many North- ern Democrats, especially those in the lower Midwest, which had been settled in large part by emigrants from the South, including his own Virginia forebears. The South and the West were natural allies, he preached, with identical interests, until the incubus of antislavery agitation began to drive them apart.

At a time when many Americans decried the destructive influence of sectionalism, Vallandigham at times envisioned it as the founda- tion for a new American political order. Speaking of the Midwest, he declared in Congress on December 4, 1860: "We have an empire equal in area to the third of all Europe, and *we do not mean to be a dependency or province either of the East or the South;* nor yet an interior or second-rate power upon this continent; and if we cannot secure a maritime boundary upon other terms, we will cleave our way to the sea coast with the sword." It was a formulation that veered perilously close to suggesting that the Midwest might be better off if it seceded, too. On February 14, he wrote to the *Cincinnati Enquirer,* "When all possible hope is gone, and the Union irretrievably broken, then, but not till then, I will be for a Western Confederacy."

"Star after star [has] shot from our political firmament," he now told his colleagues in the House. "The question today is: how shall we now keep the States we have and restore those which are lost till every wanderer shall have returned and not one be missing from the starry flock." Only a radical restructuring of the entire government could bring that about, he declared. The amendment he proposed went far beyond Crittenden's. It would divide the United States into four defined sections: New England plus New York and Pennsylvania, designated "The North"; the upper Midwest from Ohio to Kansas, "The West"; Oregon, California, and any new states formed adjacent to them, "The Pacific"; and "The South," to include all the slave states from Delaware to Texas. Votes on national legislation would require a majority of the senators from all four sections in order to pass. Election of the president would also take place by section, with two electors being appointed by each state, and a majority of the electors in each of the four sections required to choose the chief executive, putting an end to majority rule, and precluding the future election of a president by the vote of a single sectional majority, as Lincoln had been. Secession would be recognized as a constitutional right, but to take effect it would need the consent of all the legislatures of the section to which the state proposing to secede belonged. Congress also would be prohibited from interfering with the right of any citizen—this really meant slave owner—to settle wherever he wished on equal terms with all other citizens. His proposal, Vallandigham claimed, would remove slavery as a political issue, and turn sectionalism from "a sword for aggression" into "a shield for defense" by diminishing the relative power of each section. This extraordinary plan won little support, but it foreshadowed the role that Vallandigham would play in the coming months as, increas-

ingly, he became the leading spokesman for Northern opposition to
the war.

This sort of thing could be expected from Democrats, but Republicans were shocked in mid-January when two of the most respected
members of their party called for what, to many, seemed to be the
most craven surrender of principle. Rep. Charles Francis Adams of
Massachusetts, the son of former president John Quincy Adams, the
1848 candidate for vice president on the Free Soil Party ticket, and a
man with unimpeachable antislavery credentials, caused an uproar
when he proposed admitting the vast New Mexico Territory as a
new slave state. Worse yet came from Sen. William H. Seward of
New York, the most influential Republican now in Congress, the man
Lincoln had tapped to serve as his secretary of state, and who had
once famously declared that there was a "higher law" than the Constitution when it came to the rights of the enslaved. Courtly, affable,
slight of build, with a clean-shaven face dominated by an enormous
nose and once red hair now gone colorless, Seward was still widely
thought of, however erroneously, as one of the most radical leaders of the Republican Party. The *Washington Evening Star* predicted
that his speech would be the "most momentous" ever delivered on
the Senate floor, and nearly two thousand people packed into the
galleries to hear it. But instead of issuing a clarion antislavery call,
he stunned his legions of admirers by announcing his support for
the *repeal* of the North's personal liberty laws, and for a poison-pill
amendment that would bar Congress from ever interfering with
slavery. At a party at the home of Sen. Stephen A. Douglas, Seward
had even been heard to declare, "Away with all parties, all platforms,
all previous committals, and whatever else will stand in the way of
the restoration of the American Union." Seward may have cleverly
been attempting to position the Republicans reassuringly as the
party of a compromise he knew the secessionists would never agree
to, but most of his admirers felt deeply betrayed. "Is it possible that
he who has battled so manfully many years for the right is ready
to abandon his principles at the first threat of Southern traitors?"
cried an outraged Vermont abolitionist, one voice among many.
"Nobody expected anything from poor old toothless Buchanan, but
it was firmly believed that the new administration would have a little

backbone." Thaddeus Stevens was in near-despair, telling treasury secretary designate Salmon P. Chase, "Mr. Seward's course has mortified me. [It] seems to indicate that our platform and principles are to be sacrificed for peace." He wondered, "Will Lincoln have nerve enough to resist?" Seward's own wife, Frances, a devout abolitionist, could scarcely conceal her deep disappointment. Eloquent as the speech was, she wrote to him, "it fails to meet the approval of those who love you best. Compromise based on the idea that the preservation of the Union is more important than the liberty of nearly 4,000,000 human beings cannot be right."

None of these proposals stanched the streaming hemorrhage of slave states from the Union. On January 21, Mississippi's senior senator, Jefferson Davis, the former secretary of war, and protégé of the South's most famous apostle of slavery John C. Calhoun, rose beside his mahogany desk. At fifty-four, he projected an image of stony, chiseled self-control. He still stood as rigidly erect as the soldier he had once been, and as befit a lordly planter whose two hundred slaves worked some of the richest land in the Yazoo delta. Suffering from chronic rheumatism and from wounds he suffered in the Mexican War, his gaunt figure "gave the idea of a body worn by the action of the mind, an intellect supporting in its prison of flesh the pains of constitutional disease." For years Davis had preached the gospel of state sovereignty and full-throatedly defended slavery as constitutional, Christian, and nonnegotiably essential to the Southern economy.

Mississippi's declaration of secession had reached him by telegraph two days earlier. "Our position is thoroughly identified with the institution of slavery, the greatest material interest of the world," it had proclaimed. "A blow at slavery is a blow at commerce and civilization." The Declaration of Independence had been invoked by abolitionists to "assert the equality of the races," a notion that the Founders had never remotely contemplated, Davis asserted. Indeed, the Constitution had made it perfectly clear that "that class of persons" were nothing but property and were never intended to be "put upon the footing of equality with white men—not even upon that of paupers or convicts." These were the fundamental principles upon which the republic rested. "When you deny them, and when you

deny to us the right to withdraw from a government which thus perverted threatens to be destructive of our rights, we but tread in the
path of our fathers when we proclaim our independence." Under
these circumstances, he said, "my functions are terminated here,"
adding that Mississippi was breaking no federal laws by seceding,
since the laws of the United States applied only to the inhabitants
of that country. Mississippi was no longer among them: it was now
a foreign country. "Putting our trust in God, and in our own firm
hearts and strong arms, we will vindicate the right as best we may. It
only remains for me to bid you a final adieu."

With that, he left the chamber.

In the days that followed, more departing Southern senators
hurled their invective at their Northern colleagues, who sat for the
most part in stunned silence as they felt the government they knew
tottering before their eyes. Stephen R. Mallory of Florida, soon to
be named the Confederate secretary of the navy, warned, "Remember that you are dealing with a nation, and not a faction." Clement
Clay of Alabama denounced the North's "insulting" challenges to
"that domestic institution of the South which is not only the chief
source of her prosperity, but the very basis of her social order and
state polity." Alfred Iverson of Georgia dared the North to attack:
"Your conquest, if you gain one, will cost you a hundred thousand
lives, and more than a hundred million dollars. You may whip us, but
we will not stay whipped, [and] never cease the mortal strife until
our whole white race is extinguished and our fair land given over to
devastation." Robert Toombs, also of Georgia, renounced the Constitution itself, declaring that Northerners were "deluded with the
nonsense that this bond of union was cemented by the brave men of
the Revolution." Lest anyone suppose that race and slavery were not
at the root of secession, Toombs added fiercely, "We want no negro
equality, no negro citizenship; we want no mongrel race to degrade
our own." Flinging his arms wildly about him, he cried out at the top
of his voice, "Good-bye, senators, good-bye, I go, never to return!"

Up to now, Southerners and conciliators had largely defined the
terms of the debate. Then, on January 29, Rep. Thaddeus Stevens
hauled himself to his feet. He faced a chamber that had glaringly
shrunk: seven states had left the Union, and a third of the House's

ornately carved desks stood empty. Overhead, the wide-spreading skylights that overarched the vast hall "like Heaven," as Lincoln's secretary John Hay orotundly put it, "blushed and blazed with gold and the heraldic devices of the married states while, all around it, the eye was rested by the massive simple splendor of the stalagmitic bronze reliefs." (A less awed visitor thought the decor suggestive of a southwestern steamboat saloon.)

Like a general addressing his troops, Stevens laid out the ground upon which the Radicals would fight for the next four years. Although Stevens nominally hewed to his party's line that the government had no constitutional right to interfere with slavery, he saw that war must come, and that it would remake the nation in ways that most Americans hardly dared imagine. His speech was a broadside against both secession and Republican compromisers, whose panicky willingness to accommodate the South he regarded as a waste of time that would only delay the inevitable.

Among the many highly emotive orators of the day, the sixty-eight-year-old Stevens drew attention not only for his acerbic tongue and famously fiery eye, but also for his lushly curling wig and his clubfoot, which, when it suited his rhetorical purposes, he deployed as a stage prop, dragging it ostentatiously behind him as he stalked across the floor of the House. Slave owners, he declared, had for decades defended their repeated threats of secession first as a reaction to what they claimed were tariffs unfair to their section, then on the proposed exclusion of slavery from the western territories, then on alleged violations of the Fugitive Slave Law, and now on "the election of a President who does not believe in the benefits of slavery." All these were mere excuses for the South's expansionist ambitions for slavery, he charged. Southerners complained that Northerners failed to enforce the Fugitive Slave Law aggressively enough. There was some truth to that allegation, he admitted, but "they cannot expect to make us love slavery" or pretend that it was "a divine institution."

In the course of more than four decades in public life, Stevens had earned a reputation as a brilliant courtroom lawyer in Pennsylvania, and a master of parliamentary infighting. He had a deserved reputation for personal honesty and indifference to flattery, and never seemed happier than when he was engaged in a fight. His full-throated abolitionism was no secret; known only to his intimates, however, was his clandestine aid to the Underground Railroad, including the harboring of freedom-seeking runaways on his properties in Pennsylvania. Unlike many of his fellow abolitionists, whose moral hostility to the South's peculiar institution cloaked a racist distaste for African Americans as people, Stevens was a social leveler who, although wealthy himself, despised every kind of institutionalized inequality. Throughout his life he had advocated for free, nondiscriminatory public education, and in the 1830s he was almost alone in the effort to extend equal rights to black Pennsylvanians; in 1837, he refused to sign the state's new constitution because it disenfranchised blacks. Never married, he maintained a close, public, and quite possibly romantic relationship with his Negro friend Lydia Smith, who managed his property in Lancaster.

"I have no hope that concession, humiliation, and compromise, can have any effect whatever," Stevens sonorously declared, with a ghost of his native Vermont twang. (After graduating from Dartmouth, he had moved to the new town of Gettysburg, Pennsylvania, in 1815 to start his law practice.) "Those who counsel the government to let them go are preaching moral treason." If secession were allowed to proceed, he said, "Posterity will wonder whether the statesmen of today were fools or traitors." The South's road to revolution would lie only "through a sea of blood." War, he thundered, would unleash forces that would dwarf all the supposed threats that the South now complained of. "They now tremble when a madman"—he meant John Brown—"and a score of followers invade them. How then will [they] withstand the booming of cannon and the clash of arms? Let there be no blood shed until the last moment. But let no cowardly counsels unnerve the people; and then, at last, if needs be, let everyone be ready to gird on his armor, and do his duty." He predicted that war would bring about the very thing that the South feared most of all: the universal emancipation of its slaves. "Let no slave state flatter itself that it can dissolve the Union now and then reconstruct it on better terms," he warned. Once the secessionists were defeated, as they must be, slavery would be extinguished forever. "Our next United States will contain no foot of ground on which a slave can tread, no breath of air which a slave can breathe."

When he finished, the House exploded in an uproar. The remaining Southern members jumped to their feet and rushed at him hurling curses and threats of violence. Blood was barely avoided when Stevens's friends sprang to his defense and formed a protective ring around him, daring the Southerners to attack. The collision presented, in miniature, the careening rush toward war that in a few months would send Americans from Maine to Texas to the musket and bayonet. Few shared his certainties at the time, but his words were prophetic. Although Stevens stood on the radical fringe of the lame-duck Thirty-sixth Congress, in the far-reaching political realignment that was about to take place he would emerge as one of the most powerful men in government.

# 2

# Let the War Come

The federal government is dead.

—SEN. LOUIS WIGFALL

A pall hung over Washington that January. Rain turned Pennsylvania Avenue into a muddy trough. Even in the best neighborhoods, yards stank from privies and putrifying household slops. The rooming houses where most members of Congress lived, and the halls of the Capitol itself, smelled of wet woolen clothing, cigars, and the charcoal that struggled to warm the underheated chambers of Congress. Slavery pervaded the city like the stink of horse manure that everywhere bedunged the streets. Although free blacks now outnumbered slaves in the capital, investors in human flesh had merely to cross the Potomac River to the markets of Alexandria to shop. The 3,100 enslaved men, women, and children who were still inextricably woven into the fabric of Washington life—holding doors, driving carriages, cleaning the mud from boots, hawking oysters, tending stables, suckling white babies, waiting on tables, toting trunks—reminded whites at every turn that the institution that was fissuring the nation was alive and thriving in its capital.

There was a still tentative, only semiurban quality to much of the city. At the western end of the National Mall—really just a field where sheep and cows grazed—rose the ugly stump of the aborted

Washington Monument, like a finger lopped off at the first joint, abandoned for lack of financing. Little had changed since 1849, when the visiting Charles Dickens sarcastically described its scattered, mostly nondescript dwellings and its wide streets that petered out in empty fields as "a city of magnificent distances." Nothing more aptly epitomized the unfinished city than the Capitol itself, surrounded by the marble blocks for its new dome strewn around the building, like the symbolic fragments of a nation in pieces.

Washingtonians felt a palpable sense of doom. The city, Jefferson Davis's wife, Varina, felt as her husband's last days in the Senate slipped away, was "like some kind of mausoleum," with no one visiting, no dinners or parties, "just a sullen gloom impending over all things." On January 27, Ohio representative Clement Vallandigham wrote to his wife, "I am able to do no good here—no man can. So I sit, and am obliged to sit, quiet and sorrowful, condemned as one who watches over the couch of a loved mother slowly dying with consumption, to see my country perish by inches." Americans who had taken their nation's immortality for granted knew that things would never be the same again.

The empty seats in the House and Senate announced a revolution in terms more graphic than any of the stormy words that had been spoken during the months past. With the departure of the Southerners, gloom shaded inexorably into fear that events were spinning out of control, and that the worst might really come to pass. Worrying rumors flew through the air: that the defenseless capital would be attacked by a Virginia mob . . . that a coup d'état would come any day . . . that unexplained fires around the city were part of a terrorist plot. Vallandigham warned his wife that an uprising was so likely that he might have to send her to safety somewhere in the mountains. Others dispatched their wives and children to Philadelphia or New York for safety.

Of the nation's entire army of 16,367 men, few were stationed east of the Mississippi River, and most of *them* were in the seceding states. The army's general-in-chief, Winfield Scott, who loathed President Buchanan, made his headquarters in New York City. Scott quickly recognized the gravity of the danger to the capital, however. Although Washington boasted several militia companies, they were more social clubs than military units, and many of their members were sympathetic to the Confederacy. The National Rifles, in particular, had quietly been supplied with arms and artillery by Buchanan's disloyal former secretary of war, and its commander openly admitted that he intended to prevent Union volunteers from reaching the capital. Government spies also reported a plot to seize government departments, including the Treasury, and then form a provisional government. Scott urgently called back into service Charles P. Stone, a West Point graduate and Mexican War veteran he trusted, and asked him to take charge of the capital's defense. Acting decisively, Stone armed hundreds of loyal Union men, and made it clear to the National Rifles that he would order his volunteers to fire on them if they failed to hand over their weapons.

Three companies of light artillery were ordered back from the frontier, and another contingent from West Point, but it would take weeks for them to arrive. Where would the crisis end? unnerved citizens asked each other. "Not only will states secede from the Union, but counties from states, and cities and towns from both; and this the work of disintegration and dissolution will go on until the whole frame of society and government will be ingulfed in one bottomless and boundless chaos of ruin," worried Rep. John McClernand of Illinois.

The panic wasn't limited to Washington. Coastal shipping shrank by half. Shipyards and ironworks went bankrupt. In New York City, commercial firms laid off hundreds or collapsed entirely as trade with the South suddenly disintegrated. Bonds secured by property in slaves crashed. Commercial traffic began to halt on the Mississippi. Grain prices fell by 20 percent, and cotton even further. Even the ice industry, which shipped New England ice to the South, was crippled by the disappearance of Southern orders. Banks failed all over the Midwest, eventually including nearly half of those in Wisconsin, and as many as three-quarters in Illinois. Financiers prayed for a ray of hope but found none. Rumors multiplied of a secret pro-Southern organization that would seize the armories, break into banks, and sack the homes of prominent Republicans. "Depression today deeper than ever," George Templeton Strong recorded in his diary. "Most people give up all hope of saving the government and anticipate general bankruptcy, revolution, mob-law, chaos, and ruin."

Meanwhile, serving federal officers all over the South openly appealed to their troops to join the rebels. As far away as California and New Mexico, Southern-born soldiers left their posts and headed for the seceded states. As soon as Texas seceded, on February 1— wildly claiming that abolitionists had hired secret agents to burn towns and distribute poison to slaves with which to murder their masters—the commander of U.S. forces in the state, Gen. David Twiggs, handed over all the weapons, ordnance, and property under his control to local authorities, and joined the insurgents himself. A few days later, Georgia seized five New York vessels in reprisal for the federal government's halting of arms shipments to the South. President Buchanan remained supine. "Had this old mollusk become vertebrate, the theories by Darwin would have been confirmed," Strong scowled.

In the echoing halls of Congress, Republicans and the remaining Southerners sidestepped each other, too angry or too ashamed to speak. It also began to dawn on Republicans that if the departed Southerners were not coming back, they faced a potentially paralyzing conundrum: without a quorum, they couldn't legislate. The crisis was unprecedented, and as technical as it seemed, its implications were vast. What now constituted a quorum? A majority of the full house? A majority of those who had been elected? Or just of those sworn in? What should be done with the vacant seats? Did they count, or not? The problem in the House of Representatives was less acute, since that body was free to adopt new rules at the beginning of each new session. But in the Senate a quorum had always meant a majority of all the authorized seats. If that quorum was based on the inclusion of the senators from all thirty-three states, including those that had seceded, it might never be achieved, but if it was based on only the smaller number of states that acknowledged that they still belonged to the Union, then the government had already surrendered to the principle of secession by effectively admitting that the absent states were not a part of the Union anymore.

Some Northerners called for the departing senators' names to be stricken immediately from the rolls. Others asserted that although they may have *withdrawn*, they hadn't actually *resigned*, and were therefore still technically members of the Senate even if they weren't physically present. What if they reappeared and reclaimed their seats whenever it suited them? "They are either members of the body or they are not," argued the ailing Stephen A. Douglas, once such an indefatigable campaigner that he was called "a steam engine in breeches," as he watched his party's once impregnable strength evaporating before his eyes. "I cannot conceive the doctrine that a man may dissolve his connection with the body and withdraw from the obligations of a Senator, and come back when he has a mind to, and give the casting vote in a tight struggle, and then slip out again."

William Pitt Fessenden of Maine—he was known to all his colleagues as "Pitt"—cut to the nub of the problem. "I hold most decidedly and decisively that no State has a right to secede, and that consequently all these acts that have been performed by these four states are without any constitutional right, and of no sort of effect whatever." In short, he reasoned, no resignations had actually taken place. Fessenden's was a voice to be listened to, with its authoritative Down East drawl: the voice of a man who got to the essence of things without mincing words. The son of a passionate abolitionist, and trained in the law by Daniel Webster, he rejected any excess of emotion. Fanaticism annoyed him intensely. Slender and slight of build—though he stood five feet ten inches, he weighed only 130 pounds—he projected stiffness and discomfort, rarely smiling, with thin lips and a stern mouth, and a customary expression that some judged dyspeptic. He reminded others of a Roman senator with his precise and deliberate movements, and his pale, chiseled, intellectual face from which the graying hair was brushed back. Given to biting humor, he had little tolerance for fools and none for sloppy reasoning. His command of logic in debate "was like a chain," one close observer remarked, "which his hearers often hated to be confined with yet knew not how to break"; he drove home his argument with the precision of a math professor demonstrating a problem. He possessed the Senate's most sophisticated financial mind, coupled with a mastery of parliamentary process, as he now demonstrated. His legislative ideal, as he once put it, was "to be calm, thoughtful, and free of prejudice" and, when different opinions collide, to determine "how we can come together upon a common ground," a principle to which he rarely failed to adhere in these tension-fraught days.

What Fessenden was saying had vast political implications. If the states that declared themselves outside the Union were even *implicitly* granted a right to secede, he said, then the federal government, the North, the Republican Party, and President-to-be Lincoln had no claim upon them, and the entire argument against secession became no more than a smokescreen for Northern sectional power— precisely as the would-be secessionists claimed. If secession was *illegal,* however, then its senators and congressmen were still members of their respective bodies, no matter what they said. This, he argued, was the only possible position for those who held that the Union was inherently unbreakable.

But if Fessenden was right, the consequences for the incoming government, which would take office on March 4, and for the war effort, if there was to be one, were potentially crippling. If the "seceded" states retained their seats in Congress, even if they remained empty, it would mean that the Republicans would have a harder time mustering a quorum to do business, and an even harder one if the seceded states' allies in Congress—from states such as Virginia, North Carolina, and Arkansas, which were still in the Union—absented themselves when wartime legislation was under consideration. Since there was no consensus within reach, Fessenden's conundrum might accomplish just what the South wanted: a federal government unable to act, and secession achieved without a fight.

The ability of Congress to act decisively was further limited by the obsolescent way in which members of the House of Representatives were then elected. Around half the members were lame ducks, many of them conservative Democrats and old-line Whigs who had been elected in 1858 and then defeated in the Republican wave of 1860, but they would still remain in place for months to come. Since the early days of the republic, when transportation to the national capital was painfully slow and communication primitive, it had been the custom for newly elected members to wait a year or more before taking office. The amount of time varied from state to state.

Each new Congress opened on the first Monday of December in odd-numbered years. But states set their own dates for congressional elections, many of them thirteen months or longer before the December in which a congressman's term was to begin. Thus many of the ardent Republicans who had been elected along with Lincoln wouldn't take their seats until December 1861.

While Congress wavered and debated, and in desperation finally sidestepped, the chimera of quorums, yet another attempt to rejuvenate stalled efforts at conciliation was getting under way. Former president John Tyler had persuaded Virginia's legislature to issue a call for every state North and South to send delegates to a National Peace Conference, to craft "some suitable adjustment" to stave off further secessions. On February 4, representatives from twenty-one states convened at the luxurious Willard Hotel, across Fourteenth Street from the White House. This effort, like all that had gone before, was probably doomed from the start. The seceded states of the Deep South as well as several Republican-controlled Northern states shunned the conference altogether, while its chairman, the slave-owning Tyler, one of the least effective presidents of the antebellum era and, in the words of an unfriendly critic, "a tottering ashen ruin" of a man, inspired little confidence in anyone. Not insignificantly, on the day that the Peace Conference opened, thirty-eight representatives from six slave states met in Montgomery, Alabama, to form what they proclaimed the Confederate States of America.

While the delegates self-importantly haggled, the president-elect at last set forth from Springfield, heading east by rail through Indiana, Ohio, New York, and Pennsylvania en route to his inauguration in Washington. Everywhere he was hailed by cheering crowds begging for an inspiring speech and reassurance that he would deal decisively with secession. They usually begged in vain. Even now, he rarely ventured beyond the pallid generalities enunciated by the Republican platform. South of Philadelphia, the journey became less a triumphal progress than an exercise in stealth. Credible reports had reached Lincoln that Southern agents planned to kidnap or assassinate him as he passed through Baltimore, which seethed with secessionist sentiment. He declined a military escort, but allowed his security advisor, the detective Allan Pinkerton, to plan this final leg of his journey in secrecy. Lincoln's departure from Philadelphia went unreported, and when a conductor entered the president's sleeping car he was told not to wake the supposedly sick traveler in his curtained berth.

As the train trundled southward, Pinkerton men stationed at intervals alongside the track raised lanterns to indicate that the way ahead was safe. At Baltimore, while waiting for Lincoln's sleeper to be hitched to a new engine, the party listened tensely to "snatches of rebel harmony" being sung by secession-minded passengers waiting at the depot, unaware that they stood only a few yards from the president-elect. Nor was Lincoln's precise time of arrival in the capital known to anyone but a few trusted individuals. Finally, on the morning of February 23, his old friend, Illinois representative Elihu Washburne recognized Lincoln's "long, lank form" descending from the last car in the train, disguised in a "soft, low-crowned hat" and a heavy shawl, looking more like "a well-to-do farmer" than the Union's hoped-for savior. The black abolitionist Frederick Douglass, no fan of Lincoln at this time, wrote ironically that the president-elect "reached the Capital as the poor, hunted fugitive reaches the North, in disguise, seeking concealment, crawling and dodging under the sable wing of night."

When he checked into Willard's Hotel, Lincoln unexpectedly found himself virtually in the midst of the Peace Conference, which had now spent three grinding weeks toiling over a proposed constitutional amendment that differed little from the one that Crittenden had been promoting all winter. Lincoln diplomatically showed interest but declined to offer his endorsement. Crittenden, however, enthusiastically embraced the conference's proposals as his own and rushed them to the Senate floor for approval. There, in the face of opposition from both the antislavery North and the remaining Southerners, they went down to ignominious defeat.

But the compromisers had not given up. Yet another prospective amendment hewn from Crittenden's plan surfaced, this time from the House of Representatives. It trimmed off, like fat from a side of beef, every stipulation but one: that no future amendment to the Constitution could ever grant Congress the power to abolish or interfere with the "domestic institutions" of any state. Its sponsor was Rep. Thomas "Wagon Boy" Corwin, an Ohio Republican who was so known because as a young lad he had volunteered to drive a supply wagon for the army in the War of 1812. On February 28, the Corwin Amendment passed by a margin of 133 to 65, two votes more than the number required for approval. Three days later, William H. Seward introduced it in the Senate. Offensive as the amendment was to antislavery radicals, Republicans who supported it maintained, at least among themselves, that it was meaningless, since it essentially reiterated the prohibition that already existed in the Constitution. For its advocates, however, it represented the last quixotic hope of staving off civil war.

As the last hours of the Thirty-sixth Congress ticked away, Crittenden continued to plead for a compromise—his own, Corwin's, the Peace Conference's, anyone's—anything that would stop the tumbling rush of secession. He struggled to make himself heard over the near-deafening roar of voices that filled the chamber. Visitors—men in stifling black broadcloth, women in billowing silk dresses—swarmed over the galleries in a dense, heaving mass, pushing and clambering over each other, shouting that they had come all the way from "Indianny" or "Vermount," demanding a better view of the action on the floor, and filling the aisles so densely that it was impossible to remove them. When the sergeant-at-arms's men tried to clear the passages, the visitors tossed the officials out with a cheer.

Crittenden spoke of the nation's imminent ruin in words that self-consciously evoked both Shakespeare's Hamlet—a trope all his listeners would have immediately recognized—as well as Henry Clay's impassioned defense of the Union during the tumultuous debate that led to the Compromise of 1850. But his was the cracking voice of the past: urgent and reasonable, but irrelevant. The Union was being dismembered, he intoned. "It is our duty, if we can, to provide a remedy. [But] we have done absolutely nothing. We see the danger, we acknowledge our duty, and yet, with all this before us, we are acknowledging before the world that we can do nothing . . . presenting to the eyes of the world the saddest spectacle it has ever seen." Perhaps his own proposals were inadequate, he conceded. But what other policy was there that might possibly save the Union? "It must be to do something, or to do nothing. Few will say we ought to have sat here and witnessed this ruin and witnessed this revolution and done nothing."

Everyone knew that slavery was at the root of the country's terrible discontent, he said. "The controversy has infected the nation's vitals." But the rights and wrongs of slavery, whether it was a blessing or a sin, were all beside the point. The question at hand had no moral dimension at all: it was simply whether Southerners had a constitutional right to their property, and whether they, as American citizens, had equal rights in the western territories, which were the common property of the Union. "The slaveholding states only ask an increased security," he argued, "exactly proportionate to their altered condition in the Union," that is, a return to the effective veto power they enjoyed over actions of the national government, as long as it was controlled by the Democratic Party. It should be obvious to all that they deserved new guarantees for their "peculiar and special property." He proposed—he was a practical man—that the western territories be partitioned between the South and the North. The North would get the richer portion, two-thirds of the whole, while the South would content itself with the remaining third. Don't deny the South "this little item of satisfaction," he pleaded. "Was ever exaction so small to avert an evil so great?"

Turning then to the shrunken contingent of slave-state men who still remained, he urged "a generous spirit of fraternity," assuring them that someday there would be a new government more friendly to Southern interests. In the meantime, he counseled, "Be patient and bear it. Congress may err. [But] the Union is the best assurance you can have of eventually obtaining from your fellow citizens a generous recompense for all the wrongs you have received. What do I ask of you more than Mr. Clay did?"

Edward Baker of Oregon, Lincoln's closest friend in the Senate and a bellwether of conservative Republican opinion, added his silver-tongued voice to Crittenden's. Born in England, trained in lawyering in Illinois, and now a senator from the infant state of Oregon, Baker was regarded by his colleagues as one of the most splendid orators in the chamber, as well as one of the most statuesquely handsome, "rich in intellectual culture, with a mind comprehensive enough to retain the wisdom of the ages, and an eloquence to charm." He insisted that the North meant no harm to the South's cherished institution. "I do not propose to interfere with slavery in the States," he assured. "I never will do it. I will agree it never shall be done." Jettison the platform the party had adopted at its Chicago convention, he urged his fellow Republicans. There was nothing cowardly in that. Back in November, no one thought the Union was seriously threatened. "Texas is going, going, going, gone—gone even while I speak. I fear, I exceedingly tremble for the result in Virginia, and even in Kentucky. If there are fifteen states to whip, what hero will undertake it? What is the government if more than a third of those whom you attempt to govern defy it? How can you do it?" To fear disunion was not unmanly, he went on, and to endeavor to avoid it was not unworthy. "Once one drop of blood is shed, no man knows what rivers may be added to that one drop." Abandoning the platform was a small price to pay to "restore to this great country peace, to our government union, and bring us back to where we were; I would do it now, tomorrow, a thousand times, and forever, though the act would sink me into oblivion a thousand fathoms deep."

Radical Republicans were aghast at Baker's surrender. They received streams of letters from across the North decrying compromise in any form. "No more concessions, no more compromises," David Root, a Presbyterian minister from Connecticut, wrote furiously to Thaddeus Stevens. "Let us stick it to the bitter end. If civil war comes, let it come." "Stand firm," Philip Wilcox, an attorney in Atchison, Kansas, urged Ben Wade. "Don't back an inch to Carolina or any other state. They have had their way since the adoption of our Constitution. The time has come when they must knuckle under." On the floor of the Senate, Zachariah Chandler of Michigan, an outspoken abolitionist and veteran of the Underground Railroad, declared, "I will never live under a government that has not the power to enforce its laws. I would rather join the Comanches." But Baker had only said aloud what many other conservatives were thinking.

Northern Democrats were virtually unanimous in support of Crittenden. Stephen A. Douglas, coughing compulsively, dying from tuberculosis, exhaustion, overindulgence, and the flaming out of a fiery career, claimed that a comprehensive compromise was still within the Senate's grasp. The Republican Party had now caved on its most basic principles and agreed to protect slavery forever. Southerners ought to celebrate a victory, not flee the Union, he exclaimed.

But this was just wishful thinking. Henry Clay was eight years dead, the spirit of concession was but an uncertain flicker, and the hard-won compromise that had preserved the Union in 1850 was a ruin, exploded by the violent vagaries of popular sovereignty in the territories, by Bleeding Kansas, the Dred Scott decision, and John Brown's raid on Harpers Ferry. The Southerners who remained scoffed at compromise. James Mason of Virginia, the grandson of George Mason, the godfather of the Bill of Rights and one of the earliest critics of American slavery, rejected Crittenden's amendment out of hand because it implied that the federal government had a right to legislate on slavery. The amendment, Mason declared, was at best just "a placebo, a bread pill, something that was to quiet the patient by deluding him under the belief that he had taken a salutary medicine, when in fact he had taken a pill containing crumbs of bread."

Louis Wigfall of Texas, still sitting smugly in the Senate despite his state's secession a month earlier, predicted that if war came Southern armies would march on Boston. "The federal government is dead," he declared to a chorus of taunts and cheers from the galleries. "The only question is whether we will give it a decent, peaceable, Protestant burial. This Union is dissolved, never, never to be reconstructed upon any terms—not if you were to hand us blank paper, and ask us to write a constitution, would we ever again be confederated with you." Talk of compromise was mere "quack medicine." The Confederacy was impregnable—its ports could never be blockaded, and its privateers would sweep Yankee commerce from the seas. Yankee ships would rot at their wharves, machinery would rust in factories, and the public would rise up in opposition to war taxes. Lincoln would doubtless sue for peace. How could a weakling who had sneaked into the capital hidden "under a cloak and a Scotch cap" be taken seriously? "We have dissolved the Union: mend it if you can. Cement it with blood. Try the experiment."

Ben Wade—"Bluff Ben" to many—had remained remarkably restrained until now. At sixty, he was a tall, angular man with high

cheekbones, sharp bright eyes, and a manner of "bulldog obduracy,"
in the words of one journalist. In debate, he "looked at the contest
with the merciless eye of a gladiator about to close in a death-grip."
His style of speech was offhand and frequently profane. When he
warmed to a theme his iron-gray hair visibly bristled, his voice rose
to a roar, he would unbutton his vest and shove up his coat sleeves,
tear off his cravat, yank off his collar, hold his arms high, and then
jump onto his heels as he brought his arms down. His egalitarianism
was uncompromising. "I know no high, no low, no black, no white,
all are created by one God, and all are entitled to the same privileges,"
he had declared as far back as 1847. Staunch an abolitionist as he was,
he employed racist language without inhibition. On his arrival in
Washington in 1851, he had described it to his wife as "a mean God
forsaken Nigger ridden place," and during the debate over an early
version of a bill to offer homesteads to the public, he retorted to a
Southern antagonist: "The question will be, shall we give niggers to
the niggerless or land to the landless?" He readily acknowledged that
racism was woven into the fabric of Americans' minds. "Men are
not to blame for that," he said, "but they are to blame if they suffer
what they know to be prejudice to prevail on them to do injustice
to anybody." Rare for the time, he was a firm believer in equality
for women, calling opposition to female suffrage "a ridiculous old
prejudice." Contemptuous of the Southern insults that intimidated
many of his Northern colleagues, he had taken to carrying a rifle-
cane and a pair of pistols he ostentatiously laid across his desk when
he thought it useful. He regarded slavery not just as a moral atrocity but also as an economic anachronism that must succumb to the
greater efficiency of modern industry. "Once you might work the
galley slave with profit," he reminded his Senate colleagues on one
occasion. "[But] how is it when you pit the galley slave against the
steam engine? Every labor-saving machine is an abolitionist. Every
pull of the engine upon a railroad is an abolition sermon."

He now erupted like the thunder of cannon. Along with Thaddeus
Stevens, his like-minded colleague in the House, Wade accepted the
inevitability of war, and he believed that it would have to be fought
not only to reknit the United States, but for something still larger, on
behalf of "the hopes of many nations now struggling for freedom

and the rights of man." Yes, the United States was "in the midst of a great and unusual revolution," he asserted. That much was clear to everyone. But what kind of revolution? Usually revolutions arose among people who had been trampled underfoot by tyrants. But there had been no such oppression in the United States. Those who were now rising against the government weren't asserting the rights of man but hoping to erect a despotism upon the ruins of the most equitable government that the world has ever seen. "You complain of us that we have a free press and free speech, and love liberty too well," he charged. "The [real] difficulty is that you can't exert a despotism in the free states of the North." Crittenden's compromise, like every other proposed compromise, was a delusion, he said. If the North gave in now, the South would surely be back again in the next Congress with even more extravagant demands. "It is all quackery," he roared. "To reconstruct your institutions upon a basis that will be permanent and eternal, as you dream, you will have to reconstruct the throne of God, and change the principles upon which He has chosen to govern the world. Go, and upon your own heads be the consequences of war; for you shall have war, be assured of that. We are ready to meet you and your treasonable designs. If it must be, let it come now; let brother take brother by the throat, and when it comes to the worst, let the stronger party prevail and possess the whole land!"

The senators kept up their rolling fire of debate deep into the night under the flickering yellow light of the gas lamps, slipping away from time to time to the Hole-in-the-Wall, a tiny eatery tucked behind the Senate post office, for ham sandwiches and generous draughts of wine. Below Capitol Hill, the city of Washington spread out like a scattering of stars fallen to earth. Despite their efforts to stay awake, senators nodded and drowsed, heads fallen against their chests, or napped fitfully on sofas at the back of the chamber. As the dawn cracked in the eastern sky, and the bright sun of Inauguration Day stretched its fingers over the awakening city, the debate at last resolved itself into a fitful series of votes.

The Corwin Amendment, with Crittenden's fervent support, was finally approved by a vote of twenty-four to twelve, the bare two-thirds that it needed to pass. One of James Buchanan's last acts in office before the inauguration was to sign the compromise amendment—although his signature was not required by the Constitution, he hoped that it would lend the measure prestige, discounted though that commodity might be—and dispatch it to the states, begging for their ratification. But it was all, in the end, a shadow play, an exercise in panicky desperation signifying nothing. Only two states would ratify the Corwin Amendment before events overtook it. The future lay not with the obsolete Crittenden and his conciliatory ilk, but with the angry and uncompromising, and with the farsighted, who saw that war must finally come and that it must be met. Henry Clay's pacificating spirit refused to rise from the dead.

The senators were still arguing when the morning broke clear and beautiful, and unusually warm for March. They hurriedly dispatched the backlog of bills that had been held hostage to the compromise debate: legal protection for American guano miners off the coast of Peru, the allotment of a pension to a Mexican War widow, payments to Indian fighters in Oregon, the appropriation of money for a military road to Santa Fe. But greater things were afoot. Below the Capitol, the Stars and Stripes flew over every public building and from private homes, and fluttered from ropes stretched above the major avenues. A martial cacophony of fifes and drums sounded from every direction. Soldiers and gaily uniformed militiamen thronged the streets, marching and countermarching, stirring up dust in clouds that coated everything and everyone. At 9:00 a.m. the inaugural parade began to form on Louisiana Avenue, near the city courts. Marshals dressed in black except for buckskin gloves and pink batons strutted and preened, and struggled to give some kind of order to the contingents of governors and ex-governors, state legislators, judges, Republican clubs, clergymen, diplomats in their official regalia, doddering veterans from the Revolutionary War and the War of 1812, brass bands, wagonloads of pretty girls dressed to represent the states, and thousands of ordinary citizens who wanted to join in. At 11:00 a.m., the parade began to move up Pennsylvania Avenue toward Willard's Hotel, where it waited for the president-elect to emerge. Orderlies galloped up and down the lines on prancing mounts. The crowd cheered, bugles blew, and the bands played patriotic songs and popular airs. One of them was Stephen Foster's wildly popular "Way Down South in Dixie."

Lincoln at last emerged, dressed in a new cashmere suit and carrying an uncharacteristically aristocratic gold-tipped ebony cane to greet Buchanan, who had arrived in the presidential carriage with Sen. James A. Pearce of Maryland, one of the few loyalists the hapless outgoing president still had in Congress. Lincoln and his friend Edward Baker stepped in, and the four of them, in near-silence, drove east down Pennsylvania Avenue, under the watchful eyes of snipers posted on the rooftops, the first time in American history that military security had been organized for a presidential inauguration. A cloud of cavalrymen enveloped the carriage so thickly that few bystanders caught a clear glimpse of Lincoln. Even then, rumors persisted that Lincoln would be assassinated en route to his inauguration—"You will be shot on the 4th of March 1861 by a Louisiana Creole we are decided and our aim is sure," an anonymous letter warned—or that there would be outright insurrection before he took the oath of office. If Lincoln was frightened, he didn't show it. Buchanan seemed morose, as well he might, since he surely knew that Americans of most every political cast regarded him as a failure.

When they reached the Capitol, Lincoln and Buchanan pointedly walked arm in arm to the House chamber, in a symbolic image of unity, to witness the swearing in of the new vice president, Hannibal Hamlin. At five minutes before noon, Solomon Foot of Vermont, the Senate's senior member, escorted Hamlin to a chair on the dais next to the outgoing vice president, the square-jawed, slave-owning, honey-voiced John Breckinridge of Kentucky, the losing presidential candidate of the breakaway Southern Democrats in the 1860 election. "In taking final leave of this position," Breckinridge, who before the year was out would be wearing a Confederate general's uniform, began, "I can ask but a moment amidst the busy scenes around us, to tender you my grateful acknowledgments. I have never appealed in vain to your justice or your charity. And for my successor, I can express no better wish than that he may enjoy those relations of mutual confidence and regard which have so happily marked my intercourse with the Senate." After this, Hamlin drew himself up to his full height, a commanding six feet three inches, and declared in his resonant twang that with "inflexible purpose," trusting in the courtesy and cooperation of the senators, and the aid of Divine Providence, he was ready to discharge the duty entrusted to him by the American public. Placing his hand on the Bible that Breckinridge held out to him, he swore to uphold the Constitution. At noon sharp, Hamlin brought down the gavel and declared the battered, shrunken, and tragically ineffectual Thirty-sixth Congress to be at an end.

The words of both Hamlin and Breckinridge were oratorical boilerplate. But the gavel's crack marked a significant transition, a moment perhaps even more symbolic than Lincoln's arm-in-arm stroll through the Capitol with Buchanan. A slave-owning Southern Democrat had handed power over to an abolitionist, the most radical man ever to sit in the vice president's chair: the entire American political world seemed to have been turned on its head.

The senators and congressmen then made their way to the Capitol's east front, facing First Street, to muster with the members of the Supreme Court and other dignitaries. A table had been set up for the new president, facing a cheering crowd of 25,000. Smartly dressed New Yorkers mingled with Yankees from New England, blacks enslaved and free, staid Quakers from Pennsylvania, lanky Westerners from beyond the Appalachians. There were few Southerners, a reporter surmised, "judging from the lack of long-haired men in the crowd." Edward Baker stepped forward, and announced, "Fellow citizens, I introduce you to Abraham Lincoln, the President-elect of the United States of America!"

# 3

# A Wretched Humbug

With power comes responsibility,
and we must now prepare to take it.

—SEN. LYMAN TRUMBULL

In his first speech as president, Lincoln restated in his thin, high-pitched voice what Baker had said to the Senate the night before: "I have no purpose, directly or indirectly, to interfere with the institution of slavery in the States where it exists." Along with many other members of his party, Lincoln still believed that beneath the demagogic rhetoric of secession the South was teeming with quiescent Unionists who with a little encouragement would rise up and retake their states from the fire-eaters. With this in mind, he condemned the "lawless invasion" of any state—an unmistakable reference to John Brown's raid—and promised that his administration would continue to vigorously enforce the Fugitive Slave Law. In short, law-abiding states had nothing to fear from the new Republican government. He was even willing to support the Corwin Amendment. However, he added, the Constitution had intended the Union to be eternal, and it was therefore the national government's duty to defend itself, and his own duty to ensure that the Union's laws were enforced in every state. "There will be no invasion, no use of force," he said, but "if the minority will not acquiesce, the majority must or the government must cease." Secession could lead only to complete national disintegration. "If a minority will secede rather than acquiesce, they make a precedent which, in turn, will divide and ruin them; for a minority of their own will secede from them whenever a majority refuses to be controlled by such minority." He then rephrased his argument in a homely metaphor that no one could fail to understand. "Plainly speaking, we cannot separate," Lincoln said. "We cannot remove our respective sections from each other, nor build an impassable wall between them. A husband and wife may be divorced, and go out of the presence, and beyond the reach of each other; but the different parts of our country cannot do this. They cannot but remain face to face." Finally, he declared, the momentous issue of civil war lay "in your hands, my dissatisfied countrymen, and not in mine. The government will not assail you. You can have no conflict without being yourselves the aggressors. You have no oath registered in Heaven to destroy the government, while I shall have the most solemn one to 'preserve, protect and defend' it." He concluded with his now famous appeal to Americans' shared history: "The mystic chords of memory, stretching from every battlefield and patriot grave, to every living heart and hearthstone all over this broad land, will yet swell the chorus of the Union, when again touched, as surely they will be, by the better angels of our nature." When Lincoln had done, the feeble Roger Taney, chief justice of the Supreme Court, now eighty-three years old, a Jacksonian Democrat and former slave owner who had held his position since 1836, and who had written the Dred Scott decision, trembling with age and gazing upward at the much taller Lincoln, administered to him the oath of office.

The Republican New York Times approvingly declared the inaugural to be "a document of precisely the right stamp—firm in support of the Government, and highly conciliatory," but it left many other Americans deeply unsatisfied. The secessionist Charleston Mercury denounced it as "a monstrous compendium of impotence and perversity," while the Richmond Times Dispatch declared that the speech alone was tantamount to an act of war. The hostile Ohio congressman Clement Vallandigham charged that Lincoln had delivered his speech "with the forked tongue and crooked counsel of the New York politician, leaving thirty millions of people in doubt whether he meant peace or war." The New York Herald dismissed it as weak and indecisive, a packet of "vague generalities," and predicted that the administration would never find enough troops to put down the Southern rebellion, and that the Republican Party would split in two if it dared to try. At the other end of the spectrum, abolitionists were disappointed at Lincoln's apparent capitulation to the interests of slavery. Frederick Douglass called the address a "revolting declaration" that "offered immunity to traitors." The diarist George Templeton Strong, a conservative Republican, perceptively observed that many of his Northern friends, whose business interests caused them to favor the South, approved of the address for its conciliatory tone. He acutely added, "But I think there's the clank of metal in it."

Governing was a new experience for the Republicans. Few had held significant federal posts before. They had never elected a president or controlled the Senate. None had ever sat on the Supreme Court. Although Democrats still dominated the court, the rest of the government was in the midst of a revolutionary upheaval. The House of Representatives would not meet again until July, but the Senate continued meeting in special session, and the shift of power was instantly apparent. Southerners and their Northern friends who had chaired the most important Senate committees were swept aside. Pitt Fessenden of Maine became chairman of the Finance Committee; Charles Sumner of Massachusetts chairman of Foreign Affairs; Henry Wilson of Massachusetts chairman of Military Affairs; Zachariah Chandler of Michigan chairman of Commerce; Lyman Trumbull of Illinois chairman of Judiciary; John P. Hale of New Hampshire chairman of Naval Affairs; Ben Wade of Ohio chairman of the Committee on Territories. All were self-described abolitionists except Fessenden and Trumbull, and they would soon be won over. Never before in the nation's history had so many radicals, or New Englanders—Chandler, Trumbull, and Wade were all New England–born—wielded such concentrated power.

Republican office seekers deluged and harassed members of Congress with pleas for federal jobs in arsenals, customs houses, post offices, and bureaus. Some were obsequious, such as John Rawlins, who wrote to Thaddeus Stevens that he was "tolerably acquainted" with the Bible, Shakespeare, and Webster's dictionary, and hoped that it would be "possible that in some nook or corner of 'Uncle Abe's' extensive domains there might be an official place for my humble self." Other appeals were pathetic, like that of Joseph Ritner, who begged for any kind of job at all, offering by way of qualification that he was "not totally blind," and Theodore McGowan, a Princeton graduate from Pennsylvania who had been teaching for five years in South Carolina and was desperate to escape further "molestation" for his Yankee views. Bribery was not unheard of. It was widely rumored that Ohio congressman Thomas Corwin had sold clerkships to three Dayton men for $100 apiece, and more prestigious offices for $1,000 or more.

Like many new presidents both before and after, Lincoln took office with a fuzzy grasp of all that the presidency entailed. The British ambassador, Lord Lyons, appraising Lincoln for his masters in London, reported that he seemed ignorant "of everything but Illinois village politics." His cabinet choices were a mixed bag that took careful account of geographical balance and the Republican Party's varied constituencies. The appointment of his chief rival, Sen. William H. Seward of New York, as secretary of state was widely praised, and that of the notoriously corrupt senator Simon Cameron as secretary of war—a gesture to the important state of Pennsylvania—just as roundly condemned. The appointment of abolitionist senator Salmon P. Chase of Ohio to Treasury pleased the Radicals and the Ohioans, although his experience in finance was limited. The selection of the obscure Connecticut newspaperman Gideon Welles as secretary of the navy was intended to assuage New Englanders, while the appointment of Missourian Edward Bates as attorney general and Montgomery Blair of Maryland as postmaster general served as a conciliatory gesture to the slaveholding border states.

A disproportionate amount of the president's time was taken up meeting patiently with the endless "ill-bred, ravenous crowd" of job seekers who knocked hopefully at the door of the White House. Lincoln rarely turned anyone away without at least an interview. Yet more precious time was wasted on bureaucratic trivia. Lincoln, Seward irritably complained to his wife, tried to do too much himself, and "takes that business up first which is pressed upon him the most." Seward later told ambassador-designate to Great Britain Charles Francis Adams that Lincoln had "no conception of his situation—much absorption in the details of office dispensation, but little application to great ideas."

Meanwhile, the festering secession crisis worsened. The only military facilities in the South that remained in federal hands were Fortress Monroe near Norfolk, Fort Pickens at Pensacola, Fort Jefferson off Key West in the Dry Tortugas, and Fort Sumter. Fort Jefferson was too isolated to be under much threat. Fort Pickens needed reinforcement, but it was stoutly defended, as was Fortress Monroe. Fort Sumter, however, was in danger of immediate attack. Its garrison was vastly outnumbered and threatened by starvation, while its flag taunted the rebels in the very cradle of secession. In his inaugural address, Lincoln had promised both to avoid bloodshed and to defend federal property that was threatened by the rebels. But it was more clear by the day that he couldn't do both. Time was running out: the day after his inauguration, Lincoln received a report from Major Anderson that Sumter's supplies would last no later than mid-April.

Secessionist sentiment was more rampant than ever in the nation's capital. There was talk in the streets of making Washington the capital of the Confederacy. Secessionist fire-eaters were feasted and flattered, and openly formed rifle clubs that barely disguised their military intent. Nervous Unionists were sure that the strange whistles they heard in the night meant that government officials were being followed. If an uprising took place, General Scott had only five hundred men he knew he could count on.

As the administration's first weeks slipped by, Democrats damned its "disastrous, halting, and hesitating" lack of policy. Impatient Republicans charged that Lincoln seemed hopelessly devoid of leadership. "I want plain outspoken language," complained one frustrated Michigan Yankee. "Lincoln's pronouncements have been too ambiguous." The Republicans in Congress were sharply divided. Radicals urged muscular confrontation, arguing that failure to reinforce Sumter would be a catastrophe for both their party and the

nation. "Without a little bloodshed this Union will not, in my estimation, be worth a rush," Sen. Zachariah Chandler declared.

Conservatives, both Democratic and Republican, vigorously
opposed forceful action of any kind. Seward, for one, warned that
attempting to resupply Fort Sumter would likely drive the border
states out of the Union. He instead urged calculated delay, to provide time for moderate Southern Unionists to regain control of their
states. Others, including Chase, who opposed concessions on principle, warned that the government simply didn't have the money to
fight a war. "A wet buckskin string would make a better backbone
than either [Chase] or Seward exhibit," one irate Cincinnatian wrote
to Ben Wade. But even the ardently antislavery *New York Tribune*
counseled peaceful accommodation.

In truth, the compromisers were living a delusion. The supposed
moderate majority didn't exist. If anything, support for Southern
nationhood was rapidly growing. "All the powers on earth can *never*
force us back into the Same Confederacy with you," two Carolinians
wrote jointly to Ben Wade. "We have a white man's government and
will suffer death with all its horrors before we will exchange it for a
negro government like yours."

Dominating the Senate's special session through the first three
rain-sodden weeks of March was the man who might have been
president, Stephen A. Douglas, the "Little Giant," the ferociously
partisan champion of the Northern Democrats, and Lincoln's long-
ago rival in Illinois. He began on March 6 with what seemed to be
a full-throated defense of the administration and its passiveness
toward the South. Lincoln's inaugural address, he insisted, should
be seen as a *peace offering*. It was, he confessed, far more conciliatory
than he had expected. Lincoln had pledged to do nothing to provoke
war. He had not sworn to retake forts that the South had occupied,
or to defend the ones the government still held. He had even implied
that he would abandon Fort Sumter, if that would bring peace! More
than that, he promised to do everything in his power to enforce
the Fugitive Slave Law, and made clear that he wouldn't oppose an
amendment to the Constitution to protect slavery everywhere in the
territories. "What more can be said?" Douglas exclaimed. "He has
sunk the partisan in the patriot."

Douglas's apparent support for the administration was invaluable. But his motives were not unmixed. When he spoke, it was with the assumed authority of a man who, despite his defeat in November, still regarded himself as the Democratic Party's natural leader, as well as a consummate strategist who, if he played his hand well, hoped to seize the political initiative from the hands of the untried man in the White House. Although Douglas was ostensibly lending his help to Lincoln, he was also trying to box him in by forcing him to declare on the record precisely what he intended to do. If Douglas could claim credit for resolving the national crisis, he would revive the shattered fortunes of the Democrats, and hope to lead his party to victory in the 1862 elections over a Republican Party that had caved on its antislavery principles and disillusioned many of its followers. Beyond that, he foresaw the creation of a new center-right alliance combining conservatives from both parties on a platform that would call for the reconstruction of the government on principles that would allow the seceded states to return. Douglas thus had nothing to lose and everything to gain by praising Lincoln's weak statesmanship, while implicitly suggesting that the administration had embraced the Democrats' peace policy.

Douglas was challenged by the bearded and bellicose Louis Wigfall of Texas, who was or was not still a senator depending on one's angle of vision. Although Texas had officially seceded on February 1, and Wigfall himself had been appointed to the *Confederate* Senate, his beefy backside had remained tenaciously in his seat, from which he repeatedly mocked anyone, Republican or Democrat, who rose to defend the Union. Loudly bragging to all and sundry about his contempt for the United States, he passed on military information to his Southern friends, bought arms for the Confederacy, and swaggered around encouraging men to enlist in the secessionist forces.

"It is easy to talk of enforcing the laws," Wigfall drawled. "But when you come to holding, occupying, and possessing forts, [only] bayonets, and not words, settle the question." The "Union" that Douglas was so busily defending didn't even exist anymore, either legally or in fact. "I deny it in toto," Wigfall barked. "Take your flag out of our country, or you must make up your minds to have war." The seceded states were never coming back. "If you were to give them a blank sheet of paper and tell them to write their constitution on it they would not come in again. No compromise, no amendment of the Constitution, no arrangement that you enter into will be satisfactory to those states, unless you recognize the doctrine that slaves are property, and that you will protect that species of property as you will every other."

Douglas turned on Wigfall with palpable disgust. The Texan had repeatedly declared that he now regarded himself as a "foreigner" in the United States, so why was he still here?

Wigfall blithely retorted that the government of Texas had not yet officially informed him that it had abolished the office of United States senator. When it did, he would pick up his things and leave. Until then, he'd continue to show up as long as it suited him.

Fed up with Wigfall's insulting behavior, Sen. Lafayette S. Foster of Connecticut moved that since Wigfall admitted that he no longer owed allegiance to the United States, he deserved to be expelled immediately from the Senate. If Foster's proposal passed, it would be the first expulsion of a senator in American history and would lead inexorably to the expulsion of the other slave-state senators who had left their seats.

North Carolina senator Thomas L. Clingman leaped to Wigfall's defense. If the Texan said that he was a "foreigner," that was just his own opinion—Wigfall had every right to remain until he was ordered by his state to leave. To this, Robert Hunter of Virginia, an ardent secessionist, slyly added that if Congress were to expel Wigfall on the supposition that the seceded states were no longer in the Union, then it would imply the de facto recognition of those states as foreign countries, and they should hereafter be treated as such.

Pitt Fessenden's acute parliamentary instincts immediately recognized the unstable ground upon which the Senate was about to step. In January, he had warned of the risks posed by legislation that even hinted at the independence of any breakaway state. He now proposed that since the men who had been elected to represent the several rebellious states were effectively members of the Senate no longer, their seats had thereby become *vacant*, and their names should simply be stricken from the official roll. "In my opinion, the acts that took place here were a resignation," he said. It was a clever move, with far-reaching significance that was not obvious at the time. By declaring the seats merely "vacant" the resolution would strip Wigfall and the others of any claim to participate in the Senate's business, sidestep the constitutional consequences of secession, and leave the means of refilling those vacant seats up to Congress itself in the future. The maneuver would eventually form the basis for the wartime reorganization of Southern states and the strategic enlargement of Republican Party power in Congress.

Both Foster's and Fessenden's proposals hung fire while off the Senate floor impatient Republican Radicals sought to push the administration toward a more forceful stand. In a nominally secret caucus on March 13, Ben Wade boldly proposed that the party's lawmakers go to Lincoln en masse to demand that he reject all schemes for abandoning Fort Sumter. Wade reportedly declared that the fort ought to be held even if it cost 100,000 lives in the process. Zachariah Chandler, Wade's close ally, a wealthy Detroit businessman, offered to personally arrange the resupply of the garrison for just $50,000, if necessary. Neither proposal was accepted by the caucus, but it represented a first shot across the administration's bow from Capitol Hill Republicans who were determined to assert congressional power over any war-making that was to take place.

Later, on the Senate floor, Wade made his view explicit. "I do not know what the policy of this Administration may be, but I entertain very strong opinions upon the subject," he declared. The Senate, in view of the dire situation that the country faced, had a political and constitutional duty to "express itself," he said. "The president may indicate the measures that he sees fit to pursue, but we are a coordinate branch; we are his advisers; and it is right and proper that we should, in emergencies like the present, express our opinions in full, not only to the president, but to the people."

Douglas may have caught wind of the hardening sentiment among the Republicans, because on the same day as the Republican caucus he played what he clearly considered his strongest card. He offered a startling and provocative resolution that swept all other concerns from the stage: that the secretary of war report to the Senate exactly what forts, arsenals, and naval facilities the government still held in the seceded states; and whether it had the means to retain them and to recapture the ones that had already been seized. Douglas's resolution further called upon Secretary of War Cameron, and implicitly the president, to declare in detail the size of the military force that would be required to compel the seceded states to obey the laws of the United States. With this, Douglas sought to force Lincoln's hand. By compelling the administration to make public the real costs of a war that the American people would never support, Douglas believed, he would leave the government with no choice but to support his own plan for negotiation with the secessionists. "Tell us where we are drifting, so that we can decide if we're willing to be drawn into war without the approval of Congress or public consent," Douglas demanded. With this, Douglas was also opening a question that would have vast ramifications in the months and years to come: did the president have the authority to wage war without the explicit approval of Congress, or did he not?

Lincoln ought to know that he couldn't legally do anything by himself that would lead to armed conflict, Douglas said. "He has no more discretion to blockade New Orleans or Charleston than he has New York or Boston." Nor did the president have the authority to call out the army or navy, unless he was specifically asked to by a state governor in the case of internal insurrection. That was hardly the case in South Carolina, where the state itself was challenging the national government. Furthermore, it was plain that Congress had no intention of granting the president the means to make war on the breakaway states.

"The question is whether we are going to reduce the southern confederacy by military force," Douglas said. "Let us get at the facts." Why, if the government intended peace, as he had been led to think, had the navy's Mediterranean squadron been ordered to come home? Why were stocks of armament being collected at New York? Did the administration intend to retake the forts and to use them as a starting point for invading the states in which they lay? If so, how many men would it take? How many soldiers would it take just to secure Fort Sumter? Ten thousand? Twenty thousand? Rumor had it that it would require 35,000 men just to protect the city of Washington, and 250,000 more to defeat the secessionists throughout the

South—far more soldiers than had ever been gathered on the North American continent. He had further heard that it would cost $1 million for every nine-hundred-man regiment that was raised, and $300 million or more to keep the forces that were deployed in the field for a year. Such numbers were almost beyond imagining. Where would all that money come from? No tariff could bring in anything close to that. Direct taxation? Could the American people be made to pay for a war they didn't even want to fight, "a war of indefinite duration that will require a quarter of a million men and exorbitant taxation, levied on one half of the American people to subdue the other half?" Douglas was now in full rant. "Let your policy be proclaimed to the world! Silence is criminal when we are on the eve of events like these!"

Republicans were understandably furious with Douglas: the information he was asking for was vital to national security. But in fact, if anything, Douglas's estimates were far too modest. Nor were his questions unreasonable. But the Republicans were not about to let him hamstring the administration with the truth. "It is evident that he knows nothing," Fessenden savagely declared. "Who ever heard that an administration, when it first came into power and was not warm in its seat, would at once lay before the country what it designed to do when it could hardly say what it designed to do itself?" Douglas, he continued, was throwing around numbers just to scare people. How did he even come up with them? He had apparently just picked them up on the street. What was his point, except to inflame the people and increase their fears? "Are we to be drawn into a flame by the ravings of every politician who wishes to get up an excitement in this chamber or out of it?" One highly pleased supporter afterward wrote to Fessenden, "You fairly stripped the lion skin from the gentleman and showed the animal beneath to be nothing but a braying ass!"

Douglas was exhausted and ill, and it showed. His nerves frayed under Fessenden's pounding. He began to lose control. In his fury, his ego burst desperately through. "Seven states are out of the Union, commerce is interrupted, confidence destroyed, the country going to pieces, just because I was unable to defeat you"—that is, the Republicans. "You can boast that you defeated me, but you have defeated your country with me. God only knows what consequences may grow out of it."

Although Douglas had monopolized the debate, he failed to pin the administration down and bend it to his will. His resolution failed to reach a vote. "We do not attach the consequence to the senator's speech that he attaches to it himself," Fessenden dismissively announced. "We do not think that the country hangs upon his words." Douglas might still dream of overthrowing the Republicans in the next election. But his career, one of the most dynamic in nineteenth-century American politics, was on the cusp of extinction.

On the last day of the session, March 26, peering shortsightedly through large gold-rimmed spectacles, Lyman Trumbull offered a Republican counterproposal. The forty-six-year-old Trumbull, who though New England–born had taught school and studied law in the Deep South, smiled rarely, stuck to facts, and reminded some of a Puritan preacher in manner. His proposal included no boilerplate appeal for conciliation or pleas for peace: "It is the duty of the president to use all the means in his power to hold and protect the public property of the United States, and enforce the laws thereof as well as in [the seceded states] as within the other states of the Union." The resolution never came to a vote, but it made clear what Congress wanted and expected from the president: leadership and spine.

A week earlier, a naval captain grandly named Gustavus Vasa Fox, after the great seventeenth-century Swedish king, had been presented to Lincoln and the cabinet. A graduate of Annapolis and a seasoned sailor, Fox laid out an ambitious scheme he had thought up to relieve Fort Sumter. It was no secret that food was in short supply, and the garrison could not long hold out with empty stomachs. Rather than send warships to run a narrow gauntlet between the sandbars that blocked the entrance to Charleston harbor, where they would be sitting ducks for Confederate batteries, Fox offered to lead shallow-draft tugboats over the sandbars under cover of darkness. Lincoln was won over. He directed Fox to organize a cargo of supplies and two hundred soldiers to reinforce Anderson. A separate expedition was mounted to resupply Fort Pickens, under the auspices of Seward and the State Department.

Seward, still confident that he could reach a peaceful settlement if Anderson's garrison was removed, strongly advised against provoking the Carolinians. Through intermediaries, he had already conferred with emissaries of the Confederate government to negotiate terms of separation. Then, on April 1, in one of the most extraordinarily flatfooted moves in American history, he proposed to Lincoln that he provoke an international incident leading to war with Spain and France, and perhaps even Britain and Russia, over their alleged interference in Mexico and the Caribbean. This, Seward argued, would distract both North and South from the secession issue, and induce them to reunite in a paroxysm of patriotism. Seward, who saw himself as an activist prime minister to the unsophisticated president, then went on to offer to manage the American response to this new international crisis, to in effect co-opt presidential power. Seward, not unlike Douglas, took for granted that he was Lincoln's superior, and that the president would easily be outmaneuvered. Much as Douglas had been thwarted by the congressional Republicans, Seward was cut down to size by the president himself. Lincoln wisely ignored the secretary of state's presumption. "If this must be done, I must do it," he decisively told Seward, offering a glimpse of the steel that lay beneath his rough-hewn persona.

Although Charleston had been in slow decline for decades, it remained the Confederacy's most important port on the Atlantic coast. Its physical setting was sweepingly picturesque, on a narrow peninsula between the Ashley and Cooper Rivers, and buffered against the open sea by a semicircle of low, swampy islands and sandbars. A center of the slave trade since colonial times, the city had some forty slave markets still operating, retailing thousands of men, women, and children each year. Blacks, 85 percent of them slaves, comprised almost half of the city's population and filled almost every rung of the laboring classes from the most menial to the most skilled. Publicly, white Charlestonians boasted of their slaves' devotion, but they lived in constant unspoken fear of a servile uprising that would butcher men, women, and children in their beds.

No one in Charleston doubted the ultimate triumph of the Con-

federate cause. Popular feeling was reflected in the ardently secessionist *Charleston Mercury*, which dismissed federal power as "a
wretched humbug—a scarecrow—a dirty bundle of red rags and
old clothes," and that Yankee soldiers were no more than a mob of
"poor hirelings" who would never fight. Facing Fort Sumter were
three thousand militiamen commanded by Pierre Gustave Toutant
Beauregard, who had resigned as West Point's superintendent to
offer his services to the Confederacy. After three months camped on
the sand dunes and snake-infested islands around the harbor, they
were impatient to fight.

Lincoln's long internal struggle over the political consequences
of relieving Fort Sumter came to an end on April 4. He had finally
concluded that war must come, and that it would serve the federal
government's interests to provoke the rebels to fire the first shot.
With this in mind, he officially informed South Carolina's governor
that an attempt would be made to resupply Fort Sumter with food,
but that no further attempt to throw in men, arms, or ammunition
would be made without further notice.

On April 10, the first of Fox's vessels, the *Harriet Lane,* a small revenue cutter, appeared off Charleston. For the Carolinians, the sight
of her brought everything to a head. The next afternoon, a small
boat flying a white flag pushed off from the Battery. In it were three
envoys representing the Confederate States government. Slaves
rowed them three and a half miles across the harbor to Fort Sumter, where they were met by the ironically named Lt. Jefferson C.
Davis of the U.S. Army, who was no relation to his namesake, the
newly named president of the Confederacy. Davis led the envoys
to the fort's commander, Maj. Robert Anderson, from whom they
demanded immediate surrender. Anderson thanked them but said,
"It is a demand with which I regret that my sense of honor, and my
obligation to my Government prevent my compliance." He added
that he would surely be starved out in a few days anyway, if the cannon that ringed the harbor didn't blast him to pieces first.

Feeling that his hopelessly outgunned men had defended the flag
as best they could, Anderson informed Beauregard that he would
evacuate the fort by noon on the 15th, adding that he wouldn't open
fire on the rebel forces unless he was attacked first. But the Carolin-

ians had run out of patience. At 4:30 a.m., the sound of a mortar broke the stillness. A signal shell rose high into the still starry sky, curved downward, and burst directly over Fort Sumter. Batteries on Morris Island opened up, then others from Johnson's Island, then from Sullivan's Island, sending vast flocks of terrified waterbirds swirling skyward from the surrounding marshes, until the fort was surrounded by a ring of fire. Shouts of triumph rang from the rebel emplacements as geysers of brick and mortar spumed up where balls hit the ramparts.

At 7:00 a.m., Anderson ordered his men to return fire. Within an hour, the wooden officers' quarters were on fire. Stacked shells burst from the heat, while suffocating clouds of smoke and burning cinders sprayed over the defenders. Flames from the burning barracks spread rapidly, as heavy masses of brick crashed to the ground. As the fire crept toward the powder magazine, soldiers raced to move hundreds of barrels of powder that threatened to explode and to blow the entire fort and its garrison into the cloudless sky. Then, as the supply of cartridges steadily shrank, Sumter's cannon fell silent one by one. By afternoon, only six were still firing.

In the aristocratic homes of Charleston, the artillery's roar rattled even devout secessionists. "Some of the anxious hearts lie on their beds and moan in solitary misery," trying to reassure themselves that God was truly on the Confederate side, recorded Chesnut. "When we are shut in, Mrs. Wigfall and I ask 'Why?' 'Of course, He hates the Yankees,' we are told."

In mid-afternoon, Louis Wigfall—with hardly a farewell, he had finally abandoned his desk in the Senate—had himself rowed out to the fort under a white flag to again call upon Anderson to give up. Wigfall had no authority at all to negotiate a surrender. He was essentially grandstanding, as he had so often done in the Senate. He loftily offered Anderson the same terms that Beauregard had a few days earlier. This time, with the fort on fire, Anderson agreed, and ordered a white flag to be raised.

The surrender almost collapsed when three Confederate officers showed up with *official* authority to ask for Anderson's capitulation. Anderson was so furious at having given up to the freelancing Wigfall that he almost ran up the Stars and Stripes again. However, he was persuaded to wait until confirmation of the terms of surrender arrived from Beauregard. Amazingly, despite an estimated three thousand cannonballs fired at the fort, not a single man had been killed on either side and only a handful of the fort's defenders had been injured by flying fragments of concrete and brick.

The next morning, Sunday, April 14, Fort Sumter's remaining pieces of artillery began a ceremonial cannonade of what was meant to total fifty guns. Tragically, however, in the midst of this melancholy farewell, a cannon misfired and blew off the right arm of one of its gunners, killing him almost instantly and critically wounding another. They were the first fatalities of the Civil War.

At 4:30 p.m., Anderson handed the fort over to the South Carolina militia. His exhausted soldiers formed up amidst the rubble of the parade ground with flags flying and drums beating the tune of "Yankee Doodle." Within minutes, the flags of the Confederacy and of South Carolina were snapping over the blasted ramparts.

A steamboat lent by a local businessman carried Anderson's men beyond the bar to the federal fleet, past hundreds of joyful Charlestonians gathered on steamers, sailboats, bobbing rowboats, and dinghies, under the eyes of rebel soldiers poised silently on the shore, their heads bared in an unplanned gesture of respect for their erstwhile fellow countrymen as they departed. Physically and emotionally drained, dazed from forty-eight hours without sleep, starved for decent food, Anderson's men gazed backward toward the fort where, every one of them knew, they had made grim history, until it at last sank away below the horizon. The war had begun.

4

# Forward to Richmond!

War, unrelenting war, is resolved upon. It is vain
to oppose it. One might as well oppose his uplifted
hand to the descending waters of Niagara.

—SEN. JOHN BRECKINRIDGE

Sumter changed everything. News of the fort's surrender reached Washington on April 14. In the ensuing days, President Lincoln proclaimed that "combinations too powerful to be suppressed by the ordinary course of legal proceedings" were obstructing the enforcement of federal laws. He unilaterally summoned 75,000 militiamen for three months' service to forcibly retake the national property that had been seized by the rebels, directed Northern navy yards to acquire and arm civilian ships for battle, and ordered a blockade of Southern ports. With the mails and telegraph compromised by disloyal employees, he dispatched couriers to New York to authorize state officials there to spend up to $2 million in Treasury funds to equip and transport militiamen for the relief of the capital, secretly bypassing the federal administration, which the Republicans, with reason, believed to be riddled with traitors.

Lincoln's actions were only arguably constitutional, and their legality would dog his presidency for many months to come. Seward privately reflected that the administration had carried out so many extralegal actions that it might have brought all involved "to the scaffold." No previous president had ever ordered such drastic measures, none of which except the right to summon militia were explicitly granted to him by the Constitution. That he did so without the consent of Congress fed the fears of Americans who were already suspicious of the new administration, and now dreaded the complete collapse of representative government. Unilateral executive action in fact ran against Lincoln's political grain. Like most Americans, especially former Whigs, Lincoln considered Congress the real engine of government, and the president mainly the executor of its will. As a member of Congress himself, in 1846, he had outspokenly opposed James K. Polk's effort to manipulate the United States into war with Mexico. And as recently as February, en route to Washington, he had asserted that the chief executive should neither recommend legislation nor exert indirect influence to affect the actions of Congress. But in the moment of crisis he jettisoned Whiggish political theory.

On April 15, he also called for an emergency session of Congress to meet on July 4, but that was two and a half months away. In defense of his actions that spring, Lincoln said, "It became necessary for me to choose whether, using only the existing means, agencies, and processes which Congress had provided, I should let the government fall at once into ruin, or whether, availing myself of the broader powers conferred by the Constitution in cases of insurrection, I would make an effort to save it with all its blessings for the present age and for posterity."

War fever ran through the North like an electric charge. Winfield Scott, in a mood both "fierce and jubilant," declared to the president's aides, "Now let them fight or starve. The only good use for traitors is to hang them." In Republican strongholds, the popular determination to fight took on a near-religious dimension. " 'No peace to the wicked,' saith the Lord,—and if the Rebels are not *wicked—who is?*" an impassioned Michigan abolitionist wrote to Zachariah Chandler. "Cry aloud and spare not." Of the rebels, urged one Ohioan, "The traitors must be punished, and I trust in the name of Heaven there will be no parleying." Before a roaring audience in Cleveland, Ben Wade declared, "The time for argument has passed and the time for action has come. They wish to meet you hand to hand, and foot to foot. Old as I am, I'll go with a musket on my shoulder."

Patriotic drums beat in every town from Maine to Minnesota.

Women offered to make cartridges, sandbags, and bandages. Shop windows suddenly filled with prints of soldiers and battles, and little boys appeared in colorful homemade Zouave uniforms. In New York, young plutocrats from the silk-stocking districts, Irish immigrants, brawling firemen, and Tammany stalwarts flocked to the colors. Tent colonies of recruits popped up in city parks. Two days after Lincoln's call, a pair of fully armed Massachusetts regiments were on their way to Washington, and before the week was out Ohio had enrolled some thirty thousand volunteers, more than double the state's quota. "It's all excitement here," Pitt Cooke wrote from Sandusky, Ohio, to his financier brother Jay in Philadelphia. "The whole country is turning out. Oh! Such excitement and zeal as all our people show they are ready & more than ready, with men and money. It gives one such a hopeful & encouraging view of the usual silly selfish nature of our race. We are all war." Not all were welcome: Horatio Rankin, an African American, wrote to Ohio's adjutant general to ask if "some of the colored sons of Ohio" would be welcome to defend the flag "on a level with the rest of the Ohio militia," but he never received an answer. It was to be a white man's war.

Many Democrats closed ranks behind Lincoln in the name of patriotism. Stephen A. Douglas called for a firm response, declaring, "The Capital of our country [is] in danger, and must be defended at all hazards, and at any expense of men & money." Many opposition newspapers nonetheless accused Lincoln of "dictatorship" and "usurpation," and condemned Republicans as "atrocious, barbarous, heathenish in their rage for blood." The *Dayton Daily Empire*, Clement Vallandigham's mouthpiece, urged Democrats "not to vote a dollar nor give a man to carry on this Republican war upon the South."

The slave states that still remained in the Union reacted to Lincoln's call with defiance. The governor of Missouri declared the president's proclamation "diabolical," while Tennessee's governor spat that his state "will not furnish a single man for the purpose of coercion, but fifty thousand if necessary for the defense of our rights and those of our southern brothers." Virginia, claiming that the federal government had "perverted" its power by oppressing the slaveholding states, repealed its ratification of the United States Constitution, and threw in its lot with the Confederacy. Crowds filled the streets

of Richmond in a delirium of joy, shouting the war cries of secession, tearing down the national flag, and threatening to march on
Washington to drive Lincoln from the White House. North Carolina, Arkansas, and Tennessee would all soon follow Virginia out of
the Union. Agitation for secession also surged in the border slave
states of Maryland, Kentucky, and Missouri. Ordinary citizens were
hard put to sort out confusing reports of what was really going
on. "Some respectable gentleman arrives from the South and tells
in New York, Phila., or some other northern city, what amount of
troops, how conditioned and equipped, &c &c he has seen in the
South," one Ohioan reported in his diary. "Another respectable and
intelligent man arrives a few hours later from the South, and he too
has seen all, and heard all about matters in the South, and his story
flatly contradicts his immediate predecessor. And still another highly
respectable and intelligent man arrives from the South, and he too
tells his story, which contradicts both the other respectable gentlemen's stories."

Waves of rumors rattled Washington: that the Harpers Ferry
armory had been captured by Virginia militia, that the Norfolk Navy
Yard had been abandoned and the federal fleet there captured, that
a rebel force of 2,500—or was it 5,000?—was poised to attack the
capital. Secessionist militia companies openly drilled just across the
Potomac. Pro-secession Democrats were reported to be recruiting
volunteer companies in southern Ohio to fight for the Confederacy
and gathering the names of "friends of the South" who might be of
use later. Meanwhile, the army and the navy hemorrhaged officers,
including Col. Robert E. Lee of the Second Cavalry, who had personally been offered the command of the national forces by President
Lincoln, but instead resigned his commission to join Virginia's state
forces and the Confederacy. Nearly all the officers at the Washington
Navy Yard walked away from their jobs, and when clerks in federal
offices were asked to take an oath of allegiance, scores refused. "I
feel so oppressed with sadness, there seems to be no hope," Charles
Mason, a patent lawyer and staunch Democrat, penned in his diary.
No one knew if the city's volunteer militiamen would even defend
the capital if they were called upon, or if they would turn their guns

on the government. Frightened Washingtonians who were able
locked up their homes and fled the city. By April 19, Washington was
isolated from the North as telegraph, rail, and postal links through
Maryland were all cut.

Unionists scrambled to defend the capital. Sen. James Lane of
Kansas, "gaunt, tattered, uncombed, and unshorn" and dressed in
"a rough, rusty overcoat, a torn shirt, and suspenderless breeches,"
recruited a company of friends to guard the White House, posting
them "in belted and revolvered dignity" up and down its wide portico. Cassius M. Clay of Kentucky, the newly appointed minister to
Russia, armed with three pistols and a bowie knife, like a character sprung to life from a dime novel, ostentatiously drilled another
armed troop that included at least one senator and several members
of Congress. Veterans of the War of 1812 organized a third, while
loyal clerks prepared to defend the Treasury building against imminent attack.

The situation in Maryland was chaotic and critical. Secessionist
sentiment was intense, and many of its leading politicians, if not outright separatists, hoped to at least keep Maryland neutral. Mobs had
already forced unarmed Pennsylvania militiamen back to their own
state. Baltimore's streets teemed with young men brandishing clubs
and pistols, while secession flags fluttered from ships in the harbor,
and prominent Unionists were threatened and ordered out of the
city. "The heart of Maryland, and Baltimore especially, are rotten
and traitorous to the core," the *New York Times* alleged.

On April 19, the city exploded. Around 11:00 a.m., the nine hundred men of the Sixth Massachusetts Volunteers arrived by train
at the President Street station, where railcars had to be hitched
to horses and pulled a mile across town to Camden Station, then
attached to another steam engine in order to continue on to Washington. They were confronted at President Street by a mob cheering
Jefferson Davis and hurling cobblestones pried up from the street.
At least one car was dragged off its tracks, forcing the militiamen
to climb down among their attackers. Pistols were fired. Soldiers
fell. An officer ordered his men to shoot. Rioters rushed the troops.
In all, sixteen were killed, four of them militiamen, the rest civil-

ians, and many more were injured before the regiment was able to reach Camden Station and get away. Maryland's governor Thomas Hicks, a lukewarm Unionist, warned Lincoln that if any more troops attempted to pass through Baltimore they would be stopped "unless they come through blood." Federal forces later discovered caches of rifles and pistols, percussion caps, cartridges, and even cannon that had been secreted by the secessionists.

Outside Baltimore, pro-Southern Marylanders carried out systematic subversion. One of them was John Merryman, a gentleman stock breeder, slave owner, and state militia officer living near the town of Towson, north of Baltimore. Uniformed, wearing states' rights badges pinned to their coats, and armed with weapons stolen from a federal armory, Merryman and his men worked their way north along the railroad to the Pennsylvania state line, chopping down telegraph poles and burning bridges as they went. Merryman proclaimed to all within hearing that he was determined to prevent Northern troops from "invading" Maryland. "God damn them," he shouted. "We'll stop them from coming down here and stealing our slaves." For the time being, Merryman went about his destructive work uninterrupted. But he would soon become the focal point of a constitutional crisis.

Despite many members with pro-Southern sentiments, the Maryland state legislature shied away from secession, labeling it "inexpedient," but called for recognition of the Confederacy and denounced the looming war as "unjust and unconstitutional." When a delegation of prominent Baltimoreans demanded from Lincoln that he allow no more Northern troops to set foot in Maryland, the president, openly furious for once, retorted caustically: "Our men are not moles, and can't dig under the earth. They are not birds and can't fly through the air. There is no way but to march across, and that they must do." To many it seemed only a matter of time before Maryland, too, joined the Confederacy, leaving the nation's capital marooned and indefensible. On April 27, Lincoln suspended habeas corpus—that is, the right of due process—between Philadelphia and Washington, and authorized the army to arrest anyone it deemed a threat to public safety.

Any lingering doubt that Lincoln intended to fight was swept away at the beginning of May, when he called for 42,000 volunteers to enlist for three years' service, and ordered the recruitment of eleven permanent new regiments to beef up the Regular Army. He also extended the blockade—more a paper strategy than a real one at this point—to include Virginia and North Carolina. With little news, and none of it reliable, for long days no one knew what had happened to the reinforcements that had been promised by Northern governors. Lincoln, with his long legs outstretched and a spyglass propped on his toes, gazed southward searching for troopships steaming up the Potomac. Gradually the volunteers trickled in, avoiding Baltimore by way of Annapolis, and repairing the sabotaged railroad as they went. Although some arrived in Washington fully equipped, others were little more than patriotic mobs, dressed in uniforms of every imaginable hue and style. Regiments of Zouaves strutted in embroidered jackets, scarlet pantaloons, and tasseled caps copied from Algerian French troops. The 79th New York, which fancied itself Scottish, swaggered in kilts and tams. The Garibaldi Guards sported scarlet shirts and slouch hats in honor of the Italian nationalist hero Giuseppe Garibaldi.

The Capitol soon became a fortified camp bristling with guns. Troops drilled morning, noon, and night on the plaza in front of the east facade. The building's doors and windows were barricaded with sacks of flour and iron plates that had been intended for the new half-built dome. Drilling soldiers filled its halls, the clomp of their boots cannonading from the marble walls. The men of the Seventh New York took up residence in the House chamber, where they stretched on the brocade-covered sofas amid heaped slabs of bacon, quarters of beef, and saddles of mutton dumped on the luxurious carpets. New York's swaggering Fire Zouaves—"a jolly, gay set of blackguards"—amused themselves by swinging from a rope dangling from the ceiling of the Rotunda. The Sixth Massachusetts, fresh from its bloody street battle in Baltimore, settled into the Senate chamber, where its commander oversaw his troops from the vice president's chair. A blacksmith installed himself at Louis Wigfall's former desk, while a pair of factory hands occupied those of Virginia's two recently departed senators. Angry soldiers set at Jefferson Davis's desk with bayonets, until made to stop by the Senate doorkeeper. The metastasizing disorder and filth mortified the Capitol's dignified architect, Thomas Walter. "Things are more unpleasant here every day," he lamented. "The Senate Chamber is alive with lice; it makes my head itch to think of it—the bed bugs have travelled up stairs. . . . The building is like one grand water closet—every hole and corner is defiled."

Most of the members of Congress had returned to their districts. Clement Vallandigham went home to Dayton, where he took stock of his party's sorely depleted prospects. Most evenings, he gathered with supporters at the office of the *Daily Empire* to read the latest dispatches and talk politics. With the South gone and Northern Democrats split over support for the war, the remnants of the ruined prewar party might well be his to seize, if he played his hand well. He gradually settled on a strategy: to passively support the troops in the field, but to actively oppose the "Republican" war, which he felt certain must end in bloodbath and failure. At every opportunity, he challenged presidential authority, denounced antislavery measures as unconstitutional, proposed amendments to restrict the army's actions, and repeatedly clashed with Republicans over war aims, at one point offering to duel a Pennsylvania member who impugned his patriotism. Demanding Lincoln's impeachment, he repeatedly insisted that he would never vote to invade the South: "Never! Millions for defense; not a dollar or a man for aggressive and offensive civil war." To Republicans, he became anathema: merely being seen with him was regarded as evidence of disloyalty, if not outright treason.

Meanwhile, Ben Wade stumped Ohio's Western Reserve recruiting cavalry regiments among his abolitionist supporters. John Sherman funneled Ohio troops to the army that was forming in western Maryland. Pitt Fessenden roused his followers in Maine in support of the war. Edward Baker, the staunchest Republican advocate of the Crittenden compromise, donned a colonel's blue frock coat and was named to lead a unit recruited on the East Coast that dubbed itself the "California Regiment" in his honor. (Although he represented Oregon, Baker had spent most of the previous decade lawyering and politicking in San Francisco.)

Generals in every state complained to their senators and congressmen that they had no horses, cannon, tents, or rations. Ordinary soldiers begged them to arrange promotions and transfers. All the way from Kansas, a lieutenant in a company of Leavenworth volunteers wrote Senator Sherman to beg him for a senior appointment. ("I want to hang some of those traitors and to make some of them bite the dust," he encouragingly wrote.) Another young soldier complained indignantly that his entire company, from the abolitionist stronghold of Ripley, Ohio, had volunteered as a unit to enlist for three years, but had been told to go home because the state's quota of men had already been reached.

When Congress reconvened on July 4, things seemed little changed on the surface. Senators and representatives, as usual, shambled along the corridors in shapeless summer coats, light-colored linens, and broad-brimmed hats, suggesting to a British visitor "a gathering of millers or bakers" rather than dignified lawmakers. Tobacco juice puddled as ever in the marble stairwells. During debates, members still pored over newspapers, chatted with each other, scribbled letters, guzzled ice water, nibbled on pastries, and directed streams of spittle with haphazard accuracy toward spittoons placed strategically around the chambers. But a transformation had taken place. The old order was gone. The balance of power in Congress had shifted sharply in favor of the Republicans, who now outnumbered Democrats by more than two-to-one in both houses.

Henry Wilson, chairman of the Senate Military Affairs Committee, opened the session with a broadside of bills that laid the foundation for the Union war effort. Florid and beardless, gregarious in temperament, the forty-nine-year-old Wilson, one journalist wrote, was "rather loose and ramshackle" in his speech, but endowed with a tearful, sympathetic voice which partly made up for his lack of polish. Some thought in manner he suggested a village postmaster or a small-town businessman and underrated him accordingly. In an era

when even high-born politicians often claimed humble origins, Wilson was the real thing. Born in poverty to an alcoholic day laborer,
indentured to a farmer at the age of ten and later trained as a cobbler, he eventually built up a shoemaking enterprise that employed
more than one hundred workers and made him rich. His lifelong
revulsion against alcohol was surpassed only by his impassioned abolitionism and eventually carried him into state politics and the U.S.
Senate, where he was now serving his second term.

The most provocative of Wilson's bills was a blandly titled but
far-reaching joint resolution "to approve and confirm certain acts of
the President of the United States, for suppressing insurrection and
rebellion." This would give retroactive congressional approval to the
executive actions that Lincoln had taken in the weeks after the attack
on Fort Sumter, including the inflammatory suspension of habeas
corpus, legalizing them as if they had been done under the express
authority of Congress.

Former vice president John Breckinridge, now a Kentucky senator, irately charged that simply to consider such a measure at all
was tacitly to admit that Lincoln's acts were unlawful or unconstitutional. Many Americans, though mainly anti-administration
Democrats, felt genuinely shocked by the suspension of habeas corpus, which smacked of the sort of imperial high-handedness that
the Founding Fathers had warned against. No president had even
attempted it since Thomas Jefferson had failed to persuade Congress
to do so in the wake of Aaron Burr's supposed conspiracy against
the government in 1807. Breckinridge, as patrician and graceful as
Wilson was proletarian and rough-hewn, declared that Congress had
no right whatever to validate a violation of the Constitution. Worse
yet, for Congress to presume to absolve the president was essentially
to declare that it had the power to rewrite the Constitution without bothering with the process of amendment. Of habeas corpus,
Breckinridge went on, "The monarch of England cannot suspend
that writ, but transatlantic freemen seem to be eager to approve and
ratify acts which a European monarch would not dare to perform."
Such acts would haunt the country for generations to come, he
warned. "We are rushing, and with rapid strides, from a constitutional government to a military despotism."

In near-lockstep with Breckinridge, in the House of Representatives, Clement Vallandigham, brandishing a copy of the Constitution, condemned the "catalogue of daring usurpations" that he
asserted was being carried out by an administration, which was
equally contemptuous of the Constitution, Congress, the courts,
and the American people. It was not the aggrieved South but the
Lincoln administration that was guilty of treason, climaxing decades
of "violent" and "unprovoked agitation of the 'slavery question' in
the North." With these words, Vallandigham was staking out a position that he would ferociously defend in the years to come: defense
of the South's right to slaves, yoked to the conviction that Southerners would embrace peace if only they were guaranteed protection from the menace of the antislavery North and its "intolerant"
New England fanatics. By ignoring Congress, Lincoln had already
denied the representatives of the states and the people any voice in
the most momentous question the country had ever faced, while the
voice of the judiciary, "that last refuge and hope of liberty," had been
high-handedly spurned as well. Not even the sainted Andrew Jackson had dared to blockade an American port without the authority
of Congress. "Jackson! Jackson, sir!" cried Vallandigham. "The great
Jackson did not dare to do it. But our Jackson of today, the little Jackson at the other end of the avenue, and the mimic Jacksons around
him" blockade the whole Southern coast. That wasn't all. The privacy of the telegraph had been invaded, private messages seized
without search warrants, rights of property wantonly violated, the
right to bear arms overridden, free speech denied, homes invaded
and the residents dragged away by the armed minions of "the future
Tiberius of America"—a catalogue of treason that would have
cost any English sovereign his head. "A citizen of Maryland"—John
Merryman—he exclaimed with mock incredulity, had been seized in
his own home in the dead of night by armed soldiers, torn from his
wife and children, and dragged off to a fortress, where he was still
held without due process, bail, or a grain of evidence presented to a
grand jury. "Yet the president now asks us to ratify his usurpations
by a law *ex post facto,* and thus to make ourselves parties to our own
degradation, and to his infractions of the Constitution."

Vallandigham was overwrought, but his account of what had

happened to Merryman was accurate. (Merryman and his band of secessionist militia, it will be remembered, had destroyed the bridges and telegraph lines north of Baltimore in mid-April.) On the night of May 21, a party of Pennsylvania troops had arrested Merryman and interned him at Fort McHenry, in Baltimore harbor, where he had been held ever since, charged with treason. Friends of the patrician Merryman persuaded the pro-Southern chief justice of the Supreme Court, Roger B. Taney, to issue a writ of habeas corpus stating that the president had no authority to suspend due process, and ordering Merryman's immediate release. However, with Lincoln's explicit support, the fort's commander defied Taney's order. Although the Constitution allowed for the suspension of habeas corpus in time of national emergency, it did not make clear who had the right to do it. Antiwar Democrats and some Republicans believed that it was the prerogative of Congress alone, while Lincoln held that judicial dictates were irrelevant, since as commander-in-chief he was fully empowered "to preserve, protect, and defend the Constitution" by any means necessary, including the denial of rights to accused traitors.

The questions the Merryman case posed were troubling ones. What was the Constitution worth if it couldn't save the country from collapse from within? By suspending basic freedoms, was the government playing into the hands of rebels who claimed that it was Northern tyranny that compelled them to secede in the first place? If fundamental rights could be suspended in wartime, why couldn't they be taken away during peacetime too? Such questions genuinely worried many Americans, and they would provide an arsenal of political ammunition to the war's political enemies for a long time to come. No single wartime measure would shake the nation's constitutional underpinnings more violently.

With a few exceptions, the Republican press rallied to the administration's defense. Conceding that the power to suspend the writ belonged only to Congress, the *New York Times* declared pragmatically that "in the presence of an enemy, the civil power must give way, for the time, to the military [as] a part of the great law of instinct and self-preservation, which is higher than constitutions, older and stronger than the statute book." (The *Times* disgustedly dismissed Taney as "too old and palsied and weak to march in the ranks of rebellion and fight against the Union, [so] he uses the power of his office to serve the cause of the traitors.") The administration's congressional allies recognized how much was at stake. "In order to save the Union, I would take some risk of despotism," Sen. Edward Baker admitted, perhaps a bit uneasily. "I repeat that now: I will risk a little to save all."

Lincoln himself defended his suspension of habeas corpus in uncharacteristically strained prose that betrayed his own discomfort. "The whole of the laws which were required to be faithfully executed, were being resisted, and failing of execution, in nearly one-third of the states," he asserted in a special message to Congress. "Are all the laws but one, to go unexecuted, and the government itself go to pieces, lest that one be violated?"

Merryman's arrest was not the only action that could be construed as high-handed abuse of civil rights. In St. Louis, four hundred soldiers invaded a newspaper office, seized the type, ordered the paper to stop publishing because it was allegedly fabricating reports injurious to the national government. In Quincy, Illinois, the ranking officer ordered citizens to arrest anyone who furnished horses or provisions to aid secessionists across the Mississippi River in Missouri. In Cincinnati, a commission merchant was arrested for shipping butter to the South. In New York, thousands of telegrams were seized because they were addressed to the Confederacy or contained "inflammatory" sentiments. In Boston, ordinary citizens overheard expressing "treasonable" remarks were arrested. Men traveling through Maryland suspected of planning to enlist in the Confederate army were seized and interned.

Vallandigham predicted that freedom of the press would fall next, and then freedom of religion, trampled by a fanatical abolitionist clergy. National banks, a vast and permanent public debt, direct taxation, stupendous corruption, "no more state lines, no more state governments, and a consolidated monarchy or vast centralized military despotism, must all follow." Only a "speedy, immediate, honorable peace" could save the country, he cried. Speaking in what he said was "a spirit of justice and moderation," he proposed, unsuccessfully, that before the president was granted the authority to call out any more volunteers, he be ordered by Congress to appoint seven commissioners to accompany the army as it marched. Their mission would be to receive and consider any proposals that were sent by the president of the "so-called Confederate States, or any one of them, looking to a suspension of hostilities" and the peaceful return of those states to the Union. Then, to a bill appropriating pay for the volunteers, he proposed an equally unsuccessful amendment stating explicitly that no part of the money be employed in "subjugating a conquered province" or "in abolishing or interfering with African slavery in any of the states."

Both Vallandigham and Breckinridge had offered as eloquent a defense of freedom and republican government as any American had ever made, until they mentioned slavery. The Union, Breckinridge had told the Senate in all sincerity, was "not an end but a means," by which property rights and personal rights were to be protected. The "institutions of the southern states"—that is, Southerners' right to enslave—were even older than the Constitution itself, he maintained, and were meant to be protected forever. "To declare that this contest shall be prosecuted, if necessary, to the abolition of slavery in the southern states, is in principle to declare that it shall be prosecuted to the total subversion of all state authority, to the total overthrow of all rights, personal and political." Such protests revealed, of course, that the supposed idealism of states' rights politics only thinly veiled an uncompromising belief in the principle of slavery. Slavery's defenders, South and North, feared—in this they were correct—that despite Lincoln's insistence that the goal of the war was the restoration of the Union and nothing else, his expansive view of his war powers coupled with the exponentially growing power of the Radical Republicans in Congress might eventually extend to abolishing slavery altogether.

Tremors foretelling the earthquake that was to come could already be felt on Capitol Hill. As early as May, the German émigré and Radical from Missouri Carl Schurz had told Lincoln's secretary John Hay, "Slavery offers itself more vulnerable to our attack than at any point in any century, and the wild malignity of the South is excusing us before God and the world." Orville Browning of Illinois, soon to be elected to the Senate, had also suggested to Hay that once the South was subjugated, "exterminated whites" ought to be replaced by "a black republic" over which the United States might "extend a protectorate while they raised their cotton." Others talked more realistically, if unofficially, about enlisting slaves for military service. By mid-July, even a conservative Republican like John Sherman could say, "Rather than see one single foot of this country of ours torn from the national domain by traitors, I will myself see slaves set free." Around the same time, a resolution began floating around the House of Representatives calling for the "immediate and unconditional emancipation of all slaves in the seceded states." Nothing came of it, but it was a straw in the wind.

Meanwhile, the Northern public's demand for a decisive battle steadily swelled. Sen. James Dixon of Connecticut passionately declared, "The slow canker of tardy inaction will rust into the very heart and spirit of the people. They demand that [the war] be short, decisive, terrific, and overwhelming. Every day's delay is fraught with incalculable mischief to the cause of the Union. Tomorrow, next week—at the earliest possible moment—let the invincible columns move southward." Zachariah Chandler predicted that the Confederates would "run like cowards" and be captured to the last man. Even the usually circumspect Pitt Fessenden believed that a single "short, sharp blow," would crush the insurrection. The pro-war press, led by the *New York Tribune,* the most influential Republican newspaper in the country, hammered the administration daily with a taunt beneath its masthead: "The Nation's War Cry: *Forward to Richmond! Forward to Richmond! The Rebel Congress must not be allowed to meet there on the 20th of July!* BY THAT DAY THE PLACE MUST BE HELD BY THE NATIONAL ARMY!"

To many, the Union's paralysis was ponderously embodied in the dropsical person of seventy-five-year-old Winfield Scott, who had served as commanding general of the army since 1841, but was physically incapable of taking the field. Barely ambulatory, he could be seen in his antique frock coat with wide turned-back yellow lapels

and gold epaulets, hobbling feebly along the street, a dispiriting vestige of the once celebrated hero of the War of 1812 and the Mexican War. The ancient general's strategy, it seemed to the impatient
Chandler, was apparently to "surround the scoundrels, make their
case hopeless & compel a retreat to Richmond." He growled, "My
chances to *see* a fight are small." While Scott's physical disabilities
were obvious, they underestimated the depth of his strategic thinking. He proposed marching an army of eighty thousand men down
the Mississippi River, supplying it by boat, and cutting the Confederacy in half. Derided as both grandiose and unfeasible in 1861, this
was very close to the strategy that Ulysses Grant would adopt later
in the war.

Reflecting on the mood of that hectic spring, Rep. Albert Gallatin
Riddle, an Ohio Radical, wrote, "The average man then supposed
war meant to march upon the enemy by the shortest route, assail,
hang to him, and *lick* him in the shortest possible time. All the men
of that opening day had the same idea." The army also faced another
unforgiving source of pressure. Nearly all the troops under arms had
been called up for ninety days—the maximum allowable under the
Militia Act of 1792 and their term of service was about to expire. The
army's newly appointed field commander, Irvin McDowell, a West
Pointer who had considerable staff experience but none commanding in battle, knew that if he didn't use the men he had, he'd lose
them within days. Some regiments whose time was up were already
starting for home.

McDowell knew that most of them weren't ready for battle. Not
a single officer in the army had ever maneuvered troops in large bodies. Indiscipline was rife. Drunken soldiers careened through the
streets of Washington, brawling, wrecking brothels, sometimes begging passersby for money to buy a drink. Privates struggled to master the most elementary drills, presided over by officers who knew
no more of the military arts than the men they commanded. No
one seemed to have maps of the Virginia countryside through which
the army was eventually expected to march. Artillery was woefully
inadequate, out of date, poorly horsed, and served by gunners who,
caustically commented a British correspondent who had covered the
Crimean War, were "worse than the Turks." Asked by the reporter

what the meaning was of the random shots he heard at one fort, the commanding officer dryly replied, "They are volunteers shooting themselves." Nevertheless, certain that the Confederacy could easily be dispatched by a single defeat, Americans weaned on admiration for the amateur soldiers of the Revolutionary War placed a near-religious faith in the martial powers of volunteer militiamen to lick any enemy. Suffused with overconfidence, Ben Wade and many of his like-minded congressional colleagues blamed Lincoln for unmanly hesitation. "The stern demand of a united people cannot and must not be baffled by the perverseness of one man though he be the president of the United States," Wade growled.

On July 16, the first regiments began marching out of their bivouacs on the Potomac toward the rebel encampment at Manassas Junction, thirty miles southwest of the capital. On the 21st they collided with an army commanded by Pierre G. T. Beauregard, the Confederate hero of Fort Sumter, at a meandering stream called Bull Run. An army of civilian tourists, including many members of Congress, followed the army in carriages rented for the day for fabulous sums, freighted with picnic baskets and bottles of wine, and in at least some cases armed with guns with which they hoped to take pot shots at the rebels. Among them were Wade and Zachariah Chandler, a giant of a man who wore a long goatee and, like Wade, was partial to explosive profanity which he delivered, whenever required, in a sort of "menacing tremolo" that could stop men in their tracks. They were accompanied in a second carriage by the Senate's sergeant-at-arms, and several others, all of them armed. They were confident that the rebels would be captured to a man.

Wade's party drove past deserted farms and ripening cornfields, past the expectant eyes of black slaves and their sullen masters. At Centreville, twenty miles south of Washington, carriages by the hundreds pulled up on the hills overlooking the rolling, partly wooded countryside where the battle was already under way. A well-dressed lady watching the fight through opera glasses was heard to say, "That is splendid. Oh, my! Is not that first-rate? I guess we will be in Richmond this time tomorrow." Beneath the hills, the landscape churned with dust and smoke, and resonated with a cacophony of shouted orders, screams, defiant cries, the crackle of gunfire, the deep-throated whunk of cannon. "The canon balls & baum shels flew like hale stones & there was an emensed shour of rifle balls," one terrified soldier, Elijah Brown, wrote afterward. The heat was withering. Confederate battalions plunged forward. Federal fire cut them down. The survivors broke and ran. An officer on horseback galloped past the spectators, waving his hat and shouting, "We've whipped them on all points!" In the smoky chaos, a body of federal troops could be glimpsed running up a hill. There were cheers. Federal batteries rushed forward. Rebel infantry opened fire from the surrounding woods. Then the scene dissolved again into clouds of blue smoke. The first messengers dispatched back to Washington reported a great victory.

Then it all began to come apart. The Confederates overran the batteries on Henry House Hill. Civilian wagon drivers panicked. First in twos and threes, then by the score, then in the hundreds, demoralized federal troops began drifting back up the Centreville Road. Soon they were no longer walking but running, throwing away their rifles, canteens, cartridge boxes, haversacks, bedrolls, hats, and coats. Artillerymen abandoned their cannon and caissons. Officers disappeared, and soldiers cried out to strangers to lead them. Drivers lashed maddened horses. A brigade commanded by William Tecumseh Sherman, the brother of Sen. John Sherman, attempted stoutly to stem the tide and failed. Fleeing men's faces gaped like gargoyles, blackened from the powder from the cartridges they'd bitten off in battle, stained and streaked with sweat, eyes bulging with fear. There was General David Hunter in the back of a wagon, blood pouring from his head. And, there, Col. Ambrose Burnside, whose Rhode Islanders had seemed on the brink of victory a few hours before, now hatless, galloping past on a horse. And there, Sen. Henry Wilson heading away from the battle on a mule. The army that had marched off so proudly the night before was no longer an army but a mob, commandeering ambulances, carts, caissons, any kind of conveyance that rolled. Empty wagons and riderless horses galloped wildly across the open fields. "I was run over by our own Cavelry & was knocked down & was steped on & jammed into the mud but was not hurt but a little," Elijah Brown wrote. Rumors circulated that the rebels were bayoneting the wounded. With the explosion of every Confederate shell, the vast straining mass of men, animals, and wagons was seized as if by an electric convulsion. Terrified soldiers clung to the sides of carriages: passengers pushed them off and drove on. "We had to be rough with them," one civilian, disgusted at what he regarded as pure cowardice, reported in a letter. "Finally, with a pistol each, [we] kept them out."

Ben Wade and his friends were swept along against their will in the rout. Shame at what he saw metamorphosed into a towering rage as the mob drove them on pell-mell over a road that was literally paved with discarded guns and gear. Just short of Fairfax Court House, ten miles north of Bull Run, Wade convinced his friends to pull their carriages sideways across the road where it passed between a fenced-in farm and a dense wood. "Boys, we'll stop this damned runaway!" he shouted. Large of body and voice, and fearless of his person, Wade pushed his hat back on his head, levered a cartridge into the chamber of his new Maynard carbine, and cocked it. Chandler drew a heavy Navy revolver. Their friends did likewise. They pointed their weapons at the boiling mass of men who jostled against their carriages. Wade boomed that if they attempted to run any farther he'd blow their brains out. Wade's stand lasted only about twenty minutes, but it was enough to stem the tide until the arrival of the still intact Second New York Volunteers, which brought some semblance of order to the fleeing multitude. Wade's fame spread because of his sensational bravery. "Whatever credit there was in stopping that rout is due wholly to senators Wade and Chandler," wrote the *National Intelligencer*, with some exaggeration. But the statesmen had shown extraordinary courage at a time when many had not.

At the White House, early dispatches reported that losses had been heavy, but that the North had prevailed. Then, at about six o'clock, Secretary of State Seward burst into the president's office with a look of horror on his face. Only the president's two secretaries were there, Lincoln having gone out riding. John Nicolay began reading Seward the last triumphal dispatch. "That is not so," Seward cried. "The battle is lost."

In the gloomy, rain-soaked days that followed, what remained of the army struggled fitfully to regroup. The seemingly impregnable Union seemed suddenly "smashed like a China plate," wrote the deeply depressed poet Walt Whitman. Dispirited, mud- and blood-spattered soldiers wandered aimlessly up and down Pennsylvania Avenue. They dropped down anywhere to sleep, on the steps of houses, in vacant lots, on the street. Whitman watched them with pity, "these defeated soldiers—queer-looking objects, strange eyes and faces, drench'd and fearfully worn, hungry, haggard, blistered in the feet." William T. Sherman, who had managed to keep his brigade intact, threatened to shoot a volunteer officer who decided to pack his bags and go back to New York. The man stayed, but hundreds from less disciplined commands walked away and went home. Apologists wildly claimed that the Union forces had been overwhelmed by more than 100,000 Confederates, the vast majority of them imaginary. (McDowell actually had about 30,000 men, slightly more than the Confederates.)

All over Washington, there was talk of surrender, and forcing Lincoln and his cabinet to resign. The soggy air of defeatism spread across the North. In Dayton, Ohio, a lawyer "saw more sad countenances, more nervous quivering of lips, and pale and wild dismay of countenance, and heard more deep and bitter imprecations against the destroyers of our once happy, peaceful and prosperous country than I ever saw or heard before." And in New York, Horace Greeley's *Tribune,* which had so shrilly demanded an immediate march on Richmond, now proclaimed the Confederacy to be impregnable, and called for compromise. Pitt Fessenden, sunk in gloom, could not stop thinking about a young soldier he saw, with his legs shot away and begging to be put out of his agony. He wrote, "I have felt at times during the week as if I should be glad to have somebody do me the same favor—so intense has been my shame & disappointment."

Had the Confederates assaulted Washington in the days immediately following Bull Run it was universally believed that the city would easily have fallen. Fortunately, the rebels were as disorganized in victory as the Union was in defeat. What remained of the federal army was close to disintegration, however. Many of the ninety-day men were on the verge of mutiny. Thousands simply packed their bags and went home. The public, for the most part, was willing to forgive the ordinary soldiers, who had fought bravely, supposedly against huge odds. But judgment of the officers who had failed to lead them to victory was scathing. Whitman, who would spend much of the war as a volunteer nurse tending to the wounded, bitterly wrote: "There you are, shoulder straps!—but where are your companies? Where are your men. Incompetents! Sneak, blow, put on airs there in Willard's sumptuous parlors and bar-rooms, or anywhere—no explanation shall save you. Bull Run is your work; had you been half or one-tenth worthy of your men, this never would have happened."

# 5

# The Clink of Coin

Bayonets are at best illogical arguments.

—SEN. EDWARD BAKER

Northerners went into collective shock after the collapse of their hopes at Bull Run. "With men enough clamorous to go to war, with means enough to pay the bill, what in the name of our country's salvation is the matter?" a demoralized Bostonian wrote to Zachariah Chandler. Fear of imminent Confederate attack once again gripped Washington. Wild stories of battlefield atrocities filled the air: that the Confederates had tortured the wounded, burned hospitals, decapitated the dying, used Yankee shinbones as drumsticks, collected skulls for drinking cups. Minor incidents took on dire proportions: rebel pickets were glimpsed on the Potomac, an Ohio soldier who wandered away from camp was lynched near Arlington, a Union officer was assaulted in Alexandria. "We took it for granted that the rebels would be on our heels," William T. Sherman later recalled. But as the days passed without an attack the shattered regiments gradually regrouped. Rail and telegraph lines to the North were restored. Fresh troops poured into the capital. And Congress continued to meet without interruption in a courageous demonstration of faith in ultimate Union victory.

While no Northerners could pretend that Bull Run was not a

catastrophe, creative denial was made to explain the inexplicable. Many, like Walt Whitman, blamed the defeat on irresponsible officers, others on the Confederates' alleged "unmanly" tactics. Declared the Lancaster, Pennsylvania, *Daily Evening Express*, with the impassioned naïveté of the moment: "The Northern troops fight with the full front, the open, honest bravery of men who are valiant in a good cause. The Southern soldiers fight like the Indians; hide themselves behind woods, thickets, and masked batteries; have recourse to every mean and dishonorable feint and stratagem. It is the Indian against the white man. Southern bravery is that of the serpent and Northern bravery is that of the man." Rather than accept defeat, however, the great mass of the Northern public soon felt a revitalized determination to fight to the finish. Reported the *Daily News* of Philadelphia, renewed war fever spread over the land "like streams of hot lava."

Members of Congress now realized that the war could actually be lost unless they acted decisively. It was also clear that the survival of the Union would depend not just on willing volunteers and the machinery of war but, as the abolitionist Wendell Phillips put it, on "the clink of coin." However, the Treasury was wholly unprepared for an open-ended war. Admitted Salmon P. Chase, with understatement, "The augmentation of force necessitates augmentation of expenditures beyond the estimates of the Secretary of War." Even before the war, the lingering effects of depression had left the economy wounded and the federal budget deep in deficit. In March, the national debt stood at $70 million; by July, it had risen to $90 million. The prospect of prodigious borrowing prompted widespread fears of economic collapse. Up to now, federal revenues had come almost entirely from tariffs levied on shipping. No duties could now be collected at ports in the seceded states. Imports fell and trade slackened: thousands of vessels lay idle at Northern ports. Financial houses that had invested deeply in the South were prostrate. Skittish investors retreated from the markets until they knew whether secession would fail or succeed.

Chase, sounding a note of panic, begged Congress for money to pay the army, buy ships, hire clerks for the War Department, fund the new Unionist police force that had been hired in Baltimore, reimburse states for the money they had laid out to buy arms for the troops they raised, meet federal salaries that were coming due, and for a multitude of other pressing expenses. In all, Chase estimated that the government would need some $320 million for the coming year, a serious underestimate as events would prove. The entire sum of specie in all the banks in the United States was just under $100 million, of which one-quarter was in bank vaults in the seceded states. The Union's financial machinery was primitive. No system of national taxation existed. There was no national bank or organized system for raising large sums of money. The country was awash with as many as seven thousand different kinds of banknotes issued by thousands of local, often dangerously undercapitalized banks, which discounted or flatly rejected the currency issued by others. (Thaddeus Stevens complained to his colleagues, "If you get one of their notes you cannot pass it beyond the town in which it issued. If you can, you have better luck than I have. I got one from Pennsylvania, and I could not pass it at all.") As the Union's fortunes sank the government's credit slumped along with it. Bond sales flopped when Chase refused to accept bids at par and bankers' trust in the Treasury collapsed. By summer, as the fledgling armies marched and maneuvered, financing for the war reached a crisis.

As chairmen, respectively, of the Senate's Finance Committee and the House Ways and Means Committee, the responsibility for creating financial machinery commensurate with the government's need fell to Fessenden and Stevens. Both men understood better than Chase that a strong and trusting relationship between the Treasury and Northern moneymen was imperative. Their combined energies were worth entire armies in the field. The two had much in common: they were skillful tacticians, lawyers by training, single-mindedly committed to the Union, and bred from the same rocky New England soil. (Stevens, though he made his career in Pennsylvania, was born in Danville, Vermont.) Both could be harsh and imperious. Colleagues sometimes referred to Stevens as chairman of the "Committee of Mean Ways," while Fessenden was well-known to have "no patience for humbug and no tolerance for bores." The self-contained Fessenden was reserved to the point of iciness, while Stevens, by contrast, although not exactly gregarious, was one of the most flamboyant men in the House, "a driver—bitter, quick as electricity, with a sarcastic, blasting wit," a younger member wrote. While Stevens was notorious as one of the House's leading abolitionists—"the great mogul of abolitionism," a Lancaster, Pennsylvania, newspaper called him—Fessenden counted himself a pragmatist on the subject of slavery. Yet he could be unexpectedly touched. In July, a visitor to Fessenden's home brought with him a small enslaved child who played on the carpet and chattered for an hour, impressing Fessenden with his intelligence. He wrote afterward to a friend, "The thought that it was owned, like a dog, by one of its fellow creatures, made me utter fresh maledictions on an institution which upholds such an atrocity."

Fessenden's workload was immense, all the more so in an era when members had no assistants and office staff. Quite apart from war financing, all other government appropriations were also channeled through his committee. As floor manager, he drove debate forward impatiently, dismissing amendments out of hand when he could, pressing to shorten debate when he could not, occasionally mocking speakers, including fellow Republicans, when he felt they went on too long. "We come here to meet a crisis," he tartly reminded them more than once, "not for the purpose of ventilating our rhetoric upon questions that have been ventilated enough." Remarked one close observer, Fessenden believed firmly in "leaving all the jabber to others, & being content to work like a dog."

Fessenden, Stevens, and Chase all concluded that a combination of massive loans, increased tariffs, and taxes—including an income tax—would be necessary to raise the sums needed. They all knew that the largest proportion would have to come from loans, but the government would have to demonstrate that it was prepared to create new revenues to ensure that interest on the loans would be paid. "It is unpleasant to send your sons and your brethren to be slaughtered in this unholy war," Stevens declared on the floor of the House, in July. "It is [also] unpleasant to send the tax gatherer to the door of the farmers, the mechanics, and the capitalists of the country to collect taxes." But he added bluntly, "The capitalists must be assured that we have laid taxes which we can enforce." Chase hoped to raise $19 million from an assortment of direct taxes, initially targeting incomes over $1,000 per year, later reduced to $800, but still a substantial figure in 1861. As much as Americans had historically resisted direct taxation, there was patriotic support in some quarters. "The Northern people are not only ready and willing to be taxed, but they insist upon being taxed," the *Daily Alta California* extravagantly declared.

When some members urged the postponement of what they feared would prove a deeply unpopular measure, Stevens replied, "By putting it off for six months, you also put it out of the power of the government to provide arms and munitions of war for six months. Neither the capitalists in this nor any other country will ever lend the government money when it makes no provision for its redemption, and unless such provision is made the loans you have already authorized will not be taken, and the Treasury will be left without a dollar." He added grimly, "I believe that many thousand valuable lives will be lost, and that millions of money will be expended. The only question is whether the government is prepared to meet all these perils and overcome them."

A bill increasing tariffs on mostly luxury goods—ivory, silks, velvet, ginger—would, it was hoped, bring in another $10 million. It passed after a sometimes rancorous debate, which at one point saw Fessenden turn caustically on the patrician Charles Sumner of Massachusetts, the preeningly handsome chairman of the Foreign Relations Committee. Sumner had argued that higher tariffs would annoy America's trading partners and by depressing imports would harm Europe's laboring classes, who sympathized with the Union. "Why, sir," Fessenden snapped, "the country is in a state of war, incurring an expense enormous in its magnitude, which the people of this country must bear. The question is, how are they to get the money? It must be had upon some terms or other. What right has a foreign country to make any question about what we chose to do when we are in a state of war, and struggling for national existence even?" Sumner's very argument, Fessenden harshly added, was an insult to the Union they were all sworn to defend.

The loan bill, the most urgent of the revenue measures, shaped by a conference committee dominated by Fessenden and Stevens, meanwhile made its way through the Senate. Initially, Chase had sought approval for a $100 million loan. Instead, led by Stevens and Fessenden, whose foresight was greater than the treasury secretary's, Congress authorized Chase to borrow up to $250 million, in the form of bonds issued at 7 percent interest and redeemable after twenty years, and Treasury notes at 7.3 percent interest, redeemable in two years. The Republicans' power was dramatically reflected in the vote, which passed in the House by 150 to 5, with none but a small clump of conservative Democrats opposing it, and by a similarly overwhelming margin in the Senate.

However, bankers and financiers were far less willing to underwrite the government than they had been earlier in the year, when the Union's prospects looked sunnier. New York financier James Gallatin, the son of Thomas Jefferson's treasury secretary Albert Gallatin, had then helped to organize a consortium of northeastern banks to bail out the government by consolidating their capital and combining the specie in their vaults in a common fund. Chase had since then undermined the bankers' trust first by refusing to permit them to acquire the instruments below par, and then by insisting that the banks deposit their loan payments in the Treasury in coin, short-circuiting the system of credit that was customarily used as a tool of financial exchange.

The Treasury also faced the daunting challenge of distributing its notes nationwide. Although the government had borrowed heavily during the Revolutionary War and sold bonds during the War of 1812, it had never attempted anything on this scale before. As a start, Chase appointed 148 agents, mostly presidents of banks, to sell the notes in their communities, initially to businessmen and speculators whose patriotism was not averse to profiting from wartime investment. One of these agents was the upstart financier Jay Cooke, who was named to cover Philadelphia and the surrounding area. Although Cooke and his partners claimed personal worth of more than $500,000, they actually commanded liquid assets of less than $10,000—a comparative pittance compared to larger, more established banks. Tall, slender, blue-eyed, sunnily self-confident, and appealingly youthful even in his forties, Cooke inspired extraordinary trust from more established moneymen, the Treasury Department, and supporters in the crisis-driven Congress alike. His methods would revolutionize the marketing of investments and reverberate long beyond the Civil War. He unabashedly compared himself to Robert Morris, the brilliant Philadelphia financier who had personally guaranteed the loans to the Continental Congress that had kept it afloat during the Revolutionary War. "His mantle has fallen on the right Shoulders," Jay wrote to his brother Henry.

Cooke's patriotism was tinged with an evangelical fervor that saturated his family. During the war, he would personally ship thousands of prayer books to the soldiers. At the same time, the Cookes were canny and uninhibitedly self-interested businessmen. Although Jay, like the rest of his family, was intensely antislavery, he didn't hesitate to advise Chase not to hire a son-in-law of Lucretia Mott, "a violent abolitionist," for a Treasury job because it would "injure our cause" among conservative banks and capitalists. With similar circumspection, Jay's brother and partner Henry, a Columbus newspaper editor, had long promoted the careers of both John Sherman and Salmon Chase, and readily put his political connections in the service of the company. "Now is the time for making money, by honest contracts out of the govt," Eleutheros Cooke advised his son Jay. "If H.D."—that is, Henry—"don't avail himself of the hard-earned favor of the [administration], he deserves poverty." As early as April, Jay told Henry that he had confidentially urged Chase "to keep on the right side of those Capitalists who are disposed to dabble in the loans required of the government—if they *do* make sometimes a handsome margin it is no more than they are entitled to *in such times as these*. They can be useful to the Government."

Although Jay Cooke had sold small numbers of Treasury bonds earlier in the year, he really caught Washington's attention in June, when he took on the sale of $3 million in Pennsylvania war bonds, at a time when the state's credit rating was low, and more established banks shied away. Cooke surmised correctly that government securities were unlikely to sell high as investments alone. With an instinct for emotional advertising far in advance of his time, he created the first financial marketing campaign directed at the general public, by appealing to Pennsylvanians to "manifest their love for the Commonwealth," and at the same to make profit "free from any taxation whatever." Cooke personally walked Philadelphia's financial district carrying subscription papers, collecting pledges from banks, insurance companies, merchant firms, and individuals, and published the names of patriotic investors in local papers across the country to stimulate wider demand. The campaign was a sensational success.

Cooke opened a second office in Washington and proposed to make Treasury operations the firm's main business, writing to Chase that he counted on "those natural advantages that would legitimately and honestly flow towards us from your personal friendship & the fact that our firm was ardently & fully with the Administration." By the end of the first week, Cooke was selling over $100,000 of bonds per day. He outsold every other agent, and as the sales drew ever widening public support, the anxiety that overshadowed the Treasury began to fade. He wrote to Gov. Andrew Curtin of Pennsylvania, "I have been at it from 8 A.M. till after 5—a continual stream, clergy, draymen, merchants, girls, boys, all kinds of men and women— some of our citizens who came in—I mean those of *mark*—went out almost with tears in their eyes—so overjoyed at the Patriotic [sale]." Crowed one Philadelphia journalist, "Every dollar subscribed is a bullet for a traitor's heart, and a nail for his coffin."

Financing the war was at least a practical challenge. More difficult was the problem of defining the war's moral purpose to the varied and not altogether compatible Unionist constituencies, which ranged from uncompromising abolitionists, to Free Soilers who believed in white supremacy, to unreliable border state slave owners, to patriotic Democrats who opposed the administration on almost everything but the war. Much to the dismay of antislavery men, President Lincoln repeatedly asserted that the war's only aim was the restoration of the Union, a principle that was in turn founded on his unshakable belief that the fate of the United States, the world's only republican government, was a struggle of far-reaching historical significance that dwarfed all other concerns. "I consider the central idea pervading this struggle is the necessity that is upon us of proving that popular government is not an absurdity," he confided to his aide John Hay.

"We must settle this question now, whether, in a free government, the minority have the right to break up the government whenever they choose. If we fail, it will go far to prove the incapability of the people to govern themselves." No Republicans disagreed with this formulation, but for many it hardly went far enough.

At the beginning of the session, Henry Wilson had proposed a bill empowering federal forces to confiscate property that was being used for insurrectionary purposes by the rebels. At the time, most members took this to mean weapons, horses, wagons, documents, and the like. The day after Bull Run, however, Lyman Trumbull offered a provocative amendment to the bill that explicitly included slaves, declaring that "any persons claiming to be entitled to the service or labor of any other person"—that is, slave owners—who put their bondsmen in the service of the rebellion in any way, by digging trenches or erecting fortifications, for example, would forfeit their ownership "any law to the contrary notwithstanding." Trumbull's amendment struck at the heart of slavery itself by directing federal power to undermine the master's right to his slave.

"If traitors use bondmen to destroy this country, my doctrine is that the Government shall at once convert those bondmen into men that cannot be used to destroy our country," Wilson declared in support. "I hope that this Government will carry it out with an inflexibility that knows no change." More cautiously, John Sherman, reflecting the halting movement toward qualified emancipation on the part of more conservative Republicans, allowed that "Rather than see one single foot of this country of ours torn from the national domain by traitors, I will myself see slaves set free; but at the same time I utterly disclaim any purpose of that kind." Opponents of the measure reacted apoplectically. John S. Carlile, appointed to the Senate to represent the rump counties of Virginia occupied by the Union Army, exclaimed, "Because a conspiracy has been inaugurated to overthrow and destroy the government, are you to overthrow and destroy the rights of property in one-half of the states of the union? What right have you, to go into my state and to thrust yourself between me and my property, and to say that I shall not own it and dispose of it in accordance with the laws of my state?"

This was no abstract debate. In May, near Norfolk, three fugitive slaves had appeared at Fortress Monroe, one of three military bases in the seceded states that the federal government still held. (The others were Fort Jefferson off the Florida Keys, and Fort Pickens at the mouth of Pensacola harbor.) The fort was commanded by Gen. Benjamin Butler, a canny Boston lawyer and doughface Democrat who had supported the Dred Scott decision, and had cheerfully nominated Jefferson Davis for president at the party's 1860 convention. But when the war broke out he proclaimed his unswerving loyalty to the Union. (He had little choice if he hoped to have a future in Massachusetts politics.)

When a Confederate officer requested the three runaways' return under the terms of the 1850 Fugitive Slave Law, Butler declined, with an inspired reply that was to prove the foundation for one of the most consequential policies of the war: "I am under no constitutional obligations to a foreign country, which Virginia now claims to be." Butler of course knew that federal law still required the return of fugitive slaves to their masters. But he reasoned that under the laws of war he had a right to seize any kind of enemy property that might be turned against him, including slaves who would be forced to serve the rebels. Not surprisingly, more runaways began seeking Butler's protection, first by the scores, then by the hundreds, then by the thousands.

Freedom-seeking men, women, and children began pouring into the Union lines wherever federal armies marched. Absent a coherent federal policy, individual officers acted on their biases. Some, especially abolitionist New Englanders, welcomed them with open arms and put them to work. Others drove them away or conspicuously returned them to their masters. Sometimes they ordered them flogged for good measure before sending them back. In some areas, federal troops were ordered to guard the property of Southern civilians, including their slaves. Gen. John Dix, for instance, figuratively threw up his hands, exclaiming, "In the first place, I did not wish to be called upon to send them back to their masters, and in the second place, I did not wish my men charged with conniving at their escape." Worried Illinois senator Orville Browning, who had been elected to fill Stephen Douglas's Senate seat after his death in June, "When they come we cannot repulse them—we cannot butcher them, we cannot send them back to bondage. We cannot incorporate them into our population in the free states. We cannot drive them into the sea—we cannot precipitate them into any other country. What are we to do with them?"

Hostility to African Americans was deep-seated among Yankee soldiers raised in a climate of almost universal racism. "We see plenty of slaves, and I am heartily sick of it; and God speed the time when the negro shall be free and on his own side of the Atlantic," wrote a Vermont corporal, one of many Yankees who hoped that the war would lead not to racial integration but to the deportation of blacks to Africa. "Black laws" restricting the settlement, movement, and civil rights of African American residents existed in many nominally free states. In New York State, in 1860, a proposed amendment to the state constitution granting Negro suffrage was defeated by a 100,000-vote majority, and in New York City was supported by only 1,600 of the 32,000 who voted *for Lincoln*. Even Jim Lane of Kansas, who had battled proslavery guerrillas in the 1850s, urged the deportation of blacks from the United States, declaring on the floor of the Senate, "I want to see, so soon as it can be done constitutionally, these two races separated, an ocean rolling between; that—South America—the Elysium of the colored man; this the asylum of the white."

The swelling contraband problem demanded a policy, particularly since most of the freedom seekers came from volatile border states, where loyalty to the Union was precarious. Purely for pragmatic reasons then, Lincoln declined to renounce Butler's impulsive invention, which with the president's permission was endorsed by the War Department. "Contrabands," as they were now universally called, were absorbed into the Union Army's workforce as laborers, laundresses, hospital attendants, officers' personal servants, guides, and most valuably as spies who provided information on the dispositions and size of Confederate forces. The presence of the contrabands in the army's camps also imperceptibly began to change soldiers' ingrained ideas about blacks and slavery. Often for the first time in their lives, Yankee soldiers now encountered Negroes as people much like themselves, with families they loved, familiar hopes and fears, and heart-wrenching stories of grinding field work, of hunger and torture, and of children ripped away from them and sold. Eventually, these multitudes of quotidian human encounters would begin to reshape Northern opinion and change the perceived purpose of the war.

In Congress, conservatives were still bent on protecting slavery. In the House, the slave-owning Unionist John Crittenden of Kentucky, who had struggled to craft a compromise solution before the guns opened on Fort Sumter, now proposed a resolution stating explicitly that the war had no purpose but to restore the status quo ante, with slavery left intact. (Crittenden had relinquished his Senate seat to make way for Breckinridge and had accepted a seat in the House instead.) "Does war change the powers of Congress?" he demanded. Congress simply had no power to legislate upon slavery, and never had. Nothing in the Constitution permitted the government to deprive a man of his property in slaves. "Let us act our part like men," he urged. "We have declared that this war is not for the subjugation of the South, not for the overthrow of slavery, not for the overthrow of their social institutions, but simply for the noble purpose of restoring our country. Let us do no act that shall degrade this struggle." The resolution was more nuanced than it seemed. It denied that slavery's overthrow was the *purpose* of the war, a formulation that even most Radicals could agree to, since they increasingly believed that its destruction, one way or another, would be a *consequence* of the war. When the matter was put to a vote, on July 22, all but two Republicans voted in favor.

Thaddeus Stevens was not among them. "I thought the time had come when the laws of war were to govern our action," he declared in one of the most powerful speeches of the session. "Who says the Constitution must come in, in bar of our actions? It is an absurdity! When a country is at open war with an enemy, you have a right to use every means which will weaken him." Citing the eighteenth-century Swiss scholar of international law Emer de Vattel, whose influence loomed large in Civil War–era America, he continued, "If it be a just war, and there be a people who have been oppressed by the enemy and that enemy be conquered, the victorious party cannot return that oppressed people to the bondage from which they have been rescued. One of the most glorious consequences of victory is giving freedom to those who are oppressed. By what principle of philanthropy can you return them to the bondage from which you have delivered them, and rivet again the chains you have once broken?"

On this, Stevens said, there was no room for compromise: there must be no bargaining, no negotiation, no truces with the rebels, except to bury the dead, until every man of them had laid down his arms, disbanded his organization, submitted himself to the government, and sued for mercy. "If their whole country must be laid waste, and made a desert, in order to save this Union from destruction, so let it be. I would rather reduce them to a condition where their whole country is to be repeopled by a band of freemen than to see them perpetrate the destruction of this people through our agency." What he said next represented slave owners' worst fears—the arming of former slaves. The time had not yet come, but surely it soon would, he presciently predicted. "I, for one, shall be ready to go for it, let it horrify anyone else. That is my doctrine, and that will be the doctrine of the whole free people of the North before two years roll round, if this war continues."

Entangled with the argument over the war's purpose were the stubborn questions of how it was to be fought, and who—Congress or the president—possessed the paramount constitutional authority to wage it. Consensus remained elusive. Some Republicans held that the war power rested with the president alone. The Constitution had given Congress the right to *declare* war, maintained elderly senator Jacob Collamer of Vermont, but the power to *wage* war was entirely an executive one. Lyman Trumbull, a doctrinaire and sometimes nitpicking constitutionalist, retorted that in view of the hundreds of millions of dollars and hundreds of thousands of men Congress had voted to defeat the rebellion, "Shall we be told that Congress has no power? Our power is omnipotent over this army!" Trumbull and others remained particularly uneasy at the prospect of granting the president the power, "monstrous in a free society," to abuse civil rights including, as the public was reminded virtually every day by the newspapers, the suspension of habeas corpus.

Unionist fears of subversion were not groundless. Federal agencies were widely believed to be infiltrated by subversives and spies. Antiwar activity that a few months earlier was confined mostly to Maryland had continued to metastasize. (John Merryman, whose arrest for bridge burning near Baltimore first sparked the debate over habeas corpus, was indicted for treason by a grand jury on July 12.) In some, antiwar sentiment found its voice mainly in defeatism, and in what Unionists contemptuously called "the slimy track of the traitor press." Shortly after Bull Run, Benjamin Wood, editor of the New York *Daily News* and the brother of the city's antiwar mayor, Fernando Wood, declared, "It is time! Wait no longer! Democrats, arise in your might. Throw off your allegiance to the vampires of your party. Thus will you tame the hyenas of war." Particularly in the lower Midwest, however, where affinities with the South were strong—in Indiana and Illinois, 12 percent of the population was Southern-born, and in Ohio 6 percent—pro-secession vigilantes terrorized Unionists with seeming impunity. Fears were also spreading of a secret pro-Confederate paramilitary organization, the Knights of the Golden Circle, that was recruiting sympathizers to fight the government. Violent incidents were becoming increasingly common. In the southern Illinois community of Nashville, armed men ordered several Unionists to leave town, destroyed the homes of others, cut down the Stars and Stripes from a public building, and hoisted a secession flag in its place. Elsewhere across the region, Republicans feared similar attacks with a sense of vulnerability that was heightened with so many men gone to the war.

Increasingly, Unionists conflated subversives with nonviolent dissenters and troublesome Democratic Party politicians of the Vallandigham variety under the rubric of "Copperheads." (A colorful but probably apocryphal story held that the term originated when a package addressed to President Lincoln had broken open in the Washington post office, and two poisonous copperhead snakes slithered out.) Zachariah Chandler charged, "The whole Democratic party is tainted with this doctrine of rebellion and secession." In Concord, New Hampshire, the offices of the *Daily Standard* were mobbed and destroyed by returning soldiers incensed by its antiwar editorials. In New York, the stridently antiwar editor of *The Cauca-sian,* James McMaster, was arrested by federal marshals, shackled in handcuffs that had been taken from a slave ship, and thrown into a prison cell at Fort Lafayette. In a Maryland town, men were seized and marched in front of federal troops as shields against supposed attack by local secessionists. Arrests were sometimes made based on hearsay and unsubstantiated innuendo from informers. And in Val-landigham's hometown of Dayton, the young lawyer Charles Med-lar wrote nervously to his fiancée that pro-war Republicans "rant about hanging, mobbing and assassinating Vallandigham and other local antiwar Democrats" such as himself, who wished to remain as "armed neutrals." Medlar wondered, was it now treason to advocate compromise? To question the constitutional power of the president to increase the standing army? To talk about economic hardship, ruined trade, or anxiety about prospective heavy taxes?

John Breckinridge gave voice to such concerns on August 1, in what proved to be his senatorial swan song before he returned home to Kentucky. He denounced the imminent and now virtu-ally unstoppable vote to approve the use of war powers against the seceded states and their sympathizers as a political apocalypse that, he charged, "provides for the destruction of personal and political rights everywhere," abolishing not only the rights of habeas corpus and trial by jury, but also "all state governments, all the judicial, exec-utive, and legislative functions of state governments . . . and every vestige we have remaining of political and personal liberty." If neces-sity was used as justification for the violation of one provision of the Constitution, couldn't it be used to justify *any* violation? What would come next, he demanded. Would the army now be dispatched to collect the enormous taxes that were about to be enacted? Would New York, or any other state, be declared in "insurrection" when its citizens refused to pay? From the ruins of the Union, more and more confederacies would soon rise, he predicted. "You have two confed-eracies now. Fight twelve months and you will have three; twelve months longer, and you will have four."

In the midst of Breckinridge's oration, Sen. Edward Baker of Ore-gon, riding crop in hand, strode dramatically into the chamber wearing the crisp blue uniform and fatigue cap of a colonel. He laid his sword meaningfully in full view across his desk, and after listening to Breckinridge for some minutes indicated that he wanted to speak.

Will the honorable senator tell me it is our duty to stay here, the stentorian Baker cried, within fifteen miles of the enemy seeking to advance upon us every hour, and talk about nice questions of constitutional construction as to whether it is war or merely insurrection? No, sir. It is our duty to advance, if we can; to suppress insurrection; to put down rebellion; to dissipate the rising; to scatter the enemy. I agree that we ought to do all we can to limit, to restrain, to fetter the abuse of military power. Bayonets are at best illogical arguments. But it is part of the law of war. You cannot have trials according to the forms and ceremonial of the common law amid the clangor of arms. Is it not the manly part to go on as we have begun, to raise money, and levy armies, to organize them, to prepare to advance? To talk to us about stopping is idle; we will never stop. Will the senator yield to rebellion? Or would he conduct this war so feebly that the whole world would smile at us in derision? These speeches of his, sown broadcast over the land, what clear distinct meaning have they? Are they not intended to dull our weapons? Are they not words of brilliant, polished treason?

The Senate's galleries broke out in thunderous applause, as the president pro tem, Henry Anthony of Rhode Island, hammered his gavel and cried for order.

What would the senators of ancient Rome have done, Baker demanded, if one of their number had declared that Hannibal the Carthaginian had good reason to attack Rome, and that he ought to be dealt with peacefully?

"They would have hurled him from the Tarpeian rock," Pitt Fessenden shouted. (Fessenden's listeners knew, as would any American with a smattering of classical education, that to be thrown from the Tarpeian rock, in early Rome, was the punishment for treason.) "For me," Baker declared, "amid temporary defeat, disaster, disgrace, it seems that my duty calls me to utter another word, and that word is bold, sudden, forward, determined war."

A few days later, the legislative dam broke. Beneath the lash of Fessenden and Stevens, the overwhelming Republican majority enacted a raft of legislation unmatched since the republic's earliest days, raising a mighty army, providing previously unimaginable sums of money to support it, and readying the nation for full-scale war. In doing so, Congress had decisively asserted its right to participate equally with the president in shaping war policy. Arguably most important, Congress legalized nearly all Lincoln's unilateral executive actions. The legislators' support was less than wholehearted, but it was decisive. John Sherman captured the pragmatic ambivalence that was shared by most of his colleagues: "I believe the president did right. He did precisely what I would have done had I been in his place—no more, no less; but I cannot here, as a senator, under oath, declare that what he did was legal."

Passage of the Confiscation Act established Union policy toward slavery in the seceded states, and signaled the beginning of the end of slavery in America. The biggest war loan in American history was approved. An embryonic income tax was enacted, although its implementation was postponed. Money was appropriated to buy arms and ordnance, to construct fortifications to protect the capital, to develop armored ships. The size of the navy and the Corps of Engineers was increased. The president was given the power to mobilize state militias for the war's duration. Soldiers' pay was raised. Federal employees, for the first time, were required to swear a binding oath of allegiance, in an effort to weed subversives from the government rolls. Fines and prison terms—up to $5,000 and six years in jail—were imposed on conspirators against the government or its laws. Proclaimed the *Philadelphia Daily News,* without hyperbole, "This extra session has been, in many respects, the most remarkable of any held since the adoption of the Federal Constitution." Alone among the war measures, Congress failed only to approve the suspension of habeas corpus. Although Thaddeus Stevens finally muscled it through the House on the session's last day, tacked onto a pay hike for the soldiers, the Senate failed to act on it, thus tacitly allowing the executive's claimed powers to remain in force without congressional sanction, ensuring that it would continue to inflame the war's Northern enemies, and bedevil federal authorities for many months to come.

After the close of Congress on August 7, most members returned to their districts, to stump for the war and to help raise troops. Edward Baker joined his command on the Potomac north of Washington. It seemed self-evident that he was destined to play a major role in the formation of congressional war policy. Ben Wade returned to Ohio, where he organized two cavalry regiments and an artillery battery. Zachariah Chandler, at the request of Secretary of State Seward, set out personally to recruit spies to infiltrate pro-rebel circles believed to be organizing secretly in Detroit. Jim Lane headed to Kansas to rally federal volunteers against Confederate incursions from Missouri.

One member who left for good was John Breckinridge. Just after the close of the session, he traveled to Baltimore with Clement Vallandigham, where they attempted to deliver speeches justifying their views, but they were drowned out by a crowd roaring cheers for the Union. Back in Kentucky, Breckinridge told constituents that "the Constitution of the United States is as much forgotten as if it lay away back in the twilight of history. I exchange, with proud satisfaction, a term of six years in the Senate of the United States for the musket of a soldier." He would soon be leading gray-uniformed troops against his erstwhile government.

Among the new arrivals in Washington was thirty-four-year-old Gen. George B. McClellan, a favorite of Treasury Secretary Chase, named to supplant the hapless Irvin McDowell. A West Point–trained engineer, he most recently had served as president of an Ohio railroad. Years earlier, he had served on Winfield Scott's staff during the Mexican War, where he came to know many of the young officers he would lead, and fight, in the Civil War. Like many products of the prewar army, he had little respect for politicians—he contemptuously dismissed Lincoln as a "well-meaning baboon," and Seward as an "incompetent little puppy"—even less for abolitionists, and none at all for Negroes. "I confess to a prejudice in favor of my own race, & can't learn to like the odor of either Billy goats or niggers," he later wrote. He announced to one of his staff officers that if he was ever asked to fight to free slaves, he would refuse. But he was the hero of the moment, anointed by the *New York Herald* as "the Napoleon of the present war" for a pair of small victories in the mountains of western Virginia. Short, trim, mustached, and punctilious, he set out to turn the disorganized masses of volunteers into a war machine, and promised to lead them triumphantly to Richmond.

He had his work cut out for him. Recruiting was done almost entirely by the individual states. As often as not, men who turned up in camps across the North found no one to train them. A Michigan officer complained to Zachariah Chandler that his regiment wasn't even half-drilled, officers didn't know how to use their sabers, "not one in twenty can load a revolver properly," or give even one-third of the required commands. The regiment's senior captain spent half his time drunk, discipline was "a thing unknown," and overall "the regiment is a humbug and a disgrace." From Harrisburg, where Henry Cooke had gone to expedite overdue pay for Pennsylvania volunteers, he wrote to his brother Jay, "I find 'confusion worse confounded' here. Ten thousand troops, clamorous, and riotous, and almost impossible to get information from those who ought to know."

The army also had to build a huge new management structure from scratch. The breakneck promotion of Regular Army officers meant that prewar lieutenants were now suddenly captains, colonels, even brigadier generals. Staff officers were in painfully short supply at every level. A vast human machine of transport officers, quartermasters, commissary officers, medical officers, and aides-de-camp had to be put into place. Until corps were organized, every piece of division-level business had to be sent to army headquarters for approval. "You might as well have the Supreme Court of the United States act upon every $20 case," complained Irvin McDowell, who remained in Washington as a staff advisor to Scott.

McDowell also huffed that, with a volunteer army, "You are obliged, as it were, to take in all kinds of fish by a sort of drag-net." Regiments were commanded by politicians, lawyers, businessmen, and doctors, and brigades by men who had never seen a day's military service. Fumed Henry Wilson, "You find men strolling about, not knowing where their colonels and captains are. You find colonels and captains strolling about your hotels, that have not gone to the places where they belong." Officers left whole regiments unfed, unsheltered, and unled. In many camps flu, measles, and "lung fever" were rampant, and often fatal. "There are about four hundred on the sick list in our regiment now probably there are twenty five that will get A discharge and some eight or ten that will die," an ailing Vermont soldier wrote home to his wife.

Replacing the inept presented enormous problems in the highly politicized volunteer force, in which men often elected their own company officers, and company officers the regiment's field officers. (Future president James A. Garfield was defeated in the vote for colonel of his Ohio regiment allegedly "by bargains and brandy.") Not infrequently, officers discharged for incompetence were reappointed by their state governors. Would-be officers constantly besieged their senators and representatives like civilian job seekers. In one fairly typical instance, a Mexican War veteran "from one of the best families" of Painesville, Ohio, as he put it, begged Ben Wade to fix a captain's command for him, while one of Wade's neighbors offered to enlist—if Wade raised the money to pay his debts. Wade's son James received a plum appointment as a lieutenant in the Third Ohio Cavalry at the urging of Treasury Secretary Chase, very likely with a nudge from Wade himself. Three of Fessenden's sons would also serve in the army, all as officers, as would both of the childless Thaddeus Stevens's nephews. None of them had prior military experience.

Before the year was out, the North would have almost 700,000 men under arms. (The number would eventually reach more than two million—about half the North's men of military age.) Arming them presented another set of problems. After decades of peace, the government had pathetically few stockpiles of matériel. Armories were filled with obsolete guns, rusty swords, and rotting cavalry gear. Some regiments were issued two or three different kinds of guns—smoothbores, old flintlocks converted to percussion, unreliable Belgian rifles, whatever was on hand. Billions of rounds of ammunition, millions of horses and mules, blankets, uniforms, shoes, tents, crates of hardtack, and barrels of pork had to be ordered. During the war's first months, there was no centralized system of procurement. For the most part, states manufactured their own ammunition in their own arsenals. In Ohio, prisoners at the state penitentiary were put to work making everything from gun carriages to spurs and tent pins. From Bangor to Sioux City, volunteer seamstresses rushed to assemble uniforms, drawers, shoes, socks, and canteens, while arsenals and factories employed women and children to make ammunition by hand. In this difficult and dangerous work, Illinois's quartermaster general approvingly reported, young children "acquired habits of industry and became accustomed to a discipline that will have its salutary effect upon the formation of their characters."

New fortifications had to be erected everywhere, and old ones repaired. (Crumbling Fort Washington, on the Potomac below the capital, was inhabited by a single retired soldier who, it was said, would probably surrender it for a bottle of whiskey.) Everyone needed uniforms: less than a week after Bull Run, the War Department offered tenders for 700,000 yards of blue wool for uniforms, 200,000 forage caps, and 800,000 drawers, and 33,000 gross shirt buttons—as well as 200,000 brass bugles. Not surprisingly, lucrative contracts were not infrequently channeled to well-connected insiders. The New York financier J. Pierpont Morgan bought thousands of obsolete rifles for $3.50 apiece and sold them to the army for $22 each, while a Lancaster newspaper complained that contracts for the manufacture of cannon had been granted to "favored parties" in Pennsylvania "who know no more about rifled cannon than a toad knows about the use of a side-pocket."

At the same time, innumerable bureaucratic jobs had to be created and men appointed to fill them. In the War Department, the Adjutant General's Department, Quartermaster's Department, Ordnance Department, the Corps of Engineers, and the Medical Department all had to be drastically expanded, along with the divisions of topographical engineers, sappers, and pontoon specialists for bridging rivers. The Quartermaster's Department alone would eventually hire over 100,000 civilian employees, more than any civilian business of the era. Chaplains also had to be hired for every regiment. (Clement Vallandigham proposed hiring rabbis for some regiments— "men of great learning and unquestioned piety"—but he was voted down, Congress insisting that none but "ministers of some Christian denomination" would be accepted.)

Members of Congress were besieged with complaints from the disgruntled. "It has been utterly impossible for me to supply everyone fully," one frustrated cavalry officer wrote to Ben Wade, begging him to intercede on his behalf with the Quartermaster's Department. "My own animals, as well as others suffer. I can get no hay." Others complained about the quality of rations, overdue pay, drunken officers, gambling in the camps, and disrespect from the military authorities, like the company of dissatisfied Michiganders who indignantly protested to Zachariah Chandler that they had been stuck into a New York regiment, and demanded reassignment to a regiment from their home state.

Not all of these challenges were McClellan's to solve. But he took the disorder in hand. New earthworks soon jutted from the Virginia countryside. More artillery and better rifles were ordered, and Regular Army discipline imposed in the camps. He sent army regulars to clear stragglers out of the gin mills and bordellos. When a rebellious New York regiment threatened to leave for home, he ordered a detachment of regulars to shoot them if they didn't drop their guns. Where he could, he weeded out incompetents. "Confidence renewed!" trumpeted the *New York Tribune*.

McClellan at first enjoyed the unbounded confidence of Lincoln as well as the Congress. "Presdt, Cabinet, Genl Scott & all deferring to me," he wrote to his wife, Mary Ellen, in late July, revealing a degree of self-regard that would haunt his relations with the civilian government. "I almost think that were I to win some small success now I could become Dictator or anything else that might please me." Ordinary soldiers, too, responded warmly to his swaggering panache as he galloped among them "in full tog, chapeau, epaulettes, etc." On November 1, he officially replaced Winfield Scott as the commander of all the nation's armies. When Lincoln asked him if too much responsibility had been imposed upon him, he declared with sublime self-confidence, "I can do it all."

# 6

# The Moloch of Slavery

We are first, for we are the
representatives of the people.

—SEN. WILLIAM PITT FESSENDEN

As September bled into October, pressure grew for a new advance against the rebels, who had blockaded the lower Potomac and had massed what McClellan mistakenly believed was an immense force of between 180,000 and 200,000 rebels in northern Virginia, triple their actual number. Instead of action, he drilled and paraded, paraded and drilled. McClellan himself had approximately 180,000 men hunkered in the forts that now ringed Washington, increasingly well-trained as the weeks passed, but still untested in battle. Although Lincoln continued to defend the general in spite of his inaction, congressional confidence in him waned. McClellan, remarked Ben Wade, "is determined his troops shall all be veterans before he permits them to come under fire."

On Capitol Hill, impatience with McClellan turned into frustration with the president for not compelling him to attack the enemy. To his friend Zach Chandler, Wade bitterly wrote on October 8,

I begin to despair of putting down this rebellion through the instrumentality of this administration. They are blundering, cowardly, and inefficient. They seem to be devoid of all feeling of pride or even self-respect perfectly content to be besieged in the capital of the nation. Their highest aspirations seeming to be to get so that they feel safe in their own dear persons harboring no more idea of acting offensively and endeavoring to disperse the enemy that holds them in durance than they have of removing the pillars of the Capitol themselves. You could not inspire Old Abe, Seward, Chase, or Bates with courage, decision, and enterprise with a galvanic battery. I am not always sure it would not be best for the country if the rebels should take Washington, President, and all hands. True, we have vast armies in the field maintained at a prodigious and almost ruinous expense, yet they are suffered to do nothing. I begin to think it will go on so until an outraged and indignant people [shall demand] an overthrow of this imbecility and place the power in more competent hands.

On October 21, 1,700 federal troops led by Sen. Edward Baker crossed the Potomac into Virginia at Ball's Bluff, thirty-eight miles north of Washington. Baker was following the orders of Gen. Charles Stone, who had helped to organize the capital's defenses in the spring and now commanded a division deployed along the Maryland bank of the river. After the army's months of inactivity, the raid was meant as a show of force to feel out Confederate strength and, if possible, capture the town of Leesburg—"a slight demonstration," McClellan later called it, when blame was being piled on the hapless and the dead. The flamboyant Baker was hungry to make a name for himself on the battlefield.

Ferried across the river in small boats, they scaled the steep bluffs, and with great élan attacked a camp of Confederates posted on top. They made headway at first. Baker, togged out in his dress uniform like "a pretty bird," led from the front, sword in hand, all dash and bold manliness, shouting orders in the splendid voice that was so memorable on the Senate floor. (Facing him on the Confederate side were Capt. Albert G. Brown of Mississippi, who had sat alongside Baker in the Senate until his state seceded, and Col. William Barksdale, also of Mississippi, who had occupied a seat in the House of Representatives until that state's delegation withdrew.) But brio wasn't enough to carry the day. Baker's men arrived piecemeal onto

the cramped field, where they were exposed to superior Confederate fire and overwhelmed. Baker himself was shot through the head
as he attempted to roll forward a cannon, becoming the only sitting
U.S. senator ever killed in battle. The outgunned federals wavered
and then broke, tumbling pell-mell down the bluff to the river, where
they discovered that there were too few boats to carry them all back
to the safety of the Maryland shore. The Confederates poured fire
down onto them where they stood packed and helpless on the riverbank. Defeat became massacre. Those who could swim, and many
who couldn't, threw away their rifles and plunged into the frigid
water. Scores drowned. Bodies turned up as far south as Washington
for days afterward. In all, half the Union force was killed, wounded,
or captured.

"Is there any hope for us?" a distraught Ohioan begged of Ben
Wade when he received news of the new defeat. To his wife, Caroline, Wade himself wrote, "All is gloom and despondency here.
All are disgusted." The Ball's Bluff disaster only confirmed Wade's
growing fear that Lincoln and his generals were hopelessly inept, if
not derelict in their duty. (McClellan, in a characteristic effort to shift
blame, sought to pin the defeat on the dead Baker.) If Washington
was really as safe as the administration repeatedly claimed, Wade
exclaimed, it was only owing to the Confederates' inactivity, not to
the feeble caliber of federal leadership.

"We are in a world of trouble here," Pitt Fessenden wrote to
Elizabeth C. Warriner, his cousin and intimate friend who shared
his home in Portland. "Everybody is grumbling because nothing is
done," he wrote her a few weeks later, "and there are no symptoms
that anything will be done. The truth is that no man can be found
who is equal to this crisis in any branch of the Government. Favorit-
ism has officered the army with incapables. The Treasury has been
plundered and mismanaged (not by the Secretary) until there is little
left in it. No two men can agree in opinion. The truth is, there is
nothing but a great military success which can save us from terrible
calamity." Horrible weather only added to the general gloom. For
the first several weeks of the new year, snow and sleet pelted the
capital, leaving the streets a morass of slushy, icy muck. "Oh, that
I had some loving friend to cheer me," the lonely Fessenden wrote.

In the country at large, there were serious worries that support for the war was ebbing and that frustrated soldiers might rebel against the administration, alongside sinister rumors that the Kentucky-born Lincoln had "southern proclivities," and didn't really want to prosecute the war. Some disgruntled Republicans suggested replacing Lincoln with a more aggressive wartime leader, perhaps the two-fisted senator Jim Lane of Kansas, or the charismatic John C. Frémont, who had been ousted from his command in Missouri for disobedience, but remained extremely popular among abolitionists.

Frémont, famed for his exploration of the Far West, and converted to abolitionism by his wife, the daughter of the powerful Missouri senator Thomas Hart Benton, had performed unexpectedly well as the Republican Party's first candidate for president in 1856. In July 1861, he was named to the command of the strategically vital Department of Missouri, a plum appointment but beyond Frémont's limited executive and military abilities. On August 30, he thrilled abolitionists by rashly declaring free the slaves of anyone deemed an enemy of the U.S. government, a step significantly beyond Benjamin Butler's legalistic criterion of "military necessity." Within days, however, Lincoln warned Frémont that his proclamation posed grave danger to the Union cause by undermining support for the government in the slaveholding border states. When Frémont declined to retract his order, Lincoln publicly countermanded it, and on November 9 replaced him with the cautious and conservative Gen. Henry W. Halleck, who ordered that all slaves who had fled to Union lines under Frémont's declaration of emancipation be rounded up and returned to their masters. "I wish to God that we had in Old Abe's place a man who dare take the responsibility to strike a blow," Ben Wade's son James, an officer in Missouri, privately confided. "I want a man there who would commence by hanging every officer in the army who would return or suffer to be returned a slave." To Chandler, Wade himself wrote furiously, the president "has done more injury to the cause of the Union, by receding from the ground taken by Fremont, than McDowell did by retreating from Bull Run."

Wade felt more and more that his primary duty was to inject a sense of urgency into the administration, and to provoke it into launching a long overdue offensive against the Confederacy. Late on the night of October 25, accompanied by Chandler and Lyman Trumbull, Wade confronted McClellan face-to-face at the home of Postmaster General Montgomery Blair, and pressed him to set his vast army on the march. McClellan fobbed them off, blaming the enfeebled Winfield Scott for the stalemate, and claiming that he faced overwhelming odds and couldn't risk an advance without more men. The next day, Wade and his friends carried their campaign to the president himself. The "Jacobin Club," as Lincoln's secretary John Hay sarcastically called them, "came up to worry the administration into a battle," telling Lincoln at one point that if he didn't adopt a more aggressive strategy he might as well invite Jefferson Davis to Washington and surrender. But Lincoln made clear that he intended to stand by McClellan. "No country was ever cursed with such imbecility," Wade exasperatedly complained to Caroline.

Time and again, McClellan appeared to be on the brink of stirring into action, but nothing happened. Fessenden wrote despairingly to his cousin Lizzy, "I am convinced that nothing can be done so long as he is at the head of the army. It is all marching up the hill, & then down again." On November 13, Hay reported a shocking insult to the president. Lincoln, Hay, and Secretary of State Seward had gone to McClellan's residence on Lafayette Square to see him, in an effort to persuade him to act. Told by a servant that the general was attending a wedding, they went inside to wait. An hour later, the general arrived, but went upstairs without a word. Half an hour later, Lincoln sent the servant up to remind McClellan that they were still waiting. He returned to say that McClellan had gone to bed. It was, Hay recorded in his diary, "a portent of evil to come."

If things continued this way, Wade worried, by March the government would wind up mired in debt—$600 million by the most recent estimate—with "nothing yet done that seems to be at all commensurate with the exertions the nation has made. And everybody knows that our finances are not in a condition to keep this up eternally. All this is hanging upon one man who keeps his counsels to himself"— George McClellan. The army had been ready to march for months, but McClellan refused to say why it still remained idle, or what he intended to do. The discouraging state of the war seemed underscored by the rainstorms that soaked the capital well into December. So dense was the fog at times that members of Congress standing on Pennsylvania Avenue could hear the great canvas-covered army wagons rumble over the cobblestones but couldn't see them though they were only a few yards away. In the camps, besodden soldiers huddled over their cookfires eating stale bread and beef as hard as gutta-percha. In Virginia, even a little rain sank cannon, wagons, and entire supply trains in mud up to their hubs. "There are many screws loose" in the war effort, a disconsolate Republican activist in Cincinnati, Nelson Franklin, reflected, "but I fear we have no head to tighten them."

The tightening of the screws began at last on December 2, when Congress met for what would prove to be one of the most dynamic sessions in its history. It opened with a cascade of wide-ranging proposals that would begin to prepare the nation for the ultimate destruction of slavery, aggressively insert Congress into the waging of the war, permanently transform federal monetary policy, and shape the westward expansion of the country's development. The congressional Republicans, Radicals as well as conservatives, now determined to do what the generals and the Lincoln administration seemed afraid to do on their own, and to drive the war forward on as many fronts as possible. If the North was to prevail on the battlefield, Wade, Stevens, Fessenden, and other like-minded men believed, it would require steel-spined leadership, creative politics, moral courage, and a racial revolution that up to now only a few members had dared to contemplate.

One of the boldest strokes, and one of the most controversial, was the formation of the Joint Committee on the Conduct of the War, at the instigation of Zachariah Chandler, who with Wade had witnessed the disgraceful collapse at Bull Run firsthand. Over the next four years, the committee would eventually hold 272 sessions, interview almost every major Union military figure, hundreds in all, and examine virtually every aspect of the war effort, from high strategy to the procurement of cavalry horses. For most of the next four years, an invitation to the committee's room off what later became known as the Brumidi Corridor was a summons dreaded by defeated generals, timeservers, and corrupt contractors. (While the committee deliberated, in the corridor outside the Italian painter Constantino Brumidi methodically filled wall after wall with ancient designs inspired by the villas of Pompeii and oval medallions illustrating the founders of the nation, agricultural implements, sheaves of grain, American wildlife, and images of western mountains and rivers.)

The committee became, in many respects, the driving engine of congressional war policy, prodding and pressuring the president toward more decisive action against slavery and more aggressive military action. Especially at the beginning, it was an uphill battle. A shaken member of the committee recalled after meeting with Lincoln in early January, "The most striking fact revealed by the discussion was that neither the president nor his advisers seemed to have any definite information respecting the management of the war, or the failure of our forces to make any forward movement. We were greatly surprised to learn that Mr. Lincoln himself did not think that he had any right to know." Wade would do his best to fill the vacuum. "Yes, [Lincoln] is the commander-in-chief, by the consent of the people," Wade conceded. "He is their creature and agent." But the Constitution had lodged the power to declare war, make peace, and to raise armies in Congress, not the presidency. "When war is declared," Wade asserted, "it depends upon Congress, not upon him, to say whether that war will continue, and to prescribe precisely upon what principles it shall be governed. The president cannot lay down and fix the principles upon which war shall be conducted. He is as powerless as one of us or one of the people." Wade's thinking, which was shared by most though not all of the congressional Republicans, would shape and dominate nearly all the committee's work.

As the sponsor of the legislation that created the committee, Chandler could have taken its chairmanship if he wished, but instead he nominated Wade, who possessed the legal and parliamentary experience that Chandler lacked. In the months and years to come, the Joint Committee elevated Wade to the heights of wartime influence, eventually second only to Fessenden in practical power, and second to none in his unceasing advocacy of hard war. Wade's toughness sprang from a hardscrabble boyhood. Born to a laborer in western Massachusetts, he received little early schooling apart from intense patriotism coupled to a Calvinist piety that he shucked off as soon as he was old enough to think for himself. As a teenager, he walked west, earning money as he went by driving cattle, chopping wood, and pushing a wheelbarrow for the construction of the Erie Canal. Settling among fellow New England transplants in Ohio's Western Reserve, he studied law under Joshua Giddings, at one time the only outspoken abolitionist in Congress, who became his mentor, and eventually won recognition in his own right as one of the ablest lawyers in the state.

In addition to Wade, the committee's Republican members included Chandler, who made up for his lack of advanced education with moral grit, earnestness, and energy; Rep. George W. Julian, an antislavery Radical from Indiana, an alumnus of Wade's and Chandler's expedition to Bull Run, and an early advocate of extending full civil rights to Negroes; Rep. John Covode of Pennsylvania, a hard-war man who had begun his working life as a blacksmith and who was regarded as "shrewd but illiterate, a match and more than a match for men of high culture, reputation and acquirements"; and Dartmouth-educated lawyer Rep. Daniel Gooch of Massachusetts. The only permanent Democratic member of the committee was Moses Odell of Brooklyn, a Douglas man who believed in states' rights and white supremacy but wholeheartedly supported the war effort. Sen. Andrew Johnson, a lifelong Jacksonian Democrat but fiercely devoted to the Union, also served briefly on the committee until his appointment by Lincoln as wartime governor of the Union-occupied portions of his native Tennessee in March of 1862.

The committee had McClellan in its sights from the start. Gen. William S. Rosecrans, who had served under McClellan in western Virginia, when asked by Chandler if the army would be in better shape for battle if it kept drilling for another six months, replied: "It is not military knowledge, but military habits, that you want. Men have to fight, and before they fight a decisive battle—before they become very reliable troops—they must be hardened up to it." He added, "The general impression is that the snakes are torpid now, and now is the time to strike them." Gen. James Wadsworth, the commander of Washington's defenses, assured the committee that the troops were eager to avenge the humiliations of Bull Run and Ball's Bluff. But if the soldiers realized that there was no plan for battle, he warned, "it would be almost impossible to keep the volunteers here."

The committee's questioning, particularly Wade's, was blunt, sometimes bullying, and often designed to embarrass officers its members regarded as weak or politically suspect. To the chagrin of many military men, the committee regularly invited officers to criticize their superiors. When Wade asked Gen. Samuel P. Heintzelman, who was not close to McClellan, if he knew anything of McClellan's plans of operation, the general replied, "No, sir; I have not the slightest idea—not the slightest."

"I will ask you whether it is usual for a general-in-chief to conceal his great plans from commanders of divisions, &c; or, in other words, is it not necessary that they should know something of his plans?" Wade asked. To this, Chandler added, "In your military experience and reading, has it not been customary, in maneuvering a large army, even for the most eminent generals to take the opinions of his generals of division?"

Replied Heintzelman, "Yes, sir; we very frequently find that is the case."

Democrats, and some Republicans, were incensed at civilian politicians sitting in judgment on military matters about which they were presumed to know little. In opposing the creation of the committee, Republican senator Lafayette Foster of Connecticut declared, "I believe in letting the military authorities manage the army. If it is badly managed now I am sorry; I do not believe it is, but if it be, in Heaven's name do not make it worse by tampering, for worse we shall make it and only worse." To this, Fessenden, who swung his support decisively behind the committee, replied that since Congress was constitutionally responsible for declaring war and for providing the means to wage it, then it also was duty-bound to monitor the war's conduct on behalf of the public. Are we, he demanded, "to ask no questions, make no complaints, no investigations, know nothing, say nothing, and inquire nothing about it? We are not under the command of the military of this country. They are under ours as a

Congress, and I stand here to maintain it. Say what men may, we are not second; we are first, for we are the representatives of the people, and our behests, so far as they are within the limits of our constitutional authority, are to be obeyed."

Assigning responsibility for the debacles at Ball's Bluff and Bull Run stood first on the committee's agenda. Wade was notably unfriendly to what he considered the Regular Army's "aristocratic" officer caste, and frankly hated West Point, "the hotbed in which rebellion was hatched," which he felt produced graduates devoid of egalitarian values and loyalty to the country. Almost 200 of the 820 West Point graduates in the prewar army hailed from Southern states. Most joined the rebel army, including Robert E. Lee, a former academy superintendent, Jefferson Davis, Stonewall Jackson, J. E. B. Stuart, and Pierre G. T. Beauregard, who resigned from the superintendency in 1861 and ordered the attack on Fort Sumter. "There is something wrong about this whole institution," Wade had declared during the July debates. "I wish it could be done away with. I do not believe that in the whole history of the world you can find as many men who have proved themselves as utterly faithless to their oaths, ungrateful to the government that has supported them, guilty of treason and a deliberate intention to overthrow that government which has educated them and given them its support, as have emanated from this institution." Deeply influenced by the received memory of the aroused citizens—his father among them—who had taken up arms to fight the British in 1776, he believed that formal military education was a waste of time, and that inspired leaders would always rise from the ranks. "I am willing to carry on this war until, if it be necessary, the South was reduced to utter desolation," he had told the Senate just before Bull Run. "But not a war run by professional officers."

Massachusetts-born Gen. Charles Stone, who had initiated the movement at Ball's Bluff, was precisely the kind of officer that Wade meant: a rigid West Pointer and conservative Democrat, whose abrasive manner did him no good with either subordinates or civilian politicians. Although Stone had organized the defense of Washington at the war's start, he had offended many of the New England troops he commanded—as well as Massachusetts governor John Andrew and

Sen. Charles Sumner, both ardent abolitionists—by ordering his men not to "encourage insubordination" among the slaves. The committee's questioning of all the senior officers, and many junior ones, made clear that the operation was crippled by bad communications, misinterpreted orders, logistical snafus, and faulty intelligence. But public outrage cried out for a scapegoat. The committee learned that only three small boats were on hand to transport the hundreds of federal troops back from Ball's Bluff, and that even these were inefficiently put to use, ensuring that the panicked soldiers huddled on the riverbank would be trapped and massacred.

Witnesses from various Union regiments told the committee that for weeks before the battle Stone had allowed suspicious letters and packages to be sent across the river, "made signals" to parties on the Confederate side of the river, personally visited with rebel officers, permitted the enemy to erect fortifications that he could have destroyed, returned fugitive slaves to their masters, and cultivated the friendship of secessionists in Maryland. "The general feeling is that a great proportion of the officers and men do not think he is altogether on the square," testified Lt. Philip J. Downey of the Second New York, which was badly mauled at Ball's Bluff. "I thought he was more of a Secesh than anything else." Instead of defending his subordinate, McClellan deflected attention from his own faulty oversight of the operation by lending credence to the allegations of a refugee from Leesburg, who claimed that Stone was "popular" with Confederate officers there. Venomous news reports spread across the country denouncing Stone as Baker's "murderer."

The committee took hearsay too seriously and hobbled Stone's self-defense by not permitting him to question his accusers. Stone also unwisely provoked the committee by ignoring its questions about his strategy, snapping, "If I had any plans, I should not wish to tell them, even to my aide-de-camp." By the time the hearings were over, his career was ruined. He had in fact proved incompetent in managing his troops in the run-up to Ball's Bluff, but he was not a traitor. Nevertheless, he would be formally arrested in February, and spend six months imprisoned at Fort Hamilton in New York without ever being charged with a crime.

The committee's investigation into the battle of Bull Run took

The United States Capitol. In 1861, its dome was still under construction, a symbol of the fractured Union.

Abraham Lincoln shortly before his election to the presidency: unbearded, untried, and by Southerners deeply untrusted.

Vice President Hannibal Hamlin of Maine, an abolitionist plucked from the Senate to help Lincoln win support in New England.

BOMBARDMENT OF FORT SUMTER BY THE BATTERIES OF THE CONFEDERATE STATES, APRIL 13, 1861.—[SEE PAGE 257.]

Southern batteries firing at Fort Sumter. The war begins.

Outgoing president James Buchanan, one of the most experienced and least competent man ever to sit in the White House. He proved impotent to stem secession.

THE FIFTH MASSACHUSETTS VOLUNTEERS DRILLING FOR ACTIVE SERVICE—CHARGING, AT THE DOUBLE QUICK, UP A STEEP BANK NEAR THE CAPITOL. (See page 48.)

Northern volunteers rushed to the defense of Washington and trained within sight of the Capitol.

Sen. William Pitt Fessenden: a moderate from Maine, he crafted many of the financial measures that kept the Union's armies in the field.

Rep. Thaddeus Stevens of Pennsylvania: a brilliant parliamentarian and one of the most eloquent abolitionists in Congress. He served as the Republican floor leader in the House of Representatives for much of the war's most important legislation.

Sen. Benjamin F. Wade of Ohio: rough and outspoken, he was a leader of the Radical Republicans and wielded immense power as chairman of the Joint Committee on the Conduct of the War.

The collapse of the Union Army at Bull Run shocked those who expected a short and glorious war.

Sen. Zachariah Chandler of Michigan: a veteran of the prewar Underground Railroad, he was an aggressive advocate for harsh war measures and Ben Wade's closest ally in the Senate.

Sen. Henry Wilson of Massachusetts: known as the "Natick cobbler" because of his humble origins as a shoemaker, he chaired the powerful Military Affairs Committee.

Sen. Lyman Trumbull of Illinois: a former Democrat, he brought his exceptional legal skills to the Radicals' war effort and authored the Thirteenth Amendment.

Sen. Charles Sumner of Massachusetts: a staunch advocate for the rights of African Americans, he was more effective as an orator than as a legislator and often irritated his fellow Radicals.

Rep. Clement L. Vallandigham of Ohio: the most outspoken antiwar Democrat in Congress, he was accused of treason by Republicans and expelled to the Confederacy in 1863.

THE COPPERHEAD PARTY.——IN FAVOR OF *A VIGOROUS PROSECUTION OF PEACE!*

Antiwar Democrats, dubbed "Copperheads," were perceived as viperous subversives by most Republicans. Northerners would probably have seen one of them as Clement L. Vallandigham.

place simultaneously, and was equally fine-grained, revealing more evidence of incompetence, indiscipline, inadequate training, confusion in the chain of command, and grotesquely inaccurate intelligence. The committee also found a more justified scapegoat than Stone in the elderly Gen. Robert Patterson, who had failed to prevent Confederate forces in the Shenandoah Valley from reinforcing those at Bull Run. Unlike the unfortunate Stone, however, the politically well-connected Patterson was allowed to fade gracefully into retirement. Both investigations marked a political turning point in Union policy: they showed the officer corps that Congress meant to play a forceful role in the war, and that the Joint Committee was to be taken seriously.

While the Radicals were moving to assert control—or at least a significant influence—over military policy, Republicans were also staking out a position on emancipation that was far in advance of Lincoln's cautious policy. On December 2, Thaddeus Stevens released an oratorical salvo that reverberated for months to come. "Whereas slavery has caused the present rebellion in the United States," Stevens began, "and whereas there can be no solid and permanent peace and union in this Republic so long as that institution exists within it; and whereas slaves are now used by the rebels as an essential means of protracting and supporting the war; and whereas by the law of nations it is right to liberate the slaves of an enemy to weaken his power," he called upon the president to declare free all slaves who left their masters, and lent their aid in quelling the rebellion. It was a barely veiled call to slaves to take up arms in the Union cause.

Secretary of War Simon Cameron had called explicitly for arming former slaves in an early draft of his annual report to Congress, but deleted it under intense pressure from McClellan. Stevens, as chairman of the powerful Ways and Means Committee, could not be cowed. In January, he went even further. The war would not end until the rebels' power had been "utterly annihilated," he told the House, and that would not happen as long as the government feared to tamper with slavery. Their wartime economy depended on the sweat of slaves, he said. "So long as [they] are left the means of cultivating their fields through forced labor, you may expend the blood of tens of thousands of freemen and billions of money, year after year, without being any nearer the end." Slavery, by freeing white men for the army, gave the South a huge advantage over the North, where every man who donned a uniform was a man subtracted from its factories and farms. To counter this strength, the North must take a radical step. "Prejudice may be shocked, weak minds startled, weak nerves may tremble, but they must hear and adopt it. Those who now furnish the means of war, but those who are the natural enemies of slaveholders, must be made our allies. Universal emancipation must be proclaimed to all." Slavery's sympathizers might raise an outcry about the presumed horrors of a "servile insurrection," but what was more to be feared—"a rebellion of slaves fighting for their liberty, or a rebellion of freemen fighting to murder the nation?" Stevens asked. "You send forth your sons and brothers to shoot and saber and bayonet the insurgents; but you hesitate to break the bonds of their slaves to reach the same end," he taunted. "What sickly loyalty and humanity is that which would allow lawless insurgents to murder a hundred thousand freemen, rather than liberate an oppressed people to prevent it?"

In any just war, nations had a right to employ any and every measure to weaken the enemy, Stevens continued. "The slave is in a state of war with his master. Why not employ the enemy of our enemy to weaken his power?" To some, emancipation might seem a terrible weapon.

> But instruments of war are not selected on account of their harmlessness. You choose the cannon that has the longest range. You throw the shell that will kill the most men by its explosion. You grind to the sharpest edge the saber bayonet. But you object to emancipation because it liberates the slaves of traitors! Tenderhearted Christians! Benevolent philanthropists! If such men are statesmen, where are the idiots to be found? It *must* come to this, and the sooner the better. We have put a sword into one hand of our generals and shackles into the other. Let the people know that this Government is fighting not only to enforce a sacred compact, but to carry out to final perfection the principles of the Decla-

ration of Independence, which its framers expected would long since have been fulfilled on this continent, and the blood of every freeman will boil with enthusiasm, and his nerves be strengthened in this holy warfare. Give him the sword in one hand, and the book of freedom in the other, and he will soon sweep despotism and rebellion from every corner of this continent. The occasion is forced upon us, and the invitation presented to strike the chains from four millions of human beings, and create them MEN; to extinguish slavery on this whole continent; to wipe out, so far as we are concerned, the most hateful and infernal blot that ever disgraced the escutcheon of man.

Although Stevens's resolution did not pass, it served as the overture for a sustained legislative assault on slavery that would steadily push Republicans, and the president, further than they had ever expected to go toward wholesale emancipation. Amidst the public frustration with the stalled war effort, support for a decisive blow against slavery was growing. Writing to Henry Wilson, one angry constituent voiced a spreading sentiment, "Not only is this Moloch of slavery the *cause* of this infernal Rebellion and of all our troubles— but it still *stands in the way of our advancing armies, and of all progress toward putting down the Rebellion!?* What has kept back our columns for weeks and months, except the fear of *disturbing slavery?*"

Within the Republican majority, there was growing talk of strengthening the previous summer's Confiscation Act, arming freed blacks, and finding a political route toward large-scale emancipation. Even some Democrats were beginning to see some form of emancipation as inevitable. "A new order is upon us," editorialized the anti-administration *New York Herald*, "and even in behalf of the peculiar institutions of the South we must accommodate ourselves to the exigencies of a great political revolution."

# 7

# The Strong Arm of Government

It is the nation that is freed!

—WILLIAM LLOYD GARRISON

In early December, Henry Wilson and Thaddeus Stevens took a portentous step, the first in what Radicals hoped and conservatives feared would develop into a steady march toward the abolition of slavery: they proposed the emancipation of the 3,100 slaves in the District of Columbia. Washington was the only place in the United States where Congress clearly had the authority to end slavery. Although the District had adopted Maryland's slave laws in 1801, the Constitution stipulated that as a unique *federal* territory it was to be governed by Congress alone. As early as the 1820s, early abolitionists had argued for such a measure, as had Abraham Lincoln, in 1849, during his single term in the House of Representatives. But as long as proslavery Southern Democrats had dominated the government the proposals predictably died stillborn. A seismic shift was now about to take place in Republican war policy.

More was at stake than just the freedom of the capital's few slaves. Everyone knew that abolition in the District of Columbia would immediately set a precedent for the extension of emancipation to federal property everywhere from forts and shipyards to the vast territories of the West. Few if any members of Congress believed that Congress had the constitutional authority to abolish slavery outright in any state, however. Northern Democrats and border state Unionists still opposed emancipation on virtually any terms. Even some Republicans in principle preferred a slow-motion process, while others feared that a tidal wave of freed blacks would inundate their states. The Radicals were willing to compromise, but only to the extent of offering to pay moderate compensation to loyal slave owners when their human property was freed. In deference to conservatives and to the president, who retained a tenacious—if ever unfulfilled—faith in the willingness of border state slave owners to free their slaves if they were offered an incentive, the Radicals agreed to two measures: to offer individual compensation to Washington's slave owners, and to compensate any state that committed itself to some form of gradual emancipation.

Stevens argued that emancipation was not only the right thing to do—it made practical sense. He urged his colleagues to look at the numbers: he estimated that perhaps half the 429,441 slaves in the border slave states belonged to loyal men, and perhaps another 80,000 slaves belonged to presumed loyalists scattered elsewhere in the South. In all, then, compensation might be offered for some 300,000 slaves at, say, $200 apiece, adding up to a total of $60 million. "Manumit the slaves, and the war would end in six months," he predicted. "Leave them to the rebels, and I doubt if six years will end it." The war was already costing the federal government at least $500 million a year: six more years of war would increase the national debt to $3 billion, not to mention countless more soldiers' lives. If that were to happen, Stevens cried, "All the waters of the Nile can never wash the blood from our souls!" By comparison, $60 million in compensation was a paltry sum.

In the Senate, Charles Sumner, whose soaring oratory often flew beyond his effectiveness as a legislator, declared that if emancipation in Washington were enacted "the first practical triumph of freedom will at last be accomplished. This metropolis, which bears a venerated name, will be purified; its evil spirits will be cast out; its shame will be removed." A less emotional, and more persuasive, defense of the bill was articulated by Pitt Fessenden, who understood that Congress stood at one of those rare moments when speedy action could bring about real and dramatic change. Usually cautious in his utterances, he now declared himself an out-and-out abolitionist— a cool-headed, pragmatic, judicious abolitionist, but an abolitionist all the same. "I do desire to see slavery abolished in this country as soon as may be, by constitutional methods, and by those who have the power to act upon the subject," he said. He conceded that the Republican Party had repeatedly declared that the war's purpose was not to overthrow slavery. But that did not mean that they had pledged to do nothing that might *affect* slavery. "What have we been struggling for?" he asked. "It was to place this government in a position where it should not lend its aid to the support of slavery."

Fessenden allowed that Congress did not have a constitutional right to undo slavery where it existed by law. "But so far as the people of this country have the power under the Constitution to weaken the institution of slavery," he said, "to deprive it of its force; to subject it to the laws of the land; to take away the political influence which it has wielded in this country, and to render it as far as they can a nullity, they have the right to do so, and it is their solemn duty to exercise it. Do you suppose we came into power to sit still and be silent on this subject; that we came into power to do nothing; to think nothing; to say nothing lest by some possibility a portion of the people of the country might be offended?" The civilized world was waiting impatiently for the American government to do something—*anything*—to demonstrate that it was not forever shackled to the protection of slavery. Act now, he begged. "We can at any rate strike it out from the national capital. We can break it down here. The day has arrived, the hour has presented itself."

Opposition to the bill was led by Garrett Davis of Kentucky, a onetime protégé of the great Henry Clay and erstwhile Know Nothing, who was elected by the state legislature to fill the defector John Breckinridge's seat. Small-boned, almost skeletal in appearance, legalistic by bent, and both Unionist and proslavery by conviction, though Davis claimed to believe in gradual emancipation, he was racist to the core, and found the very idea of freed slaves—"vicious," "thievish vagabonds"—almost physically repellent. Emancipate them, he predicted, and they "will become a sore and a burden and a charge upon the white population." Slavery, he asserted, was

Negroes' natural condition, and the *only* state in which they could coexist with whites. Yes, Congress might technically have the *power* to wreak the injustice of emancipation upon the hapless whites of Washington, but he predicted that actually carrying it out would unite the entire pro-Union population of the border states against the national government. And if ever the government dared to abolish slavery in the Southern states, he warned, their white inhabitants would ruthlessly reduce the Negroes once again to servitude, "or they would expel them and drive them upon you, or they would hunt them like beasts and exterminate them." The proposed bill represented a sinister abolitionist tactic, "an entering wedge," Davis scathingly declared. "You want to get the head in, and then you intend to push the monster through. That is what you are after. This is but a preliminary operation." Didn't the residents of the District have any right to say whether they wanted slavery or not? "Why do you not go out into this city and hunt up the blackest, greasiest, fattest old Negro wench you can find and lead her to the altar of Hymen? You do not believe in any such equality; nor do I."

Fessenden replied that if the bill was but an opening wedge, "so much the better, for so much nearer shall we be to the final accomplishment of the object."

Realizing that the bill's proponents had the votes to pass it, its enemies launched a rearguard assault on its most vulnerable salient: the fraught question of what was to be done with the freed slaves. They hardly needed to point out that behind the more than three thousand slaves in Washington loomed the terrifying specter of almost four million more who might soon be loosed upon the country. "How long would it be until this miserable population, like the frogs of Egypt, would be infesting your kitchens, squatting in your gates, and filling your almshouses," cried Sen. Waitman T. Willey, who represented the rump end of Virginia that was occupied by federal troops. (Willey also still identified himself as a Whig, one of few who remained in public life, "like fragments of a wreck, tossed to and fro on the billows of this revolution," as he put it.) If slaves were to be freed, he said, then they must be gotten out of the country, as far away as possible from white Americans.

The mass deportation of freed slaves beyond American shores

had been promoted since 1816, with the founding of the American Colonization Society. Though regarded as an enlightened approach to race and slavery by its friends, "colonization" appealed to few blacks; it was advocated most warmly by Americans who were embarrassed by slavery but resisted any policy that seriously undermined it as an institution. Even now, Lincoln and some other prominent congressional Republicans supported colonization as the best permanent solution to the "Negro problem." Find a place for them in some tropical country, such as "Hayti," or Central America, urged Missouri Republican Frank Blair Jr. Insist on that, and the Negroes would flood away "like the outpouring of the Mississippi when a crevasse is opened." Negrophobic conservatives like Blair were more realistic than the antislavery Radicals in acknowledging the root-deep racism that pervaded the country. There was no question that the government would eventually be able to dictate terms of peace to the beaten rebels, he asserted. But he warned, presciently as it would ultimately turn out, "We cannot emancipate the slaves of the South and maintain them in the condition of freemen upon the soil of these United States without the presence of an immense army sufficient to prevent the white race from reenslaving the black, and by waging a constant war upon the people of our race for the protection of the black race." How long, he asked, would Northerners be willing to endure such a burden?

At that very moment, interrupting Blair, the Speaker of the House, Galusha Grow, announced that he had just received a message from the president stating that Lincoln had signed the joint resolution offering compensation to border states. This might well have proved to be a decisive stroke had Lincoln been correct in his belief in the essential right-mindedness of Unionist slave owners. But not a single border state embraced it, including even tiny Delaware with its few hundred remaining slaves.

As a sweetener for Washington's loyal slave owners, Congress agreed to appropriate $100,000 in compensation, up to a limit of $300 per slave. Owners had ninety days to apply to the commission empowered to assess the value of each slave. (One of its three members was a commercial slave trader, who was presumed to bring a necessary professional eye to such things.) Significantly, the measure also empowered slaves to testify as to the loyalty of their former owners, a shibboleth-shattering precedent, given that wherever slavery existed they had been barred from testifying against whites in court.

Garrett Davis argued relentlessly that innocent Washington slave owners would be cruelly victimized by the bill. He cited the pathetic case of a Mrs. Beall, a woman "of intellect, of cultivation," a widow suffering from heart disease and goiter—"the largest I ever saw"— who was totally dependent on income from the several slaves she leased out, one as a nurse in an infirmary, another as a seamstress, another as a cook, another as a house servant, another as a laborer, who altogether brought in for Mrs. Beall $800 or $900 per year. At a mere $300 apiece, they would be worth just $1,500, when each one was worth $1,000 or more on the open market. "Is she to be deprived of that property for the pittance that is proposed in this bill?" Davis demanded. "The men who remove these slaves from their plentiful and contented home will outrage humanity and benevolence by the act." Davis's gentle empathy with slave owners was unmatched by any comparable feeling for their slaves.

Davis's appeals were to no avail. In mid-April, Congress voted by two-to-one in both houses to free the capital's slaves, in the first outright act of emancipation by the federal government in the nation's history. In its way, it represented hardly less of an assault against the bulwarks of the rebellion than the shot hurled by federal field guns just days earlier in the thickets of Shiloh, in Tennessee, the bloodiest battle of the war to date. Abolitionists were ecstatic. "It is the nation that is freed!" crowed William Lloyd Garrison in *The Liberator.* "It is our government that has been emancipated! The President walks upon free soil. The birds will sing sweeter. The grass will grow greener. Mothers own their daughters! Men own their wives! Washington is free!" Every black church in Washington held special services of prayer and thanksgiving. Men and women alike shouted, prayed, and wept. *The Christian Recorder,* the newspaper of the AME church, captured the volcanic joy that everywhere erupted. "All hail the day of emancipation here! All hail the day of prospective emancipation everywhere! Thou rattle-snake slavery! And art thou at last humbled in the dust! FREEDOM—ALL HAIL!"

When Thaddeus Stevens hailed emancipation in Washington as a glorious precedent, the considerably more cautious William Sheffield of Rhode Island, a fellow Republican, worried aloud that to go any further would only inflame Southerners. To this, replied Stevens, "I dislike slavery and I am willing to go every way I can to abolish it. There are others who are loud in their protestations of dislike for slavery, and yet when they come to a practical proposition for its abolition, where we clearly have the power in the premises, they meet us with all sorts of objections."

But mightn't more forceful policies on slavery just prompt the Southerners to resist federal authority all the more vigorously? Sheffield asked.

That kind of reasoning, Stevens said slyly, reminded him of a certain timid captain in the Revolutionary War, "perhaps from Rhode Island," who raised a company to fight the British. When his company came face-to-face with the enemy, "he cried out when they were about to shoot, 'For God's sake, don't fire, for don't you see it will only make them madder!'"

The embarrassed Sheffield, amidst his colleagues' laughter, peevishly replied, "I've heard another story, and it may be the man was from *Pennsylvania* . . ." But before he could tell it, Stevens said, "I don't propose to have any difficulty with the gentleman." Said Sheffield, "Neither do I, for I would as soon get into difficulty with a porcupine!"


No less a contribution to the war effort was the replacement, in mid-January, of the incompetent secretary of war Simon Cameron by Edwin M. Stanton, a prominent Pennsylvania lawyer, Free Soil Democrat, and rock-solid Unionist who had served briefly in James Buchanan's cabinet. It didn't hurt that he was also an intimate friend of Charles Sumner and Salmon P. Chase. Fessenden, initially skeptical of the appointment, was quickly won over: "He is just the man we want. We agreed on every point. The Negro question and everything else." With his irritable personality, cherubic face, gimlet eyes, and prematurely receding hairline, Stanton hardly suggested a forceful personality. But he quickly proved to be a talented, often ruthless administrator, one of Lincoln's most valuable advisors, and skeptical of McClellan, whom he was known to regard as "a dead failure." Stanton's decisiveness, one abolitionist wrote to Wade, "sent a thrill of joy through the loyal heart."

On March 11, Stanton reported that 672,878 men were under arms—almost 200,000 more than the government had supposed. The expense of maintaining them sent shock waves through the government. So hopeful were congressional leaders that victory was in sight—and so fearful were they that the government couldn't afford to wage war beyond the summer—that on April 3 they advised Stanton to close recruitment offices across the North. The *New York Times* delusionally declared, "The army of the Union is now complete."

As early as October it had become clear that estimates of the war's cost had been too optimistic. In fact, it was already closer to $1 billion, double what Stevens had projected. Many army units were still unpaid, and the printing of bonds was running hundreds of thousands of dollars behind sales. Gold and silver were becoming scarce. Counterfeit currency proliferated. And in some localities retailers were resorting to postage stamps and "shin-plasters," fractional paper money issued by banks, merchants, and private companies. After a Union naval officer seized two Confederate envoys from a British ship on the high seas in November, sparking fears of war with the Crown, stocks plunged even further. "I'm resigned to speedy and total insolvency," George Templeton Strong confessed to his diary. "War, taxes, and cessation of business will have done their work before long. Poverty will soon drive me to enlist, if patriotism does not."

The government's debts were mounting fast. Henry Cooke wrote repeatedly to his brother Jay that the government was "hard up," and that Treasury officials were "grab[bing] for every dollar they can to get the wheels moving." Conservative New York moneymen were predicting that the government would soon beg for peace just to escape bankruptcy. But Chase's relationship with the banks continued to erode as he required them to pay their loans back in gold even as their reserves melted away. Some bankers threatened to break their ties with the Treasury entirely, and several did so at the end of December, refusing their options on $50 million worth of loans, and leaving the Treasury nearly empty. Many accused Chase of sheer ineptitude. "He is as much out of place in the Financial department of the Govt as he would be as an engineer on an ocean steamer, or locomotive," one exasperated investor exclaimed. Despite Chase's best efforts, it was now estimated that the government could run out of money as early as February. European markets were in no mood to help the Union out. The *Economist* of London declared, "It is utterly out of the question in our judgment that the Americans can obtain either at home or in Europe anything like the extravagant sums they are asking."

But there was a signal bright spot. Jay Cooke's bond sales continued unabated. A few months earlier, the *Philadelphia Inquirer* had reported that bond buyers were swarming Cooke's offices on Third Street in Philadelphia, buying $100,000 of the loan in a single day. "One gentleman had $10,000 in a bag slung over his shoulder. Another offered $20,000." Fifteen hundred employees of the Philadelphia and Reading Railroad authorized the company to deduct a sum from their monthly pay, and subscribe it to the national loan. And so it went. By December, Cooke had sold about one-fourth of all the notes sold by the 160 agents outside the sub-treasuries. Cooke wrote, "Their charge of money bags is quite as efficient as a charge of bayonets."

The Cookes were selling bonds so fast that the understaffed Treasury Department couldn't keep up with them. When Jay expressed irritation with the backlog and delay, Henry apologetically replied, "They promise to shove me through as fast as possible," and reported that the Treasury Department's overworked register, one Chittenden, had complained to him that he had to sign his name three thousand times a day—six times per minute—on top of all his other business. But the government needed more money, and faster, than even the indefatigable Cookes could produce it.

Chase hoped desperately that the war could be "brought to an auspicious termination before midsummer" of 1862, but he was realist enough to accept that it probably wouldn't. On top of the $318 million that Congress had appropriated in July 1861, the Treasury Department had determined that it would need as much as $214 million more to make up the "deficiencies" just for the current fiscal year, plus a *further* $413 million for the following year. Thaddeus Stevens was nothing short of alarmed. "We will thus have to appropriate more than $600 million without the addition of a single dollar [in income] beyond what is estimated for," he told the House. "I confess I do not see how, unless the expenses are greatly curtailed, this government can possibly go on over six months. If we go on increasing expenses, as we have been doing, the finances, not only of the government but of the whole country must give way, and the people will be involved in one general bankruptcy and ruin." Stevens, too, was a realist. He knew that belt-tightening, however desirable, would not be enough. He and Chase both understood that the need for immediate federal action was imperative.

Chase was willing to accept direct taxation, long anathema to most Americans, as well as a sharp increase in tariffs. A hard-money man to his core, however, he strongly disliked both borrowing the huge sums that he knew would have to be raised, and the prospect of issuing currency unsecured by gold. "The idea of perpetual debt is not of American nativity, and should not be naturalized," he stiffly asserted. He offered two possible schemes: first, the complete replacement of the nation's plethora of privately issued banknotes by a uniform national currency that would, in theory, be payable in coin on demand. But he considered this too dangerous, since there would always be a temptation to print money beyond the government's ability to redeem it, risking radical depreciation and ultimately bankruptcy. His second, preferred, option was to encourage banks to invest their capital in government bonds—that is, essentially, to loan it money. The banks would then deposit the bonds with the Treasury Department as collateral. The Treasury would in turn issue new banknotes secured by the federal government, which the banks would circulate in lieu of their own less reliable notes, thus drawing the banks into a de facto alliance with the national government.

Regardless of what Chase wanted, the decision rested with Congress, and most particularly with Stevens's Ways and Means Committee, where all revenue bills originated. The bill-crafting subcommittee worked doggedly, "more hours daily," Stevens said, "than any laborer, mechanic, or manufacturer, sweating over every line and punctuation." Brushing aside Chase's wishes, the House called for the government to issue its own notes that would go directly into circulation as the government paid its bills. They would not be redeemable in specie, but rested instead on a presumed confidence in the government's good faith rather than hard coinage. On January 22, Stevens's ally Elbridge Gerry Spaulding introduced what would become the Legal Tender Act, authorizing the issue of $100 million in non-interest-bearing notes for use in the payment of all public and private debts, and redeemable "at the pleasure of the government." The bill also authorized another $500 million in interest-bearing bonds, for which the new notes could be exchanged at par. "This bill is a measure of necessity, not of choice," Stevens told the House on February 6. "No one would willingly issue paper currency not redeemable on demand and make it a legal tender. But it is not a fearful measure; and when rendered necessary by exigencies, it ought to produce no alarm." Given the current rates of discount, he added, were the government to attempt to rely upon bonds alone, it would require a sale of $1.5 billion to produce enough currency to make $1.1 billion. "The sum is too frightful to be tolerated."

Stevens admitted that the Constitution did not explicitly sanction a national currency. However, the eighth section of the Constitution's first article empowered Congress to make laws that were "necessary and proper" to carry out the defined powers of the government. (This was the same section that Alexander Hamilton had cited in 1791 to justify the establishment of the first National Bank.) He saw the proposed currency as a new pillar of national authority and a bond of unity among citizens, government, and business. Stevens brushed off fears of inflation, saying that it was likely to occur whether paper currency was issued or not. "If this bill shall pass," he declared, "I shall hail it as the most auspicious measure of this Congress; if it should fail, the result will be more deplorable than any disaster which could befall us."

There was considerable public support for the measure. "We want a currency which will not be hoarded, like specie, in times of instability," editorialized the *Philadelphia Daily News*. "The Treasury notes will supply to the people what they most want. We cannot have too many of them, for the more plentiful they are the more employment there will be for those willing to work and the greater will be the power of the loyal people to sustain an expensive war." Anti-administration Democrats, however, claimed that the powerful central banking system that the bill contemplated would exercise a far more oppressive monopoly than state banks ever had. On January 30, cried Clement Vallandigham, "The Ship of State is upon the rocks." Forcing paper currency on the country, he claimed, was a "dangerous experiment" that would inevitably lead to the complete disappearance of gold and silver, catastrophically high prices, extravagant speculation, false wealth, and immense inflation. "Cheap in materials, easy of issue, worked by steam, signed by machinery, there would be no end to the legion of devils which shall pour forth from the loins of the Secretary" of the Treasury, he claimed, predicting that the new notes would be universally rejected by the public and business alike "though you should send them forth bearing ten times the image and superscription—the fair face and form of Abraham Lincoln, now president and Caesar of the American republic."

Democratic critics were joined by some hard-money Republicans, who feared that federal currency would quickly turn into the "fetid trash" that Confederate money had already become. Writes historian Heather Cox Richardson, "Taking their cue from the rural world of small enterprise from which they had come, most Republicans conceived of national finance as simply a larger version of individual finance. A penniless person could not buy goods with a mere promise to pay sometime in the future; nor could a nation, they thought." Only gold and silver could be trusted to retain value, "as solid a foundation as the everlasting hills," argued Rep. Justin Morrill of Vermont, who on most issues voted with the party's most progressive members. He scoffed at the notion that so much money would ever be needed in any case—the war couldn't possibly last into 1863. "The ice that chokes the Mississippi is not more sure to melt and disappear with the approaching vernal season than are the rebel armies upon its banks when our western army shall break from its moorings and rush with the current to the Gulf," he confidently predicted. Morrill failed to persuade, however. Stevens's bill, adjusted upward to authorize $150 million in notes, passed comfortably by a vote of ninety-three to fifty-nine.

The bill went to the Senate on February 7, where the legal tender provision was vigorously opposed by Fessenden, who, influenced by friends in the northeastern banking community, believed that it would ruin the government's credit. New York financier James Gallatin feverishly warned him against embracing any "wild and reckless" paper money "scheme" that he and his colleagues feared would glut the money market and cripple the nation's finances. Fessenden felt painfully divided between principle and pragmatism, however. "This thing has tormented me day and night for weeks," he wrote privately. "The thing is wrong in itself but to leave the government without resources at such a crisis is not to be thought of." He considered the measure a virtual confession of bankruptcy and moral failure. If the currency shrank in value, as it surely must, it would encourage debtors to pay their loans at a discount, victimizing honest creditors. It would also stain the honor of the nation itself by undermining the trust of potential foreign lenders. Instead, he argued that the most honorable means to maintain the government's credit was through taxation and aggressive cost-cutting. He had in mind contracting fraud that was metastasizing at an alarming rate: arms merchants were found to have overcharged the government by $1,500 per cannon, mattresses for soldiers were filled with whalebone chips instead of cotton stuffing, and the New York clothier Brooks Brothers had sold the army uniforms made from pressed rags that melted off soldiers' backs; reports of contracts for rotten meat, knapsacks that fell apart in the rain, and boots soled with wood scraps were ubiquitous.

That said, he made clear that forceful action was required to deal with the financial crisis. "I would advocate the strong arm of the government to any extent in order to accomplish the purpose in which we are engaged. I would take the money of any citizen against his will to sustain the government, if nothing else was left, and bid him wait until the government could pay him. Thank God, we have not arrived at that. But I am not certain that it would not be a more manly course to meet the matter straight in the face, and if we are to compel a man to part with his property, to do it without offering him what may appear to be security."

Never in the best of health, Fessenden felt crushed by the competing pressures of the Senate chamber, the committee room, consultations with the president and cabinet secretaries, correspondence, and the ever-annoying battalions of office seekers. Working day and night to reshape the Legal Tender bill, he experienced chronic depression, excruciating headaches, and persistent insomnia, lying restlessly awake long after going to bed and waking too early in the morning. "When a man feels as if he could cut everybody's throat, and that everybody wants to cut his, he is in a pretty bad condition, and such is mine, almost, when I contemplate public affairs, and think how powerless I am to stay the tide," he wrote to Lizzy Warriner.

Pummeled by the Finance Committee, the bill reappeared in the House freighted with amendments that left Stevens chagrined. Senate-approved amendments created sinking funds to eventually pay off the national debt, and to meet the interest on bonds. Another allowed large investors in the new Treasury notes to earn interest on them. A third permitted the Treasury to sell bonds at market rates. The most controversial amendment required that interest on federal bonds be paid in coin, rather than in "greenbacks," as the new notes would be called.

Stevens, who was usually in alignment with Fessenden on appropriations, but far more populist in his sympathies, was disgusted by the revisions, particularly the amendment that called for interest payments on bonds to be paid in coin, which he saw as a giveaway to unpatriotic capitalists and biased against both the poor and soldiers in the field, who would have to accept paper money as pay. Fessenden had "too much of the ingredient called conservatism," he privately grumbled. At his most deliciously sarcastic, without mentioning Fessenden's name, Stevens declared to gales of laughter from the House visitors' gallery that "a doleful sound came up from the caverns of bullion brokers, and from the saloons of the associated banks," whose lobbyists "fell upon the bill in hot haste and so disfigured and deformed it that its very father would not know it." The bill's Senate version, he said, "makes two classes of money— one for the banks and brokers, and another for the people. Was ever before such a machine got up for swindling the Government and making the fortunes of the gold bullionists in one single year?" Despite his appeal, the House narrowly rejected Stevens's attempt

to kill the amendment, and then adopted the Senate's language by a
large margin. The bill was so "mutilated" by markups by the time it
finally passed, on February 24, that even many members were con-
fused about what it actually contained. But Lincoln went on to sign
the Legal Tender Act the next day, and soon the new notes, the first
national currency in American history, began flooding the country.

The act also provided for a new issue of $500 million in bonds
at 6 percent interest payable in twenty years, an immense boon to
the Cooke brothers, whose relationship with the administration was
cozier than ever. Their Washington office, on 15th Street, lay within
shouting distance of Chase's at the Treasury Building, and to the
Cooke brothers the door to the secretary's home was always open.
"You should push your influence—or else it is good for nothing," Jay
urged Henry. "I wish you to see the *importance* at the start of getting
ahead of all the others." In November, Jay Cooke had offered to buy
Chase a carriage, a one-horse coupé, for his personal use. The secretary demurred, but he did allow Jay to pay for a set of bookshelves
for his daughter Kate, who served as the widowed secretary's hostess
in Washington. At one point, Chase at least passingly entertained the
possibility of going into business with the Cookes.

The Cookes were in virtually daily consultation with Chase and
his assistants, who gave the brothers prior private notice of every shift
in Treasury business, and ensured that they received new issues of
bonds before any of their competitors. The arrangement was secre-
tive, with Henry sometimes reporting the latest insider information
to Jay in code, and Jay assuring Chase privately that "the business
matters entrusted to our house will be entirely and strictly confiden-
tial." Chase, Jay reminded Henry, "knows that such an arrangement,
while it is pleasant and profitable for us, yet is the very best thing that
can be done by the government—in fact, is absolutely necessary. We
must all study by our watchful care of the interests confided to us
to justify this confidence and to show [Chase] that the Treasury is a
gainer." On March 7, Cooke was officially appointed a Treasury sub-
scription agent, which enlarged his field of activity as a semiofficial
agent of federal financial policy even further. Two weeks after that,
the Treasury authorized him to dispose of yet another $750,000 in

bonds to pay troops embarking for the battlefield. Then on May 1, the firm was assigned still another $500,000. Many more commissions would follow.

Outside Washington, the wintertime despair that had clouded Union spirits was beginning to lift. Union armies were finally on the march. In early February, an amphibious assault captured Roanoke Island, in North Carolina, giving the Union a purchase on the Confederacy's Atlantic coast. A few days later, an obscure brigadier general from Illinois named Ulysses S. Grant captured a pair of strategically placed Confederate strongholds, Forts Henry and Donelson on the Tennessee and Cumberland Rivers respectively, opening the way to Nashville, Tennessee's capital, which fell on the 25th. Although Grant was surprised by the Confederates at Shiloh, on April 6, he recovered to deliver them a stinging defeat, leaving some 24,000 men from both armies dead, wounded, and missing. Three weeks later David Farragut astonished the Confederates by sailing a fleet of federal warships under fire up the Mississippi River to capture New Orleans, the South's biggest port, choking off the bulk of its export of cotton. Another Union force drove southward from Missouri into Arkansas, and still another captured St. Augustine, Florida, while the navy extended its blockade of the Confederate coastline from the Carolinas to Texas. There were rumors—later proved to be false—that North Carolina regiments had revolted against their commanders in Charleston, and that in Memphis the rebel authorities were so desperate to fill their ranks that they were snatching old men and boys from their beds. Surely the "Waterloo of the war" must be imminent, crowed the *New York Herald*.

Even McClellan had at last roused himself, spurred, at least in part, by a peremptory order from Lincoln to get moving by Washington's birthday, February 22, a date that was allowed to lapse once it became clear that the "young Napoleon" was actually stirring. Finally, on March 10, long blue-uniformed columns began to snake out of the camps around Washington, headed toward the Confederate defenses near Centreville. The reorganized and newly christened

Army of the Potomac now numbered more than 110,000 men, who after the long months of drill and more drill were eager to fight. "We are on the eve of the great battle of the war—and I believe the decisive victory which shall put an end to the rebellion," Henry Cooke breathlessly reported to his brother Jay. The next act was an embarrassing anticlimax. When McClellan advanced on the enemy fortifications that had intimidated him all winter he found them not only empty but also armed with "Quaker guns"—logs that had been painted to look like cannon. The Confederates who had been posted there had probably never numbered more than fifteen thousand men, one-fifth the number that McClellan had claimed to justify his procrastination. The novelist Nathaniel Hawthorne, who visited Manassas soon afterward, wrote, "It was as if General McClellan had thrust his sword into a gigantic enemy, and beholding him suddenly collapse, had discovered to himself and the world that he had merely punctured an enormously swollen bladder."

"Everybody feels annoyed and mortified that the [rebel] army at Manassas should have been suffered to escape, and more especially at the wooden guns," Fessenden complained to his father. "Humiliating." McClellan, he disgustedly decided, was "utterly unfit" for his position, and the responsibility for keeping him in it fell squarely upon the president. "Every movement has been a failure. And yet the president keeps him in command, and leaves our destiny in his hands. I am about in despair. We went in for a rail-splitter, and we have got one."

For his own part, ever the epitome of Napoleonic self-confidence, McClellan shrugged off criticism with disdainful aplomb, and fell back on a plan that, at least on paper, justified the reputation for strategic brilliance with which he had initially been credited. In other hands than his, it might well have led to the capture of Richmond, and dealt a death blow to the Confederacy. Outflanking the several west-to-east rivers that served as lines of defense on the direct overland route from Washington to Richmond, McClellan proposed to transport his immense army by ship to the peninsula that lay between Virginia's York and James Rivers, and to advance on the Confederate capital from the southeast, from its soft and lightly defended underbelly, so to speak. To move this armed behemoth, McClellan mobilized a grand armada comprised of more than one hundred steamers, some of them brought from as far away as the Hudson River, and nearly three hundred ferries, sailing craft, canal boats, and barges that set sail from Alexandria on March 17 as regimental bands played "Dixie" and "The Star-Spangled Banner." "The greatest expedition ever fitted out is now going South," boasted young, battle-hungry Lieutenant George Armstrong Custer, newly graduated from West Point. The transports carried more than 120,000 troops, hundreds of artillery pieces, thousands of horses, mountains of foodstuffs and matériel, and the hopes of the entire Union. "The moment for action has arrived," McClellan proclaimed to his assembled host, the largest yet to face the rebels. "God smiles upon us, victory attends us, yet I would not have you think that our aim is to be attained without a manly struggle." Although McClellan couldn't fully conceal his strategy from the Confederates, enough troops were left behind in northern Virginia to keep them guessing.

# 8

# Beneficent Reform, Hothouse Capitalism

———————◆————————

> Proslavery men seem to suppose that the
> Ruler of the universe is a proslavery Being.
> But if I have not mistaken Him greatly, He
> is at least a gradual emancipationist.
>
> —SEN. BENJAMIN F. WADE

Pitt Fessenden was near collapse. He had toiled for weeks on the "infernally" difficult tax bill and foresaw weeks more of unremitting work ahead of him. "It will be odious, of course, and overwhelm us all with curses," he wrote his cousin Lizzy. "I have made up my mind, however, to put it through in the best shape I can." As the costs of war mounted, everyone knew that a sweeping tax bill was imperative. "We are ready—the whole country is ready—more than this, it is willing, even desirous to be taxed, heavily taxed to furnish all needful means," one patriotic constituent wrote to Fessenden. A single regiment of infantry cost about $20 million a year to maintain, while estimates of the war's overall cost now ranged upward from one million dollars a day. Assuming that war ended in 1863, as most members of Congress hoped, the nation's debt would stand somewhere between $833,000 and $1.2 billion, with debt service alone running at between $50 million and $70 million annually.

Taxes would compensate for only a fraction of the debt, but they would demonstrate to lenders and bondholders that the government was serious about repaying the gargantuan sums it was borrowing. "Is the tax really necessary?" Thaddeus Stevens had rhetorically asked when he introduced the plan to the House, in March. Crushing the rebellion "requires armies and navies," he then said. "To sustain them, money is absolutely necessary, for the soldiers of the Republic must not go unpaid, no matter what it may cost the civilian. Money can only be had through loans; but loans cannot be had unless, at the same time, means be provided for paying punctually the interest."

In a nation that had for the most part regarded domestic taxes as a plague, the plan was one of the war's most monumental under-takings. It had to somehow reconcile countless conflicting local, sectional, commercial, and financial interests without instigating a citizens' revolt. As Stevens's gentlemanly ally Justin Morrill of Ver-mont, who floor-managed the debate, put it, the bill spread "its fingers out in all directions, ready to clutch" whatever it could "to buoy up the sinking credit of a nation which has hitherto generally sheltered its capital and its labor from all tax gatherers." The lion's share, $16 million, Morrill said, was to be raised by taxing alcohol, for "a tax upon the habits or vices of men is the most reliable of all taxes." The rest, mostly at a rate of 3 percent, would be levied on tobacco, licenses and official stamps, patent medicines, candles, lard, gas for lamps, slaughtered cattle, candy, starch, ginger, watches and pianos, boots and bonnets, auctions, candles and soap, billiard tables, yachts, railroad tickets, and hundreds of other manufactures, goods, services, and professions—including circuses. (Ohio Democrat Sam-uel Cox snidely remarked that Republicans "must have forgotten all their days of sunny childhood. A man must be lost to all sensibility who will tax a circus.") The plan also proposed a much more com-prehensive and efficiently designed income tax than the one enacted the previous summer, but not yet activated, along with a new federal agency, an "Internal Revenue Bureau," to collect the revenues.

Like the broadening assault on slavery, the tax plan represented yet another front in the Republicans' steady march toward more effec-tive and centralized government. It was a trend that did not escape the House's bitter core of states' rights Democrats. "When this vast system goes into operation, and these tax gatherers are abroad in the land," menacingly predicted Copperhead representative George Pendleton of Ohio, a Vallandigham ally, "there will go up a voice in the country that will make this legislature tremble. A tax bill like this

which goes into every house, into every business, every neighbor-
hood, which taxes everything a man eats and all that he wears, which
puts a tax on every conceivable subject of taxation, such a tax bill
has never before appeared in this country." Although no Republicans
challenged the plan, at least a few were less than eager to put themselves on record supporting it. The *New York Herald* reported that all
sorts of excuses were made by members to avoid the votes: one is
"called out by his wife, another by the telegraph, another was 'exces-
sively hungry.'" Stevens, the *Herald* added, was "obliged to crack the
parliamentary whip vigorously over the team to keep them in the
traces." Stevens's bullying was rewarded when, one day after the battle of Shiloh, the bill passed by a vote of 125 to 14, with but a single
Republican defection.

Piloting the bill through the Senate proved a greater challenge.
Members of Fessenden's own Finance Committee quarreled over
many of its provisions. He begged, threatened, and cajoled, impatiently reiterating that the taxes were supposed to go into effect on
July 1, a date that was fast receding toward the realm of the impossible. "The country is waiting for and expecting it," he pleaded. "It
has been delayed so long that the impression and fear is getting up
in the country that Congress really means to shirk it, and give it the
go-by." To cousin Lizzy, he wrote, "My hair has gone almost as grey
as my beard under all these labors and tribulations, and I expect you
will hardly know me when I come home." For relief, when he had
a rare hour to spare, he strolled through the botanical garden at the
foot of Capitol Hill and dreamed of his own beloved garden in Portland, where hyacinths, tulips, fuschias, wisteria, and arbored grapes
flourished in a soothing silence that was not to be had in Washington. Fessenden fought hard to prevent other legislation from interfering with the tax bill. But he was finally forced to yield time to his
colleagues' "confounded" demands.

Among these were a quartet of interrelated bills that have often
been treated as near-flotsam on the great tide of wartime legislation, but which were among the most transformative measures ever
to appear on the floor of Congress: the Homestead Act, the Pacific
Railway Act, the Morrill Land-Grant College Act, and the creation
of the Department of Agriculture. All had been dammed up for

years, in some cases even decades, by implacable opposition from the slaveholding South. Now, with the obstructive slave states out of the Union, the bills faced little more than a rearguard action.

The centerpiece of the quartet, the Homestead bill, promised 160 acres of free federal land in the West to any head of a family who was twenty-one years old and a loyal citizen (or declared the intention of becoming a citizen), lived on the land for five years, and "improved" it, typically by clearing timber, farming, and erecting a home. Union soldiers who had served at least two years in the army could receive title to their homesteads after just one year; rebels were excluded altogether. Although the national government had organized the sale of frontier lands since the founding of the republic, never before had public land been given away free. In the *New York Tribune*, Horace Greeley, long a journalistic megaphone for western settlement, trumpeted it as "one of the most beneficent and vital reforms ever attempted in any age or clime."

The Homestead bill was introduced in February by thirty-two-year-old House Speaker Galusha Grow of Pennsylvania, who a colleague dryly recalled as "a man of safe and steady views, moderate ability, and a tendency towards adjectives." Reuniting the country and settling the West represented two linked fronts in a single epic struggle, Grow orotundly declared, framing the bill as both a war measure and a soaring vision of postwar Manifest Destiny that would reward "the soldier now in the field fighting the battles of constitutional free government" along with the "soldiers of peace—that grand army of the sons of toil, whose lives from the cradle to the grave are a constant warfare with the elements, with the unrelenting obstacles of nature, and the merciless barbarities of savage life. Their battlefields are the prairies and the wilderness of your frontiers; their achievements felling the forests, leveling the mountains, filling the valleys, and smoothing the pathway of science and civilization in their march over the continent." Homesteading, he argued, would usher in an era of unparalleled prosperity. "The greater the ability to consume the greater the consumption, and the greater the consumption the greater, of course, must be the production, and, consequently, the greater the revenue collected on it."

Similar bills had been proposed like clockwork since the mid-

1840s, usually by Andrew Johnson, then a populist member of the House from eastern Tennessee, and now the wartime governor of the liberated portion of his native state. They had several avowed goals: to convert the prairie into productive farmland, to lessen social strife in eastern cities by transforming the landless urban poor into independent property owners, and to create a ribbon of white settlement across the continent. Although a slave owner, Johnson articulated the hopes of the white rural poor to rise in the world by acquiring land where they would not have to compete with slave labor; Southern elites feared, with good reason, that this would soon lead to the formation of more free states hostile to slavery. Typically, in 1860, the extreme Southern nationalist senator Louis Wigfall protested that session's Homestead bill for "providing land for the landless, homes for the homeless, and leaving out the important matter, in my opinion, of niggers for the niggerless."

Although fanatics like Wigfall were now gone, proslavery Unionists in Congress continued to protest that giving away public land represented the same kind of radicalism that, by threatening to emancipate the slaves, would "strike out of existence at one blow two billions of dollars of personal property subject to taxation." Others asserted that the federal government ought to sell public land as it had always done. But support for the bill largely transcended party divisions since land-hungry Democrats were as likely to benefit from it as Republicans. It sailed through the House with a lopsided majority with both Vallandigham and Stevens voting for it, one of the exceedingly rare moments when they found themselves on the same side of anything, and then cruised through the Senate by a similarly large margin.

Wedded closely to the Homestead Act was the bill to commit the resources of the federal government to the creation of a transcontinental railway from the Missouri River to the Pacific coast. Proposals for such a project had also been stymied by Southerners, who would only agree to a route that would facilitate the westward expansion of slavery. California representative Timothy Phelps, a hawk-faced

Forty-niner turned land developer, led the debate in the House. The railroad's construction was first a matter of critical national security, he maintained. The Pacific states and territories were isolated and exposed, "almost wholly defenseless" against assault by a foreign power—a fairly potent argument at a time when intervention in the Civil War by England and France seemed possible. The railroad, Phelps said, offered the only means to speedily dispatch reinforcements from the East. Moreover, such an undertaking would demonstrate to the European powers that the United States still possessed both the determination and the resources to simultaneously undertake a spectacular expansion of the nation's infrastructure and fight off a massive rebellion against national authority.

Thaddeus Stevens, an ardent supporter, acknowledged that the government would have to borrow heavily to subsidize the railroad, but he argued that the growth in the West's population brought about by homesteading and the railroad would so enrich the country by expanding its agricultural economy that it would soon be able to pay off the loan's interest and principal alike. Moreover, by speeding commercial transportation across the continent, the railroad would open vast new Asian markets for American manufacturers from China to India. He added a warning: the moment was now ripe, but it wouldn't last. Build the railroad now, he urged, before the seceded states were returned to the national fold, as they must eventually be, when "we shall find them with the same arrogant, insolent dictation which we have cringed to for twenty years, forbidding the construction of any road that does not run along our southern border."

Everyone knew that private capital alone was neither willing nor able to shoulder the expense involved. To induce capitalists to invest, the bill therefore granted the railroads a strip of land for right-of-way along with ten alternating sections of land per mile on both sides of the track for its entire distance, eventually a total of 127 million acres, which it was free to sell to settlers. It also provided for a government loan to the companies in the form of thirty-year bonds at 6 percent interest, in amounts ranging from $16,000 to $48,000 per mile, depending on the difficulty of the territory through which the line would pass. In effect, the government was inventing what the historian Richard White has termed "hothouse capitalism," by nursing private investment and protecting it from risk.

Not surprisingly, businessmen ranging from Wall Street moneymen, to land speculators, to the manufacturers of iron rails and spikes saw a bonanza. Behind the scenes, brigades of lobbyists harried legislators, seeking federal subsidies for a spider's web of branch lines that would feed into the transcontinental trunk. The California businessmen backing the Central Pacific Railroad, which would lay track eastward from Sacramento, succeeded even in placing their own Washington lobbyist as clerk of the House subcommittee responsible for the bill, and empowered him to generously spread the railroad's stock around where it would be most effective. As bribery flourished, Rep. William Sheffield of Rhode Island disgustedly denounced the bill as "one of the most stupendous swindles ever forced upon a people." But his was a lonely voice. The conclusion was foregone. Like the Homestead Act, the Pacific Railway bill breezed through both houses with many votes to spare.

Sheffield's skepticism lit the path to a future in which the railroad's construction would deliver immense (and often unearned) riches to the businessmen who managed to find space at the federal trough. But Northern support for the project was virtually universal at a time when Americans were beginning to see their nation as a continental empire whose destiny must not be impeded by war or expense, much less by the Native Americans across whose lands the steel rails would be made to go. Ben Wade, speaking on behalf of the railroad bill, expressed the feelings of the vast majority of Americans. "Everything that conspires to build up the great West, to people it with a thrifty, industrious set of inhabitants, pleases me. I am glad to lend aid to it anywhere and everywhere."

On May 5, Wade introduced in the Senate yet another familiar, deceptively modest-sounding bill "to provide colleges for the benefit of agriculture and the mechanic arts." The bill was so well understood, and had been introduced in so many previous Congresses, that it scarcely required debate, Wade said. It would provide every state in the Union with thirty thousand acres of public land for each of its representatives and senators in Congress as an endowment for tuition-free agricultural colleges where students would learn the science of soil chemistry, different types of grains and seeds, techniques of deep plowing and drainage, the use of new farming implements, animal husbandry, the treatment of diseases that affected plants and animals, chemical fertilization, and "the philosophy of manures." It was the genesis of what would eventually become the nation's state university systems.

The bill would be known as the Morrill Land-Grant College Act, after Justin Morrill, its House sponsor and primary author. Morrill was a complex figure, an egalitarian blacksmith's son who had "the tastes of the English gentry," a self-educated advocate of higher education for both men and women, a hard-money man expert in the arcana of tax policy, and an abolitionist who found the physical proximity of blacks discomforting. He had pressed for the establishment of federally supported working men's schools since the 1850s, believing that farmers and mechanics deserved specialized training as much as doctors and lawyers did. "We have schools to teach the art of man-slaying and make masters of 'deep-throated engines' of war; and we shall not have schools to teach men the way to feed, clothe, and enlighten the great brotherhood of man?" he declared during a protracted debate in 1858, when the bill seemed on the very cusp of becoming law. His initiative, along with parallel efforts to establish a federal Department of Agriculture to coordinate the dissemination of new scientific knowledge, had met with ferocious resistance from Southern Democrats, who, as they had with the proposals for homesteading and the Pacific railroad, scorned any legislation that might even tangentially interfere with slavery. Sen. Clement Clay of Alabama had then denounced it as a "monstrous" measure, and Sen. James Mason of Virginia raged that it would allow Congress to "fasten upon the Southern States that peculiar system of free schools [as] in the New England States." Despite their vitriol, the bill passed both Houses, but was vetoed by President Buchanan, unwavering in his defense of slavery's proclaimed interests, asserting that in his opinion it was neither constitutional nor "expedient."

This time, there were no serious challenges to the bill. There was, however, a remarkable intervention by Sen. Joseph A. Wright of Indiana, a War Democrat who had replaced his disgraced predecessor, Jesse Bright, who had been ousted from the Senate for disloyalty. Wright startled his colleagues by suggesting that they ought to devote similar resources to the education of women. "Do not be startled, gentlemen," said Wright. "Look at your half a million men in the army, with neglected daughters and sisters to be raised and educated. It would much better become the Senate if they were providing some means by which labor could be furnished to a thousand females in this city by means of copying, or something else, or in educating the females of the land. They must do one of three things: either go to teaching, or sewing, or they must, many of them, lead abandoned lives. If you have anything to give to colleges, you could be much better engaged in devoting this fund for the education of the females of the land." This was apparently the only instance in which anything close to a feminist argument was advanced during the Thirty-seventh Congress, and perhaps the entire course of the Civil War. But it was ignored by Wright's fellow senators. If only inadvertently, however, the Homestead Act created what may have been the era's single most significant legislative benefit to women, by allowing homesteading by single women and widows as heads of family: women would eventually file 10 percent of all claims.

The creation of the Department of Agriculture was also treated as a war measure that by helping farmers to improve their agriculture would strengthen the Union and help defeat the rebellion. Declared Wright fulsomely, "The great agricultural interests of the Union underlie its prosperity," and indeed formed the "very foundation of our national greatness." The department, explained its sponsor, the Radical abolitionist representative Owen Lovejoy of Illinois, would foster scientific research and disseminate the latest knowledge to farmers across the nation, enabling them to arrest the decline of their land, improve their crops, and restore tracts that had already become exhausted, bringing it back "to its pristine vigor."

All four bills passed by commanding margins. They demonstrated the gathering Republican commitment to a broad new concept of the public interest, as well as a long-term vision for the nation's future, one that was vividly expressed by Phelps in his argument on behalf of the Pacific railroad:

> It is claimed by the anti-progressives that it is illegitimate for a government to give aid in this way or in any way to any purpose of the kind. On the contrary, it is to carry out such great enterprises, which are demanded for the safety of communities, and the wants of commerce and civilization, and are beyond the means and ability of individual and corporate enterprise, that governments are formed. . . . Are we to follow in the footsteps of the old-school politicians, who could find no power in the Constitution to do anything but plunder the national Treasury, by distributing the spoils of office among wrangling adherents? Or shall we rather seek the public good, and fertilize all the fields of enterprise in which our citizens are engaged.

Phelps might have been speaking collectively of all four acts, whose transformative effects still continue to shape the United States a century and a half later.

To Fessenden's continuing chagrin, Radicals also pushed what he called the "confounded" matter of the confiscation of rebel property back onto the floor. To his son William, Fessenden irritably wrote, "The confiscation bill is *entre nous* a humbug in any shape—but Sumner and Wade have got up an excitement about it, and something must pass." Debate over it took place simultaneously with the domestic bills, as day after day, often within the same hour, both the House and Senate toggled back and forth between the nation's aspirational future and its violent present. The previous summer, Congress—in what then seemed a daring move—had approved the confiscation of slaves whose owners could be shown to have allowed them to be used in direct support of the Confederate war effort. Radicals were now calling for a more stringent bill that applied to all rebels. Initially, more than twenty versions competed for attention. Rafts of knotty questions vied for support, and for precious floor time: Should all rebel property of every type be confiscated? If only part of their property, then what part, and for how long? Should that property always include their slaves? Should the confiscated property be sold to retire the Union war debt? Should confiscated lands be turned over to former slaves, or perhaps to Yankee homesteaders?

Lurking behind virtually every proposal was a knotty conundrum: what would the consequences be if slaves were freed wholesale? Fear roiled the free states. "Most of them must come north, and here there is no employment for them," worried the *Philadelphia Daily News*. It was plain that as their numbers swelled "they would become vagrants and paupers, and they would eventually share the fate of the expelled Aborigines"—that is, extermination. No one really knew. In the House, Charles A. Wicliffe, a conservative Kentucky Unionist, cried that the administration seemed bent on a nefarious "John Brown raid upon the Negro property of the country," and "turning them loose upon defenseless women and children, to commit rapine, murder, and conflagration of defenseless habitations," while an apoplectic senator Willard Saulsbury of Delaware warned that Northerners would never admit the savage hordes of freed slaves into their own states. To considerable applause from the visitors' galleries, Saulsbury prophesied that by "1870, let this war terminate as it may, whether you conquer the seceded states or not, there will then be more slaves in the United States than there were in 1860. If the people have a right to make their own laws, and to govern themselves, they will not only reenslave every person that you attempt to set free, but they will reenslave the whole race. By your legislation you cannot bring up the filthy negro to the elevation of the white man. The United States of America, from the northern lakes to the southern Gulf, from the Atlantic on one side to the Pacific on the other, shall be the white man's home; and not only the white man's home, but the white man shall govern, and the nigger never shall be his equal."

Momentum was now on the side of the Radicals, however. In the House, Albert Riddle of Ohio declared, in defense of confiscation, "We are to punish as the parent and brothers would punish the members of his family who had deliberately set fire to the family mansion, overturned the family altar, and aimed their dagger at the bosom of the mother who bore them." And in the Senate, Ben

Wade boomed, "We might not only forfeit and confiscate the property of the rebels, but take the life of every man of them. I go for the largest forfeiture. I am in favor of visiting just punishment on every man who has raised his accursed hand to strike down the institutions of our fathers. I will take their property, and I will relieve the loyal North, and the loyal men of the South, and indemnify them with the confiscated property; yes, to the last dollar of these scoundrels. I say to every traitor who holds a slave, 'so far as my hand can reach that slave is free and a much better man than you.'"

Although the Radicals agreed among themselves that the Constitution empowered the government to seize any rebel property, they differed as to whether that power belonged primarily to Congress or to the president. While Wade, always an outspoken defender of legislative prerogatives, warned against magnifying the president "into an irresponsible despot" by endowing him with powers that belonged to Congress alone, Thaddeus Stevens by contrast held that in wartime the Constitution endowed the president with virtually unlimited power. "If no other means were left to save the Republic from destruction, I believe we have the power, *under the Constitution and its express provision,* to declare a dictator," he told the House. "Rather than the nation should perish, I would do it."

The bill that finally emerged was a strong one, although it did not resolve all the questions that had been raised. It called for the complete forfeiture by rebels of "every species of property," either when a rebel was convicted by a court of treason, or by direct order of the president. The bill further declared free all former slaves who sought refuge with the army, and explicitly barred the military from surrendering fugitives to anyone who claimed them, thus ending the army's controversial role as what one abolitionist contemptuously termed "a slavery saving machine." The bill also authorized the employment "by the president" of as many "persons of African descent" as needed for the suppression of the rebellion, and to "use them in such manner as [the president] may judge best for the public welfare." Although most legislators supposed that the liberated slaves would be set to manual labor, such as digging trenches, the bill's wording clearly permitted the army's recruitment of former slaves and free blacks alike, potentially adding hundreds of thousands of new volunteers to the Union forces. In yet another stroke against slave owners, the bill neutered the Fugitive Slave Law, by requiring masters to prove both their ownership of a fugitive, and that they had never lent aid to the rebellion. Finally, in a nod to Negrophobic Unionists, the bill authorized but did not mandate the resettlement of as many blacks as could be induced to emigrate to "some tropical country beyond the limits of the United States."

The debate caused enormous stress for Fessenden, quite apart from his impatience to return to the stalled tax bill. "The question has given me great trouble," he wrote to his abolitionist father, Samuel, in March. The whole subject seems to be full of constitutional difficulties. While he wholeheartedly supported confiscation in principle, as policy he saw any number of troubling nuances. Like Lincoln, he believed that a harsh policy of confiscation was likely to alienate Southern Unionists even further, while ever at his ear was his father's impassioned plea: "If you would save your name from the curses of coming generations and receive the blessing of all the good and virtuous of the present vote slavery out of existence wherever it is found to exist." Although Fessenden frequently voted with the Radicals, his intellectual agonizing continued to set him apart from them, and he sometimes judged them harshly. Of the self-important Sumner, who had theatrically unrolled a seven-hundred-foot-long petition signed calling for the total extinction of slavery, Fessenden the erstwhile gardener privately remarked, "If I could cut the throats of about half a dozen Republican Senators, (figuratively speaking), I should use the knife as readily as I ever did upon an ugly looking shrub. Sumner would be the first victim, as by far the greatest fool of the lot."

When Wade complained that the bill was too weak, "a mere milk-and-water concern, a laughing stock," Fessenden exploded. "I am in favor of a stringent bill, and I think this is a stringent bill. If I did not think it was, yet as it was agreed upon by the majority, and is the only thing to be got, I would not stand up here, because I did not like it, and advertise the country that this bill which is to be passed by my friends, will be good for nothing after it is passed."

Wade thundered back, "I do not like to be lectured and scolded for the course that I see fit to take."

Snapped Fessenden, "The chairman of the Committee on the Conduct of the War seems to have imagined ever since he was thus appointed, that he not only had the war under his control, but the Senate, too. I doubt whether he will succeed in regulating me quite as well as he regulates the war." He added sarcastically, "I think there is a little wisdom left in this Senate when we leave out the Senator from Ohio."

"I should like to see it manifested," Wade retorted.

"That is undoubtedly the expression coming from the Senator's heart—that he would like to see that there was any wisdom here except what he has got," replied Fessenden, as laughter erupted from their colleagues, many of whom enjoyed the spectacle of the blustery Wade taken down a peg. "He cannot see it, I will admit, but we do. I am sorry he is so blind. We do not look through his spectacles at himself in the glass."

Wade grumbled that he was merely reacting to Fessenden's "dictatorial tone," adding, "I laid no claim to any superior knowledge on subjects and matters not pertaining to the war, except the war of words in the Senate, and there I shall always yield to him."

The debate over confiscation bled inevitably into the fraught problem of postwar Reconstruction, now an increasingly urgent concern since, like most Northerners, congressional leaders had high hopes that McClellan's spring campaign would prevail on the battlefield, and that the war might be brought to an end by summer. In late March, McClellan had led an army of more than 100,000 men to the peninsula between the York and James Rivers in a grand maneuver to turn the Confederates' right flank. Landing near Yorktown, where the surrender of the British Army in 1780 brought the Revolutionary War effectively to a close, McClellan prepared to march inland to assault Richmond from the rear. And then he stopped. And the excuses began.

Confronted by what he judged to be impassable Confederate fortifications, he sat in place for a month, digging entrenchments, ordering up heavy siege guns and demanding reinforcements, claiming that the rebels outnumbered him by at least two-to-one. If he had only been given enough men, he swore to anyone in Washington whose ear he could command, he would already have been in Richmond. Dismissing accurate intelligence from fugitive slaves, McClellan continued to insist that he faced at least 100,000 rebels; in fact, at this point, he was opposed by no more than 11,000, and perhaps even fewer. Meanwhile, the Confederates gained valuable time to collect troops from as far away as the Carolinas and the Shenandoah Valley to block his path toward the rebel capital.

Lincoln's frustration became positively volcanic as he feared that yet another opportunity to deal the South a death blow was slipping away. "And once more, let me tell you, it is indispensable to you that you strike a blow!" the president wrote to the dilatory general. "The country will not fail to note—is noting now—that the present hesitation to move upon an entrenched enemy is but the story of Manassas repeated." In reply, McClellan exuded his usual overweening certainty. "I am confident of success, not only of success but of brilliant success," he wrote to Lincoln on April 20. He promised to smash the enemy within weeks, and "break up the rebel cause" once and for all. To his wife, Ellen, he confided: "I will finish the matter by one desperate blow. I have implicit confidence in my men, and they in me!" McClellan remained immensely popular with the army, with most of the public, and with much of Congress, who still took him more or less at his word. But he didn't fool everyone. Lincoln's secretary John Hay wrote privately to his White House colleague John Nicolay, who was out of town, "The little Napoleon sits trembling before the handful of men at Yorktown afraid to either fight or run." One disgusted Republican sarcastically suggested to Ben Wade that the army ought to ship McClellan 150,000 camp stools and 300,000 stilts since he seemed bent on staying uselessly bogged down in the Virginia mud.

By the beginning of May, McClellan finally felt ready to assault the Confederate works, only to discover that the enemy had simply disappeared under cover of night. During the days and weeks that followed, McClellan gradually inched up the peninsula. He stalled again at Williamsburg, once again convinced that he faced an army many times its actual size, complaining incessantly. "They are concentrating everything for the last death struggle—my government, alas, is not giving me any aid!" he whinged to his wife. Again he called for siege guns while his caution created precisely the problem that he feared. As he hesitated, the Confederate army grew until it numbered some 85,000 men, still smaller than McClellan's, and far less than the 200,000 McClellan now believed opposed him, but strong enough to face him in open battle.

# 9

# Tax Is Patriotic

Is it any worse to kill [the] enemy with
a musket in the hands of a black man than
in the hands of a white man?

—SEN. ORVILLE BROWNING

Meanwhile, on Capitol Hill, the possible outlines of the postwar world were beginning to form in legislators' minds. Reconstruction, as historian Eric Foner has written, offered Republicans the opportunity to create a "perfect republic" purged of the legacy of slavery. What would that republic be like? Should the rebels be punished as individuals, or as states? Should their leaders be executed, or barred forever from government? Would the breakaway states remain the same entities they had been before the war, or "sponged out" completely from the body politic? If so, what was to prevent them from restoring their wartime leaders to power? What would happen to slaves? Even if slavery were to be abolished, might not the Southern states simply vote it into existence again? Or would the old states be broken up? Or ruled indefinitely by the federal government, with governors, courts, and legislatures all imposed by Washington?

These were all open questions, and in the years to come they would open deep fissures not just between Democrats and Republicans, but among opposing factions of the Republican Party. Many still hoped, as did Lincoln, that once the secessionists were defeated now silent Southern Unionists would flock back to the national colors and take charge of the errant states, bringing them into line with the rest of the country. The Radicals harbored no such illusions. As their influence grew, they increasingly embraced what was essentially a revolutionary program. Some argued that the entire political and military leadership of the Confederacy ought to be executed, along with every former member of the U.S. military who had betrayed his oath, and former members of Congress who had cast their lot with the rebels. Charles Sumner, who enjoyed an ardent following among the abolitionist public, had suggested in April that by rebelling the seceded states had lost their standing in the Union, and ought to be reduced to the status of federally controlled territories. The national government, he reasoned, would then have the authority to legislate an end to slavery in them as it just had in the District of Columbia, and to reorganize them in any way it saw fit. The more politically potent Thaddeus Stevens agreed. "I would plant the South with a military colony if I could not make them submit otherwise," he declared. "I would send those soldiers there with arms in their hands to occupy the heritage of traitors, and build up there a land of free men and of freedom, which fifty years hence would swarm with its hundreds of millions without a slave upon its soil." Pitt Fessenden, reflecting the views of more cautious Republicans, sharply disagreed, arguing that such a principle would undermine the basic justification for the war: the premise that no state could take itself out of the Union, and that those states which *claimed* to have seceded had in fact merely been taken over temporarily by rebels and traitors.

Even as Congress argued, an experiment was already taking place on the military-occupied Sea Islands of Georgia that provided an embryonic model for what the postwar South might look like. Federal troops had seized Tybee and Cockspur Islands in March. In April, the federal officer commanding the district, Gen. David Hunter, a native of Troy, New York, an abolitionist, proclaimed all slaves in his area officially "confiscated" and free. This was well within the parameters of the Confiscation Act of 1861. Newly liberated blacks were left largely to run their own affairs, work for themselves, engage in trade, pray without interference, and learn in new schools run by literate slaves and white abolitionist volunteers. They were also given guns and trained to defend themselves by federal officers.

Then, in May 1862, Hunter went a step further, issuing a ukase similar to Frémont's ill-fated 1861 proclamation of emancipation in Missouri. Hunter unilaterally declared the wholesale emancipation of all slaves in the entire states of South Carolina, Georgia, and Florida, all but slivers of which were beyond the reach of his actual power. "By one stroke of the sword he has liberated *a million of slaves*," exclaimed an ecstatic abolitionist officer under Hunter's command, with pardonable exaggeration. (The actual number was a few tens of thousands.) Northern Democrats reacted to all this with predictable horror. The *New York Herald* predicted that "bloodthirsty Jacobins of the abolition school [were] poisoning the Great irrepressible Sambo" with ideas that could only lead to servile insurrection and "rapine"—a faintly veiled euphemism for the unbridled rapes that whites typically claimed would ensue from emancipation. Notwithstanding such fulminations, the former slaves on the Sea Islands were demonstrating that they could thrive quite well as free men and women.

Under pressure from conservatives, the War Department demanded to know from Hunter if he had, as reported, actually dared to organize a regiment of "fugitive slaves." Indeed, he had. (Fessenden's son James, a lieutenant in the army, was one of the new regiment's instructors.) "No regiment of 'fugitive slaves' has been or is being organized in this department," the unapologetic general replied wittily. "There is, however, a fine regiment of persons whose masters are 'fugitive rebels,' men who everywhere fly before the appearance of the national flag, leaving their servants behind them to shift as best they can for themselves. So far, indeed, are the loyal persons composing this regiment from seeking to avoid the presence of their late owners that they are now, one and all, working with remarkable industry to place themselves in a position to go in full and effective pursuit of their fugatious and traitorous proprietors."

More important was the president's reaction. Hunter's second proclamation infuriated him. Ten days after it was issued, he declared it void. "No commanding general shall do such a thing, upon my responsibility, without consulting me," he told Treasury Secretary Chase, who supported Hunter. That kind of proclamation "I reserve to myself," he added, explaining that only he had the legal authority to issue an order of emancipation purely as a war measure in areas not yet controlled by federal armies. Lincoln's nuanced language did not repudiate Hunter's intent and hinted that the president might at least be contemplating such an action himself. Nor did he fire Hunter, despite demands from conservative Unionists that he do so. Although Lincoln continued to preserve a conservative posture in public, he was now edging, in private, toward the abolitionist position that the congressional Radicals had advocated for months.

On May 21, Fessenden was finally able to muscle the Senate's attention back to the long-delayed tax bill. His hope of initiating the new taxes by July 1 had fallen by the wayside, but with time ticking rapidly away it was imperative that the legislation be enacted before Congress recessed in mid-July. Beneath his impatient parliamentary lash, the senators plowed ahead, meeting every day, sometimes twice on Saturday, and often far into the night with members debating in the hazy glow of hundreds of whale-oil candles. Decorum ebbed with the hours. Senators, traditionally more inclined to dignity than their House colleagues, pulled off their boots and broadcloth coats, puffed cigars, and napped on settees at the back of the chamber. Zachariah Chandler was particularly notorious as a disruptive snorer, on one occasion making so much noise that Vice President Hannibal Hamlin asked the doorkeeper to wake him up, which he did by violently shaking his leg. "Are they voting?" Chandler sleepily asked. Replied the doorkeeper, "No, sir, but you snore so loud that you disturb the Senate." Said Chandler, "Is that all I am doing? Well, I will continue snoring until they adjourn."

Day after day, through the rest of May and deep into June, the senators haggled over amendments to strike out taxes on watches, dogs, and billiard tables, reduce the levies on tobacco and real estate transfers, change the formula for taxing insurance companies, omit a penny of tax on cotton, and myriad other proposals urged by the legions of lobbyists—at least fifty by one count—who coagulated in the halls. Every commodity had its enemies and defenders: paint, perfumes, molasses, lumber, yarn, artificial flowers, umbrellas and parasols, firecrackers, castor oil, even imported sea shells. Samuel C.

Pomeroy of Kansas, a strict temperance man, complained that Congress, instead of sanctioning the use of alcohol by licensing its sale ought to prohibit its use altogether. Ira Harris of New York begged an exception for the lowly glove manufacturers of one upstate town, many of them allegedly widows and orphans, who couldn't afford more than two cents a pound on dressed deerskins. Edgar Cowan of Pennsylvania protested that it was plainly unfair to tax anthracite and bituminous coal at different rates.

The dwindled voice of the Democratic minority rarely managed to make itself heard. When it did, it was usually in the weary and fatalistic voice of Willard Saulsbury, a states' rights ideologue, who stoutly maintained that the federal government had no constitutional power to license any kind of business whatever. If such a hypothetical right *did* exist, he meaningfully pointed out, it would logically imply a right to regulate virtually any and every kind of activity. What would then be left to the state governments? Very little, if anything. "This would be consolidation with a vengeance."

Sumner set off a verbal firefight among his fellow abolitionists by proposing, to the shock of many, that a tax of $10 "per head" be levied on the owners of slaves. Pomeroy furiously declared that he could never support any measure that treated human beings as property. John Sherman, a conservative on racial issues, suggested that the tax was "inexpedient," since it would only further alienate the alienated slave owners of the border states. Hadn't Sherman already voted to tax auctioneers, jugglers, and the slaughterers of cattle? sarcastically demanded Sumner. Well, slave-driving was but another business. "It is the business of the slavemaster to make the slave work," Sumner said. "This is his high vocation. He is an auctioneer of human rights; a broker of human labor, a juggler of human sufferings, I might say a slaughterer of human hopes. Shall we run about the country seeking class after class that we are to visit with taxation, and under the lead of the senator excuse this largest and most offensive class of all?" Saulsbury, his voice dripping with disdain, shot back, "Upon every occasion when this subject of slavery can be lugged into your legislation, it is dragged in." After more acrimonious debate, the proposed tax was reduced to $5, then to $2, and then the amendment itself was defeated when Pomeroy, Sherman, and several other Republicans joined with conservative Democrats and Unionists to kill it completely.

When Harris, a business-minded, middle-of-the-road Republican, worried that the bill might annoy so many different sectors of the economy that it would ruin any political party that took responsibility for piloting it through Congress, Fessenden, at the end of his rope, harshly turned on him. "I am tired and sick to death of hearing men get up here in the Senate and talk about the effect of a tax upon a political party, that it is going to ruin our party," he said. "I do not want the country to be told that we legislate with reference to protecting the Republican Party against being overthrown. We do not legislate upon any such principle, I trust. At least, I do not."

Wade, too, was growing impatient. "If we do not intend to have the whole of this tax fall on our grandchildren, we have got to stop talking. This generation will be entirely exculpated from its payment if we go on as we do over every item."

Despite Americans' aversion to taxation, there was surprisingly little debate over the income tax, which had widespread support from the patriotic press. "Tax is patriotic," editorialized the *Lancaster Daily Inquirer*. "It is the plain duty of every loyal citizen to offer his cooperation." Even the *New York Herald* vigorously backed the tax as "one of the necessities of this war." Although Congress had enacted what was technically the country's first income tax in 1861, it still had not been implemented. Fessenden now undertook to craft a stronger, more graduated measure that would both reap greater returns and shift more of the burden to the wealthy. A tax of 3 percent would be imposed on incomes between $600 and $10,000, and of 5 percent on incomes over $10,000, and 7.5 percent on incomes over $50,000. He further emphasized that the new Internal Revenue Bureau—it would double the size of the Treasury Department—created by the bill would ensure that the wealthy, who were likely to "resort to every possible evasion," would be compelled to pay their fair share. Those who do not cooperate—men "rolling in wealth and bloated with stocks . . . who walk off whistling and paying nothing"—could be arrested and jailed.

Fessenden did his utmost to hurry the bill along to a vote. For the most part, he succeeded in deflecting amendments that would seriously harm the bill. But debate repeatedly ground to a halt for want of a quorum, and the sergeant-at-arms was sent scuttling through the Capitol's corridors to hunt up absent members, often without any success. "The public business requires that this bill be finished very soon," Fessenden complained on May 31. "I am entirely over-ruled, and have been repeatedly, not by votes of the Senate but by gentlemen taking themselves off and leaving us without a quorum."

The problem was not members' laziness, nor was it a question of mere parliamentary custom. Before South Carolina's secession, sixty-eight senators represented the thirty-four states of the Union. A quorum had always meant a majority of the total, thirty-five in 1860. Since then, eleven states had seceded. Some senators had resigned, others had simply failed to show up; of those from the seceded states, only Andrew Johnson of Tennessee remained. The Senate had also expelled both of Missouri's pro-secession senators, and in January 1862 Jesse Bright of Indiana, who, it was judged, had given "aid and comfort" to the enemy by personally recommending a Texas arms merchant to Jefferson Davis, in language that acknowledged Davis as the president of the Confederacy. The border state men were eventu-ally replaced with Unionists, and Bright with a War Democrat, while two new Unionist members from the western counties of Virginia—the future state of West Virginia—were also added. The Senate now effectively consisted of only forty-nine sitting members, but a quo-rum still required thirty-five of them to be present. On any given day, any number of senators might be ill, traveling, or absent for other reasons, leaving fewer, even far fewer, members than that on hand. As long as no member called for a quorum, the rules permitted the body to continue to function, as it had done for the past year and a half. But if a member objected, a quorum call had to be taken, and if the number fell short, the session had to cease immediately.

Even on major votes it was not uncommon for only the barest majority to be in the chamber, leaving little if any margin for error. The House, which was free to change its working rules at the begin-ning of each session, had dealt with the problem by declaring that a quorum consisted simply of a majority of all those members who had been "elected and sworn," thus subtracting from its total all but a handful of Unionists from the seceded states who remained. Rule changes were far more cumbersome in the more institutionally conservative Senate. To that obstacle was added the fear of many senators that eliminating the right of the seceded states to elect members would imply that secession was an accomplished fact.

As the session's end neared and radically controversial measures such as confiscation, emancipation, and the arming of Negroes deepened the existing divisions, fears grew among the majority that a small group of hostile senators could effectively block, or at the very least slow the passage of essential legislation, including money bills needed to finance the war. As early as April, John Sherman—Fessenden's younger protégé on the Finance Committee—had suggested unsuccessfully that the Senate adopt the House rule, which he called the "true constitutional quorum," but debate on it was thwarted for—lack of a quorum. "It is impossible, in my judgment, to pass either the confiscation bill or this tax bill while you require thirty-five senators in their seats," Sherman warned at the end of May. In June he tried again, proposing a reduction of the quorum to twenty-five, but for reasons that remain unclear, it sank beneath the paper waves of the Judiciary Committee, and did not reappear. Nothing more would soon happen to reduce the leadership's anxiety.

In the absence of a will to act, the Senate did its best to hobble along without reform. The retooled tax bill made its debut on June 6, pummeled, kneaded, clipped, and trimmed, but still largely intact. "I acknowledge its defects," Fessenden admitted. "The undertaking is new in the country. We have had to find our way comparatively in the dark." When the vote was taken on what the *New York Herald* proclaimed "a stupendous system of taxation," it passed thirty-seven to one, a triumph for Fessenden, with only one of Kentucky's senators dissenting. Saulsbury, disgusted, boycotted the vote. After a few more tweaks in conference committee stipulating that a new tax regime would begin on August 1, except for the income tax, which would be deferred until the following May, the Senate adopted the committee's report, which would serve as the foundation of Republican tax policy for the rest of the war, without a division, and the House by a decisive 106 to 11.

The tax bill was only one part of Congress's desperate campaign to shore up federal finances, and to demonstrate to Americans and skeptical Europeans that the government was committed to paying its debts. At the end of June, Stevens introduced a sweeping new system of tariffs on imported goods. The bill's author was the tireless Vermont agrarian Justin Morrill, fresh from the triumphant passage of his Land-Grant College bill. The new system cut in half the existing list of duty-free items, and imposed an average duty of 37 percent on imported goods and materials. Its purpose was twofold: to raise new revenue, and to protect domestic industries against the competition from cheaper foreign imports. "If we bleed the manufacturer, we must see to it that the proper tonic is administered at the same time," Morrill said, in an effort to reassure restive businessmen. The immensely detailed bill covered hundreds of items, from iron in a multitude of forms—pig iron, cast iron, rolled iron, scrap iron, bolts, hinges, nails—to iodine, pimentos, licorice root, absinthe, borax, food coloring, perfumes, carpets, mittens, clock parts, tassels, preserved fruits, mohair, wool, drugs, silk, steel and iron, alcohol, white marble statuary "in block, rough, squared, or sawed," ammonia, and much else.

There was little argument over the specifics until June 25, when an extraordinary confrontation, nominally over rice, erupted between Stevens and Aaron A. Sargent, of California, who asked for a sharp increase in the duty on "clean rice." A native of Massachusetts, Sargent had gone west as a Forty-niner, where he became a newspaperman and eventually a district attorney. He counted as a forward thinker on most issues that mattered to Republicans, including abolition, and was considerably more radical than most of them on women's rights; after the war, he would craft the language that years later became the Nineteenth Amendment, giving women the right to vote. But he hated the Chinese.

Addressing the House, Sargent now explained that two types of rice were imported into California, a total of 25 million pounds of it annually. "Clean" rice hulled in China was eaten almost exclusively by the state's fifty thousand Chinese, while "unclean" rice was hulled in California by American-owned mills. Unless imported "clean" rice was taxed more heavily, Sargent said, foreign "cooly" labor would continue to benefit at the expense of American workers. Imposing a large duty on "clean" rice would thus deservedly penalize the Chinese, who, he went on, "are, as a class, characterized by vicious habits" such as smoking opium and "intoxicating themselves with other drugs."

Stevens theatrically rose from his desk. He was not a tall man, but his sonorous charisma commanded rapt attention whenever he spoke. "We invite immigrants to this country without inquiring from what nation they may come," he began. China, as everyone ought to know, had been cruelly oppressed by the European nations, and forced into ruinous wars because it had attempted to fend off England's "importation of poisonous drugs that demoralize its society and destroy its people." In his opinion, the Chinese "were the most sober and industrious people upon the earth before they had the misfortune to become acquainted with English civilization." Yes, large numbers of them had immigrated to California—and there they had been singled out for abuse and "disgraceful" punitive state legislation. "They had the right to go there," he went on, "and I hold it to be in violation of every rule of law which should have sway in a civilized country to discriminate against them. Such laws are wholly in conflict with the generous spirit of our free institutions. They are a mockery of the boast that this land is the asylum of the oppressed of all climes." The very idea of imposing a special duty on the rice they ate was intolerable.

Sargent was undeterred. "In morals and every other respect they are obnoxious to our people," he retorted. "The women are prostitutes, and the men are petty thieves . . . a people of strange tongue, vile habits, impossible of assimilation, and with customs difficult to penetrate, [who] swarm by thousands to our shores, like the frogs of Egypt, and yet we are upbraided by the intelligent gentleman because we put a state tax in them to discourage their influx. We are overrun by these pagans, and we are doing what we can to relieve ourselves in the mild form of taxation."

The exchange was brief, and Sargent's amendment was voted down. But no other moment so vividly illustrated the reach of Stevens's tolerance. He probably never met a Chinese, and none lived in his district, or for that matter anywhere outside California and Nevada. With nothing to gain politically by speaking up, he made clear that his empathy was remarkably all-encompassing in an age

when racism was ubiquitous, even among his allies, and widely justified both by Scripture and by what was counted then as science. As
much as his unflagging advocacy of rights for blacks, his defense of
the Chinese pointed the way toward the far more ethnically diverse
nation that still lay in the future.

Even taken together, the new tariffs and taxes would still raise
only a fraction of the money that was required for the war, perhaps about $175 million of the $1 billion or more needed for the
coming year. In June, Chase was forced to admit that the Treasury
had already exhausted the $150 million in greenbacks that Congress
had authorized in February, and begged Stevens to persuade his
colleagues to approve another issue of $150 million immediately.
Elbridge Spaulding of New York, speaking for the Ways and Means
Committee, delivered the grim truth to the House: "No man, not
even the President, the Secretary of War, the Secretary of the Navy,
the Secretary of the Treasury, or the Chairman of the Committee of
Ways and Means, or all of them together, can give even an approxi-
mate estimate as to the whole cost of this war, because they do not
know the number of years it will continue, nor what will be the final
solution of the grave questions involved." Only a few weeks earlier,
giddy congressmen had been predicting that the war would end by
summer. But confidence was fast disintegrating once again. It was
now becoming painfully clear that McClellan's campaign in Virginia,
upon which Northern hopes rested, was failing.

On May 31, the Confederates struck the left wing of McClellan's
army at Fair Oaks, six miles from Richmond—so close that the Yankees could hear the church bells ringing in the city. The battle was a
draw, but it caused McClellan to once again halt his glacial advance.
The battle's most significant single casualty was the Confederate
commander, Joseph E. Johnston, who was severely wounded and
had to be carried off the field. He was replaced by Robert E. Lee,
who had spent most of the past year in obscurity as an advisor to
Jefferson Davis. McClellan's judgment of his new adversary, whom
he had known during the Mexican War, may have been the most
wildly inaccurate assessment of any general made by another during
the entire war. Lee, McClellan wrote to President Lincoln, may be
"personally brave & energetic to a fault, he yet is wanting in moral

firmness when possessed by heavy responsibility & is likely to be timid & irresolute in action." McClellan then sat down to passively while away the days, promising Lincoln, Stanton, and his army that the decisive battle was at hand, and victory was imminent. To his wife, Ellen, he wrote, "We will have Richmond & I shall be there with God's blessing this week." But the decisive battle never came, at least not the one McClellan had in mind.

McClellan's boasts faded by the week, as he once again consumed himself with fears of the Confederates' numerical superiority, convincing himself that he faced an enemy at least 200,000 strong. Increasingly, he spoke less of conquering the enemy than of preserving the army's honor by organizing a successful withdrawal. And, as always, of his desperate desire for more men. "Had I twenty thousand fresh & good troops we could be sure of a splendid victory tomorrow," he wired Stanton on June 27. The next day, he unblushingly insulted the secretary of war, declaring histrionically, "If I save this Army now I tell you plainly that I owe no thanks to you or any other persons in Washington—you have done your best to sacrifice this Army."

The series of battles that followed during the next week—Oak Grove, Mechanicsville, Gaines's Mill, Savage's Station, Glendale, White Oak Swamp, and Malvern Hill—would become known as the Seven Days. The supposedly timid and irresolute Lee slammed into first one detached segment of McClellan's army and then another, punching and counterpunching. In almost every action, he achieved parity of numbers if not tactical superiority by deftly concentrating his forces where the federals were comparatively weak. Only one of the battles was a clear-cut Confederate victory, and several qualified as tactical defeats for Lee. Yet McClellan kept retreating, backing down the peninsula the way he had come, treating each battle as a setback, until he finally came to a stop against the James River at Malvern Hill. There McClellan decisively prevailed over Lee, who threw brigade after brigade in suicidal frontal attacks against massed federal artillery. Despite huge Confederate losses, the campaign was an unmitigated defeat for the Union. McClellan's overwhelming advantages in numbers, weaponry, and supplies meant nothing. He was back where he began. Self-pitying and demoralized, he blamed subordinates who had let him down, and politicians who had betrayed him—everyone but himself. He wrote to Lincoln the day after Malvern Hill, "I have not yielded an inch of ground unnecessarily but have retired to prevent the superior force of the Enemy from cutting me off." As the military historian John Keegan succinctly put it, "Fearing failure, he did not try to win."

In an extraordinary letter to his wife that he wrote on July 10, McClellan ultimately attributed the dismal outcome of the campaign to God's inscrutable but nonetheless "wise purpose." He confessed that "if I had succeeded in taking Richmond now the fanatics of the North might have been too powerful and reunion impossible. However that may be I am sure that it is all for the best." In other words, he had decided that his defeat was really in the best interests of the Union, or at least the prewar, slavery-protecting Union that he wished to preserve: by losing to Lee, he had saved the nation from the abolitionists.

The congressional Radicals saw it differently. McClellan could have crushed any army on the face of the earth, Zachariah Chandler raged on the floor of the Senate. "One hundred and fifty-eight thousand of the best troops that ever stood on God's footstool were sent down to the peninsula. What did we do? We found the worst swamp there was between Richmond and Williamsburg, and sat right down in the center of it and went to digging." For weeks, the army "lay in ditches, digging, drinking rotten water, and eating bad food, and sleeping in the mud. Still they conquered in every fight, and still they retreated, because they were ordered to retreat." The Radicals would never forgive McClellan.

On Capitol Hill, the long, often rancorous, and stunningly productive session wound toward a close with headlong haste. One of the last measures to be addressed was also one of the most far-reaching. The act, really an amendment to a law dating from 1795, stipulated that members of state militias were liable to be asked to serve for nine months, instead of just ninety days. Although it was passed without great fanfare or public debate, it would soon provoke the first, and to date the worst, rioting against administration war policy. The act antagonized defenders of states' rights, still a potent force even in the North, by providing the president with the authority to nationalize state militia units, a power that traditionally had belonged to states alone. Even more provoking, it was, in effect, a half-disguised conscription measure, requiring states that did not meet their quota of volunteers to draft members of their militia to make up the deficit, and it was quickly followed by a War Department call-up of 300,000 militiamen to fill the army's depleted ranks.

Two additional sections of the act were revolutionary. Like other legislation that irreparably chipped away at the edifice of slavery, these were couched in purely pragmatic military terms. They explicitly authorized the president to enroll for "any military or naval service for which they may be found competent, persons of African descent," and provided that any slaves who had belonged to owners who had lent any form of aid to the enemy were to be considered no longer "contrabands"—always a legally muddy term—but forever free. This, as slave owners well knew, represented a giant step toward true emancipation. It was also perfectly clear to everyone that the bill opened the army's ranks to the recruitment of blacks as combat soldiers.

The once unthinkable had migrated into the political mainstream. Just months earlier, the enlistment of blacks seemed outlandish, the fancy of none but flaming abolitionists such as Stevens and Wade. But as Lincoln prepared to call for 300,000 more volunteers, on top of 200,000 he had mobilized in May, Negroes represented the largest as yet untapped pool of potential manpower. Even conservative Republicans were coming around. Lincoln's friend Orville Browning of Illinois argued that it would simply be stupid not to use black manpower. "Is it any worse to kill [the] enemy with a musket in the hands of a black than in the hands of a white man?" he asked. Besides, he added, revealing the virulent racism that often lay just below the surface of many Northerners' public opposition to slavery, military discipline would restrain blacks' natural "ferocity," and "be the very best, if not the only protection we can give to the women and children of the rebel states against the frightful scenes of carnage and conflagration which may otherwise sweep them from the earth."

In the House, Virginia-born Robert Mallory of Kentucky indignantly declared of "the Negro" that "knowing his depraved nature as I do," putting a gun in the hands of a slave to shoot down white men was an unspeakable insult to the rules of civilized warfare. "I would as soon think of enlisting the Indian, and of arming him with the tomahawk and scalping knife." In addition, he sneered, they were all cowards and not worth the expense of organizing them. "One shot of a cannon would disperse thirty thousand of them."

Thaddeus Stevens slowly unfolded himself from his desk, "rising by degrees, as a telescope is pulled out," his heavy toupee falling over his brow and his "cold little eyes" bristling with anger. "Why, then, object to them as a savage and barbarous race, if one gun will disperse an army of them?" he sarcastically rejoined, pointing out that "civilized" nations—the Portuguese, French, Dutch, and British, as well as the patriots during the Revolutionary War—had all armed blacks. "I am for sending the army through the whole slave population of the South, and asking them to come from their masters, to take the weapons which we furnish, and to join us in this war of freedom against traitors and rebels. I do not view it as an abolition or as an emancipation question. I view it as the means, and the only means, of putting down this rebellion."

In the Senate, Willard Saulsbury, the overmatched but indefatigable voice of slavery, assailed the bill as yet another attempt "to elevate the miserable nigger—Do you believe that the free white soldiers of this country will fight side by side with negroes?" McClellan, still camped in Virginia with his idle army, and as convinced as ever that he faced an overwhelming rebel force, substantially agreed. He informed Lincoln that he violently opposed the arming of Negroes. "Neither confiscation of property . . . or forcible abolition of slavery should be contemplated for a moment," he fulminated. "Military power should not be allowed to interfere with the relations of servitude. A declaration of radical views, especially upon slavery, will rapidly disintegrate our present Armies." But McClellan's star had waned, stained by his months of procrastination and empty boasts, and his dismal performance on the peninsula. No one was calling him the "young Napoleon" anymore, except in mockery. Salmon Chase, once McClellan's leading booster, confided to one of Jay

Cooke's associates that the general was "the cruelest imposition ever forced upon a nation," while on the Senate floor Zachariah Chandler accused him openly of "wholesale murder" and "constructive treason," thundering, "That criminal, should not only be deprived of his office, but, in my humble opinion, he should suffer the extreme penalty of the law." Nothing so drastic happened, of course, but it was clear to almost everyone, including the general himself, that not only was he out of step with the administration's fast evolving policy on emancipation, but that his days as commander of the Army of the Potomac were numbered.

John Sherman spoke for the Republican majority when he declared, "It is a question of whether the rebels alone shall have the benefit of slavery, without feeling its weakness, or whether the United States shall employ the labor of a race of men whose interests, whose sympathies, whose whole hearts are with the people of the United States in suppressing this rebellion." Pausing to assure his fellow senators that he didn't believe in racial equality, he added, "I think the law of caste is the law of God; you cannot change it. But they are our natural friends in subduing this rebellion." The bill would easily triumph over the conservatives' objections.

A last-minute glitch threatened to derail the confiscation bill, over which Congress had fought to the point of exhaustion since the beginning of the session. The president had made it known that he might veto the bill, over which so much verbal blood had been spilled, because the bill implied that seized property might be confiscated permanently with no provision for forgiveness, a detail that he believed was contrary to the Constitution. "The severest justice may not always be the best policy," Lincoln wrote in a draft letter that was delivered to Congress that night. "Would it not be wise to place a power of remission somewhere, so that these persons may know they have something to lose by persisting and something to gain by desisting?" Although Wade and other Radicals threatened to defy the president, in the end Fessenden's persuasive powers prevailed. "Is it better that no bill be passed with regard to this object?" he asked. The session would expire within hours, and if members failed to act now, the entire bill would die on Lincoln's desk. Sumner, no less a Radical than Wade, declared his support for Fessenden. "The navigator is sometimes called to save his ship by casting into the sea a part of his cargo," he offered. The most important part of the bill was its promise of emancipation. "To save this part, I willingly abandon all the rest." An explanatory note was hastily crafted to alleviate Lincoln's concerns, the crisis was averted, and the bill, which had caused so many months of bloodletting, was at last passed.

During the session's final hours, long-delayed, pedestrian measures flew through votes in rapid succession: bills to punish the fraudulent sale of postage stamps, to ban the confinement of soldiers in the Washington city jail, to enlarge the Lake Superior land district, to transfer the administration of the western gunboat fleet from the War Department to the Navy Department, to settle the land titles of "half-breed Kansas Indians," to accept the donation of millionaire Cornelius Vanderbilt's private yacht to the navy, and many more. Messengers sped back and forth between the chambers, and between Capitol Hill and the White House, and back again, as bills were passed and signed into law by the president.

About midnight, while the Senate's sergeant-at-arms raced through the halls in an effort to scare up a quorum, two senators, James Nesmith of Oregon and Henry Rice of Minnesota—"both being in a very good humor," in the Senate doorkeeper's restrained words—spontaneously leapt from their seats with their canes in their hands "gave vent to a war whoop," and began dancing around the chamber, "whooping like Indians," continuing for half an hour for the amusement of their fellow senators, until enough members were found to get back to business.

At last, at 2:00 p.m. on July 17, venerable Solomon Foot of Vermont, the Senate's president pro tem, prepared to bring down his gavel on what by any measure had been one of the most dynamic sessions in the history of Congress. The session had sat uninterruptedly for more than seven months. Its record was astonishing. Three landmark domestic acts—providing for western homesteading, the Transcontinental Railroad, and land grant colleges—would forever reshape the face of America. The series of similarly precedent-setting money bills—providing for a national tax regime, new tariffs, and the issuance of greenbacks—would lay a solid financial foundation for the war, and for the first time put the federal government in control of the nation's money supply. Another spate of bills—the abolition of slavery in Washington, D.C., the Confiscation Act, and the new Militia Act, along with acts recognizing black-governed Haiti and Liberia, permitting blacks the right to testify in federal court, and offering federal aid to states that passed their own acts of emancipation—moved the eventual destruction of slavery from the fringe of the war effort to its core. The beginning of the long and bitterly divisive legislative struggle over postwar Reconstruction, while it did not result in legislation, left its lingering smoke thickening in the political air. As the *New York Herald* rightly put it, "These and similar propositions were the preliminary movements in the scouting, picketing, skirmishing, and reconnaissance preparatory of the great battle between slavery and its foes." Not least, without debate, Congress voted to issue the nation's first military award for heroism: the Congressional Medal of Honor.

"May we not be allowed to indulge the hope and confidence that after a few passing months we may come back to these seats with renewed vigor of health and strength, of heart and of hope," Foot ventured by way of farewell, as his fellow senators shook the stiffness out of their limbs, gathered their papers, and shuffled out into the steamy Washington afternoon. "May we not even hope to come back amid the rejoicings of a mighty though now distracted and warring people, restored once more to union, to peace, and to harmony?"

# 10

# The Slaves Must Be with Us

Abolition—*yes!* Abolish everything
on the face of the earth but this Union.

—REP. THADDEUS STEVENS

Alone among Pitt Fessenden's four sons, twenty-one-year-old Sam gave his father cause for worry. Frank, twenty-three, was serving with the army in Tennessee, and had been wounded at Shiloh. James, twenty-eight, a sharpshooter, had been detailed to train some of the first black troops raised from among ex-slaves in South Carolina. Twenty-seven-year-old William was capably handling his father's business affairs in Maine. Sam, always impulsive, had as a teenager run off to join John Brown in Kansas, and had to be hauled home before he got killed. Now a student at Bowdoin College, he was squandering his allowance on carousing and costly clothes, and evinced little interest in academics. "Choice must be made between a life of manly usefulness and honor, and one of worthlessness and disgrace," his father admonished him in January. "The great defect in your character is self-indulgence without thought either for yourself or others."

Driven by both his craving for adventure and the desire to redeem himself in his father's eyes, Sam enlisted in the army and was immediately commissioned a second lieutenant—he was a senator's son, after all—in the artillery. Posted in the Shenandoah Valley, he proved popular with his superior officers, as well as an unexpectedly sensitive observer of war's corrupting effect on otherwise decent men. Shaken by what he saw, he wrote to his father, "I have witnessed one continuous course of plundering, robbing, insulting women and destroying what could not be used. Not content with taking from poor people whatever they had to eat [our men] have broken into cupboards, smashing to pieces what household utensils they could not carry off; heaving up clothes of no use to any but the owners; have insulted the women they first robbed, striking them in some instances with the muskets they held in their hands. We are a disgrace to our country, and if we are whipped I shall not be sorry," he added, shockingly.

In July, Sam's unit was deployed to reinforce the newly formed Army of Virginia, under the command of Gen. John Pope, who had been called east from Missouri after winning several small strategic victories along the Mississippi River. Pope's army was originally intended to shield Washington while McClellan attacked Richmond, and then to move south against the Confederates in a grand pincer movement. With McClellan supine at Harrison's Landing on the Peninsula, the North's hopes now rested with Pope and his seventy thousand men. The press, the public, and the Republican leadership all demanded a decisive battle that would destroy the Confederate army at a single blow, open the road to Richmond, and end the war. "This is the crisis of the rebellion," declared the *New York Herald*. "Henceforth we must have only action, action, and again action. We are done with playing with war, and must fight now in earnest."

Pope, whose pluming self-regard surpassed even McClellan's, was prepared to oblige, and said so loudly. In early July 1862, he boasted to the Joint Committee on the Conduct of the War that if he had had command of the 200,000 men under McClellan's control before the Seven Days battles, he could have marched them clear to New Orleans. "We have come to you from the West, where we have always seen the backs of our enemies, from an army whose policy has been attack and advance," he proclaimed to his troops in the imperial plural. "Advance is the Order of the Day. Success and Glory in the Advance. Shame Lurks in the Rear."

With action looming, Sam's spirits rose. "We expect marching orders every moment," he wrote to his father on August 22. "There is no doubt that a severe battle will occur." No longer were the senator's letters freighted with barely controlled disdain, but now with the pride that he, and doubtless Sam, had long wished for. "Your army is the center of all eyes, for the hopes of the country are resting upon it," he wrote. "May you do your duty, and may God preserve you."

Pope's modest experience in the West failed to prepare him for what ensued, as much from his fellow officers as from the enemy. McClellan, jealous of Pope's new favor in Washington, wrote to his wife in mid-August, "I have a very strong idea that Pope will be thrashed during the coming week—& very badly whipped he will be & ought to be—such a villain as he is ought to bring defeat upon any cause that employs him." His remarks were prescient, if close to treasonous. Despite direct orders from Lincoln, McClellan persistently refused to provide reinforcements to Pope from his own army. When, belatedly and grudgingly, he finally did so, they were still disembarking at Alexandria when Pope collided with an entrenched force under Stonewall Jackson near the old Bull Run battlefield, on August 29.

Pope hammered the rebels all day with assault after assault. Thirty miles away in Washington, the sound of cannon fire could be heard like a distant drumbeat in the withering summer heat. The city pulsed with anticipation. Hospitals were cleared and churches taken over to make way for casualties. On street corners, in hotel lobbies and taverns, crowds of men begged impatiently for the latest news. Early news reports claimed erroneously that the rebels had been driven from their positions with great slaughter. From Portland, where he was riveted waiting for the latest telegraphic reports, Pitt Fessenden wrote hopefully to his son Frank, "It seems Pope has fought a great battle and won it. I am most happy to believe it to be so, but shall be very curious to hear of Sam."

The next day's reports were more equivocal, then catastrophic. Pope confidently claimed in a predawn message to the War Department that the rebels were "badly used up" and in retreat, even as Confederate reinforcements poured onto the field. When they struck, they rolled up the Union line, sowing panic, and nearly bagging Pope's entire army. Among the dead was Col. Fletcher Webster of the 12th Massachusetts, the son of the great orator Daniel Webster. And among the wounded was Sam Fessenden, now a captain, who was serving as an aide to Gen. Zealous Tower of Pope's Third Corps. Sam was shot in the gut when Confederate Gen. James Longstreet's corps overwhelmed Pope's exposed left flank.

The senator entrained immediately for Washington as soon as he learned that Sam had been injured. By the time he got there, Sam was dead. He wrote to a friend a few days later, "For the loss of a beloved child there is no such thing as consolation. There is however a melancholy satisfaction in knowing that he died in a just and holy cause. I am assured too by all persons who knew him that he was calmly and unostentatiously brave, bearing all hardships cheerfully and uncomplainingly. His death was that of a Christian patriot." Sam was just one of the Union's 16,000 casualties, far outstripping the Confederates' 9,200.

It was clear that the war would not end before the November elections—a perilous prospect for the Republicans, as public disillusionment grew. As the North struggled to come to grips with yet another lost opportunity, Zachariah Chandler impotently raged: "Are imbecility and treason to be retained and promoted to the end of the chapter?" But there was little time for recrimination. Lee's army was already on the march, thrusting boldly north toward Maryland, brushing aside disorganized federal opposition, and sowing terror in Pennsylvania. By September 5, Pope was gone, and McClellan was back in full command. "Unquestionably, he has acted badly toward Pope," Lincoln told his secretary John Hay. "He wanted him to fail. That is unpardonable. But he is too useful just now to sacrifice." Lincoln added, more hopefully than confidently, "If he can't fight himself, he excels in making others ready to fight."

Lee's aim was to draw the federals into battle, defeat them on their own ground, thereby win recognition of the Confederacy by the European powers, and bring the war to an end. He also expected, erroneously as it turned out, that tens of thousands of Maryland volunteers would flock to his banners once he entered the state. Lee might well have prevailed, but for a singular stroke of fate. On September 13, a copy of Lee's battle plan was discovered wrapped around three cigars in a field in Maryland. McClellan was thus handed one of the rarest miracles in warfare, a blueprint of the enemy's intentions showing exactly where his troops were heading, when they were expected to arrive there, and, by deduction, how many men he had. A more enterprising commander than McClellan would have instantly moved to destroy Lee's army piecemeal. Instead, precious days ticked away while he reorganized his troops, demanded more supplies, and lobbied for reinforcements since, no matter what the captured document said, he remained convinced that he faced at least 120,000 rebels, three times their actual number.

When McClellan's 70,000 men finally moved, it was with his usual glacial deliberation, allowing Lee still more time to consolidate his forces around the town of Sharpsburg, Maryland, between Antietam Creek and the Potomac River. The two armies met on September 17, on a tightly packed two-square-mile battlefield of low hills, cornfields, and wood lots that allowed little space for tactical flair. McClellan negated his several advantages by repeatedly hurling forward courageous but cripplingly uncoordinated assaults that gave the enemy time to shift troops from one part of their line to another to meet new attacks over the course of twelve blood-soaked hours. Despite many missed opportunities, the Union was on the brink of breakthrough when the timely arrival of Stonewall Jackson's "foot cavalry"—so called because of their speed on the march—stanched imminent collapse. By the end of the day, dead men and horses lay strewn in mounds over the trampled cornfields and shattered wood lots. When losses were tallied, the Union had lost 12,400 men, and the Confederates 10,300. (McClellan claimed baselessly that the Confederates had lost 25,000.) It was the bloodiest single day not just of the Civil War but in all American military history. His ego unscathed, McClellan preened. "The spectacle yesterday was the grandest I could conceive of—nothing could be more sublime," he wrote to his wife the day after the battle. "Those in whose judgment I rely tell me that I fought the battle splendidly & that it was a masterpiece of art." Apart from his circle of headquarters sycophants, he was the only one who thought so.

The Confederates were bruised and depleted, and assumed that

McClellan would attack again the next day. He had some 32,000 completely fresh troops—more than the total number left to Lee—as well as tens of thousands of bloodied but still combative troops who had fought on the 17th. But he declined to renew the battle that day or the next, and then passively allowed Lee to withdraw unmolested across the Potomac to Virginia. Fessenden, along with many others, was beside himself with frustration. To Salmon Chase he wrote, "I was silent during all the last session upon the pig-headed obstinacy and stupidity which kept incompetent generals in command, and was destroying our armies to no purpose. May God forgive me! If I live to take my seat once more, and this horrible abuse continues, I will try to redeem my errors."

Antietam was a draw by any military measure. Politically, however, Lee's retreat allowed the administration to construe it as a victory. That, in turn, permitted the president to take a step he had been contemplating for several weeks, one that made the battle a symbol of moral triumph that transcended McClellan's unimpressive battlefield performance. On September 22, Lincoln informed his cabinet that he intended to proclaim the liberation of all slaves living in areas under rebel control as of January 1, 1863. He had, he said, "made a covenant, that if God gave us victory in the approaching battle," he would consider it a sign of divine will in favor of general emancipation. Although a few members of the cabinet demurred, none opposed Lincoln outright. This preliminary Emancipation Proclamation further promised to protect the freedom of former slaves, and to interfere in no way with any efforts they made to liberate themselves, effectively negating the Fugitive Slave Law of 1850. Finally, and significantly, the proclamation invited former slaves to enlist for service in the North's armed forces.

Although the proclamation said nothing about the long-term future for freed slaves, it carried an implicit corollary: that, when feasible, emancipated blacks would be sent out of the country, willingly if they agreed, and forcibly if they didn't, probably to a cheerless region on the west coast of the Isthmus of Panama, then part of Colombia, known as Chiriquí. Lincoln, who personally preferred what a later age would call voluntary "self-deportation," reported Navy Secretary Gideon Welles, "thought it essential to provide an asylum for a race which could never be recognized or admitted to be our equals."

The proclamation was devoid of idealistic pronouncements; rather, it evaded the legally fraught question of emancipation's constitutionality by appealing pragmatically to military necessity by defining slavery not as a moral evil but as a part of the Confederate war machinery. "The slaves must be with us or against us in the war. Let us have them," Welles wrote, adding uneasily, "It is, however, an arbitrary and despotic measure in the cause of freedom." It also had the practical effect of deterring the European powers—all of them opposed to slavery in principle—from recognizing Confederate independence, at least for now. But most Republicans recognized the proclamation's implications. "There has been no more important and far reaching document ever issued since the foundation of this government," editorialized the *New York Times*. Ben Wade, so often disappointed with the president, cheered, "Hurrah for Old Abe and the proclamation!" Charles Sumner, overcome by emotion, speaking at historic Faneuil Hall in Boston, declared, "Thank God I live to enjoy this day. The skies are brighter and the air is purer, now that slavery has been handed over to judgment." Although some soldiers denounced the proclamation, others, probably the majority, took a more calculating view. "Harsh experience has destroyed in them all feeling of sentiment in regard to the Negro, and they only wish to know how he can be put to service in the crushing of the rebellion," the *New York Times* reported.

Democrats, predictably, cried doom. A Circleville, Ohio, paper squarely blamed the abolitionists, calling for them to be lynched "till the flesh rot off their bones and the winds of Heaven whistle Yankee Doodle through their loathsome skeletons." The racist but pro-war *New York Herald* predicted that Southern whites would now unite even more firmly "in a furious hatred of the North," adding savagely, "The nigger-worshippers assert that the proclamation will end the war, but men of sense know that [now] the war will really begin." McClellan, mortified, told a civilian supporter that, along with the president's imminent suspension of habeas corpus across the North, the proclamations were "inaugurating servile war, & at one stroke of the pen changing our free institutions into a despotism."

What no one disputed was that "on this pontoon [Lincoln] has crossed the Rubicon," as a correspondent for the *Boston Post* put it. At a celebratory gathering at Salmon Chase's home, members of the cabinet, as well as "a few old fogies," reported John Hay, "all seemed to feel a sort of new and exhilarated life; they breathed freer; the President's proclamation had freed them as well as the slaves. They gleefully and merrily called each other and themselves abolitionists, and seemed to enjoy the novel sensation of appropriating that horrible name."

While Lincoln's announcement of the Emancipation Proclamation was a bold political stroke, it had only been made possible as a result of the many months of debate in the House and Senate, and the ceaseless personal prodding of the Radicals in Congress. The proclamation's more immediate foundation was laid by the Second Confiscation Act, which showed the president that even conservative Republicans such as Fessenden had fully accepted the once extreme notion that victory could only be achieved by completely destroying the South's society and economy. Thaddeus Stevens was skeptical that the proclamation would have much direct effect, but he recognized that a political watershed had been crossed by Congress, "agreeing with me where a year ago not fifty could have been found."

At seventy and in precarious health, Stevens had risen from his sickbed to accept the Lancaster Republicans' nomination for the crucial October elections, demonstrating that his faith in the liberating tide of history was undiminished: "Abolition—*yes*! Abolish everything on the face of the earth but this Union; free every slave—slay every traitor—burn every rebel mansion, if these things be necessary to preserve this temple of freedom to the world and to our posterity."

Meanwhile, Copperhead ranks dramatically swelled. Some even began quietly rooting for the Union's defeat: when news came that the Confederates had slipped away from a battle in Mississippi without a fight, one Washington Copperhead, Charles Mason, a federal employee who was careful to keep his politics secret, confided to his diary, "It is better for them to have retreated than to have been beaten." In the army, racist soldiers threatened to throw down their arms, or to revolt against abolitionist officers. Fury at emancipation fused with defeatism and distress at rising food prices in an incendiary mix. In Toledo, striking white stevedores—charging that blacks were paid the same rate as they were—attacked innocent African Americans wholesale. In Cincinnati, Irish workers replaced by contrabands set fire to blacks' homes and roamed the streets shouting "down with the niggers."

The spring's optimism had evaporated as decisive battlefield victory once again proved elusive. Hundreds of millions of dollars had now been squandered on lost battles and stolen by crooked contractors, and thousands of lives lost seemingly to no purpose. "The bones of our dead soldiers would make a Golgotha monument higher than that of Bunker Hill," cried the *New York Herald*. "In return for this immense quantity of blood and treasure, what have we gained? Are the rebels subdued? On the contrary, they seem stronger than ever."

Resistance to the Militia Act grew. In response, a series of War Department orders in August authorized the arrest of any man trying to leave the United States to escape the draft, and imprisonment of violators. Reaction and counterreaction fed suspicion on all sides, most seriously in the Northwest. Democratic judges issued subpoenas for the demobilization of soldiers who no longer wanted to serve. Doctors welcomed appeals from draft dodgers claiming to have newly discovered ailments. Copperhead editors openly urged men to defy the draft and to reject the income tax. In some towns, troops had to be called out to break up antidraft rioting. Everywhere, desertion spiked. A steady stream of deserters could be seen passing through Lancaster, Pennsylvania, some still carrying their guns, a distressed informant reported to Thaddeus Stevens. By the end of the year, military authorities in Indiana would be arresting four hundred deserters a week, and by February 1863, the War Department would list 282,000 men—36 percent of the army's full strength—as absent from their commands.

Two days after issuing the preliminary Emancipation Proclamation Lincoln further inflamed Democrats, including many who had thus far supported the administration, by proclaiming the suspension of habeas corpus across the entire country. This proclamation authorized trials by military commissions of "all Rebels and Insurgents, their aiders and abettors within the United States, and all persons discouraging volunteer enlistments, resisting militia drafts, or guilty of any disloyal practice." Declared Thomas H. Seymour, a former governor of Connecticut, and prospective Democratic candidate for president in 1864, "We must denounce the two proclamations lately made by Mr. Lincoln, or consent to be white slaves for life."

With the initiation of martial law, stories circulated of homes invaded by provost marshals' men, of closets and bureaus rifled, and young men arrested merely because they "talked saucily" to soldiers. In Washington, services in one Episcopal church were temporarily banned because the priest declined to read a prayer that the administration had asked to be offered for the Union forces. Hundreds of Northern civilians, including editors, doctors, lawyers, judges, ministers, were arrested, many of them charged with expressing disloyal thoughts in print or in casual conversation.

The threat of subversion was real enough. Confederate agents were active in many states, and the shadowy pro-Confederate secret society known as the Knights of the Golden Circle was widely believed to be forming armed units in Illinois and Indiana, and infiltrating the army. (Members had to be Protestant and born in a slave state, although free-state-born Catholics might be eligible if they could prove "evidences of character as a southern man.") But the government's methods could be heavy-handed and capricious. A New Hampshire doctor was arrested for declaring at a recruiting rally that three-fourths of the men who enlisted would be killed and go to hell. In New Jersey, the editors of the *Newark Evening Journal* were seized for encouraging citizens to break up a recruiting rally. In Wilkes-Barre, Pennsylvania, several men were jailed when they called for the election of men who would peacefully bring the Southern states back into the Union. A federal marshal in Iowa seized the editor of the *Dubuque Herald* for allegedly discouraging enlistments. Ordinary citizens were hauled in for questioning the war, cheering for Jefferson Davis, or insulting Abraham Lincoln. One, a man named McDowell, was arrested for declaring that he "wouldn't wipe my ass with the stars and stripes." In Missouri, an average of 106 civilians a month were arrested; by November, more than five hundred political prisoners had been interned at a single camp near

Columbus, Ohio. Most were held for no more than a few days, but at least some were jailed, allegedly in "rat-infested cells," for more than a year. In Dayton, a law student, the son of one of Clement Vallandigham's best friends, was arrested for stating his opinion that Democrats shouldn't help the Republicans attack the South, while two Presbyterian ministers who had been guests in Vallandigham's home were jailed as alleged Confederate spies.

It had been a dispiriting session for Vallandigham. Despite his dogged efforts to participate in floor debates, Speaker Galusha Grow rarely recognized him, and when he did it was only on procedural points. Otherwise, his attempts to intervene were ignored. On one typical occasion, when he asked for unanimous consent—usually pro forma—to present petitions calling for a "peaceful adjustment" of the national crisis, a single Republican objected. Vallandigham then moved to temporarily suspend the rules to enable him to introduce the petitions. When a vote was taken, his plea was rejected outright. "Where has the right of petition gone?" he cried impotently. He morosely told a friend that he expected to hear yet another proposal to censure or expel him every time a Republican addressed the chair.

Vallandigham believed that foreign intervention and Union defeats would soon force an end to the war. Although he paid lip service to restoration of the Union in its prewar form, he foresaw—though he avoided specifics—a complete reorganization of the Mississippi Valley states, either in a new autonomous relationship within the United States, or in affiliation with the Confederacy. To Republicans, he remained a lightning rod for opprobrium: "filth" to be "purged" from Congress, the *blackest traitor* of all, a man "whose every breath is devoted to" the nation's destruction. Wrote one contemptuous Ohioan, "There are thousands of good men in his district that would [put] his dead body in a position that the northern soldiers could pass under it."

Antiwar Democrats heroized Vallandigham as a prophet who had seen the futility of the conflict sooner than most. At the beginning of July he left Washington for the Ohio state Democratic convention in Columbus, the most enthusiastic such conclave in living memory, and so heavily attended that one-quarter of the delegates could not get into the hall, causing the organizers to move it outdoors to the statehouse grounds. Addressing the delegates, he savagely attacked the federal government: "Today they who are our servants, creatures made out of nothing by the power of the people, would now become the masters of the people; while the organs and instruments of the people—the press and public assemblages—are to be suppressed; and the Constitution, with its right of petition, and of due process of law and trial by jury, and the laws and all else which makes life worth possessing—are to be sacrificed now on the tyrant's plea that it is necessary to save the government, the Union." Gathering force as he spoke, to tidal roars of approval, he warned of "bayonets at the ballot box," and soaringly declared, like a latter-day Constantine the Great, " 'The Constitution as it is, and the Union as it was.' In that sign you shall conquer. Let it be inscribed upon every ballot, emblazoned upon every banner, flung abroad to every breeze, whispered in the zephyr and thundered in the tempest, till its echoes shall rouse the fainting spirit of every patriot and freeman in the land."

Vallandigham knew that he would be a prime target in the October state elections since the Unionist-controlled state legislature had gerrymandered his once secure district to include a strongly Republican county in an effort to oust him. As he stumped for reelection, he served up unstinting portions of the rawest racism, repeatedly condemning Congress for its alleged obsession with the "Almighty African," claiming that "from the prayer to the motion to adjourn, it is negro in every shape and form in which he can, by any possibility, be served up." He claimed that just blocks from the Capitol—"within whose marble walls Abolition treason runs riot"—contrabands by the thousands were being fed at public expense while Union soldiers went hungry "without so much as a cracker or a crust of bread."

In speech after speech, he equated "the Secession rebellion South, and the Abolition rebellion North and West," asserting that the "Abolition rebellion" must be put down before the government could ever hope to suppress the secession rebellion. The war, he charged, had divided the North and West, ruined the army, inspired Confederate resistance, driven the federal debt beyond $1 billion, cost the lives of many thousands of brave soldiers, produced a tide of worthless federal currency, and ruinous taxes. "Stand in the doorway of your farmhouse and behold and feel nothing, nothing not taxed, except the air you breathe, and the bright sunlight or starlight of heaven! And yet you must pay it to the uttermost farthing." And why? "For all this, abolitionism is responsible."

Increasingly, he saw himself as a Christian martyr and his political purgatory as part of a spiritual mission. To his mother, he wrote, "I am weary, very weary . . . after all I have done and suffered." But, "God has been very good to me in the midst of sore persecution, and has delivered me out of the hands of my enemies." The Bible, he wrote, promised that "whoever will do right, firmly and wisely, will be sustained if he endure to the end. I am still hopeful of the future, even amidst the darkness which surrounds us, and the evil and wickedness which I see on every side." In the midst of his trials, he said, he found an uplifting solace in the music of a regimental band that serenaded him one evening in June. (He didn't mention that the soldiers of another Ohio regiment chased him out of their camp as soon as they recognized him.)

His feeling of persecution wasn't irrational. He received many death threats and was understandably rattled when the editor of his mouthpiece, the *Dayton Daily Empire*, was shot dead on the street. Fearing his assassination, armed volunteers surrounded his home. Despite the threats, Vallandigham continued to speak throughout his district, and at antiwar rallies further afield, often for hours at a stretch. On August 2, he told an enthusiastic crowd, "It is appointed to all men to die; and death never comes too soon to one in the discharge of his duty. I have chosen my course, have pursued it, have adhered to it to this hour, and will to the end, regardless of consequences. My opinions are immovable; fire cannot melt them out of me. I scorn the mob. I defy arbitrary power. I may be imprisoned for opinion's sake. Other patriots, in other ages, have suffered before me. I may die for the cause; be it so. . . . The knife of the assassin shall [never] move me from my firm purpose."

Election campaigns across the country were exceptionally vicious. The *New York Tribune* predicted alarmingly that a Democratic victory would result in the immediate recall of all the New York regiments from the army. Democrats railed against "niggers, [and] high federal taxes," asserting that the only way to prevent the ruin of the country was to vote against the administration, and look to an "immediate settlement of the present troubles." Everywhere, "runaway negroes" were alleged to be stealing white men's jobs. Newspapers likened Vallandigham to Benedict Arnold and Aaron Burr, and published unfounded rumors linking him to the Knights of the Golden Circle. In New York, Democratic gubernatorial candidate Horatio Seymour declared, "The scheme for immediate emancipation and general arming of the slaves throughout the South is a proposal for the butchery of women and children, for scenes of lust and rapine; of arson and murder unparalleled in the history of the world." To punctuate such warnings, Democratic newspapers hyped stories—real or fictitious—about attempted rapes of terrified white women by "lusty black fiends." Pervasive fears of uncontrollable inflation further undermined Republican support. By early October, gold was worth 23 percent more than paper money, and it kept on rising. Voting for the Democratic Party, trilled one partisan sheet, would restore the nation to the peace and plenty it had once enjoyed: "While it ruled, blessings fell from the wings of the Angel of Peace like dew drops from heaven."

The first elections took place in October. They set in motion a rolling disaster for the Republicans, who failed to sell emancipation and their management of the war to many tens of thousands of voters who had supported them in 1860. The Democrats took control of the legislature in Indiana and won most of the House seats in both Ohio and Pennsylvania, where they ousted Speaker of the House Galusha Grow in one of many upsets. "Today the shackles of the white man have been loosened!" the *Dayton Daily Empire* gleefully crowed. Then, in November, Democrats captured the statehouses and scores of state offices in Illinois, New Jersey, and New York. New York's new lieutenant governor, John Van Buren, the son of former president Martin Van Buren, called for a new constitutional convention acceptable to the seceded states, and declared, "The war has gone far enough and it is time to make peace with the South." Nationally, the Democrats gained more than thirty seats in the House of Representatives.

Overall, Democrats regarded their showing as a triumph: a year and a half earlier, their party had seemed close to death. No more. The voters had delivered a clear and unmistakable message: either deliver victories, or end the war. "Total rout," the New York diarist George Templeton Strong wrote despondently. "A vote of national suicide. All is up. We are a lost people. The Historical Society should secure an American flag at once for its museum of antiquities." The election, pronounced the pro-administration *Cincinnati Times*, was no less than "a political revolution."

Many Republicans blamed Lincoln personally for political ineptitude and weak leadership. "The folly of the president has lost Ohio and Indiana, and I am surprised that its effects have not been even more calamitous," wrote Fessenden in October. "As it is, the West is disgraceful in every way." An incipient rebellion within the party sought to dump Lincoln and draft Fessenden as the Republican candidate for 1864, but he quickly quashed it. It was a harbinger of troubles to come for the president, however.

The news for Republicans wasn't all bad. Owing to shifts in some state legislatures, they actually increased their majority in the Senate by five seats. In Pennsylvania, Thaddeus Stevens was reelected by a large margin, despite Democrats' denunciation of him as "the most pestilent abolitionist that ever disgraced this district." And thanks to the gerrymander, Clement Vallandigham was defeated by Gen. Robert Schenck, a war veteran and antislavery lawyer. The editor of the newspaper in Vallandigham's boyhood hometown of New Lisbon wrote: "That arch-traitor and chief of Copperheads—that pimp of Jeff. Davis and standing disgrace to his state, Clem Vallandigham, is laid out cold and stark in the embrace of political death. He is dead, dead, dead—and a loyal people will bury him so deep in the mire of his own infamy that the stench from his putrid carcass will never offend the nostrils of good men." This was wishful thinking.

Despite his defeat at the polls, Vallandigham spent most of October and November on what resembled a sort of triumphal tour around Ohio and Indiana, proclaiming his unflaggingly fiery message to rally after wildly cheering rally. Even the churches, he charged, had abandoned the doctrines "of Christ and him crucified, and taken up the negro and him glorified." There could be no peace, he said, "until you drive out those who have defiled the temple of the Savior of mankind, and restore the gospel in its purity." Among his followers, his star soared. The ladies of Dayton ceremonially presented him with an elegant gold-headed cane. In other towns, he was pelted with bouquets and floral wreaths. Declared the *Dayton Daily Empire,* he "has obtained the greatest personal and political triumph ever won by any public man in the United States in the face of a storm of abuse, obloquy, slander, and denunciation." From all over the country, antiwar Democrats lauded him as a martyr, advocate for the interests of the white man, voice for oppressed Democrats, defender of free speech, and champion of the Constitution. Some proposed him as a future senator or governor. They were ambitions that Vallandigham quietly, but increasingly optimistically, shared.

# 11

# Folly, Stupidity, and Wickedness

You will not be surprised when you see this
great army melt away with frightful rapidity.

—GEN. CARL SCHURZ

At the end of November, Pitt Fessenden returned to Washington, feeling ill-prepared for the start of the final session of the Thirty-seventh Congress. He suffered from a cold and uncontrollable coughing—"the most severe attack of 'the Fessenden' that I have had in a course of years"—as well as diarrhea and lingering grief over his son Sam's death. He wrote to cousin Lizzy, "I am in hopes that there is a better time coming even in this world, though at times I get pretty much discouraged." Although his spirits were briefly lifted by the arrival of a keg of Malaga grapes, a barrel of bananas, and two quarts of champagne—a Christmas present from a New York financier—the nation's prospects offered nothing to cheer him. To his son William he lamented, "Folly, stupidity, and wickedness rule the hour. I anticipate nothing but disaster. The president gives no signs of improvement. I shall not be surprised at a blow-up in Congress." Given the gloomy outcome of the autumn elections, he feared the balance of power would slip into the hands of the exultant Democrats. "The country has little to hope [for], I fear, from either Mr. Lincoln or his advisors," he ruefully reflected. There was much to be done, and very little time in which to do it during the scant three months that Congress had left.

Congress reassembled in a city that felt increasingly like a vast military base. For much of the autumn, more than a thousand cots had filled the House chamber and the Capitol's Rotunda and corridors with the wounded survivors of Second Bull Run and Antietam. The stench of sickness, filth, excrement, and even livestock quartered inside the building forced U.S. Capitol architect Thomas Walter outside to work in the street. Pennsylvania Avenue's cobblestones racketed beneath the tramp of arriving regiments and the weight of wagons freighted with the munitions of war. Embalmers' establishments advertised themselves to soldiers' bereaved families with mountainous stacks of coffins at curbside. Off-duty soldiers, stragglers, and deserters wandered among legions of shell-shocked veterans and amputees. Cheap eateries, variety theaters, and gambling houses catering to soldiers had sprung up along the sleazy blocks between Pennsylvania Avenue and the stagnant canal. Flocks of gaudy prostitutes dressed in furs and ostrich feathers serviced them in other ways. (Prostitution was no secret: the provost marshal's office compiled official lists of seventy-three "white brothels," and twelve "coloured bawdy houses"; there were doubtless many more.) In the city's hotels, the visiting author Nathaniel Hawthorne remarked, "office-seekers, wire-pullers, inventors, artists, correspondents, long-winded talkers, clerks, contractors, railway directors, state officials, congressmen, lobbyists, generals, and all manner of loafers traded war news, inked contracts, and sipped mint juleps and brandy smash and unadulterated rye whiskey, while enveloped in a constant atmosphere of cigar smoke." Sometimes at night the president's gaunt figure, a gray shawl pulled across his shoulders, might be seen, moving like a shadow on some errand to the War Department or the secretary of state's home, "an apparition as unexpected and as welcome as the sight of the shining dome" of the Capitol.

The city's once bucolic outskirts had frayed into a shabby patchwork of muddy wastelands, forts bristling with cannon, military tent cities, briar patches, the rotting carcasses of dead horses and mules, and hacked-down woodlands. Thousands of penniless contrabands

dressed in pieces of cast-off blue army uniforms crowded into sprawling, disease-ridden encampments thrown together from scrounged
barrels, blankets, and scraps of wood. Huge, newly erected hospitals
were shoehorned everywhere, "like a giant fungus-growth, bursting with mercy and with pain, battening on human blood." Across
the Potomac in Union-occupied Virginia, a booming black market
thrived among soldiers and civilians alike. Sentries on the lookout for
illicit goods found bologna sandwiches stuffed with quinine, kegs of
whiskey hidden beneath cargos of manure, coffins filled with bottled
wine, and canteens of liquor beneath ladies' hooped skirts. An officer detailed to search travelers crossing the Long Bridge remarked
that "as a school for the study of human nature" the bridge might
have been "styled a university [since] what could not be seen anywhere else in the way of subterfuge, double-dealing and duplicity
could be found there." No-man's-land began just beyond the outskirts of Alexandria. There, no one was safe. Confederate guerrillas raided pacifist Quaker and Unionist farms, bushwhacked isolated
Union soldiers, and carried off horses and blacks, both slave and free.

The wracking physical insecurity so close to the capital was an apt
metaphor for the instability of the country. Fessenden was ragged
with anxiety. On December 11, he wrote Lizzy, "I am fearing a great
crash and blow-up, but cannot tell you wherefore." It came two days
later at Fredericksburg, fifty miles south of Washington, on the Rappahannock River, in the form of yet another battlefield disaster.

George McClellan had finally been relieved of command on
November 8 and replaced by the stolid and reluctant Ambrose
Burnside, the thirty-seven-year-old commander of the Ninth Corps.
Burnside, in the words of a contemporary, had "a tall and robust
frame, buoyancy of manner, and a spirit of perpetual elasticity," as
well as a high, prematurely bald dome, and a pair of dramatically
flourishing side whiskers that, ever after, would be known as "side-
burns." His successful operations in coastal North Carolina, in early
1862, remained one of the few clear-cut Union triumphs in the East.
Twice he had declined earlier War Department invitations to take
charge of the Army of the Potomac, explaining with a humility rare
in the upper ranks of the officer corps that he felt incompetent to
command so many men. He finally accepted this third appeal only

when he concluded that he had no right to disobey a direct command by the president. "Poor Burn feels dreadfully, almost crazy—I am sorry for him," McClellan condescendingly wrote to his wife. "They have made a great mistake—alas for my poor country." In the army, there was a widespread feeling that McClellan had been driven out by pressure from Wade and the other Radicals in Congress. There were rumblings of mutiny, even of a possible coup d'état by Little Mac's loyalists, and a march on Washington to "clear out the Abolition crew." Nothing came of this, but a sense of grievance ran deep among McClellan's many supporters in the army.

Burnside assumed command in the midst of an ill-omened snowstorm, with only the barest knowledge of where all his troops were posted. Compelled to come up with a plan, he proposed to move his army of 110,000 men to Fredericksburg, fifty miles south of Washington, to cross the Rappahannock there, outflank the Confederate army, and force it to retreat southward to protect Richmond. It wasn't a bad plan on paper, but it depended on speed, requiring the delivery of hundreds of pontoons that would enable the army to bridge the Rappahannock before the Confederates realized what was happening. Burnside planned for the pontoons to begin arriving within three days: it took them more than three weeks. Torrential rains flooded the rivers, roads turned to muck, orders went astray or were ignored, rations were delivered to the wrong depots, burned bridges and broken rail links slowed troops further. By then, the Confederates had occupied the heights that commanded the city, and dug in. To attack them there, behind abatis, trenches, and stone walls, was at best a high-risk proposition, if not suicidal. Burnside, fixed in his plan, did it anyway.

On December 12, pontoons at last in place, Burnside pushed his army across the Rappahannock. The next day, in a series of head-on assaults, they attacked the six-mile-long Confederate front. William B. Franklin's "grand division," comprising two corps, attacked first on the left, where a division of Pennsylvanians led by Gen. George G. Meade found a hole in the enemy's lines. The West Point–trained Franklin, a McClellan acolyte, was a capable subordinate but an uninspired leader who lacked the initiative to exploit the break-through. Meade's men drove the enemy back half a mile until, out-gunned and unsupported, they were pushed back again while tens of thousands of Franklin's unused troops stood idle. Then, when the battle was already effectively lost, Burnside ordered his right wing forward across an open plain swept by Confederate cannon to assault the enemy's best-fortified positions of all. Regiment after reg-iment, brigade after brigade, division after division of federal troops went bravely forward against intense and concentrated enemy fire. None managed to get closer than 150 feet from the Confederate line. "The grape and canister tore through their ranks, the fearful volleys of musketry from invisible foes decimated their numbers every few moments," recalled a survivor. "The conflict was hopeless."

Telegraphic reports from Fredericksburg reached Washington almost immediately. That evening, Fessenden wrote grimly to Lizzy about the "terrible fighting and slaughter." Still sick, "unable to get my system decently regulated"—he had resorted to dosing himself with "blue pills," a compound of mercury, liquorice root, and con-fection of roses—he struggled to make sense of what had happened. The battle, he concluded, had been a terrible blunder, exacerbated by the lackadaisical actions of politically untrustworthy officers. A few days later, he lamented to his father, Samuel, that the army suf-fered from too many officers who "have no feeling in common with the true cause." Poor Burnside, he allowed, was "a true man," fully committed to the war, but as a general he was yet another failure.

Ordinary soldiers were disgusted. Morale plummeted among the survivors as their hopes of a quick Union victory burned way. They all knew they'd been badly led and badly beaten. Harlan Paige, a Vermonter whose regiment lost over fifty men killed and wounded in what he sarcastically called "the grand squeegee" at Fredericks-burg, wrote home, "We have accomplished nothing. I do not think our leaders performed what they advertised; if they did, the rebel-lion would have been crushed long ere this." Antiwar Democrats accused the administration of trying to conceal the extent of the debacle. "The widow's wail and the orphan's cry has not yet reached the callous hearts of the men who have brought this terrible state of things upon us," cried the Copperhead *Dayton Daily Empire*. The truth demoralized even the war's ardent supporters. The Union Army had lost more than 12,000 men, over 1,200 of them killed, and gained nothing. The Confederates lost 4,200, four hundred of them killed. It was the most lopsided result in any major battle of the war. Civilians, too, knew that the government couldn't afford many more such defeats, if it could afford any at all. "Many loyal citizens like myself, ready & anxious to sustain the government to the utmost [are] almost hopelessly discouraged," an influential member of the Boston Board of Trade, Joseph P. Ropes, wrote to Fessenden. He was but one of many.

In a measure of the power now possessed by the Joint Committee on the Conduct of the War, Ben Wade and several of the other members appeared at Burnside's headquarters less than a week after the battle to determine firsthand what had gone wrong. It was a precarious moment for Wade. His leadership of the committee had dramatically raised his congressional profile. But he also had many enemies in Ohio, who loathed equally his radical politics and his bullish style. His Senate term was due to end in March, and both pro- and antiwar candidates were circling, including, it was rumored, Treasury Secretary Chase, who was said to see the seat as a useful stepping-stone in his widely suspected quest to replace Lincoln as the Republican presidential candidate in 1864. Fessenden, who disliked Wade's bluster but needed his vote, expected his defeat, most likely to the opposition, since the Democrats had just won a majority in the Ohio legislature: "He may have faults, but I shall be very sorry to lose so true a man," he confided to a Senate friend.

However anxious Wade was about his political fate, it did nothing to weaken his resolve to get to the bottom of the Fredericksburg disaster. With fresh graves and the grim detritus of war punctuating the shattered landscape, the committee established itself at Burnside's headquarters across the Rappahannock at Falmouth. In the course of hearings that would later continue in Washington, they interviewed nearly every major officer who had taken part in the battle in an effort to expose incompetence and to fix blame: Why had the pontoons taken so long to arrive? Why did the crossing have to be made at Fredericksburg? Why not at the fords farther upriver? Or the fords downriver? Why didn't the army's leaders realize how formidable the Confederate defenses were? Why weren't troops sent across the river earlier by boat to secure the bridgeheads and the heights when they could have done so at little cost? Why wasn't the Union's superiority in artillery enough to drive the Confederates from their positions? Why had only half the available troops been committed to the battle? Why hadn't Meade's Pennsylvanians been adequately supported when they broke the Confederate line? Why had Burnside fruitlessly continued to hurl men against Confederates protected behind stone walls? These were blunt, even brutal, questions that few officers were eager to answer.

Wade and his colleagues gradually teased out the sorry story. Too many of the pontoons were far up the Potomac near Harpers Ferry and could never have been gotten to Fredericksburg on time: bureaucrats in Washington had failed to take responsibility for them, and Burnside had failed to make the need for them sufficiently clear. Burnside blamed Henry W. Halleck, the army's general-in-chief, and Halleck blamed Montgomery C. Meigs, the quartermaster general. Meigs blamed Burnside for underestimating the amount of labor involved. "Here was an army [the size of] the population of a great city, suddenly to be whipped up to break off from its lines of communication, and be transferred to a new position, and their supplies to be landed from a narrow channel," Meigs exasperatedly told the committee. "[T]o supply them with all the necessaries of life was like undertaking to supply Boston without any previous provision being made."

George Meade, the only field officer who could claim any glory at all from the battle, fairly seethed with anger at William Franklin, who had ordered him forward with too few men, and the fellow generals who had failed to send reinforcements when his foothold in the Confederate lines began to give way. Meade testified that he had repeatedly called for aid, to little effect. Finally he had personally ridden back to the reserves and commandeered an idle division. But it was by then too late. He lost 40 percent of the 4,500 men he had led into battle.

"And if you had held your ground you would have broken their line?" Wade asked.

"Yes, sir." The Confederates, Meade asserted, would undoubtedly have been forced to retreat from their entire line.

Joseph "Fighting Joe" Hooker, Burnside's most aggressive senior officer, who had commanded the center of the army and who had his eye on Burnside's job, testified that his own efforts to pierce the enemy line hadn't been supported either. In his own opinion, he told the committee, Burnside should have thrown all his weight against the Confederates' right flank. But had it been up to him, Hooker declared, he wouldn't even have fought at Fredericksburg—he'd have crossed the river higher up and outflanked the Confederates from the West.

William Franklin, who had presided over Meade's assault, made every effort to shift the blame away from himself. Like his patron and friend George McClellan, Franklin had compiled a sterling record at West Point, but proved weak and indecisive in battle, a reputation that his performance at Fredericksburg did nothing to enhance. "I knew nothing at all about the defenses on the other side; it was not my business to know about them," he testified. "Wherever we appeared we found [that the enemy had] a great many more men than we had." Astonishingly, he claimed not even to have known that his attack mattered in Burnside's battle plan. "At the time I had no idea that it was the main attack, but supposed it was an armed observation to ascertain where the enemy was," he lamely protested.

"Didn't you understand that you were to use all the troops necessary to seize the heights" and to ensure the attack was successful, he was asked.

"No, I did not," Franklin replied. He claimed that Burnside had never told him to use his whole force. In fact, Burnside had told Franklin that Meade's attacking column seemed too small. But Franklin had ignored his orders to put in more men.

It became clear that in the weeks before the Rappahannock crossing repeated miscommunications, Burnside's lax leadership, and ordinary military bureaucracy had made the battle close to unwinnable even before it was fought. Franklin's reputation was left in tatters. Although he would serve in other, marginal theaters of the war, he would never again hold a major command. Only Meade emerged from the hearings with an enhanced reputation and as a man with a future.

Burnside's formerly spotless reputation was damaged, but not yet wholly ruined. Within days after the Fredericksburg debacle, he was making preparations for another attack, this time south of the city. But before he could get the army under way he was suddenly ordered by the War Department to make no further movements, a considerable surprise to him since up to now he had been pressured relentlessly to mount an aggressive campaign. In testimony later published by the Joint Committee, it was revealed that two of his generals—John Newton, a highly regarded Regular Army man, and John Cochrane, a politically well-connected former congressman from New York—had gone directly to the president in a secret campaign to undermine Burnside's leadership. They told Lincoln bluntly that Burnside's new plans would lead to another disaster. Although they claimed to be acting on their own, they had at least the tacit encouragement, if not the active collusion, of William Franklin, the McClellan loyalist whose passivity crippled the Union assault at Fredericksburg. Their aim was clearly an unprecedented attempt to undermine their commanding general. By the time Burnside learned what had happened, the details of his plans were common knowledge throughout the army, and now worthless.

Interviewed by the Joint Committee, Newton said that since Fredericksburg confidence in Burnside had collapsed. "I felt that the very existence of the army was at stake." Asked by Wade if the army would still fight, Newton replied, not with "that rush and impetuosity" that won battles.

Was that feeling a result of the failure at Fredericksburg? Wade asked.

"That was undoubtedly the provoking cause—the starting point."

"What other cause?" asked Wade.

"Troops and officers possess a certain knowledge of character," Newton devastatingly replied. "They see a man under certain circumstances and judge of him."

The insubordination of Newton and Cochrane was a shocking breach of military protocol. Burnside understandably felt that both men should be dismissed forthwith. But his star was already on the wane. Cochrane, the politician, was sidelined, but Newton's career was barely affected. The committee favored Burnside, weighing his unimpeachable commitment to the war effort against his manifest ineptitude. But it was all too apparent that what the generals had told them was merely the truth: the army no longer trusted its commander.

The Fredericksburg defeat sent the North's morale spiraling down to its lowest point yet. There were alarming spikes in resignations among officers and desertions among the men. By January 1863, an estimated 10 percent of the troops on the rolls of the Army of the Potomac had abandoned their units. Carl Schurz, the commander of the Eleventh Corps, warned Lincoln that if such losses continued, "you will not be surprised when you see this great army melt away with frightful rapidity." In the camps on the Rappahannock, pay was months overdue, fresh food was in short supply, and diarrhea was almost universal. Some men lacked proper shoes and trousers, and others couldn't even afford to buy stamps to write home to their families. Benumbed Yankees once again damned the government's "blundering and imbecility."

In the West, Ulysses Grant was maneuvering fruitlessly in the bayous around Vicksburg, Mississippi, the linchpin of the Confederacy's control of the Mississippi River, and a revivified Confederate army was thrusting northward into Tennessee. Meanwhile, financial crisis loomed yet again. The war's cost had again outstripped projections, and the outlook for the coming year was no better. Assuming the war continued, Treasury Secretary Chase estimated that the national debt likely would rise to $1,222,207,203 by July 1 of 1863, and by another $500 million more by July 1, 1864. Even this was no more than conjecture. The Treasury was borrowing at a rate of $30 million a month. "Unexpected military delays," in Chase's words—in reality, defeats—the growing cost of supplies, and flagging confidence had made it much more difficult for banks to dispose of federal bonds "except at ruinous loss." Capitalists feared runaway inflation and were dumping government securities, while specie was virtually unobtainable and rampant speculation in gold rocked the New

York financial market. Gold, which had commanded a premium of 38 percent in October, was at 50 percent by December, and still on the rise. An alarmed Chase confided to Stevens, "It is next to impossible to collect the internal revenue in lawful money of the United States; and I see no ground for belief that the funds necessary for the pay of the army and the prosecution of the war can be in any way provided" without a new infusion of money.

Rumors swirled of upheaval in the beleaguered White House. After Fredericksburg, the congressional Republicans' patience with the administration was at an end. On one thing alone they agreed with the carping Democrats: the North wouldn't stand for another defeat, or for continued incompetence in the government's leadership. Three days after Fredericksburg, the senatorial Republicans, led by Fessenden and Wade, launched what amounted to an attempted political coup. Its immediate aim was the ouster of Secretary of State Seward. Their ultimate, if less bluntly stated, target was to galvanize a president nearly all of them felt was too passive, too disorganized, and too timid to wage the kind of hard war that now must be fought. If they were successful in evicting Seward, the Senate would gain effective control over cabinet and high military appointments, and possibly the president himself.

Seward's radicalism of the 1830s and 1840s had long since dissipated. Although he was a founder of the Republican Party, and had been its leading presidential prospect in 1860, he had become increasingly unpopular among his former congressional colleagues, who regarded him at best as meddling and opportunistic, and at worst as a malign "back-stairs influence" who dominated the president, ignored the rest of the cabinet, and preferred a negotiated peace with the Confederacy to outright victory. Thaddeus Stevens at one point told Seward to his face that he had betrayed the abolitionist faith he had once espoused and charged him with holding Lincoln back from arming blacks. For months now, Treasury Secretary Chase, Fessenden's closest confidant in the cabinet, had been filling his ears with reports of Seward's dark machinations.

On the evening of December 16, the Senate's Republican members huddled in a reception room just outside the Senate chamber. The mood was somber. At least one senator expressed the view that the war was already lost. The less fatalistic majority agreed that Seward, "the source of all difficulties," must be removed. Charles Sumner, the chairman of the Foreign Relations Committee, charged that Seward's diplomacy had drawn ridicule upon himself at home and abroad, and worried that he might agree to British offers to mediate in the war. The impetuous Wade proposed an immediate vote of no confidence in Seward, a censure of Lincoln himself "for placing armies under commanders who did not believe in the policy of the government and had no sympathy with its purposes," and a threat to withhold funds from the administration unless it acquiesced to the Radicals. Fessenden, more cautious, countered that although the Senate had to act decisively to save the country, it must do so with care and unanimity if it was to be effective.

The caucus finally voted to call for a "partial reconstruction" of the cabinet—that is, the eviction of Seward—and approved a paper drawn up by Sen. Jacob Collamer, a Vermont conservative, informing the president of their desire that all important decisions and appointments be approved by the cabinet as a whole, a situation that "does not now exist." The paper further stated—one can surely hear Wade's growl here—that "it is unwise and unsafe to commit the direction, conduct, or execution of any important military operation or separate general command or enterprise in this war to anyone who is not a cordial believer and supporter" in the justice of the war and the urgency of suppressing the rebellion.

Nine senators led by Fessenden and Wade delivered the paper to Lincoln in person. Wade, with characteristic bluntness, told Lincoln that it was his fault that the Republicans had lost the autumn elections, because he had placed "the direction of our military affairs in the hands of bitter and malignant Democrats." Perhaps at the war's outset there had been no alternative but to rely on Regular officers such as McClellan, who shared "the southern feeling," Wade said. But it was now high time that "the war should be conducted by its friends." Fessenden then told the president that as his "constitutional advisors" the Senate had both a right and a duty to provide its "advice" in time of crisis. Too many important measures were being decided—implicitly by Seward and the president alone—without even the cabinet's knowledge, a habit that "could not fail to be attended without evil consequences."

The senators had seriously underestimated the president. On the evening of the 19th, the committee—minus Wade, who had gone to Falmouth to interview Ambrose Burnside—arrived at the White House for a second meeting. Seward, meanwhile, aware of what was afoot, prepared to accept what seemed inevitable and handed Lincoln his resignation. Lincoln, however, was determined to allow no faction to dictate cabinet policy, which, he was convinced, almost certainly correctly, would cause his administration to collapse and set an "evil example" for the future. Having no intention of surrendering Seward, he confronted the senators head-on. To their surprise, they found the entire cabinet assembled to meet them, with the exception of Seward.

Lincoln made himself clear: as far as he was concerned, Seward was entirely "earnest" in his support for the war and hadn't interfered in anyone's business unasked. Calculating that none of his cabinet members would break ranks if they were confronted face-to-face by the senators, he asked them collectively if they felt that they had been adequately consulted. By doing so, he adroitly cornered Chase, who caved, declaring that he "fully and entirely" endorsed the president, and that—this was the opposite of what he had been telling senators—there was no lack of unity at all in the cabinet. (Secretary of War Stanton later told Fessenden, however, that everything the senators had said about the cabinet was in fact true.)

Nevertheless, according to Navy Secretary Welles, the senators once again accused Seward "if not with infidelity, with indifference, with want of sympathy with the country," and virtual control of the president. Lincoln then asked his visitors: "Should Seward resign?" Fessenden, "skillful but a little tart," in Welles's words, said that the senators were not willing to discuss his "demerits" in front of the rest of the cabinet. Lincoln then directed the cabinet members to leave. When they were gone, Fessenden then made what his biographer Robert J. Cook deemed "his boldest move of the evening, indeed of the entire war." He advised Lincoln to accept Seward's resignation, saying, "Mr. Seward lost my confidence before he became secretary of state, and had I been consulted I should not have advised his appointment."

"I had no opportunity to consult you," Lincoln mildly replied.

"No," said Fessenden, but you should have come to Washington first to meet with the Senate. "I am sorry you did not do so. Do you wish us to advise with our fellow senators on the point suggested?" That is, would Lincoln permit them to put Seward's future to a vote in the Republican caucus?

Lincoln, who could easily guess the outcome of this maneuver, replied, "I think not." He feared, he told the senators as they wearily left his office at 1:00 a.m., "a general smash-up" if he let go of Seward.

In the aftermath of the senators' visit, the embarrassed Chase penned his own resignation. Lincoln now had letters from both Seward and Chase. (Welles reported that when Lincoln's "long arm and fingers" reached for it, Chase "held on, seemingly reluctant to part with the letter," but eventually let go of it.) Lincoln relied especially on Seward, though not to the limitless degree the Radicals supposed, and he liked him personally. He was respectful of Chase, the only avowed Radical in the cabinet, but there was no warmth between them. Wrote Welles, "Seward comforts him; Chase he deems a necessity." The resignations stayed in his pocket.

The failed coup strengthened Lincoln in the end, demonstrating his firm command of the cabinet, as well as a stubborn resistance to what he regarded as bullying congressional interference. Although the senators had not succeeded in unseating Seward, much less turning Lincoln into a tool, the very act of trying to get rid of him would be "productive of good," Fessenden wrote to his father the day after the second meeting with the president. In time, Lincoln would be seen to make an effort to consult more with his cabinet. And Seward would eventually, if unenthusiastically, embrace more radical war measures. Fessenden could congratulate himself, though it was not in his blood to do so, that he had masterfully maintained unity in the potentially fractious Republican caucus; he had also managed the delicate challenge of confronting the president without wounding or humiliating him. Wade, more than anyone, was furious at the outcome. However, he could at least draw some satisfaction from

the fact that the president did not withdraw the Emancipation Proclamation, as Wade feared he might. Nor did any more McClellans
rise to command the Army of the Potomac.

Wade was buoyed, a few weeks later, by his own improbable
reelection, a paradoxical result of the antiwar Democrats' victory in
the Ohio polls. Pro-war Democrats in the state legislature loathed
Wade but they swallowed their bile and joined the Republicans to
reseat him before the legislature's new members could elect a Copperhead in his place.

Fessenden bore his tactical defeat with his characteristic stoicism.
But the episode did little to alter his misgivings about Lincoln. "The
country demands success and nothing short of that will appease the
public," he wrote to his son William. And to his father: "Our great
trouble, after all, is not in the cabinet but in the president. He is an
earnest and true man, but lacks dignity, order, and vigor—three terrible defects in times like these."

Meanwhile, with the wind of the recent elections still billowing their
sails, Democrats continued to attack the Republicans with burgeoning self-confidence. After less than two years of war, they tirelessly
reiterated, untold millions of dollars had been squandered, hundreds
of millions more in property had been destroyed, and the national
debt had soared, while new taxes crushed ordinary citizens, a vast
federal bureaucracy fattened on their inflated salaries, and torrents
of runaway slaves threatened to flood the country. "How much longer will the people be willing to have their sons, their husbands, and
their fathers sacrificed, massacred, butchered?" demanded Clement Vallandigham's hometown newspaper, the *Dayton Daily Empire*.
"What prospect is there that the war will be brought to a successful
termination? Not the slightest."

With Christmas approaching, the *Daily Empire* flanked its columns of defeatist war news and nasty accounts of alleged crimes
committed by blacks upon whites with announcements of holiday
concerts by Tyrolese and Swiss singers, and seasonal ads for freshly
arrived oysters "for saloon and family alike," fresh meats—"No bet-

ter slaughtered"—Dr. Roback's Stomach Bitters, "the poor man's friend," and jolly presents for children. Perhaps facetiously, on the same day that it advertised luscious gumdrops, liquorice, jujube bars, rabbit houses, bird cages, birds, toy soldiers, and circus figures at Brandenberg's on Third Street—"Toot! Toot! Toot! Kris-Kinkle is Koming!"—it also printed a bogus report that twenty-four guillotines had been shipped from Europe "for the president to use on Americans."

Vallandigham had returned to Washington girt for renewed combat, assuring a friend, "I am alive and well & and carrying on 'a vigorous prosecution of the war' against abolition." Fired by his swelling support among the angry and the disillusioned, including serving soldiers—"Vallandigham is one of the most cheering signs of the times," wrote one alienated Indiana infantryman—he called again for an immediate end to hostilities. Although he knew he lacked the votes to thwart the Republicans' agenda, he attempted to stall their initiatives by means of parliamentary challenges and a fusillade of resolutions that sought to define much of the Republicans' new legislation as treason. One of his proposals would declare any federal official who attempted to "pervert" the war's purpose to overthrow any state's "established institutions" guilty of a "high crime against the Union and the Constitution." Others defined as a crime any attempt to establish a territorial government within any state, or to propose peace on any terms but the "integrity of the Union." None of these stood a chance of passing, but they served as emotive rallying points for the reinvigorated opposition, and perhaps more importantly as prospective planks for the Democratic Party's 1864 presidential platform.

In his speeches that winter, Vallandigham portrayed himself as a lonely prophet who had long warned Americans of the evils that abolitionism would inexorably wreak upon them. "But the people did not believe me, nor those older and wiser and greater than I," he opined. "They rejected the prophecy and ignored the prophets." Now, "though slander sharpened his tooth [and] falsehood crushed truth to the earth," he proclaimed that he alone had remained unblemished by compromise. "Today I bless God that not the smell of so much as one drop of blood is on my garments," he cried. "Perish office, perish honors, perish life itself; but do the thing that is right, and do it like a man. I did it."

The Confederacy was stronger than ever, he assured his colleagues in the House. Although the war had begun with "fanatic enthusiasm," with seemingly inexhaustible wealth, resources, and credit, "yet victory strangely follows the standards of the foe." The government had "signally, disastrously—I will not say ignominiously— failed to subdue ten millions of 'rebels,'" whose aspirations were, in truth, little different from those of George Washington, who— Vallandigham at this point doubtless gestured theatrically upward toward the portrait mounted over the Speaker's dais—gazed down over the chamber "so sadly upon us, the false, degenerate, and imbecile guardians of the great republic which he founded." And now an honorable if tragically wrongheaded war for the Union had been abandoned for a war to emancipate the Negro. "With what success?" he demanded. "Let the dead at Fredericksburg answer."

# 12

# Men, and More Men

When a nation has a war upon its hands, with
traitors in every state of the Union, mixing up
everywhere—it is not a time to stand upon trifles.

—SEN. WILLIAM PITT FESSENDEN

Lincoln had been a disappointment to abolitionists. They complained that he had failed to end slavery, coddled slave owners, catered to the proslavery demands of the border states, and rebuked military officers such as John C. Frémont who had unilaterally declared emancipation in their areas of control. Such policies, charged Frederick Douglass, were "calculated to shield and protect slavery," while fighting the rebels "with the olive branch." Lincoln had indeed made his priorities clear. As recently as August, he had publicly declared, "If I could save the Union without freeing any slave, I would do it, and if I could save it by freeing all the slaves, I would do it; and if I could save it by freeing some and leaving others alone, I would also do that." In December, William Lloyd Garrison disgustedly scorned the president as "a man so manifestly without moral vision, so unsettled in his policy, so incompetent to lead, so destitute of hearty abhorrence of slavery, [that he] cannot be safely relied on."

As if to prove the justice of Garrison's and Douglass's accusations, in his State of the Union message, on December 1, Lincoln called upon Congress to support a series of constitutional amendments that, far from abolishing slavery, would protect it for decades to come. One would offer federal compensation to every slave state that abolished slavery by January 1, 1900. A second would authorize Congress to appropriate money to colonize freed slaves anywhere outside the United States. A third would guarantee that slaves liberated during the war be recognized as free, and that loyal slave owners be reimbursed for their losses by the United States. Taken altogether, Lincoln claimed, this plan would benefit not only slave owners but also the enslaved, because it would save them "from the vagrant destitution which must largely attend immediate emancipation in localities where their numbers are very great, and assure them that their posterity would be free forever."

Essentially, to the dismay of abolitionists, Lincoln was once again offering to leave it to the individual states to abolish slavery in their own time, at little or no cost to themselves. His plan rested on ideas that, decades earlier, might have forestalled war and peacefully put an end to slavery. The problem was that compensated emancipation had always been a political nonstarter: Southerners had no interest at all in liquidating their human capital. "Colonization," as the deportation of freed slaves was politely called, had long appealed to some Americans who disdained slavery but didn't want to live among blacks. Lincoln presented it now as a sort of magic formula that would discourage Negroes from flooding the North, as many whites feared, because they would supposedly look forward patiently to new homes "in congenial climes, and with people of their own race and blood." This ignored the inconvenient facts that barely any blacks wanted to leave their American homes for uncertain futures in alien lands, and that no countries apart from unstable and ill-governed Haiti and Liberia wanted them. Taken together, the amendments reflected Lincoln's own deeply held beliefs. But they received scarcely a murmur of support in the loyal border states, where he hoped they would be most enthusiastically embraced.

There were those who doubted literally up to the last hour that Lincoln would even issue the Emancipation Proclamation that he had promised back in September after the Union Army's marginal victory at Antietam. Since then, the military situation had deteriorated still further. On January 1, abolitionists gathered in anxious anticipation of the news from Washington, but as the hours passed nothing happened. Although the proclamation was in fact ready by 10:45 a.m., Lincoln had noticed an error in the text, and sent it back to the State Department for correction, while he hosted a New Year's Day reception at the White House. It thus wasn't until mid-afternoon that the document was finally released to the public.

Although couched as an executive fiat, the proclamation rested on long months of legislative groundwork by the Republican Congress. Its language was uninspiring, declaring the freedom only of persons held as slaves in areas in rebellion, and specifically excluding the loyal slave states and areas already occupied by federal troops. Lincoln justified this act of qualified emancipation not with the clarion call to high principle that abolitionists longed for, but rather "as a fit and necessary war measure." Only as an afterthought, it seemed, had the president tacked on a fleeting statement that he believed it to be "an act of justice."

And yet, something momentous had happened. "Whatever may be its immediate results, it changes entirely the relations of the National Government to the institution of slavery," editorialized the *New York Times.* "Hitherto slavery has been under the protection of the Government; henceforth it is under its ban." In Boston, a racially mixed crowd gathered at the Tremont Temple, sang "Blow Ye Trumpet Blow," and cheered a succession of fiery speakers, including Frederick Douglass, who declared that if he could not yet see the abolition of "the curse" he at last "saw the beginning of the end." At Cooper Union in New York, "crowded to suffocation," a celebratory crowd, three-fifths of it black, sang "John Brown's Body" and hymns of praise, and cheered Lincoln, William Lloyd Garrison, and Horace Greeley. Quiet prayer services were held in many black churches. During a reading of the proclamation in Washington, according to a sympathetic newsman, resorting to dialect that even friendly whites commonly used at the time, contrabands were heard to exclaim, "Dat's me—I'm free," and "Dat means dis chile." *The Liberator,* enthusiastically if not quite accurately, pronounced in giant boldface type: "Three Million Slaves Set Free! Glory Hallelujah!"

Wartime emancipation was, in any case, not at all the same thing as permanent abolition. The anti-abolitionist *New York Herald* accurately pointed out, since all wartime proclamations were only temporary they would expire at the termination of hostilities: even if some state abolished slavery today, it could restore it again as soon as the war ended. The proclamation did not destroy the legal right to own slaves anywhere, or make slaves citizens of the United States. "It was," as historian James Oakes aptly put it, "the skeleton, but not the flesh, of a sweeping revision of emancipation policy." If nothing else, it was an official invitation to slaves to drop their tools and flee their masters' plantations for Union lines, and whether Yankee soldiers approved of it or not, it transformed the army to one of liberation.

Even the skeptical Douglass's initial reservations ebbed as he considered the proclamation's implications. Later that winter, speaking at the Shiloh Presbyterian Church in New York, he reflected, "The change in the attitude of the government is vast and startling. We are all liberated by this proclamation. The white man is liberated, the black man is liberated. Every general and every soldier that now goes in good faith to Old Virginia goes there for the very purpose that sent honest John Brown to Harper's Ferry."

There were of course vehement nay-sayers. Inflamed slave-state Unionists and Democrats saw the proclamation as proof of the abolitionist agenda that they had always claimed lurked behind the Republican Party's repeated promises that it would not tamper with slavery where it already existed. In Kentucky, Governor James F. Robinson urged his legislature to reject Lincoln's edict, and declared that "the saddest fact of the Proclamation will be to fire the whole South into one burning mass of inexhaustible hate." Many saw it as evidence of the president's impotence and desperation. In the Senate, Willard Saulsbury of Delaware mocked, "Why not issue another declaring that the eyes of the rebels shall all immediately drop out? They could not then see to fight. Still another that Richmond is taken? They would have no capital." In Copperhead country, where racism ran as deeply as it did in the South, the proclamation gave new fuel to defeatism. "In this war for the negro, under the proclamation, we will take no part," seethed the *Dayton Daily Empire.* "We will wash our hands of all connection with it. Let those who have more love for the negro than the white men, women and children of the South—blood of our blood and bone of our bone—urge on the hell-hounds of war for their destruction."

Vallandigham declared in a flaming proslavery speech to the House of Representatives that the war had by now taught the North a painful but necessary lesson: that the South was neither weak nor corrupted by slavery, but warlike and enduring, and that slavery was actually the source of its greatest strength. The people of the South could never be "whipped back into love and fellowship at the point of the bayonet," nor slavery abolished either by the sword or proclamation, any more than such equally fundamental human institutions as marriage or paternity could be, he said. Echoing John C. Calhoun, the archpriest of proslavery ideology, he asserted that it was in fact slavery that made possible "the absolute equality of the white race everywhere." As an alternative to emancipation and unending war, Vallandigham proposed an immediate armistice and withdrawal of federal troops from the seceded states, followed by the reduction of both Southern and Northern armies to the barest minimum, and the resumption of trade between the sections. The South had already achieved its effective independence; the rebellion had triumphed. So be it. "Better triumph today than ten years hence," he said, when far more blood and treasure had been wasted. In time, he hoped, a peaceful reunion of the two nations might take place, if the North proved its worthiness by adopting Calhoun's principle that the South deserved a constitutional veto over any measure that threatened its essential interests—namely, slavery. Vallandigham's agenda and—though he didn't put it in so many words—the Democratic Party's as it looked forward to the 1864 elections, would thus not just aim to restore the United States to the prewar status quo, but reshape it entirely to ensure that the supremacy of the Slave Power was never again challenged. Vallandigham's speech had laid out the agonizing and unpopular challenges that even the most ardent Republicans realized they would have to face if they were ever to bring the war to a victorious conclusion.

———

The man upon whom much of the session's Republican agenda depended was the nearest there was to Vallandigham's polar opposite in the House: Thaddeus Stevens. Where Vallandigham stood as an unapologetic partisan for racism, weak government, and cramped interpretation of the Constitution, Stevens was an equally ardent apostle of racial equality, constitutional pragmatism, and a national government vigorous enough and flexible enough to lead the nation toward a future that few other Americans yet clearly glimpsed. Stevens was perfectly aware that he was an outlier even among his fellow Republicans. "I have always been a step ahead of the party," he truthfully if not so humbly remarked in a speech to the House that winter. But, he said, "They are coming along behind, and will be up shortly, but they are not up yet." He contemptuously dismissed all talk of restoring the Union "under the Constitution as it was"— the Peace Democrats' mantra—as sheer absurdity. "This Union can never be restored as it was," he scoffed.

Too cavalierly for some, he impatiently dismissed hand-wringing over constitutional concerns that he felt inhibited the war effort. During the continuing debate over war powers that infused the waning weeks of the session, he declared, "You cannot justify nine out of ten of the acts of the government, or of our own acts here, if you consider the Constitution a valid and binding instrument with reference to those in arms in the rebellious states." The Constitution, he said, was obviously "a total nullity" in the seceded states, and the war "must be carried on upon principles wholly independent of it." The proposed admission of Virginia's western, Unionist-controlled counties as the new state of "West Virginia" was a case in point. Some members protested that the Constitution disallowed the division of a state without the approval of its legislature—in this case, that of secessionist Virginia. Contradicting many of his Republican friends, Stevens in principle agreed with them: the creation of West Virginia in this manner certainly would be unconstitutional—in normal times. It was nonsense, however, to suggest that "the traitors in Richmond" would ever consent to their state's division. However, he wholeheartedly supported the newly invented state because it would add another free state to the Union, and because it could be done "under our absolute power which the laws of war give us."

He freely acknowledged the laborious challenge of pushing unpopular legislation past the opposition not just of "disloyal" Copperheads but not infrequently fellow Yankees who feared the consequences of his egalitarian racial policies. In a sharp jab at the conservatives of both parties, he offered a wittily arresting image whose power every Bible-reading American could recognize, of the Hebrews saved from the chariots of Pharaoh's pursuing army. "It seems to me as if the waters were standing on each side until those oppressed people would pass through," he said. "And I have thought that the almighty Power was taking the wheels, one by one, off the chariots of Pharaoh and his host, and I see rising up all around me a thousand tinkers to put them on again, and to help to detain them on the passage."

For a man of seventy, Stevens's workload as chairman of the Ways and Means Committee was prodigious. Quite apart from his responsibility for critical war measures, he was forever half-submerged in the workaday demands for appropriations: allocating $4,000 for stationery and $5,000 for furniture and packing boxes from the clerk of the House; money to hire 120 more clerks for the quartermaster general's office; $25,000 to hire investigators to detect counterfeiting; increased salaries for federal employees down to porters and gardeners, and the "honest, sober, industrious" men who clean the Capitol's toilets. Battalions of businessmen pleaded incessantly with him to protect American exports of perfume . . . to lower taxes on manufactured hoops for barrels and wholesale tobacco . . . to raise them on the importers of refined sugar . . . There was no end to it.

Though many Republicans found Stevens abrasive, none challenged him as floor leader or faulted his pounding determination to force through critical war measures before the session's time elapsed. Most urgent was the need to replenish the army's depleted ranks. Although, on paper, the Union could claim a million men under arms, Stevens doubted that after subtracting losses from combat, sickness, and desertion as many as half that number were actually available to fight. The once mighty flow of volunteers had almost dried up after the frightful bloodletting at Fredericksburg, Antietam, and other battlefields despite generous bounties for enlistment offered by states, cities, and towns. Desertion had become epidemic:

some men left in disgust at the incompetence of their officers, others were repelled by the prospect of emancipation, others went home to support their suffering families. Particularly in the West, sometimes whole regiments deserted. Resistance to the conscription of state militiamen was also spreading. In some areas, Democrats deliberately discouraged men from serving, and even in Stevens's hometown of Lancaster, militia members had avoided voting in the state elections for fear that their names would wind up on the list of draftees. By summer, the two-year enlistments of 300,000 troops would expire, along with the nine-month terms of the men who had been called up after Antietam. Meanwhile, the need for men kept growing as the theaters of war expanded: on the Atlantic coast of the Carolinas, inland from New Orleans, across Tennessee and into northern Alabama, along the Mississippi, and deeper into Virginia. Occupied territory had to be held, railroad lines protected, cities and forts garrisoned. All of it required men, and more men.

Expanded conscription now seemed inescapable. There was growing support for it among businessmen and public officials who resented being constantly asked to contribute to ever-larger bounties for volunteers and substitutes of poorer and poorer quality. "Horse jockeys and negro traders never made a more regular business than did the substitute brokers," complained Gov. Thomas Hicks of Maryland. "The very worst class of men were brought from New York, Philadelphia and Baltimore to the Eastern Shore" to fill out the state's quotas. Boston alone had appropriated $300,000 from the city treasury for bounties, and many other communities, had done the same, starving local budgets. In addition, the War Department disliked the militia system because too many governors declined to enforce it, and because its nine-month restriction on service left too little time for men to be properly trained. Among the general public, however, conscription was almost universally unpopular, conjuring up images of armed soldiers dragging protesting men from their beds and the arms of their weeping wives. Even if the bill passed, Vallandigham said, he dared the government to try to enforce it and "like the destroying angel in Egypt, enter every house for the first-born sons of the people." Americans would never submit, he warned—they would revolt first.

The battlefield slaughter at Antietam, in September 1862, brought home to Northerners the horrific human cost of a war that seemed to have no end in sight.

As the war continued, dramatic debates in Congress drew avid audiences of journalists, women, tourists, soldiers on leave, and sometimes African Americans, who packed the galleries to watch the political combat below.

## RUNNING THE "MACHINE".

*Above:* Democrats, and some Republicans, regarded the creation of a national currency to finance the war effort—known as "greenbacks"—as a potential catastrophe and feared the new paper money would prove worthless.

*Left:* The deceptively boyish financier Jay Cooke, shown in an earlier portrait, proved to be a genius at raising money for the Union war effort.

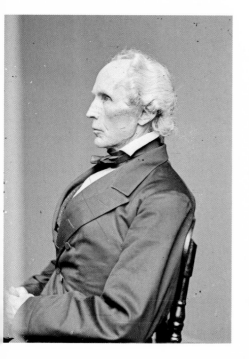

*Above left:* Sen. Garrett Davis of
Kentucky: although a Unionist,
like many border state members of
Congress, he became a bitter opponent
of any legislation that undermined
slavery.

*Above right:* Sen. Willard Saulsbury of
Delaware: regarded by some as the most
handsome man in the Senate, he joined
Garrett Davis in challenging legislation
that infringed on slavery and on the civil
rights of those who opposed the war.

*Right:* Rep. Samuel S. "Sunset" Cox
of Ohio: known for the erudition
and humor of his colorful oratory, as
well as his unadulterated racism, he
became the de facto leader of the anti-
administration Democrats in the House.

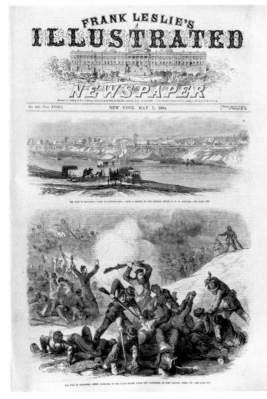

*Above left:* Fugitive slaves seeking freedom flocked to Union lines by the tens of thousands. Some federal officers returned them to their masters, but many others welcomed them and offered protection, such as these Union soldiers dressed in civilian clothes.

*Above right:* Some 170,000 African Americans, most of them former slaves, would eventually serve in the federal forces.

*Left:* In the worst war crime perpetrated on American soil apart from the Indian wars, nearly two hundred black federal soldiers were slaughtered by Confederates under Nathan Bedford Forrest at Fort Pillow in 1864, most after they had surrendered.

DARK ARTILLERY; OR, HOW TO MAKE THE CONTRABANDS USEFUL.

Northern Democrats savagely mocked Republican plans to send blacks into battle.

Black troops repeatedly proved their mettle on the battlefield, most notably at the storming of Fort Wagner in Charleston harbor, in 1863.

In the spring of 1864, Ulysses S. Grant was brought east from the western theater of war to take command of all Union armies. He committed those armies to the kind of relentless campaigns that congressional Radicals had been urging for years.

The Democrats in 1864 nominated Gen. George B. McClellan, a conservative who professed a commitment to continuing the war but hinted that if elected he would ignore the Emancipation Proclamation.

McClellan's running mate was Rep. George Pendleton of Ohio, a Copperhead close to Clement L. Vallandigham. The Democratic platform called for an immediate cease-fire as a prelude to peace.

In hope of winning border state votes in the election of 1864, the Republicans dumped Vice President Hamlin for Andrew Johnson of Tennessee. It was a fateful choice, which ensured that after Lincoln's assassination instead of an abolitionist president the country would be led by an unapologetic racist with little interest in the rights of newly freed African Americans.

Democrats claimed that armed black troops would keep veterans away from the polls. In fact, Lincoln overwhelmingly won the soldier vote, ensuring his reelection.

Members of Congress erupted in cheers and tears at the passage of the Thirteenth Amendment in 1865. It climaxed a process of universal emancipation that was virtually unimaginable before the war.

Rep. James Ashley of Ohio: young, passionate, and skillful in debate, he led the campaign to pass the Thirteenth Amendment in the House of Representatives.

Richmond in ruins. The war is over.

———————

Apart from conscription, there was of course the other untapped source of recruits, ones who would not have to be cajoled and coerced to enlist: Negroes. No wartime issue was more emotive and politically fraught, because the enlistment of blacks threatened to place Negroes on an equal plane with white men for the first time. Alarmed Democrats warned that it might well spark a white rebellion across the Midwest, where racism ran exceptionally strong. They predicted that hundreds of thousands of Union soldiers would throw down their guns in protest. In Congress, Henry May, a Maryland Unionist, pronounced the very notion that blacks could be made into soldiers "delusional," given the "African's" "inert nature, his slovenly habits, his clumsiness, his want of vigilance, and his timidity." And Kentuckian John Crittenden, the most eminent of all border state Unionists, spluttered that blacks had been deemed slaves time immemorial "by the decree of Providence," and to enlist them was both an insult to the army and "a crime against the civilization of the age."

No member of Congress had pressed for the recruitment of blacks more consistently than Stevens. "The arming of the Negroes is the only way left on earth in which these rebels can be exterminated," he told the House yet again, in January 1863, shortly before introducing a bill for the enlistment of 150,000 Negro volunteers, both free men and slaves, with the guarantee that they and their families would remain forever free. Although black troops had already been enlisted in Louisiana and South Carolina, in local initiatives by abolitionist officers, their numbers were small. In line with the Emancipation Proclamation, the War Department now authorized Northern governors to recruit blacks in their states. Some, like Gov. John Andrew of Massachusetts, were ardent antislavery men, others less so: Gov. Samuel J. Kirkwood of Iowa, also a Republican, declared simply that he wanted to see "some dead niggers as well as dead white men."

Stevens could have defended his bill merely as a pragmatic war measure. Instead, he attacked white racism head-on and challenged Congress, and implicitly all Americans, to transcend it. Racism, he implied, lay at the nation's very core. Even supposing that the army could be rebuilt with white volunteers alone, he asked, "is that any argument against employing blacks?" To those who kept reiterating that white soldiers wouldn't fight beside Negroes, he caustically snapped, "It would be a strange taste [in white soldiers] that would prefer, themselves, to face the death-bearing heights of Fredericksburg, and be buried in trenches at the foot of them, than to see it done by colored soldiers." But if there really were soldiers who would throw down their weapons rather than fight with blacks, then, "In God's name, let them go. They are rebels in heart, and ought to be in the Confederate army rather than in ours." He went on to condemn "narrow and selfish" patriotism "which embraces only one's own race, and leaves the other numerous races of mankind to bondage and to misery." But he ruefully acknowledged the era's limitations. "I do not expect to live to see the day when, in this Christian land, merit shall counterbalance the crime of color," he reflected. "True, we propose to give them an equal chance to meet death on the battlefield. The only place where they can find equality is in the grave. There all God's children are equal." On the battlefield that was the House floor, Stevens never doubted the ultimate outcome, however. He knew that few of his colleagues shared his generous sentiments on race, but they all knew that they couldn't afford to turn away 150,000 fresh men.

Stevens was less confident that he could muster a decisive majority for the comprehensive Enrollment bill, which would empower the War Department to call up, by lottery, able-bodied men between the ages of twenty and forty-five, to serve for up to three years. (Draftees were allowed to either furnish a substitute or pay the War Department a commutation fee of $300.) Although the draftees would be assigned to existing regiments designated by state, the draft would be carried out by federal officers, bypassing state officials, thereby creating the country's first true national army.

The bill also established a system of military provost marshals charged with arresting deserters, punishing "treasonable practices," and seizing traitors and enemy spies. The bill further provided that any person who enticed a soldier to desert or concealed a deserter be fined up to $500 and imprisoned for two years, and that anyone who resisted the draft or counseled a draftee to resist it be subject to summary arrest. Popular opposition to the bill would lead, in some localities, to massive resistance, and in a few to rioting and bloodshed. But there was no alternative, if the federal armies were to be kept in the field. Despite rhetorical appeals to the Constitution by both advocates and opponents, the challenges the bill faced were really less legal than political. While Republicans maintained that the Constitution plainly empowered Congress to raise armies, antiwar Democrats insisted that the federal government lacked any constitutional sanction to order national conscription.

What did these "strange, ominous" words "treasonable practices" really mean, demanded Vallandigham—these "cast-off rags filched by this administration from the lumber-house of other, more antiquated despotisms." Apparently they meant that men, women, and even children could now be hauled off to prison for nothing more than the exercise of free speech. "Words, and still less, thoughts or opinions are not acts," he cried. The bill's real purpose could only be the destruction of the remaining opposition to the administration. Where were any constitutional protections to be found in the bill? Nowhere! The Constitution explicitly required the right to a speedy and public trial. Yet no "prisoner of state" had yet been allowed to confront the witnesses who had condemned him, and none had ever been allowed to employ counsel to represent him. Invoking the bronze image of *Freedom* that was soon to be hoisted to the top of the Capitol dome, he declared that it would "stand erect in colossal mockery, while the true spirit, the living Goddess of Liberty, veils her eyes and turns away her face in sorrow." The bill represented yet another fateful step toward "legislative tyranny," which, he said, ought to be no more tolerable to freeborn Americans than Lincoln's despicable executive tyranny. "There is but one further step to take. Put down the peaceable assembling of the people; the right to petition for redress of grievances; the right of the people to keep and bear arms; and finally the right of suffrage and elections, and then these United States, this Republic of ours, will have ceased to exist. Does any man believe that it will end here? The guillotine! The guillotine! The guillotine follows next!"

The root of Vallandigham's charges lay in the suspension of habeas corpus, which had hung like a political sword of Damocles over the war effort ever since the arrest of the Maryland saboteur John Merryman in 1861. Previous attempts to lend congressional approval to the president's actions had repeatedly stalled. Since the beginning of the war, thousands of Confederate sympathizers, Northern dissidents, including newspapermen and lawmakers, as well as ordinary citizens had been arrested for allegedly disloyal activity.

For almost two years, Congress had failed to legislate clear criteria for such arrests and for the treatment of detainees, who by almost any definition were political prisoners. In the absence of law, federal officers were still carrying out arrests that would unarguably be illegal in peacetime, when they would be liable to prosecution for false imprisonment and unwarranted seizures. Demanded Sen. James Bayard of Delaware, how could a government be called free when "you may be arrested by officers unknown to the law, on offenses unknown to the laws, not described, for disloyal practices, which may mean anything that an executive officer pleases?"

Bayard and other Democrats exploited every opportunity to make their case that federal officers were already trampling ruthlessly on civil rights. They cited, for one, Ulysses S. Grant, who in December found himself at the center of a firestorm for summarily expelling all Jews from the entire Department of the Tennessee on twenty-four hours' notice because, he alleged, some Jewish merchants had violated the regulations controlling trade with the army. On January 5, Lazarus Powell of Kentucky—probably motivated less by philo-semitism than by desire to undermine one of the army's rising stars—rose in the Senate to condemn Grant's order as "illegal, cruel, and unjust." Powell asserted that in Paducah alone some thirty Jews—two of whom had even served in the Union Army—and their families had been driven from their homes, even though none of them had been doing business within the army's lines. Although Lincoln promptly countermanded Grant's order, Powell potently argued that it set an ominous precedent at a time when the rights of all citizens were at stake. Grant, he said, "might just as well expel the Baptists, or the Methodists, or the Catholics, as a class." Republicans defended Grant halfheartedly at best. Henry Wilson allowed that although "no man in the Senate approves" of Grant's order, "the rights of these persons have been promptly vindicated, and therefore I think we may let the matter drop." After the matter was tabled by a

vote of thirty to seven, no more was heard of it. But it cast a lingering shadow over both Grant's career and the administration's ongo-
ing treatment of civilians. Politically, John Sherman had warned even
before Grant's anti-Semitic gaffe, "We cannot afford these arrests."

Even Frederick Douglass, who was surpassed by no one in his
encouragement of hard-war policies, called for greater respect
for the liberties he so much wanted extended to black Americans.
Observing that many of the same men who only a few years earlier
had urged the mobbing and lynching of abolitionists for daring to
denounce slavery were now loud in their defense of their own civil
rights, he wrote, "Detestable as are the motives that have brought
them to the defense of free speech, I think they have the right in the
controversy. I do not know where I would limit the right of simple
utterance of opinion. If anyone is base enough to spit upon the grave
of his mother, or to shout for Jefferson Davis, let him, and do not
lock him up for it."

In December, Stevens, working in tandem with Sen. Lyman
Trumbull, proposed an indemnity bill that would shield the president and his agents against future lawsuits for any act they committed during the suspension of habeas corpus. Put another way, this
would retroactively legalize the executive actions of the past two
years as if they had been carried out at the direction of Congress
itself. Although the bill nominally enhanced presidential power, it
also represented an assertion of Congress's determination to wage
the war alongside the president. Stevens whipped the Indemnity bill
through the House at breakneck speed, with debate so truncated
that even some Republicans grumbled. The bill faced stronger head-
winds in the Senate, where no parliamentary mechanism existed for
easily shutting down debate.

Senate Democrats charged that the Republicans were carrying their "doctrine of necessity" intolerably far. "When our fathers
formed the Constitution, they understood what they meant, and
they formed it for war as well as for peace," declared James Bayard,
arguing that mere good intentions couldn't overrule the Constitution. More emotionally, Lazarus Powell proclaimed, "I will trust no
man with my liberties, I care not how wise he may be." A former
governor, the bearded and bearlike Powell had almost been expelled

from the Senate in 1862 for having advocated Kentucky's neutral-
ity at the start of the war. (Of this stolid Democrat, his biographer
wrote with elegant irony, "The placidity of his mind was such as to
foil observers in their attempts to detect the riches concealed in its
depths.") Almost daily, Powell claimed, he received letters from the
wives, children, mothers, and fathers of men who had been thrown
into prison for no reason. "I have gone and demanded of the proper
authorities why certain of my constituents were held, and I can get
no accurate information. I want to know the cause of these arrests,
and I want to know the names of the persons who made the charges.
If they are guilty, I want them punished; if they are innocent, I want
the prison doors opened."

To this, Pitt Fessenden retorted savagely, "I hear a long, low howl"
about political arrests from certain men—Senate courtesy precluded
him from calling out Powell and Bayard by name—who upon closer
inspection looked like "a pack of wolves" more in sympathy with
the rebels than with the Union. In fraught times like these, he added,
sounding much like Thaddeus Stevens, "when no man hardly knows
what or who his neighbor is, and when the country is trembling
upon the verge of ruin" many things had to be done that couldn't
be in ordinary times. "When a nation has a war upon its hands, with
traitors in every state of the Union, mixing up everywhere—it is not
a time to stand upon trifles, or to exact too strict an account of our
rulers."

The pressure on Fessenden was intense. Like Stevens, he was nearly
overwhelmed by unceasing demands on his time—crafting amendments to the Internal Revenue Act, managing recurrent budget-
busting deficiency bills to make up for the rising cost of cavalry
horses, artillery, forage, and military transportation, not to mention civil appropriations bills for virtually everything from coastal
lighthouses to the completion of the Capitol dome. Fessenden was
admired by his colleagues for his tireless attention to detail and intol-
erance for backlogs, but the unending work told on him. At times,
he went without sleep for days on end, fortifying himself as best he
could with his dreams of his garden in faraway Portland and the fra-

grance of its vinery. Worrying letters came at him in a steady stream from alarmed New York and Boston moneymen reporting increasingly wild speculation in U.S. notes and bonds and "imminent disaster" if confidence in the administration sank much further. Inflation was running at nearly 30 percent. Gold, which in mid-January commanded a premium of 54½ in New York, had climbed by the end of the month to 60, and showed no sign of faltering in its upward spiral.

Thanks to Jay Cooke, bond sales continued to surge, but much more money was needed than even his energies could supply. The country's chaotic currency situation further complicated the government's problems. Since the termination of the Second Bank of the United States by Andrew Jackson in the 1830s, Washington had enjoyed little leverage over banking and currency. Across the North, almost fourteen hundred banks operated by dizzyingly diverse systems: some were chartered as corporations, others were based on securities; some were regulated by state banks, and others completely unregulated. The multitude of idiosyncratic currencies they issued—much of it valueless outside a bank's own locality—fostered counterfeiting, bank failures, and an estimated $9 million each year in overall losses. Most Republicans believed that stabilization was desperately needed, and supported the creation of a new centralized system to hold and disburse government funds. "We might as well do without a sun for our solar system, as to allow the present disorderly condition to continue," complained one financier.

The result was a watershed bill that ranks among the Thirty-seventh Congress's most significant pieces of legislation. The National Bank Act proposed a network of federally certified and closely monitored national banks that would serve as the repositories for public money collected by tax and customs officials; in turn, the enormous federal deposits would amplify the banks' lending power, and profits. The bill also authorized the printing of an initial $300 million in national banknotes that would be distributed through the new banks, backed by the credit of the United States and secured by government bonds. This meant that a dollar bill issued in Maine or New Hampshire would for the first time be equally good in Ohio, Kansas, or California. (Someday, John Sherman predicted, with visionary extravagance, American dollars might even become as trustworthy as the notes of the Bank of England and be recognized as a standard medium of exchange all over the world.) The entire system was to be overseen by a new "Comptroller of the Currency," the forerunner of today's Treasurer of the United States.

The prospect of paper money further replacing specie made many Americans uneasy: unlike the earlier issues of legal tender, the new money could not be exchanged for hard coinage in gold and silver. When currency was unmoored from specie, history offered innumerable examples of governments succumbing to the temptation to keep printing money whenever expenses exceeded revenues. The danger of even worse inflation was obvious, but Treasury Secretary Chase considered it a risk worth taking. He felt confident that considering the country's immense reserves of gold and silver in the Far West—in 1862 alone, mines would produce $100 million worth of precious metals—eventually specie payment could be resumed and the nation's debts paid off.

Democrats charged that the government's financial policies were already wrecking the country's credit and that the federal government had no constitutional authority to charter banks, certainly not without the consent of the states. (Chase justified the new system as "auxiliary" to the government's explicit constitutional power to borrow money, collect and disburse taxes, and to regulate commerce.) In the Senate, Garrett Davis of Kentucky sarcastically denounced the bill as no less grandiose than the soaring architecture of the U.S. Capitol itself—unlike the Capitol, however, it was an edifice built on sand, and would soon sink of its own weight to be left a ruin as pathetic as those of ancient Baalbec or Palmyra. Some eastern Republicans also resisted the idea of a national system, which they feared would ruin efficiently operating state-chartered banks in their own states. Jacob Collamer of Vermont, who spoke for such Republican opponents, doubted both the bill's constitutionality and its expediency, and suggested that it smacked of panic, declaring that "to begin a general pecuniary revolution at this time, when there is an armed rebellion in the country, and every nerve should be strained against our enemies, seems to me very inauspicious." Fessenden himself had qualms—Maine's state banks were among the stablest in the country—but he saw little practical alternative. Although he did not lead the campaign for the bill, he declined to impede it, reminding nervous fellow Republicans that, in the sphere of finance, too, "we are obliged to do in times like these what we would not do in times of a different character."

He handed over management of the bill to John Sherman, his right-hand man, the look-alike younger brother of Gen. William Tecumseh Sherman. At thirty-nine, Sherman was seventeen years younger than Fessenden, but he was expert in the arcana of financial policy, and the Mainer's heir apparent should he relinquish the chairmanship of the Finance Committee. (There was backroom speculation—none of it instigated by Fessenden himself—that he might replace Chase or Seward, or even challenge Lincoln for the Republican nomination in 1864.)

Introducing the bill on February 9, Sherman eloquently interwove idealism and pragmatism, cold reason and menace. Without the bill, he threatened, the war would come to a halt, and the North would be overrun by their Confederate enemies. "Every man knows it—that without the issue of paper money it would be impossible to carry on the operations of the government, and there would be nothing to prevent Jeff Davis from encamping within sight of New York City." But the Union's mighty financial resources were virtually infinite, he reassured, if they were only properly harnessed. There was no lack of capital to sustain the war: an estimated $12 billion sat in private hands, begging for investment opportunities—more than enough to carry on the war for years to come. What *was* lacking was confidence, "a want of system," coupled to "a fear that that which the people have will fall suddenly on their hands utterly worthless." Contrary to such fears, Sherman predicted, the bill would not feed speculation but stanch it by bringing stability to the money markets and giving new confidence to investors.

The time had come, he said, to form a new community of interest among banks, their shareholders, the public, and the federal government. Unsupported by private capital, paper money simply could not be maintained in a time of war. The public faith of the nation alone was not sufficient to sustain a paper currency without "a combination between the interests of private individuals and the government. A good national currency as a substitute for gold and silver can only exist by combining the two systems, so that the government may issue notes of uniform tenure properly secured, and the banks shall redeem and maintain their credit." By voting for the bill, he told his colleagues, "You will harmonize these interests so that every stockholder, every mechanic, every laborer who holds one of these notes will be interested in the government—not in a local bank, but in the government of the United States—whose faith and credit and security he will be more anxious to uphold." Furthermore, the new system would undermine the kind of corrosive localism and states' rights ideology that had brought on the war and help to replace it with "a broader and more generous nationality." Strictly speaking, banking reform was not a war measure, despite what Sherman said. Most of its effect would not be felt until after the conflict had ended. However, the bill perfectly summarized the essence of Republican ideology, and its fundamental rationale for the war. "The policy of this country ought to make everything national as far as possible," Sherman said, "to nationalize our country, so that we shall love our country."

If the bill were to be defeated, he warned, the only alternative left to the government would be to print unlimited, unsecured paper money: prices would continue to rise, the expenses of the government would grow, and speculation would careen recklessly beyond control. To lose the bill would be worse than losing a battle.

> In comparison with this, the fate of three million negroes held as slaves in the southern states is utterly insignificant. I would see them slaves for life as their fathers were before them, if only we could maintain our nationality. I would see them free, disenthralled, enfranchised, on their way to the country from which they came, or settled in our own land in a climate to which they are adapted, or transported anywhere else, rather than to see our nationality overthrown. I regard all those questions as entirely subordinate to this. We cannot maintain our nationality unless we establish a sound and stable financial system.

The Bank Act passed the Senate by just two votes, squeaking through thanks to Sherman's persuasion, Chase's lobbying, and Fessenden's tacit agreement. Its margin in the House was almost equally narrow: just six votes out of 142 cast. Nonetheless, its passage was a triumph for the overarching Republican vision of a strong centralized government, and the first great resounding note in the crescendo of legislation that climaxed the last days of the Thirty-seventh Congress.

# 13

# Resistance, Conspiracy, and Martyrdom

You have now broken open my house
and overpowered me by superior force.

—REP. CLEMENT L. VALLANDIGHAM

As always happened at the end of a session, backlogged bills came in a rush, sometimes so quickly that members hardly knew what they were voting for: bills enabling the inhabitants of Nevada and Colorado territories to move toward statehood . . . removing Dakota Indians from their lands in Minnesota . . . approving a treaty with Peru . . . selling off disused military sites in Wisconsin . . . establishing a home for destitute newsboys in Washington . . . chartering a school for "colored youth" in the District of Columbia . . . liquidating Indian lands in California . . . purchasing from the estate of Uriah Levy the former home of Thomas Jefferson at Monticello for conversion into an agricultural school. (One bill that failed sought to reject as a mere "nondescript ornament" the bronze statue of *Freedom* that was supposed to crown the Capitol's new marble dome.)

On more controversial measures, parliamentary trench warfare continued into the early hours of March 3 as the session ground to a rancorous close. Anti-administration Democrats mounted a last-ditch effort to stop the inclusion of black troops in the Enrollment bill instituting the national draft. When that effort failed, they tried, this time with some conservative Republican support, to ensure that no Negroes would be commissioned as officers. "We can make them work to raise corn, pork, and beef to feed our soldiers [but] that is the only sensible use we can put them to," fulminated the Negro-phobic William Richardson, just elected to the Senate by the new Democratic majority in Illinois. But if you put "this inferior race in the army for the purpose of fighting you will lose every battle in which you use them. You cannot make inferiority of intellect fight in the field with superiority of intellect." With the bill amended to stipulate that nothing in it could be construed to authorize any Negro to exercise authority over any white man, and that enlisted men be paid not the $13 a month that whites received but $10, sym-bolically ensuring that Negroes' "inferiority" was enshrined in the law, the bill passed.

Down to the session's very last moments, the Senate wrestled, as they had for almost two years, with the most difficult issue of all: the politically volatile Habeas Corpus Suspension bill, now in the form of a measure known at this point technically—but significantly, it would be seen—as the "report of the Committee of Conference." As the hours ticked away, anti-administration Democrats used every delaying tactic that remained to them to slow, cripple, and if possible kill the bill: repeated quorum calls, roll calls, recounts, and finally a filibuster intended to run out the clock and prevent a conclusive vote. If they succeeded the bill would fail, potentially crippling the admin-istration's efforts to crack down on subversion of the war effort and the seeming spread of armed Copperhead resistance, especially in the Midwest. Both Democrats and Republicans knew that the bill would be hard to resuscitate in the next Congress, when the Republi-cans' House majority would be diminished and public opinion might well be even more opposed than it already was to what many consid-ered government overreach on behalf of a failing war.

Lazarus Powell, the ursine Kentuckian who led the Senate debate for the opposition, warned menacingly that for just "one-tenth" of what Americans had already endured under Republican domination a king of England had once lost his head. Citizens needed protection from federal power, he cried. "There is a point when forbearance ceases to be a virtue." James W. Wall of New Jersey, another Demo-crat vaulted into office after his party swept the state elections in the autumn, attacked the bill in a flamboyant speech that cited, among other erudite references, Shakespeare, Edmund Burke, Thomas Jefferson, the poet William Cowper, ancient Roman history, and the French Reign of Terror. "Let this bill pass," he declared, "and it places the liberty of every citizen in the loyal states at the will of the president of the United States, with no check, no controls, and it reopens the iron-studded doors of the casemates in your bastilles, to be filled by men against whom no accusation has been lodged." Unlike other congressional Democrats, Wall, a Princeton-educated lawyer and editor of the New York *Daily News*, at least knew whereof he spoke. He had been arrested for antiwar agitation in 1861 and incarcerated for two weeks at Fort Lafayette, in New York harbor.

Powell, Wall, and their allies adamantly refused to yield the floor, repeating arguments that they had reiterated for weeks, calling for peace and compromise, denouncing the administration, fending off hostile questions, handing the floor back and forth between themselves hour after hour. As he had many times before, slave-owning James Bayard of Delaware denounced the "lawless" Emancipation Proclamation for destroying the value of the South's slaves, then recognized Powell, who read out lengthy excerpts from the Constitution, condemned military "satraps," and decried Lincoln's "war" against the Constitution as no less evil than the one between the Northern and Southern armies. Sometime around 5:00 a.m. on March 3, in a typical time-wasting ploy, Powell announced that Bayard, who had much more to say, was for the moment "indisposed"—he had likely gone out to the privies on the west slope of Capitol Hill. He requested an adjournment until Bayard returned to "enlighten" the Senate further. The vote was fourteen to four against adjournment, but it revealed the absence of a quorum, which meant that the Senate could no longer continue business. Zachariah Chandler, fully alert despite the hour, called for the yeas and nays, while clerks were sent racing to round up, and wake up, senators still in the building. By the time the roll had been fully called—perhaps with exceptional slowness—the vote was thirty-two to four, including the suddenly no longer "indisposed" Bayard, against adjourning, and the debate went on.

The filibuster continued, now with Bayard holding the floor, claiming that the bill would soon lead to armed resistance if the government attempted to carry it out: "You will drive the people into revolution and resistance!" When Bayard had spent himself, though he remained standing, Powell moved yet again for an adjournment.

What ensued was the subtlest parliamentary maneuver of the session. The Republicans had finally worked out a strategy for ending the filibuster and were waiting for an opportune moment to put it into action. It hinged on the smallest parliamentary technicality but its consequences for the bill, and ultimately for the war effort, were immense. The Democrats were completely blindsided.

James Harlan of Iowa, a Republican stalwart, said that the rules required that when a senator had finished his speech, he must sit down, which Bayard had not done.

"Sit down!" Powell shouted to Bayard. "I'm moving to adjourn."

The flustered Bayard then yielded to Powell.

When the vote was taken, it was found that once again there was no quorum, although those present voted eighteen to four against adjournment.

"It's not necessary to have a quorum to defeat a motion to adjourn," Trumbull said.

"But you can't proceed to do any business if a quorum isn't present," Powell announced triumphantly.

James Grimes, Harlan's fellow Iowa Republican, then moved that the Senate suspend all prior business and proceed to consider an innocuous bill to fund public schools in the District of Columbia.

"I have no objection," Powell said, adding that it was still impossible to conduct business without a quorum.

Without realizing it, Powell had relinquished the floor, in effect terminating the filibuster. The Republicans, who now had the floor, would never give it back.

"Well, I'll withdraw the motion," Grimes said amiably.

Fessenden, who had said nothing else all night, now suddenly called for the yeas and nays on the adjournment.

They were called, and the adjournment was defeated, this time by thirty-three to four.

The presiding officer, Samuel Pomeroy, a Radical Republican from Kansas, then announced, in a voice which, apparently deliberately, could not be heard throughout the chamber, that the question now on the floor was on "concurring to the report of the Committee on Conference," which was, of course, the Habeas Corpus bill, though Pomeroy refrained from reminding the Senate of that. To drowsy and distracted Democrats, it sounded like just another piece of legislative housekeeping. The "report" was quickly approved by a voice vote. Without the Democrats noticing, the Senate had just passed the Habeas Corpus bill. The Republicans raced onward before the opposition could cotton on to what was happening.

Lyman Trumbull then moved that the Senate proceed to the consideration of yet another piece of legislative trivia that had been stalled by greater matters. "It is a bill relating to the validity of deeds of public squares in the city of Washington," he blandly explained. Trumbull's motion was agreed to by voice vote.

What had become of the Habeas Corpus bill? Powell asked.

"It has passed," he was blandly told.

"No, it has not passed," exclaimed the astonished Powell. "I want the yeas and nays on its passage"

"I believe I am entitled to the floor," said Trumbull.

Yes, Pomeroy ruled, the Illinoisan indeed had the floor—and Powell was out of order.

"I should like to know . . ." began the nearly apoplectic Powell.

"I had the floor!" cried Bayard, who was just beginning to grasp what had happened. He protested that he had only yielded it for Powell's motion to adjourn!

Would Trumbull care to yield the floor, Pomeroy politely asked.

"No, sir," Trumbull replied. "He gave up the floor, and I was recognized." When Bayard again protested, Trumbull barked, "The senator is out of order."

Bayard fulminated that nothing could deter him from his rights. He had yielded for nothing but the motion to adjourn, he said, which was standard courtesy, and nothing more.

"The chair did not know for what purpose the senator yielded," Pomeroy declared. He had recognized Trumbull as the first senator on the floor after the vote. He was entitled to the floor unless he chose to yield it.

But he had never heard the chair, Powell protested.

Bayard cried, "I appealed the decision, and I have a right to do that if there are any rights remaining."

Said Wall sourly, "There are none."

The beaten Democrats then watched helplessly as the Republicans brought the session to a close.

The session, in the generous words of weary Republican senator James Doolittle of Wisconsin, was "the most laborious, the most momentous, in our whole history." Its achievements went far to justify such self-congratulatory rhetoric. Few members felt proud of the suspension of habeas corpus, but it was nonetheless a major legislative achievement, and one that had eluded resolution since the beginning of the war. While the Enrollment bill's offensive discrimination against black soldiers disappointed Radicals who wanted more, it was still a political triumph that was virtually unimaginable to anyone but Thaddeus Stevens two years before. Conscription would bring the war home to every American community, but it guaranteed the flow of men that was necessary to continue fighting. The Bank Act and its creation of a national currency would utterly remake America's financial landscape. While the issuing of the Emancipation Proclamation on January 1 was of course an executive act rather than a congressional one, it could not have been put into practice without the foundational support of Republicans in Congress. The proclamation overshadowed another watershed event that took place the same day, one that would also remake the nation in other ways. A few minutes after midnight on January 1, at the federal land office in Nebraska City, Nebraska Territory, a Union Army scout, Daniel Freeman, filed his claim for forty acres of free land under the Homestead Act, the first of 1.6 million homesteaders who would transform the West well into the twentieth century.

"With all its faults and errors, this has been a great and self-sacrificing Congress," wrote Fessenden, whose towering performance, and uncompromising commitment to hard-war policies and the destruction of slavery, had given him one of the most radical voting records in the Senate, behind only Wade, Sumner, and Wilson— a remarkable evolution for a man who still liked to think of himself as a cautious conservative. "If the rebellion should be crushed, Congress will have crushed it. We have assumed terrible responsibilities, placed powers in the hands of the government possessed by none other on earth short of a despotism, borne contumely and reproach, taken the sins of others upon ourselves and forborne deserved punishment of flagrant offenses for the public good, and suffered abuse for our forbearance. Well, future times will comprehend our motives and all we have done and suffered." The session over, the Thirty-seventh Congress having reached its end, he could at last go home to Portland.

Ben Wade hardly noticed the session's end and the departure of his fellow senators and congressmen for their homes. He did his best to ignore the endless nattering of office seekers and constituents begging appointments as provost marshals, conscription administrators, army and naval officers, camp sutlers, postmasters, and promotions—an artillery captain offering to "organize contrabands at any point or place where I can do the most good," an Ohio Republican pleading for a shipment of pro-administration campaign literature "as we are unfortunately represented by a *thing*"—Clement Vallandigham—"who never sends anything but Secesh documents." He toiled on with heroic concentration, his brawny figure bent over towering heaps of foolscap notes and War Department correspondence, writing the monumental volumes that comprised the report of the Joint Committee on the Conduct of the War.

The committee's initial report culminated sixteen months of exhaustive work and encompassed the firsthand testimony of nearly two hundred officers. The United States, he wrote magisterially in his introduction, was engaged in a struggle for its very existence. "Upon the 'conduct of the present war' depended the issue of the experiment inaugurated by our fathers, after so much expenditure of blood and treasure—the establishment of a nation founded upon the capacity of man for self-government." Innumerable subjects— the movement of armies, the competence of commanders, weaponry, logistics—demanded its attention, any one of which alone might have absorbed the complete attention of Congress by itself.

The committee had therefore set as its primary focus the reasons for "the delay and inaction" that had plagued the federal armies, most particularly the Army of the Potomac, which, Wade said, had been treated as an object of special care and high expectation by every department of the government. (Although he didn't say so, the committee also focused on the Army of the Potomac for the more practical reason that its main theater of operations lay only a few hours' travel by buggy or steamship from Washington.) In any case, they saw the experience of that great but chronically frustrated army as a microcosm of the entire Union war effort.

Wade delivered the good news first. When the season of secession began, the army was puny and demoralized, and the navy's ships were scattered around the world. "There was treason in the executive mansion, treason in the cabinet, treason in the Senate and the House of Representatives, treason in the army and the navy, treason in every department, bureau, and office connected with the government," he wrote. Since then, Union forces had seized most of the Confederacy's Atlantic coastline, captured New Orleans, opened much of the Mississippi River, secured the border states, and occupied parts of Tennessee, Mississippi, Louisiana, North Carolina, and Virginia. If only the Army of the Potomac had matched this success, he went on, the war would already be over. The verdict he delivered was a harsh one: "Had that army fulfilled all that a generous and confiding people were justified in expecting from it, this rebellion had long since been crushed," he wrote. "The failure of that army to fulfil those expectations has prolonged this contest to the present time, with all its expenditure of life and treasure, for it has to a great extent neutralized, if not entirely destroyed, the legitimate fruits which would otherwise have been reaped from our glorious victories in the West."

Wade handed over the manuscript to the Government Printing Office on April 14. The first volume was published one week later, and the two others a few weeks after that. The report caused an immediate sensation when excerpts were published in newspapers around the country. For the first time in the nation's history, the American public was permitted to see more or less the entire machinery of war-making revealed. Clocking in at 754 pages, Volume One presented an almost minutely detailed exposé of George McClellan's tragic penchant for wringing failure from the promise of imminent victory.

The committee's fixation on McClellan might seem like vengeful overkill, as it indeed did to Little Mac's many friends. Pro-McClellan sentiment still ran strong in the spring of 1863, especially after the Fredericksburg fiasco. His shortcomings and outright failures on the battlefield were not yet as clear to Americans as they would later become. For at least some soldiers his charisma remained undimmed. "Ask the soldiers of the Army of the Potomac where their confidence is [and] their answer will be, 'In God and McClellan,'" wrote home Vermont Brigade infantryman Harlan Paige. "Give us little Mack again is all I ask, and that is the cry generally among soldiers here." Well aware of such feelings, the congressional Radicals worried, with some reason, that pressure from the emboldened Democrats could lead to McClellan's restoration and a repeat of his failures.

Combining copious documentation from the War Department with extensive testimony by McClellan's peers, rivals, friends, allies, and subordinates, the report chronicled in painful detail the months of inaction during the autumn and winter of 1861. "Every energy of the government and all the resources of a generous and patient people were freely and lavishly placed at the disposal of General McClellan," in expectation that he would move speedily and decisively against the rebels, Wade wrote. But it amounted to largely wasted effort and squandered opportunity. Copious testimony underscored the "Little Napoleon's" chronic aversion to aggressive action, his secretiveness, his conceited self-promotion, his obsessive inflation of Confederate numbers, and his ineptitude when he was finally prodded to battle.

Volumes Two and Three of the committee's report incorporated sixteen separate investigations great and small: the mismanagement of the army at the first battle of Bull Run, alleged Confederate atrocities, the battle between the *Monitor* and the *Merrimack,* convalescent camps, trade in military districts, the functioning of the Paymaster's Department, fraud in the procurement of supplies for the army, the protection of rebel property, the return of fugitive slaves, and other subjects. Particularly significant sections largely absolved

Ambrose Burnside of culpability for the defeat at Fredericksburg, instead charging Franklin and other McClellan allies with responsibility, evaluated (rather too generously) John C. Frémont's tenure as commander of the Western Department in 1861, and blamed the cruel defeat at Ball's Bluff primarily on McClellan. Gloated Zachariah Chandler, "McClellan is as dead as a herring."

To the committee's credit, the report also bared members' own shortcomings. In January 1862, for instance, Wade had wrongheadedly (and ineffectually) advised the War Department to stop forming cavalry regiments because he overoptimistically supposed that no more would be needed since, like many at the time, he couldn't believe that the war would really last as long as it now had. (Having raised a cavalry regiment himself, he also considered them to be a budget-straining expense.) On display as well was Wade's sometimes naive approach to military strategy, which chronically praised élan over tactical skill. Nevertheless, the report served notice that the committee's demolition of McClellan could be visited upon any general who failed to wage war without sufficient aggressiveness. "Let no officers be placed or kept in command of such men who have not the ability to command and the will to do," Wade wrote. "Thus the errors and mistakes of the past will be avoided in the future, the fond hopes and anticipations of a true and loyal people realized, the government vindicated, and rebellion speedily and forever crushed."

Wade had barely returned home to Jefferson, Ohio, when he received the unwelcome news that yet another defeat had befallen the Army of the Potomac. At the beginning of May, Burnside's swaggering replacement "Fighting Joe" Hooker, a favorite of the Radicals, had crossed the Rappahannock with 117,000 men, boasting that he would drive the Confederates back against Richmond. He collided with Robert E. Lee's Army of Northern Virginia in the tangled forested country west of Fredericksburg known as the Wilderness. Lee, in one of the most daring feats of the war, split his 60,000-man force and sent a portion of it under Stonewall Jackson marching virtually across the front of Hooker's army through dense woods to attack the federals at their most vulnerable point. Caught completely by surprise, Hooker's entire right flank disintegrated in a stampede of men, horses, and careening cannon. Hooker himself, paralyzed by a concussion and indecision, succeeded only in preventing a complete rout, and retreated north humiliated and chastened. "Lost, lost, all is lost!" Charles Sumner disconsolately exclaimed to Gideon Welles when he heard the news. Northerners tried to convince each other, as they did after many defeats, that the South must have suffered heavier losses than they did, but it wasn't the truth. The federal army lost 17,000 men, killed, wounded, and missing; the Confederates a few more than 13,000, including Stonewall Jackson, who was accidentally shot dead by his own men.

Wade raced back to Washington in an effort to at least control the political damage. With Chandler, Henry Wilson, and the evangelical senator James Doolittle of Wisconsin, who blamed Hooker's defeat on his lack of religious faith, Wade hurried to Falmouth, in Virginia, to appraise the condition of the army. Dismayed as they were, they agreed that criticizing Hooker would only play into the hands of McClellan, whose partisans were already calling for his reinstatement. Returning to the capital, Wade managed at least temporarily to defang the opposition to Hooker by offering his blustery support. Lincoln, too, was still determined to hold on to Hooker, and fended off pressure for his replacement. But events soon outran Hooker's rehabilitation campaign. Scarcely had the blood dried on the ravaged red earth around Chancellorsville when Robert E. Lee, with an infusion of fresh troops and reinvigorated spirits, was once again on the march, headed north.

The defeat at Chancellorsville, coming on top of disappointing reports from Grant's stalled campaign against Vicksburg, lent new vigor to the antiwar movement, and to Clement Vallandigham's prospects. While Wade sweated over the Joint Committee's report, Vallandigham had traveled back to Ohio in a sort of royal progress, greeted everywhere by cheering crowds of well-wishers who reassured him that although he had lost his seat in Congress he was still a power to be reckoned with. In Philadelphia, he disingenuously assured a huge rally that he had always supported the Union and only differed from the administration on the method of preserving it. In New York City, he told a different story, accusing the administration of initiating a "reign of terror," and hinting at revolution if the Republicans dared tamper any further with the freedoms of speech and assembly. In Albany, he was met by brass bands and saluted as "a faithful sentinel upon the watchtower of public liberty." Upon his arrival home in Dayton, the *Daily Empire* crowed, "He has passed through the furnace of persecution unscathed, with not even the smell of fire upon his garments."

Many Republicans believed without actual evidence that Vallandigham was at least implicated if not leading a well-organized Copperhead conspiracy that was bent on sabotaging the war effort, thwarting the draft, and fomenting armed rebellion. In the absence of reliable information, spreading paranoia tended to see deliberate subversion behind almost anything from declining enlistments and local acts of antiwar protest, to provocative speech that had always come under the protection of the First Amendment. Mass desertion was in fact encouraged and in some cases actively abetted by Copperheads as well as by disillusioned family members. In December 1862, military authorities in Indiana alone were arresting an average of four hundred deserters a week, doubtless just a fraction of the total. Especially after the Democrats won control of the Indiana and Illinois state legislatures in 1862, there was a spike in talk of creating a "Northwestern Confederacy," an idea that Vallandigham had long, if ambiguously, hinted at. Indiana governor Oliver P. Morton, a staunch Republican, was sufficiently spooked that he warned that if the war effort failed, several western states might well secede and join the Confederacy, setting off a new civil war. (When Democrats in the state legislature attempted to strip Morton of his executive powers he ordered soldiers to surround the statehouse, while Republican members bolted in order to deny the Democrats a quorum; for the rest of the war Morton governed without the legislature, as a quasi-dictator.)

By mid-1863, violent resistance was virtually epidemic across wide swaths of Ohio, Indiana, and Illinois, and in some areas of Pennsylvania, Michigan, and Wisconsin. Just outside Indianapolis armed horsemen fought a pitched battle with soldiers sent to recapture deserters. In Union County, Illinois, gunmen shot dead a federal provost marshal and wounded another. (By the end of the war, thirty-eight provost marshal agents had been murdered in the line of duty, and another sixty wounded.) In Brown County, Indiana, a Copperhead state senator killed a cavalry trooper who was attempting to arrest deserters and was spirited away by a mob hundreds strong. Elsewhere, armed men seized draft records, held mass meetings where they cheered Vallandigham and Jefferson Davis, and drilled openly with draft resisters and deserters. The coercion was not entirely one-sided. In some counties Unionists bullied their antiwar neighbors, and in March, irate soldiers from Camp Chase, just outside Columbus, destroyed the office of *The Crisis,* Ohio's leading Copperhead newspaper. "It was a secesh paper and aided the rebels and as such should be put down," shrugged Samuel Trescott, who participated in the sack. And in Kentucky, the state Democratic convention meeting in Frankfort was forcibly dispersed by the military, and its members threatened with arrest if they attempted to reassemble.

It was into this climate that Vallandigham arrived home to find Ohio, Indiana, Illinois, and Kentucky organized into a new military district under the command of Ambrose Burnside. Burnside's brief was twofold: to plan an invasion of eastern Tennessee to relieve the beleaguered Unionist population there, and to crush draft resistance. He issued three draconian edicts to be enforced by the military authorities: one barred the public from bearing arms; the second banned criticism of the administration's policies by either newspapers or public speakers; and the third, the soon to be infamous General Order No. 38, threatened a death sentence for anyone deemed guilty of proclaiming support, offering aid to or communicating secretly with the enemy, or carrying out "treason, expressed or implied." These weren't toothless edicts. Spies and journalists felt their sting. Two alleged Confederate recruiters were condemned to death by a Cincinnati court-martial, while the *Cincinnati Enquirer* was subjected to censorship, the *Chicago Times* suppressed, and circulation of the *New York World* banned in the district.

Burnside's orders were a burst of political adrenaline to Vallandigham. He began denouncing them almost as soon as he stepped off the train in Dayton, in speech after speech. On May 1, at the town of Mount Vernon, at a mass meeting attended by thousands of Democrats—many of them sporting Copperhead pins, flags, and banners—he stridently denounced the surrender of American liberties and the conversion of the government into a despotism. He said little that he hadn't said publicly before: that the war was being waged "for the liberation of the blacks and the enslavement of the whites," that the administration was bent on suppressing free speech, that he "spit" and "trampled" on General Order No. 38. But this time there was an army captain in civilian clothes taking notes. The officer, J. M. Cutts, reported that Vallandigham had explicitly invited his listeners to resist the order, "all of which opinions and sentiments he well knew did aid, comfort and encourage those in arms against the government."

Three days later, Vallandigham was asleep at his home in downtown Dayton when, at 2:30 a.m., he was awakened by pounding on the front door. Flinging open the shutters, he saw scores of soldiers filling the gas-lit street below. An officer called on him to come down and surrender. Vallandigham refused, loudly proclaiming to a rapidly swelling crowd that Burnside's order to arrest him was illegal. He shouted for the police as the household's women—Vallandigham's wife, sister-in-law, and two servants—alternately wept and shrieked as the soldiers chopped their way through the front door and then the bedroom door with axes. At this point, clinging to his wife and small son, he announced, "You have now broken open my house and overpowered me by superior force, and I am obliged to surrender."

The soldiers marched Vallandigham to the railway depot, where a special train with its steam up waited and escorted him to Cincinnati, to join some two hundred other political prisoners already incarcerated at Kemper Barracks. There he became such an attraction that gawkers offered his guards up to $10 for a peep at him; reported one guard, "Unless their eyes, however, are more acute than mine, they would have seen nothing at all remarkable in his appearance, only that he looked decidedly crest-fellen, and that he has a very large mouth." Vallandigham's was not the only arrest of a dissident public figure during the war, but it was far and away the most widely publicized.

By daylight, news of Vallandigham's arrest had raced through Dayton and the surrounding countryside. Fire bells rang. Street corner orators whipped up mobs with bitter threats against the government. "VALLANDIGHAM KIDNAPPED," blared the *Day-*

*ton Daily Empire.* "A Dastardly Outrage!!" The time had come, the paper declared, to decide "whether we are to remain free or bare our necks to the despot's heel," and predicted massive bloodshed before that question was answered. A mob armed with pistols and bowie knives attacked the office of the local Republican newspaper, the *Dayton Daily Journal,* breaking up everything it could lay hands on— furniture, type, newsprint, presses—then set fire to the building, which quickly burned through a full city block. Only with difficulty did Democratic leaders prevent the mob from lynching prominent Republicans and burning their homes. Other rioters split off to cut telegraph wires and tear up the railroad tracks into town, but they didn't manage to succeed in time to prevent the arrival of federal troops from Columbus and Cincinnati. The soldiers drove the mobs off the streets at bayonet point and, with the city now under martial law, arrested forty-five citizens and marched them off to jail.

Crestfallen Vallandigham may have been, but he immediately turned his arrest to political advantage. Heretofore he could only claim to be a martyr to free speech: now he really was one. On May 5, he smuggled out a letter addressed to "the Democrats of Ohio." In it he declared, "I am here in a military bastille for no other offense than my political opinions, and the defense of them and of the rights of the people, and of your constitutional liberties. I am a Democrat— for Constitution, for law, for the Union, for liberty—this is my only 'crime.'" The next day, he was brought before an eight-member military commission and formally charged with "declaring disloyal sentiments and opinions, with the object and purpose of weakening the power of the government in its efforts to suppress an unlawful rebellion."

The trial, such as it was, quickly became an embarrassment for the administration. Vallandigham knew that the transcript would become public and he exploited his predicament for maximum political effect. Although the trial provided the appearance of due process, the outcome seemed predetermined. He was nominally represented by two nationally known Democrats, former senator George Pugh of Ohio and Rep. George Pendleton of Indiana, but they were not permitted to join him in the courtroom. A skilled lawyer in his own right, Vallandigham grandiloquently denied the commission any authority to try him and refused to enter a plea, forcing the court to enter a plea of not guilty on his behalf. Allowed to cross-examine Captain Cutts, the government's key witness, Vallandigham claimed that in his speech at Mount Vernon he had merely defended civilian courts over military ones, and had advocated peaceful compromise, a position held by countless Northerners. And if he had called the war one for abolition, wasn't that simply a statement of fact based on the Emancipation Proclamation? He protested that he had never counseled "resistance to law or lawful authority," or urged anyone to change the government except at the ballot box.

After three hours of deliberation, the commission, as expected, pronounced Vallandigham guilty of the charges, and sentenced him to imprisonment for the duration of the war. Pugh immediately applied for a writ of habeas corpus to federal district judge Humphrey Leavitt, a Democrat and Buchanan appointee Vallandigham had recommended for the office. If Vallandigham thought that he had an ally in the judge, he was sorely mistaken. Leavitt's ruling was uncompromising. "When the life of the Republic is imperiled, he mistakes his duty and obligation as a patriot, who is not willing to concede to the Constitution such a capacity of adaption to circumstances as may be necessary to meet a great emergency, and save the nation from hopeless ruin. Self-preservation is a paramount law." Condemning "artful politicians" who disguised treason under hollow pretensions of loyalty to the Union, Leavitt continued, Burnside had judged that the emergency required Vallandigham's seizure; whether the general acted wisely or discreetly was not a subject for review by the court.

Vallandigham's arrest brought to a head both the immediate question of the suspension of habeas corpus, and the broader one of whether any suppression of dissent could be justified. It also made clear that strong-arm repression was likely to put further strain on the alliance between Republicans and pro-war Democrats. Virtually the entire Democratic press was erupting with volcanic rage, while mass meetings from Vermont to Wisconsin denounced Vallandigham's arrest, trial, and the tyranny of military rule. In New York City, a large public meeting adopted resolutions demanding an end to the war and denounced as "monstrous in theory and execrable in practice" the trial of any citizens by military courts. "The blow struck" at Vallandigham, declared the organizers of a tumultuous gathering in Albany, was "aimed at the rights of every citizen of the North." In a public statement, New York's Democratic antiwar governor Horatio Seymour further charged that the proceedings against Vallandigham were "not merely a step towards revolution, it is revolution." Vallandigham's arrest even gave some Republicans pause. "The proceedings were arbitrary and injudicious," Navy Secretary Gideon Welles reflected in his diary. "Good men, who wish to support the administration, find it difficult to defend these acts." In defense of the administration's actions, Abraham Lincoln maintained that the arrests of Vallandigham and others like him were made less for what they *had* done than "for probably would be done." Had Robert E. Lee and other Southern officers in the United States Army in 1861 been seized and detained then, he argued, the Confederate cause would have been crippled. Vallandigham, wrote Lincoln, "was warring upon the military," adding in words that resonated powerfully among the Northern public, "Must I shoot a simple-minded soldier-boy who deserts, while I must not touch a hair of a wily agitator who induces him to desert?"

All the same, Lincoln realized that Burnside had gone too far. Imprisoning Vallandigham would only inflate his martyrdom and serve the antiwar Democrats' political agenda. However, he hesitated to undermine Burnside, who had been trying, however clumsily, to carry out the administration's orders. Faced with this Solomonic dilemma, three days after the trial Lincoln opted to expel Vallandigham to the Confederacy. (Vallandigham was not the first prominent figure to be deported. Earlier in May, among others, Thomas K. Robson, the editor of a "mischievous" newspaper in Maryland, had been summarily expelled for the remainder of the war "among rebels in arms whose cause and course he so manifestly prefers.")

On May 22, the erstwhile congressman was placed on a federal gunboat and dispatched southward. In a letter to Ohio Democrats written that day, histrionic as ever, Vallandigham declared that he went into exile "not of my own will but by the compulsion of an arbitrary and tyrannic power which I cannot resist." In another letter, to Horatio Seymour, he ventured that his expulsion amounted to an act of "desperation" on the administration's part and enthused that the entire fiasco had "reserved the best possible issue for us"— the protection of civil rights. After remaining a few hours at Louisville, a military train then carried him to Murfreesboro, Tennessee. At 2:00 a.m. on the morning of the 25th, he was roused from his bed and escorted by a detachment of cavalry twelve miles across no-man's-land to the Confederate lines. (The order for his transit was written by James A. Garfield, the future president, then a major general serving in Tennessee with Rosecrans's Army of the Cumberland.) After several hours of waiting—"They were hours of solitude, but calmly spent—the bright sun shining in the clear sky above me, and faith in God and the future burning in my heart," Vallandigham later wrote—a message from Gen. Braxton Bragg directed that he be brought to Confederate headquarters at Shelbyville, where he was billeted in the home of a thrilled local admirer who unsettled him by professing that she had been expecting him to defect to the Confederacy since the beginning of the war.

Bragg ceremoniously congratulated Vallandigham on his arrival "in our land of liberty, where you will find the freedom of speech and conscience secured to all." But in truth his hosts didn't know what to do with him. Although his Northern enemies assailed him as a rebel at heart, the Confederate authorities officially regarded him only as a private citizen who had been exiled by a "foreign government." Moreover, Vallandigham was of no use to the South as an exile, but of immense value to it as a gadfly undermining federal morale in the North. As Robert E. Lee later wrote to Confederate president Davis, "It is plain to my understanding that everything that will tend to repress the war feeling in the federal States will enure to our benefit."

Vallandigham, for his own part, had no desire to remain in the Confederacy, which would only lend plausibility to his enemies' accusations—which of course was Lincoln's intention. He feared being murdered by federal soldiers if he went back to the United States, but he also knew that he had no political future except in the North, where he was confident that the Democrats would continue to build on their victories in the 1862 elections. His plight was finally solved by Davis, who on June 2 ordered the Confederacy's problematic guest to be escorted to Wilmington, North Carolina, where he could board a blockade runner bound for neutral British territory. En route to Wilmington, Vallandigham stopped in Lynchburg, Virginia, to confer with a Confederate official, Col. Robert Ould, whom he assured that if the Confederacy could just hold out for another year the antiwar Democrats would drive the Republicans from power and bring about a peaceful settlement. Despite his sojourn in the Confederacy, Vallandigham seemed not to grasp that the South was no longer interested in formulas of reunion but determined to win its independence on the battlefield. He had staked his entire wartime career on his belief that the prewar Union could be restored as it was, and he was unwilling even now to allow reality to intrude.

Meanwhile, back in Ohio, "Vallandigham fever" swept the Democratic state convention that met in Columbus on June 11, the largest ever seen. Boys hawked his pictures in hotel lobbies and taverns, while despite pelting rain impromptu pro-Vallandigham speeches were made all over town and from three different platforms erected on the grounds of the towering statehouse. When his name was put into nomination for governor, it was ratified by near-acclamation with a vote of 411 to 13. Days later, on the evening of June 17, Vallandigham successfully ran the Union blockade aboard the *Cornubia*, along with a cargo of contraband and several Confederate agents. Still wearing the same rumpled clothes he had thrown on during his arrest, he arrived three days later at British-governed Bermuda, where he transferred to a ship bound for Halifax, Nova Scotia. Although Canada had banned slavery in the late eighteenth century and provided asylum to thousands of fugitive slaves, Canadians were deeply suspicious of Yankee designs on their territory. Americans had invaded Canada in 1775 and 1813, and there was significant concern both north of the border and in London—Canada was of course still governed by Britain—that Union forces might attempt to annex all of Canada after the Civil War. Canadian businessmen invested liberally in Confederate blockade runners, and draft dodgers found safe haven there alongside the refugee slaves.

From Halifax, Vallandigham continued on to Montreal and then up the St. Lawrence River to Niagara Falls, which he reached on

July 15, to be joyfully greeted by his Copperhead friend Rep. Daniel Voorhees of Indiana, and a delegation of supporters from Dayton. The next day, in an open letter, he formally accepted his nomination for governor. The nomination, he declared, "was an act of courage worthy of the heroic ages of the world," and a rebuke to "the usurping tyrants who, having broken up the Union, would now strike down the Constitution." The choice was clear: upon one side liberty and peace, and on the other despotism. If the war were to be allowed to continue, he prophesied, "the infant of today will not live to see the end of it." His southern odyssey had only strengthened his conviction that the Confederacy could never be defeated.

# 14

# Dire Warnings

——————————

We may have to acknowledge, before
this war closes, that it was closed by the
negro to a very considerable extent.

—SEN. JAMES LANE

Dust blossomed in suffocating clouds along the pitted roads of the Potomac Valley beneath the shuffling boots of the Army of the Potomac as it trailed Lee's elusive army northward day after sultry day. Screened by his cavalry and the Blue Ridge Mountains, his 70,000 men thrust boldly across Maryland, hoping to crush Union morale and win recognition of the Confederacy from the European powers by proving that the Union couldn't even defend its own heartland. Panic once again percolated through the capital. Lincoln called out 100,000 militia from Pennsylvania, Maryland, and Ohio, in an effort to protect Harrisburg and Baltimore. McClellan's partisans begged for his reappointment. Hooker's mismanagement at Chancellorsville had now alienated almost everyone who mattered.

On June 26, one of Lee's columns, under Gen. Jubal Early, barely missed capturing Thaddeus Stevens, who had been inspecting the ironworks that he owned near Shippensburg. Instead, they looted and destroyed everything they could lay their hands on, seizing stocks of bar iron, horses, carriages, mules, eighty tons of fodder, and tons of provisions, including four thousand pounds of bacon. What they couldn't carry they destroyed, from fence rails, to the windows of his workers' homes, bellows for the furnaces, and burned the forges, rolling mill, and saw mill. Stevens estimated his losses at between $65,000 and $75,000, an astronomical sum. (For a time, he thought he might have to resign from Congress and return to lawyering to make up his losses and pay his debts.) However, to his cousin Simon Stevens he wrote, with remarkable sang froid, "We must all expect to suffer by this wicked war. I have not felt a moment's trouble for my share of it. If, finally, the government shall be reestablished over our whole territory; and not a vestige of slavery left, I shall deem it a cheap purpose."

On June 28, Lincoln replaced Hooker with George Meade, the commander of the Fifth Corps. Though a protégé of McClellan, the thoroughly professional Meade was one of the few senior men to enjoy nearly universal respect among his fellow generals. Irascible in disposition, with sad, baggy eyes nested in a weary, thickly bearded face, he seemed much older than his forty-seven years. No one expected charisma or brilliance: "He is considered rather a 'smooth bore' than a rifle," Navy Secretary Gideon Welles reflected in the privacy of his diary. But he had served capably since the Mexican War and had performed well in all the army's major battles in 1862.

Meade caught up with Lee three days later at the strategic town of Gettysburg, a few miles north of the Maryland line, where Stevens had first hung out his lawyer's shingle in 1816. The first day's battle was disastrous for the Union. Despite hours of heroic struggle against overwhelming numbers, the shaky Eleventh Corps and then the stout First Corps were battered from their positions and nearly destroyed before darkness put an end to the fighting. During the night, the rest of the Army of the Potomac reached the field and formed a defensive arc on a fishhook of hills and ridges just south of the town. The following day, Lee ordered assaults against both ends of the federal line but failed to break it.

The battle climaxed on its third day with the attempt by thirteen thousand Confederates to break the center of the federal line in a single bold stroke, known ever after as Pickett's Charge. Breaking from wooded cover a mile to the west, they walked—"charged" is a misnomer—over gently rolling ground bisected by split-rail fences. "Behind the front line another appeared and finally a third and the whole came on like a great wave of men, steadily and stolidly," recalled Union Gen. John Gibbon, who was among the troops waiting for them. Step by step, massed federal artillery blew them to pieces. "Arms, heads, blankets, guns and knapsacks were thrown and tossed into the clear air," another Yankee recorded. The weakened attack foundered in sharp but ultimately suicidal hand-to-hand fighting, in what has aptly been called the high-water mark of the battle and, metaphorically, of the Confederacy.

On July 4, Lee withdrew. Although Meade had managed the battle skillfully, he failed—ignominiously, in the view of many in the administration—to follow up his victory by destroying the Confederates before they crossed the Potomac to safety in Virginia. To John Hay, Lincoln bitterly remarked, "We had them within our grasp. We had only to stretch forth our hands and they were ours," adding dejectedly that Meade's hesitancy was "a dreadful reminiscence of McClellan." Gideon Welles concurred, lamenting that Meade had wasted the best opportunity he would ever have to annihilate Lee and bring the war to a close. Overall, the three days' losses were staggering: 23,000 on the Union side, including 3,149 dead, and about the same number on the Confederate.

Meade's generalship after Gettysburg would later be aggressively investigated by the Joint Committee on the Conduct of the War. But for now, the North could still rejoice in what was unarguably the Army of the Potomac's first great unequivocal victory. On July 5, news from the battlefield spread across the anxious North in staccato telegraphic bursts, then in a mounting crescendo. Wrote the diarist George Templeton Strong, "The woman-floggers are badly repulsed and retreating. So much seems certain, and that is enough to thank God for most devoutly, far better than we dared hope a week ago." Almost simultaneously, reports arrived of Grant's capture of Vicksburg and its thirty thousand irreplaceable defenders after a months-long siege, splitting the Confederacy in two and opening the full length of the Mississippi River to federal gunboats. In Washington, bells rang, cannon fired, strangers congratulated each other on the street; in New York the price of gold dropped by fifteen cents. Strategically, Vicksburg actually represented the greater victory, although

Gettysburg, just hours from Washington and New York, made the more dramatic impression on the public mind.

Strong's triumphal mood lasted barely a week. The introduction of the draft had spurred scattered acts of resistance as the federal government reached into every Northern community to pluck both the willing and the unwilling from their homes. The worst disturbances by far began in New York City on July 13, where as many as five hundred people died over three torrid days of horrific chaos. Two days after the drawing of names began, a mob of mostly Irish working men destroyed the draft office at Third Avenue and 46th Street. Within hours Manhattan ignited into anarchy. Rioters roamed lower Manhattan by the thousands, overwhelming provost marshals and detachments of police. Armed with clubs, fence-palings, pitchforks, axes, iron bars, and eventually, having pillaged an armory, pistols and rifles, the rioters derailed streetcars, pulled up tracks, cut telephone lines, burned police stations, wrecked the homes of known abolitionists, looted stores, and assaulted anyone they suspected might be an affluent Republican, cheering Jefferson Davis, cursing the draft and "the niggers." Unoffending Negroes were burned out of their homes, hunted down, lynched and mutilated, stomped to death, and hurled into the East River to drown. The Colored Orphan Asylum at 43rd Street and Fifth Avenue was torched, the terrified children barely escaping with their lives. (When the children were given refuge in a police station on 35th Street, white inmates jailed there tried to strike at them through the bars of the cell doors.) Hand-to-hand battles were fought in Broadway, along 42nd Street, and in front of Horace Greeley's *Tribune* building. Not until veteran troops rushed from Gettysburg reached the city was the rioting fully brought under control. Although no conclusive proof was found, it was widely believed that the riots were instigated by Confederate provocateurs and local Democratic Party operatives, who were sometimes seen cooperating with the rioters. "If a quarter [of what] one hears be true, this is an organized insurrection in the interest of the rebellion and Jefferson Davis rules New York today," wrote Strong.

---

Fearful that insurrection would spread, draft officials in many communities including New York postponed the further drawing of names. The shortage of manpower remained, however, and would have crippled the war effort had it not been for the surging enlistment of blacks that had been made possible by the Thirty-seventh Congress. Eventually, about 180,000—146,000 of them from the slave states—would serve in the Union Army, comprising about 10 percent of the total. "Nigger recruiting prospers," enthused Strong, in whom unalloyed support for emancipation coexisted with bigotry that extended to the Irish as well as blacks. "Why not? Paddy, the asylum-burner, would swear at the dam Naygurs, but we need bayonets in Negro hands."

Negrophobic politicians issued dire warnings that white troops would mutiny if they were forced to serve alongside blacks. Copperhead propagandists predicted even worse: the *Dayton Daily Empire* blared (probably apocryphally) that two Rhode Island soldiers in Louisiana had been executed for refusing to be consolidated with "a nigger regiment." Meanwhile, black leaders such as Frederick Douglass, Henry Highland Garnet, William Wells Brown, and Martin Delany, among others, fanned out across the North and Canada to passionately make the case that combat service would prove black men's "manhood" to white Americans and overcome the color prejudice that even in the North sustained unjust laws that squelched black aspirations. "The paper [Emancipation] proclamation must now be made iron, lead and fire," Douglass urged an audience at the Shiloh Presbyterian Church in New York. The Negro, he said, deserved the same chance as white men to win distinction and glory on the battlefield, and not to be merely the army's "hewers of wood and drawers of water. He will fight, but he must have a reasonable prospect of whipping somebody."

Racists scoffed: a Cleveland editor invited his readers to imagine a scene in which "the swords of the charcoal officers protrude between their legs like a monkey's tail." (In fact, at this stage of the war no blacks held ranks higher than sergeant.) But by the first week in August there were fourteen black regiments under arms and another twenty-four in training, all but five of them made up of men who had been slaves just weeks, or even days before. Among them were the soldiers of the First Arkansas (African Descent), who marched into battle singing, to the tune of "John Brown's Body," as written by one of its officers, an ardent abolitionist:

We hab done wid hoein' cotton, we hab done wid hoein' corn,
We are colored Yankee soldiers now, as sure as you are born;
When de Massas hear us yellin' dey'll tink it's Gabriel's horn,
As we go marching on.

The new Bureau of Colored Troops within the War Department dispatched more than two hundred recruiters to Union-occupied regions of the slave states to drum up volunteers for newly minted federal regiments, while Northern states sent their own agents to contraband camps to woo former slaves whose numbers could be credited to their respective state draft quotas, easing pressure on draft-eligible whites at home. The border states' last chance to accept the compensation that the federal government offered if they voted to abolish slavery evaporated as slaves simply walked away from plantations and farms and into the Union Army. For black volunteers, military service offered the surest route toward emancipation for themselves and their families. It also crippled slavery in the loyal slave states, drawing 57 percent of Kentucky's eligible blacks and remarkable numbers in Missouri, Maryland, Delaware, and Tennessee.

Black volunteers faced a particular risk that whites did not. The Confederacy defined armed blacks as slaves in rebellion, for which the traditional punishment was death. On May 1, the Confederate Congress authorized the reenslavement or execution of black enlisted men, and the summary execution of their white officers. Blacks who surrendered were often murdered on the spot. Even before black regiments took the field, the Confederates had massacred thirty unarmed black teamsters at the battle of Murfreesboro, in Tennessee, and twenty or more black crewmen taken from captured federal steamboats on the Cumberland River. After the battle of Milliken's Bend, in June, a Texas officer wrote, "We took no prisoners, except the white officers, fourteen in number; these were lined up and shot after the negroes were finished." In response, at the end of July, the War Department stated officially that for every Union soldier, white or black, killed in violation of the laws of war a rebel soldier should be executed in retribution. This warning was never acted upon. Although it may have caused some Confederate officers to think twice before they murdered their prisoners, it still left the threat of summary execution hanging over every black man who donned Union blue.

Despite such savagery on the part of the Confederates, the two regiments of recently freed Louisiana slaves who fought at Milliken's Bend astonished those who witnessed the battle by successfully driving off a force of Texans four times their size. Wrote a Yankee officer after the battle, "I never more wish to hear the expression, 'the niggers won't fight.'" Then, less than a week after the New York draft riots, on July 18, a watershed in public opinion was breached when the all-black 54th Massachusetts led a gallant but suicidal assault against the Confederate bastion of Fort Wagner, at the entrance to Charleston harbor. They attacked across a half-mile of exposed beach under enemy fire, crossed the fort's moat, scaled its sloping earthen walls, and seized a portion of the battlements until concentrated rebel artillery and rifle ravaged the survivors. Although it was a tactical defeat, the regiment had demonstrated extraordinary courage and discipline against heavy odds. Of the 650 men who charged the fort, more than 40 percent were killed, including the regiment's white colonel, Robert Shaw. Among the dead was one Cpl. James Gooding, who had just learned that his home in New York had been burned to the ground by the draft rioters.

Many racist federal officers continued adamantly to resist incorporating black soldiers into their armies, even when it would significantly augment their strength. One of them was William Tecumseh Sherman, who wrote to his brother John, "I wont trust niggers to fight yet. I dont oppose negro arming, further than I have no confidence in them & dont want them mixed up with our white soldiers." But as it became manifest to growing numbers of Northern soldiers and civilians that black men fought with uncommon bravery and tenacity, opposition to their recruitment diminished. Their performance converted Ulysses Grant from an agnostic to a true believer. "This, with the emancipation of the negro, is the heavyest blow yet given to the Confederacy," he wrote to Lincoln on August 23. "By arming the negro, we have added a powerful ally. They will make good soldiers and taking them from the enemy weakens them in the same proportion they strengthen us."

Three days later, in a public letter, Lincoln defended black recruitment and attacked racism in equal measure. "You say you will not fight to free negroes," he wrote to a correspondent in Chicago, "[but] some of them seem willing to fight for you." When at last peace came, as it eventually would, Lincoln added significantly, "There will be some black men who can remember that, with silent tongue, and clenched teeth, and steady eye, and well-poised bayonet, they have helped mankind on to this great consummation; while, I fear, there will be some white ones, unable to forget that, with malignant heart, and deceitful speech, they have strove to hinder it."


Among those with malignant heart and deceitful speech were Clement Vallandigham and his allies. They were relying, in part, on virulent Negrophobia to help carry them to victory in the autumn's gubernatorial elections in Pennsylvania, where Governor Curtin was fighting for his political life, and even more so in Ohio, where Vallandigham's surrogates believed themselves to be on the crest of a towering wave that would sweep the state. Vallandigham presided over his gubernatorial campaign from his new command post in Windsor, in Canada West—later redesignated Ontario—where he could easily be reached by his Ohio supporters. From the hotel where he lived on Sandwich Street he enjoyed a panoramic vista of Detroit: he also couldn't miss the federal warship anchored in the Detroit River whose guns seemed to point directly at his bedroom window. He soon became something of a tourist attraction. Southern sympathizers invited him to dinners, fetes, and rallies, and streams of visitors—Democratic politicians, well-wishers from all over the Midwest, parties of students, even delegations of firemen—turned up at his door to shake his hand, collect his autograph, or just to gawk at him. Federal spies alleged that he also met regularly with Confederate agents.

Like a gunner directing artillery on the battlefield, he fired off volleys of letters to be detonated at tumultuous party rallies across the state of Ohio. Democrats campaigned for him on a platform of free speech and assembly, rejection of the Emancipation Proclamation, the restoration of habeas corpus, and a constitutional convention to propose new amendments that would restore what they asserted was the Founders' "original intent"—code for accommodating the South and slavery. Pro-Vallandigham parades were gala affairs. Marchers in Dayton pulled a miniature "Lincoln Bastille" replete with downcast "prisoners of state," and in Springfield a procession of colorful political floats included one carrying sixty virginal girls wearing white dresses and red sashes inscribed "Vallandigham and Pugh," beneath a banner emblazoned "Give Us White Husbands or None at All." The campaign took on the dimensions of a crusade as Vallandigham's followers sanctified his birthplace at New Lisbon, Ohio, as hallowed ground on a par with Jefferson's Monticello and Washington's Mount Vernon. Predicted a local newspaper, Americans of the future would make pilgrimages there for centuries to come "from every point of the compass where the fire of liberty is unquenched."

Everywhere, marchers trilled and bellowed new campaign songs. One, to a martial beat, went this way:

> We are coming, Abraham Lincoln,
> With the ghosts of murdered men.
> Yes! We're coming, Abraham Lincoln,
> With curses loud and deep,
> That will haunt you in your waking,
> And disturb you in your sleep.
>
> There's blood upon your garments,
> There's guilt upon your soul,
> For the lust of ruthless soldiers
> You let loose without control;
> Your dark and wicked doings
> A God of mercy sees,
> And the wail of homeless children
> Is heard on every breeze.

Increasingly optimistic, Vallandigham was thrilled to learn that his Ohio platform had in its essentials been adopted by Democratic candidates all across the North. Republicans who imagined that the war was nearly over were "delusional," he laughingly wrote to the New York Copperhead editor Manton Marble. He felt certain that if the Democrats regained control of Congress and the White House, as he expected, the great mass of Southerners would turn away from the most hard-line Confederate leadership and happily reunite with their Northern brethren. All the same, the political landscape remained fraught with danger. The election was an existential one for American democracy, he warned. "If we fail this fall, *we shall have no presidential election next year,*" he advised Marble. "And we shall probably have a convulsion."

Vallandigham's running mate, George Pugh, tirelessly proclaimed Vallandigham "a brave, honest, persecuted man," denounced government calls for more troops, and predicted imminent military defeat. Declaring his open defiance of General Order No. 38—"I trample [it] under foot!"—he claimed that at any moment he, too, might be dragged before a military inquisition and jailed. If that happened, he demanded at his rallies, "Will you act?" In unison, thousands of voices cried, "We will! We will!" The *Dayton Daily Empire* predicted that though "stricken down by the hand of arbitrary power," Vallandigham would soon "be lifted up by the irrepressible will of a free and mighty people."

As the campaign progressed, Democratic rallies swelled in size: fifteen thousand at Bellefontaine, ten thousand at Marysville, almost twenty thousand at Delaware, forty thousand at Circleville, or so *The Crisis* asserted. Valuable support was also lent to the Copperhead cause by the eminent inventor of the telegraph, Samuel F. B. Morse, whose innocuously named Society for the Diffusion of Useful Knowledge, based in New York, spewed an unending torrent of Negrophobia, religious fundamentalism, and proslavery propaganda. In one tract, published in August, Morse proclaimed with emphasis that *"Slavery to God was Man's highest Freedom,"* and that disobedience was a "disease" whose only remedy was obedience, as ordained by God: obedience between the ruler and the ruled, husband and wife, parent and child, and master and slave. He wrote, "If the Servile relation is an essential and indispensable divinely arranged part of the Social system, is not the attempt to blot it out altogether . . . sacrilegious?" Confederates and their Northern friends couldn't ask for more.

Republicans regarded Vallandigham's candidacy as a national emergency and feared that "a quasi–civil war" would result if he managed to slip back into Ohio. Conceding that no Republican was likely to win against Vallandigham, Ohio's two senators, Ben Wade and John Sherman, along with Treasury Secretary Chase, threw their critical support behind John Brough, a tough-minded pro-war Democrat and railroad executive running on the Union ticket, who scorned abolitionism and Vallandigham alike. They pulled no punches in their rhetoric. Stumping the state for Brough, Sherman denounced Vallandigham as a "convicted traitor" who in every utterance merely mouthed the words that the Confederates "dictated" for him. Wade received death threats. "It is your purpose to instruct your sucking blood abolitionists to destroy the Union with slavery—Well, you will be responsible for a severe penalty by death when the old Union is restored but not by your party," warned one hater. Wade remained uncowed. In September, at Marietta, a city whose early settlers from New England had made it a center of Underground Railroad activity, Wade boomed, "I am a Radical and I glory in it! But I believe all who have benefited the world, from Jesus Christ to Martin Luther and George Washington, have been branded as Radicals." Although he wanted peace as much as the next man, he declared, "I would sacrifice all—sons, kindred, friends and everything before I would get down on my belly to satisfy all these scoundrels" such as Vallandigham, who counseled compromise.

As the election approached, the military authorities tightened security further. Perhaps not entirely coincidentally, just two days before the election, federal agents unearthed a half-baked Copperhead plot to attack a prisoner-of-war camp near Columbus that held over two thousand captured rebels, who were then to be armed to fight their way south to Kentucky. Proof that the plot actually existed was never produced. But the conspirators were alleged to have met in the editorial offices of the strident antiwar and pro-Vallandigham newspaper *The Crisis,* which was now publishing again after its sack by soldiers in April. The authorities arrested Samuel Medary, the newspaper's editor, several local businessmen, a pair of paroled Confederate officers, and the Ohio state schools commissioner as core members of the plot. Some military men suggested that Copperheads be banned from voting at all. "Disenfranchise them," William Tecumseh Sherman bluntly advised. "If they wont fight they should certainly have no voice in the Councils of the Nation."

Democrats and Republicans alike believed that the election would likely turn on the soldier vote. Not all states permitted soldiers in the field to cast ballots, but Ohio did, and interest among serving troops ran high. "We will open up Polls here in Camp and all qualified voters have the right of suffrage and I for one intend using it," one enthusiastic infantryman wrote home to his parents in Dayton. When the votes were counted, Vallandigham was crushed by a stunning margin of more than 100,000. The anticipated Democratic wave had proved a phantom. When news of Vallandigham's defeat reached the Army of the Cumberland, future president James A. Garfield, a major general, recalled, "There arose a shout all along the line on that rainy midnight from every tent, which rent the sky with jubilees." The chastened *Dayton Daily Empire* admitted: "Well—the gubernatorial contest is over; we have met the enemy, and—we are theirs." Similar results were reported from other states, most importantly Pennsylvania, where another Copperhead candidate for governor, George W. Woodward, who had been supported by George McClellan, was edged out. In Kentucky, despite a Democratic majority of some forty thousand in the state, the Democratic candidate for governor, Rep. Charles A. Wicliffe, was also defeated by a Unionist, furious Democrats said because soldiers had taken over the polls in many places and allowed no one to vote who opposed the views of the party in power. Relieved Unionists were jubilant. Crowed George Templeton Strong, "The tail of the national Copperhead is out of joint."

Ohio Democrats blamed their failure on a combination of interference by secret Union Leagues, "stupendous frauds," ballot-box stuffing, voter suppression, manipulation of the soldier vote, the wholesale importation of out-of-state voters, and outright intimidation. Soldiers in the field voted almost seventeen to one for Brough. In Julius Wood's unit of Ohio volunteers—"Somewhere I don't know where," in Louisiana—only five of 230 men voted for Vallandigham.

There was at least some truth to the Democrats' allegations. Many officers barred campaign material they deemed subversive from the camps, in effect censoring Democratic antiwar propaganda. And more than a few simply caved in to pressure from their fellow soldiers. One told his local newspaper that there were only two Vallandigham men in his company, and that one of them received "a good whipping" and then deserted; the other became "ashamed," and voted for Brough. Such incidents aside, countless soldiers simply rejected candidates who denigrated the cause for which they had fought and suffered, such as Lucius Wood, who disliked the Lincoln administration, but couldn't bring himself to vote for Vallandigham, "that old arch instigator of treason [and] High Priest of sin and iniquity."

Vallandigham's reaction to the election was surprisingly sanguine. "As to the future, *posterity will vote for me,* and there will be neither chance nor motive for violence or fraud," he wrote confidently to his wife the day after the election. To his supporters, he counseled patience. He was still certain that the Republican administration would fail and that Democrats would once again have the nation's reins in hand. He was, he reflected, "just entering upon the full vigor of manhood," and he had faith that God yet had much in store for him. More darkly, he expected that the nation would have to endure terrible punishment yet, for how long no one could say. "No people ever recover liberty once surrendered, except in the baptism of blood. It seems to be a divine law that without the shedding of blood there is no remission of the sin of political servitude. . . . It is indeed a melancholy spectacle to see so many people eager to be made slaves, and all the rest overborne by fraud and violence." To Rep. Samuel S. Cox, a congressional ally, he wrote, "It is a bad year for us [but] I have no doubt of final triumph." As for himself, he added, though the smears against him grew more outrageous by the day, "yet under no circumstances will I yield an inch."

He had reason for optimism. Despite the Democrats' defeat, reports of unrest and violence continued unabated. In November, just thirty miles from Springfield, Illinois, some fifty deserters and hundreds of civilians banded together and threatened to fight to the death anyone who came after them. In Greene County, Illinois, an escaped rebel prisoner was reported to be drilling armed Copperheads. In Indiana, soldiers hunting deserters encountered bands of armed antiwar vigilantes. Enrollment officers continued to be attacked. Shots were fired into provost marshals' homes, and others were ambushed and killed on the road. In Holmes County, Ohio, "hundreds" of armed men openly fortified themselves against federal troops and dared them to attack. Rumors that Confederate arms had surreptitiously been infiltrated into Detroit caused the authorities there to fear a general uprising.

Meanwhile news from the battlefronts was mixed at best. It had seemed for a brief few weeks in midsummer that the end of the war was once again within sight. Lee's invasion of Pennsylvania had been beaten back. The Mississippi had been opened to the Gulf of Mexico after Grant's triumphant capture of Vicksburg. Unionist eastern Tennessee had at long last been occupied by a federal army. But by autumn, the glow of victory had once again dimmed. On September 19 and 20, the Confederates administered one of the Union's worst defeats of the war in a dazzlingly successful surprise attack against the outnumbered federal army of Gen. William Rosecrans camped along Chickamauga Creek, in northwest Georgia. (One of the dead was Thaddeus Stevens's nephew Alanson, killed when his battery was overrun.) The shattered remnants of Rosecrans's force straggled back into Tennessee, where they were soon bottled up in Chattanooga, demoralized, dispirited, short of food and ammunition, outnumbered, and dominated by the triumphant Confederates dug in atop the steep ridges that overlooked the city. Fortunately, victory was snatched from the jaws of imminent starvation and defeat by a combination of brilliant logistics and the replacement of Rosecrans with Ulysses Grant. The War Department dispatched twenty thousand reinforcements from the Army of the Potomac under Joe Hooker and managed to get them to Chattanooga in just eleven days, an unglamorous but astonishing feat. On November 24, Hooker's troops stormed precipitous Lookout Mountain, and the following day a separate eighteen-thousand-man force under Gen. George Thomas swarmed up eight-hundred-foot-high Missionary Ridge, crying "Chickamauga! Chickamauga!" and drove off its Confederate defenders. It was a miraculous victory, and it made Grant the Union's most celebrated commander.

In the eastern theater, George Meade spent most of the autumn jousting for advantage with Robert E. Lee over the war-battered landscape of northern Virginia, lunging in one direction then another, first at Bristoe Station, then at Centreville, once again on the Rappahannock, then on the Rapidan, neither army managing to gain strategic advantage. By mid-November, they faced each other across Mine Run, a tributary of the Rapidan. Meade aimed to force a crossing and finally bring Lee to battle. His elaborate battle plan would simultaneously pitch five corps across the river, surprise Lee, turn his flank, and either roll up the Confederate line or force Lee out of his entrenchments and send him packing toward Richmond. The plan required only vigorous and decisive action, neither of which it got. The leading corps commander squandered critical hours, the spearhead division twice lost itself in the woods, the element of surprise was lost, the enemy fell back to a more formidable line, and the sudden onset of frigid winter weather put an abrupt and fizzling end to the campaign. "General Meade's budding laurels have all died down in a killing frost," morosely editorialized the *Chicago Tribune*. The season that had begun so soaringly with the victories of July now froze in the bleak landscape of wintry December, just short of a year after the debacle at Fredericksburg.

# 15

# An Event Without Parallel

———————

Slavery has always been an outlaw.

—SEN. CHARLES SUMNER

Shortly after noon on the afternoon of December 2, workmen hoisted the classical head of a goddess over the scree of construction detritus, blocks of marble, and thousands of expectant, freezing citizens three hundred feet to the top of the Capitol's dome, and lowered it onto the shoulders of the cast-iron effigy of the *Goddess of Liberty*. Her figure, it was hoped, would gaze forever over the federal city with its multitudes of battle-worn soldiers, ragged contrabands, government clerks, and harried politicians, and beyond them toward a nation soon to be triumphantly reunited by the armies of the Union. Cannon boomed and onlookers huzzahed as the head settled into place. Beneath the magnificent new dome, however, all was not well. In the marble halls below, a parliamentary coup was afoot that threatened to unravel the coalition that had steered the nation through almost three stormy years of war. Wrote an anxious Rep. Henry Dawes of Massachusetts, "I can think of nothing but a Bull Run so disastrous to our cause as that they might hear in Richmond and abroad that our own House of Representatives was in a state of revolution."

In keeping with the laws of the time, the new Thirty-eighth Congress that had been elected in 1862 was only now, more than a year later, being seated. Anti-administration House Democrats had made substantial and worrisome gains. Although the Republicans retained a nominal majority in the House of Representatives, its final makeup remained undecided since balloting had only recently been held in the areas of several rebel states occupied by the Union Army, and it appeared just possible that the men elected there could hold the balance of power. Into this political minefield stepped the embittered Tennessee Unionist Emerson Etheridge, whose modest title of House clerk belied the immense power he had to approve or reject the credentials of members at the start of a new session. A former Whig, Etheridge had opposed secession in 1861 so vigorously that he was spoken of as a potential appointee to Lincoln's cabinet. But he endorsed slavery and, like many border state men, had turned against the administration after the Emancipation Proclamation. In collusion with Samuel Cox of Ohio, a leading antiwar Democrat and Vallandigham ally, Etheridge planned to reject the credentials of as many Republicans as possible on technical grounds and validate those of conservatives who had been elected under sometimes questionable circumstances. The two men had collaborated for months with Democrats in several Northern states to ensure that their men's credentials were flawless. With their votes, Cox hoped to be elected Speaker and become the chieftan of a new coalition potent enough to thwart the emancipation and Reconstruction legislation that everyone knew would dominate the session. Ironically, Etheridge's power to approve credentials rested on a law passed by the previous Congress that gave the clerk wide latitude to exclude any member he deemed had not been elected in accordance with "the laws of the United States"—that is, it was intended, disloyal men from the rebellious states. The Copperhead *New York World* later sniggered that "the pit which these [Republicans] digged for their enemies inconveniently yawned under their own feet."

But the plot was not as secret as the conspirators thought. Rumors of some kind of Democratic sleight of hand had percolated into the newspapers as early as November. The day before Congress opened, Republican House members led by Thaddeus Stevens met with Lincoln and discussed various ways they might outflank Etheridge and seize the initiative. Someone proposed that before Etheridge could exclude any Republicans, Stevens would move to immediately name a reliable Republican as presiding officer—Speaker pro tem. If that didn't work, they could physically drag Etheridge out of the chamber. Lincoln offered homespun advice: "If Mr. Etheridge undertakes revolutionary proceedings, let him be carried out on a chip"—a split log. At least half-seriously, Lincoln suggested that if Etheridge refused to yield, soldiers might be invited to see him out.

When Etheridge called the House to order on the morning of December 7, the galleries were packed as they always were at the start of a new session, while eminent guests—among them Horace Greeley and the poet Henry Wadsworth Longfellow—hobnobbed with members on the floor. As Etheridge self-confidently read the roll it quickly became clear that he had added two Copperheads from Missouri and three conservatives from Union-occupied Louisiana and excluded no fewer than nineteen administration men from Maryland, Missouri, West Virginia, Kansas, and Oregon. Their credentials, announced Etheridge blandly, "did not show what they ought to have shown." In effect, he reduced the Republican majority by at least twenty-two votes. The Republican *Chicago Tribune* irately called his behavior "a high-handed outrage," adding, "If there be anything more pitiable than the baffled meanness and malice of his recent course there is no record of it."

The Republicans then made their move. As they had secretly decided, Massachusetts Radical Henry L. Dawes proposed that the names of the Maryland members Etheridge had excluded be added to the roll. An Etheridge ally then moved to table Dawes's motion, that is, essentially to discard it, while another protested that it was out of order. Etheridge was a deft enough parliamentarian to sense immediately that the Republicans might be on to his intentions. He grew visibly nervous, his defiant air evaporated, and he allowed Dawes's motion to proceed. This was Cox's opportunity to muster the majority he believed was at his command. But to the schemers' dismay, when the motion to table came to a vote, their revolution failed by a vote of seventy-four to ninety-four. Etheridge, in the words of the *Chicago Tribune's* reporter, suddenly became "exceedingly obsequious and manifestly cowed."

The victorious Republicans swiftly added to the roll the administration men Etheridge sought to exclude, and the House went on to elect Schuyler Colfax, a stalwart Indiana Radical, as Speaker. (Lincoln would have preferred either the conservative Frank Blair of Missouri or his old Illinois ally Elihu Washburne, but neither candidate gained traction.) Although Cox's insurrection failed, it left the Ohioan's reputation among his fellow Democrats largely undiminished. He would soon emerge as de facto minority floor leader in the bitter contests that were to come. Like many Democrats, Cox professed to support the president "whenever he is upon the proper path," but violently condemned administration policies in practice. In contrast to the prickly Vallandigham, the elfin and generously mustachioed Cox was friendly and witty, and renowned for his oratory. (He was affectionately known by almost everyone as "Sunset" Cox for a particularly orotund allusion to a sunset that he had once deployed.) Likable he may have been, but he was second to none in feral Negrophobia. In the last session of Congress, he had denounced antislavery legislation as "diabolical" in its "extermination" of property and states' rights, and entertained his colleagues with a satirical "Ten Commandments," as they were allegedly practiced by Republicans, among them: "Thou shalt not make unto thee any graven image of ebony, before which to bow thyself, nor to serve it," "Thou shalt not degrade the white race by such intermixtures as emancipation will bring," and "Thou shalt not covet they neighbor's servants." Although the Slave Power had *temporarily* lost much of its political influence due to the war, Cox admitted, from this current danger, he confidently predicted, eventually "southern slave owners will pluck the flower safely," once a restored Union could again properly protect human bondage.

The unfortunate Etheridge's moment of high drama on the national stage was brief. On December 8, the Republicans unceremoniously ousted him and replaced him as clerk with Thaddeus Stevens's close friend Edward McPherson. When it was suggested to Lincoln that he punish the Tennessean further, the president memorably replied, "Emerson ain't worth more than a squirrel load of powder anyway."

Much more was at stake in this parliamentary imbroglio than was immediately apparent. The coup's failure ensured that the Republicans would be able to proceed with the work of emancipation and, no less crucially, that they had the votes to continue funding the war and to sustain future calls for draftees. Significantly, the margin of victory in the pivotal vote had been provided by a group of War Democrats and border state Unionists who revealed that, however grudgingly, they had come to accept the reality of emancipation. Rep. James Brooks of New York, a notably racist anti-administration Democrat, later remarked, "When the border States by their vote organized this House, it was written, it was decreed, irrepealably decreed, that slavery is abolished, and there was no help for it."

In the days and weeks that followed, the new Congress gradually took stock of itself. Many familiar faces were gone: House Speaker Galusha Grow had sunk under the Democratic wave. John Crittenden of Kentucky, who fought so hard and fruitlessly to replicate the compromises of the antebellum era, had finally given up and retired. The new Democratic majority of Illinois's state legislature had replaced Lincoln's friend Orville Browning with a quasi-Copperhead, William A. Richardson. Maryland had elected the conservative Unionist Reverdy Johnson to the Senate, and the prewar Know-Nothing-turned-Radical Henry Winter Davis to the House: both would make a mark in the new Congress. Maine sent the dynamic young James G. Blaine, who was destined to become a titan of Republican politics during the Gilded Age, and Ohio two new generals fresh from the battlefield: the erudite abolitionist and future president James A. Garfield and Robert Schenck, who had been elected to the seat that had been held by the exiled Clement L. Vallandigham. Vallandigham's extremism lived on, however, in the person of the notorious former New York mayor Fernando Wood, a Tammany boss who had encouraged the city to secede from the United States in 1861.

Thaddeus Stevens returned to Washington so infirm that he sometimes had to be carried in a chair to his desk on the House floor, but he was still a personality to be reckoned with. Henry Winter Davis described the ravaged old abolitionist as "Grim, savage, sarcastic, mordant as ever—living on brandy & opium to subdue perpetual pain & mocking at the powers that be, in the most spicy way." The correspondent for the *Boston Evening Journal* reported that when Stevens cracked down on an offender against party discipline, a not infrequent occurrence, he would glare menacingly, "sweeping at him with his large, bony right hand in uncouth gestures, as if he would clutch him and shake him," and that when he launched one of his famous fusillades of sarcasm "he was as impassive, his visage as solemn, as if he were pronouncing a funeral oration." Within days of the session's opening, he called for bills to repeal the Fugitive Slave Act, completely abolish slavery, and equalize the pay of black soldiers.

At least eighty thousand black men were now under arms. It was obvious to all but the most irretrievably prejudiced that not only would blacks fight, but that they could do so with both discipline, spirit, and the "manliness" that racists claimed they didn't possess. Largely as a result of their willingness to fight, a transformation was taking place in Northern public opinion. When the war began, perhaps as little as one-tenth of the citizens of the loyal states supported immediate and unconditional emancipation. Even Democrats, at least some of them anyway, were now coming around. "I took the ground that Buckwheat flour & molasses might cure a cold but it would not cure typhoid fever," a former compromise-minded Douglas Democrat wrote to Stevens. "I am now in favour of the amancipation proclation." The ever-Negrophobic *New York Herald*, too, considered slavery dead: "The nigger is done with, and would have been as certainly done with [even] without the President's proclamation." To espouse such sentiments as certainties was one thing. But politically and legally how were Negroes to fit into the United States that emerged from the war? Semi-slaves still? Citizens? Equals? In their efforts to answer these questions, Republicans faced a task that was in some ways harder than any that Congress had addressed.

The significance of the change was captured in the remarks of Missouri senator John B. Henderson, a Virginia-born conservative Unionist, who was appointed in 1862 to fill out the term of Trusten Polk, who had defected to the Confederacy. Though a slave owner himself, who did not oppose slavery on moral grounds, Henderson cooperated with Missouri's powerful Radical faction, and had come to the conclusion that the war had made slavery untenable and emancipation inevitable. "We cannot save the institution if we would. We ought not if we could," he told the Senate in April. If slavery were the blessing that it was claimed to be, he would, he said, defend it to the last. But, "It is a curse, and not a blessing. Therefore let it go." Henderson contemplated, albeit tentatively, the possibility that emancipation would even transform the Negro. "I will not be intimidated by the fears of negro equality. The negro may possess mental qualities entitling him to a position beyond our present belief. If so, I shall put no obstacle in the way of his elevation."

From the beginning of the session, it was clear that radical legislation was in store. Stevens, whose views were once anathema to Republican conservatives, pointed the way toward the party's evolving consensus. On January 7, in reply to Cox's Negrophobic tirade, he went beyond mere defense of administration policy to daringly denounce the irrationality of racial prejudice, which attributed the supposed "natural" supremacy of whites to the "accidental color of the skin or the shape of the face" rather than an individual's intellect or merit. Such backward notions were incompatible with the promise and destiny of America: freedom would and must win out. "Our political laws are either to give equal rights to every human being, or they are to crush the one and elevate the other upon his ruin," Stevens said. As the republic continued to expand across the continent, "so will the principles of liberty expand, and they will not be confined by Mason and Dixon's line or by any other line, but will spread throughout the whole continent and over every human soul upon its soil." Not all Republicans had yet caught up to Stevens, but many were not far behind.

On January 14, the first day of regular business, Rep. Thomas D. Eliot of Massachusetts proposed the establishment of a "Bureau of Emancipation." Stevens, George Julian of Indiana, and James Ashley of Ohio, a foursquare abolitionist in the mold of Ben Wade, all introduced bills to repeal the Fugitive Slave Act, which remained on the books and was still enforced in parts of the border states. Owen Lovejoy of Illinois, whose older brother had been murdered by proslavery rioters in 1836, offered a bill requiring equal pay for both black and white soldiers in the Union Army, and another to "protect freemen and to punish anyone for enslaving them." But the session's single most radical initiative was embodied in a competing barrage of bills proposed in the House by Stevens and Ashley, and in the Senate, initially, by Henderson, and later by Charles Sumner, calling for a constitutional amendment to decisively abolish slavery everywhere. In its final form, it declared, "Neither slavery nor involuntary servitude except as punishment for crime, whereof the party shall have been duly convicted, shall exist in the United States or any place subject to their jurisdiction."

For much of the previous decade Sumner's clarion oratory had made his name a national byword for the imperative claims of antislavery. His life's ambition, he said during the winter's debate, was to "clean the statute books of all existing supports for slavery, so that it may find nothing there to which it may cling for life." His savage caning on the floor of the Senate by an inflamed South Carolina congressman in 1856 had endowed him with an aura of personal martyrdom for the cause, along with a quality of sanctimony which many of his colleagues, Pitt Fessenden in particular, found almost intolerable. Physically, he was an imposing figure, standing six feet three inches, extremely tall for the time, with a heroic profile, a face that suggested "a poetical turn of thought," and a handsome sweep of graying hair. However, even his admirers often regarded him as overly fastidious, even foppish, forever straightening his cravat, flicking dust specks from his stylish morning coat, brushing back his forelock, and restlessly scanning the crowd when he was nominally engaged in conversation.

Although he had proved an adequate chairman of the Foreign Relations Committee, he had so far played little role in shaping domestic war policy. In contrast to Fessenden, Wade, Trumbull, and Wilson, all masters of the machinery of committee work and willing to compromise when necessary, Sumner was largely ineffectual in caucus, rigid in his views, inept at drafting legislation, and clumsy in debate. Remarked a friend, George Hoar, later an influential member of the U.S. Senate, "He had no genius for detail. He lacked that quality which enables the practical statesman to adjust the mechanism of complicated statutes." Navy Secretary Gideon Welles dismissed him as "egotistical, susceptible to flattery," and hypocritical in his professed devotion to the cause of black Americans: "With all his studied philanthropy and love for the negroes in the abstract, he is unwilling to fellowship with them, though he thinks he is." Still, whatever his shortcomings, his commitment to legislate slavery to the death was unequivocal, and he now figuratively rubbed his hands in delight at the debate that was beginning to unfold. "Only a few years ago the proposition [of immediate emancipation] would have created a storm of violence," he wrote excitedly to a British friend. And to another, former British prime minister and ardent abolitionist William Gladstone, "The way seems open at last."

Sumner had always had a gift for the theatrical. At his behest, on February 9, two strongly built Negroes marched into the Senate carrying a gigantic roll of petitions organized by the New York abolitionist and women's suffragist Susan B. Anthony, calling upon Congress to embark immediately upon the universal abolition of slavery. The petitions bore signatures from more than twenty states—17,706 from New York, 15,380 from Illinois, 33 from Nebraska, 21 from Kentucky, the vast majority of them from women. The two men crossed the chamber and placed them—the "Prayer of the Hundred Thousand," he called them—on Sumner's desk. They came, he trumpeted, from East and West, "from the families of the educated and uneducated, rich and poor, of every profession, business, and calling in life," the advance of a mighty army, an army without arms or banners, praying only for equality before the law. Sumner followed up this tour de force by introducing a constitutional amendment declaring that "all persons are equal before the law, so that no person can hold another as a slave." The language, he said, "gave precision to that idea of human rights which is enunciated in the Declaration of Independence."

Sumner had hoped and expected that the amendment would be assigned to his own select committee on measures that concerned slaves and freedmen. His colleagues let him have the petitions but—a deliberate slight—they handed the proposed amendment, the more important responsibility, to the Judiciary Committee, which was led by the less radical Lyman Trumbull. Sumner was embarrassed. But there was nothing he could do about it. As a result, apart from the

driving engine of his oratory, he had little to do with the shaping
of the amendment whose passage he felt should have been the capstone of his career.

With the amendment bottled up in Trumbull's committee, all
through the blustery and bitterly cold weeks of February, Sumner
pumped out antislavery resolutions: measures to prohibit racial discrimination in testimony in federal courts, to require Washington's
streetcars to allow blacks to ride inside with whites, to enforce equal
treatment for black soldiers, to repeal the Fugitive Slave Law, so
many, complained Garrett Davis of Kentucky, that he might as well
just go all the way and "petition the Congress to change the Negroes
into white people." Repeatedly, when one measure was defeated,
Sumner moved it as an amendment to some other measure, calling
it up at every opportunity, reintroducing it, stalling for time, ignoring his critics. The conservative Unionist Reverdy Johnson wearily
claimed that half of the session's business so far had been taken up
with Sumner's human rights proposals.

When the battle over the amendment at last got under way at the
end of March it was recognized by everyone as a test of just how far
Congress was prepared to go to uproot slavery. Trumbull spoke first.
Fifty years old, still "straight as an arrow, of faultless physique, and in
manners a cultivated gentleman," he had been born into one of the
most distinguished New England families, whose lineage stretched
back to 1637 and included three governors of Connecticut, the painter
John Trumbull, and the Puritan churchman Cotton Mather. Originally a Jacksonian Democrat, he detested slavery on moral grounds,
but had long considered it a matter best left to the states. After moving to Illinois to establish himself as a lawyer, he worked to eliminate
slavery there, where it persisted as indentured servitude, and eventually migrated to the new Republican Party. Although he often voted
with the Radicals, he had never quite been one of them on matters
of race, reflecting the resistance of his Illinois constituents, many of
whom violently opposed equal rights for blacks. That changed on
March 28.

There could be no question that slavery lay at the core of the
nation's woes, he began, in a seemingly tough-minded speech that,
when read carefully, revealed Trumbull's doubt that the amendment

would actually pass. Too optimistically, the Founders had predicted that slavery would naturally fade away, but the last seventy years had proved them grievously mistaken. Slavery had in fact grown ever stronger until by 1860 its advocates demanded control of the nation, "failing in which they attempted its overthrow." He went on to summarize the several Confiscation Acts and the Emancipation Proclamation; significant as they were, he said, they fell far short of eliminating the curse of slavery because they only had force where the armies of the Union marched. "If then we are to get rid of the institution, we must have some more efficient way of doing it." Rebutting Ben Wade and other Radicals, who held that Congress could simply vote slavery out of existence, he argued that if slavery was nominally abolished merely by proclamation or an act of Congress, there was nothing in the Constitution to prevent a state from voting it back into existence in the future. The only way to wipe out slavery once and for all was by means of an unambiguous amendment to the Constitution. The real question was therefore not a moral one but a political one: could two-thirds of each house of Congress be found to support such an amendment? Although he *supposed* that the amendment would pass both houses, he was not entirely confident of it. And it would then have to gain ratification by three-fourths of the states, including at least several states that had only just begun to take steps to end slavery within their borders. But if ratification *could* be achieved, it would finally free the nation from the crippling problem whose solution had defied generations of its greatest statesmen. "We relieve Congress of sectional strife, and, what is better than all, we restore to a whole race that freedom which is theirs by the gift of God, but which for generations [was] wickedly denied them."

Slavery's defenders responded with predictable, if impotent, venom. Garrett Davis spat out a spray of mocking amendments to the bill. One proposed combining Maine, New Hampshire, and Vermont into a single state named "North New England," and Massachusetts, Rhode Island, and Connecticut into "South New England"—to diminish their sway in the Senate. Another proposed that "no negro or person whose mother or grandmother is or was a negro shall be a citizen of the United States, or be eligible to any civil or military office, or to any place of trust or profit under the United States." A third proposed settling all the country's Negroes evenly across the states, in proportion to their white populations—a prospect guaranteed to inflame racist whites in Northern states. The main attack was carried out by Willard Saulsbury of Delaware, the most merciless proponent of slavery still in the Senate. At forty-three, he was also one of the body's youngest members, with deep-set, exceptionally piercing eyes, and a haughtily belligerent manner when provoked. Once called by a reporter "the most handsome sen-ator when sober," in February of 1863, "while fast in the clutches of John Barleycorn," he had been forcibly ejected from the Senate for brandishing a revolver on the floor in a fit of drunken rage.

Saulsbury raked the Republicans for being so foolish as to imagine that they "could improve upon the workmanship of the Almighty," who had obviously decreed the existence of slavery for eternity. "I regard [slavery] neither as unconstitutional, illegal, immoral, impi-ous, or sinful in any aspect," he said, but since the beginning of time "in perfect accordance with the ways of Providence to man." Imme-diately after the Flood, the Almighty "for purposes inscrutable to us" had cursed an entire people—the Canaanites, the ancestors of the Africans—with eternal servitude. To blame slavery for the nation's crisis was as absurd as blaming the existence of fire for a conflagra-tion that had burned down part of New York City, or the existence of water for a flood, or the existence of the sun for heat stroke. The great majority of the nation's Founders were slave owners, so it was preposterous to imagine that when they spoke of "all men being created equal" they meant anyone but men like themselves. The pro-posed constitutional amendment would "blot out" hundreds of mil-lions of dollars' worth of private property. But it was just the latest campaign in an even more revolutionary war against *all* property. Should it ever be enacted, it would mean that existing property of any kind—including even the mills and factories of New England—could be swept away by a vote of Congress. Worse still, it meant the potential encroachment of the government into every sphere of life. "If you can go into the states and attempt to regulate the relation of master and slave, you can go into a state and attempt to regulate the relation between parent and child or husband and wife, or for that matter to legislate an end to all property, or distribute property equally throughout the country wherever" the federal government wanted. Moreover, the amendment could never be ratified in states such as Arkansas, Louisiana, or Tennessee, where federal power rested on bayonets alone. "Take away your soldiers and there would be scarcely one man in fifty in either of those states that would either approve your amendment or recognize your authority."

Sumner weighed in with a stellar performance, lifted by flaming oratory of an eloquence that had rarely been heard since the days of Clay and Webster. "Constitutionally, slavery has always been an outlaw," he sonorously declared, restating his belief that the Constitution was inherently an antislavery document because it nowhere used the words "slave" or "slavery." Universal emancipation could be achieved only by complete emancipation of the Constitution itself, "which has been degraded to wear chains so long that its real character is scarcely known." The only practical question left, he said, was whether slave owners deserved to be compensated for their liberated slaves, as even some of his Republican colleagues maintained. This utterly unpalatable proposition still hung in the air, he said, only "because the national representatives have so long been drugged and drenched with slavery, which they have taken in all forms, whether of dose or *douche,* that, like a long-suffering patient, they are not yet emancipated from its influence." To repay slavemasters would be a moral monstrosity. If anyone deserved to be remunerated for slavery it was the slaves themselves. It was easy for a master to estimate the loss of income from a freed slave's work on a balance sheet, "but where is the tariff or price-current by which those other losses which have been the lot of every slave shall be determined? Mortal arithmetic is impotent to assess the fearful sum total."

Lazarus Powell, an unapologetic slaveholder, dismissed Sumner's words with a Shakespearean flourish as "'a tale told by an idiot, full of sound and fury, signifying nothing,'" then damned him in a vicious ad hominem attack, sneering that "the Negro absorbs your every thought. For him you will destroy the country; for him you will allow the liberties of the white man to be stricken down, and every sacred guarantee of liberty in the Constitution put under foot without a whimper."

In the view of most who heard it, the best speech of the debate, possibly of the entire session, was delivered by courtly Reverdy Johnson, often a bellwether of conservative sentiment. Jowly, nearly blind—he had accidentally shot himself in the eye years earlier—he had first served in the Senate during the Mexican War, then as Zachary Taylor's attorney general, and was widely respected as one of the most learned lawyers in the country. He was in many ways a typical border state Unionist, a former Whig who often seemed nostalgic for the prewar United States. Although he had freed the few slaves he owned, he never outspokenly challenged slavery as an institution, and had opposed the Emancipation Proclamation, warning that encouraging officers to free slaves would be fatal to the war effort. What he now said must have shocked anyone who expected to hear a well-reasoned demolition of the amendment.

"To manumit at once nearly four million slaves is an event of which the world's history furnishes no parallel," Johnson began. "The only question in my view that presents itself to statesmen is, first, whether the measure itself be right, independent of its consequences; and, secondly, whether those consequences may be such as to render it inexpedient." *Whether the measure itself be right.* Such words had never before been spoken on the Senate floor by a slave-state senator during the previous three years of Negrophobic rants, moral evasions, legalistic hair-splitting, and biblical claptrap. Johnson declared that he would vote for freedom. He had long felt—though he had never before said it publicly—that the day must eventually come when slavery would be exterminated by a convulsive effort on the part of the bondsmen. That day had arrived. Each senator was now compelled to decide for himself how to rid the nation of an institution "so pregnant with mischief, so full of peril." It no longer mattered whether slavery had caused the war or not. However, "One thing, in my judgment, is perfectly clear, now that the war is upon us, that a prosperous and permanent peace can never be secured if the institution is permitted to survive." No executive edict could accomplish it. Nor could any ordinary piece of legislation. If the war ended without any provision being made for the future of the slaves who were not under military protection undoubtedly the courts would deem them slaves still. Only an amendment to the Constitution could do what must now be done.

The Founders could have written slavery's abolition into the Constitution, but obviously they hadn't, Johnson continued. "Remember, now the question is, can that institution which deals with humanity as property, which claims to shackle the mind, the soul, and the body, which brings to the level of the brute a portion of the race of man, cease to be within the reach of the political power of the people of the United States, not because it was not at one time within their power, but because at that time they did not exert the power?" The Preamble to the Constitution made clear, he said, that the Founders wanted above all to establish justice, preserve tranquility, maintain the common welfare, and, most important of all, secure liberty. "Is there no justice in putting an end to human slavery?" he asked. "Is there no danger to the tranquility of the country in its existence? May it not interfere with the general welfare? And, above all, is it consistent with any notion which the mind of man can conceive of human liberty?" There was nothing divine in slavery's origin, he said. True, "the Savior of mankind" had not declared slavery illegal in a lawyer's terms. Rather, "he aimed at the heart." He had taught to man "the obligation of brotherhood, and designed His doctrine to be equally applicable to the black and to the white, to the race of man as he then existed, or as he might exist in all after-time." Because slaves happened now to live in degraded circumstances were they never to enjoy freedom as other men did? "Are they by nature," he rhetorically asked, "and in spite of whatever education tyranny may have left them, so mentally and morally deficient that they do not know what are the blessings of human freedom? What do we see? Wherever the flag of the United States, the symbol of human liberty, now goes, under it from their hereditary bondage are to be found men, women and children assembling and craving its protection." All men were brothers, he said. "It is an instinct of the soul." Tyranny might oppress it for centuries, the pall of despotism might hang over it, but the truth of it was ever there. Slavery, he said, "is a sin, is a wrong, cries for redress." Once, he had believed that abolition could be attained through patience and persuasion. But that time had now passed. "Let the institution be abolished." Henceforth, whites and Negroes deserved to "share the same dangers, enjoy according to our power and our means and our ability the same prosperity, and when we die, die as men, and not as chattels."

This was not Charles Sumner or Ben Wade. Johnson was a product of the world of slavery, a man who only months ago had rejected the Emancipation Proclamation. He now addressed every proslavery argument and demolished them one after another. The speech was one of the most widely discussed and reprinted of the debate. How much direct influence it had on other senators is impossible to say, but he had made it easier for thinking conservatives to come to grips with the moral dimension of slavery, and the obligation that it placed on decent men to change their minds about it.

On April 8, the Senate voted overwhelmingly, by thirty-eight to six, to approve Henderson's amendment, the first time in American history that either chamber of Congress had voted unequivocally to abolish slavery. But this was, everyone knew, just the first battle in a legislative campaign that would soon face a different and less lopsided configuration of power in the House of Representatives.

# 16

# No Quarter!

———————●———————

Everyone says that the Union must
be reconstructed in some form, but how?

—SEN. BENJAMIN F. WADE

By spring, more than one hundred black regiments were under arms or in training. Whenever they were given a chance to fight they won praise from once skeptical officers. General Alfred Terry, who commanded federal forces in South Carolina, declared that the caliber of men in his black regiments was second to none, while the colonel of a regiment raised from among former Alabama slaves told visiting abolitionist Levi Coffin that the men were the best disciplined in his command: "It was the first time that their manhood had been recognized, and they were anxious to prove that they were worthy of the confidence reposed in them." Not all military men concurred. William T. Sherman, who still refused to accept Negro regiments in his armies, wrote to Henry Halleck, "We want the best young white men of the land. I have had the question put to me often: 'Is not a negro as good as a white man to stop a bullet?' Yes, and a sandbag is better." And in a letter to Secretary of War Stanton, Sherman added, no less bluntly, "If negroes are to fight, they too will not be content with sliding back into the status of slave, or Free Negro either. I much prefer to keep negros, for yet some time to come, in a subordinate state, for our prejudices, yours as well as mine are not yet schooled for absolute Equality."

Such ingrained prejudice would not easily dissipate. But reports from the battlefield underscored the glaring unfairness of the disparity in pay between black and white troops. Negro soldiers received just $10 a month, less $3 a month for their equipment and uniforms, while whites were paid $13 and charged nothing for their equipage. In addition, when white soldiers were killed, their families were usually paid a lump sum by their communities, while black soldiers' families were left destitute. It had at first been supposed that most black recruits would be grateful for whatever they were given. But many black volunteers were Northern free men who deeply resented the humiliation of being told that no matter how bravely they fought their lives were worth $3 less than a white's. The men of the 54th and 55th Massachusetts Regiments, in particular, had initially been promised parity, and they had collectively refused to take any pay at all until they received it. Many of those who died in the storming of Fort Wagner in July 1863 had never received a dollar and were in debt to the government for $30 or so in clothing when they fell on its ramparts.

The issue was a significant embarrassment to the government, particularly in New England and other abolitionist strongholds at a time when Radical disillusionment with President Lincoln was threatening to undermine his chances for both renomination and reelection. In mid-February Henry Wilson, the chairman of the Senate's Military Affairs Committee, denounced the disparity as a "gross injustice," called for equalization, and proposed that those men who had been promised parity also be granted retroactive pay from their day of enlistment. (Thaddeus Stevens introduced an identical measure in the House.) To many members, this seemed fair enough, but it ran into unexpected resistance from Pitt Fessenden, whose support, as chairman of the Finance Committee, was most essential.

Fessenden insisted that his opposition had nothing to do with racial animus. Indeed, he protested, one of his sons was serving as an officer in a black regiment. He asserted a bit defensively that he had always supported equal pay not just on the ground of fairness, but also "in order that there should be no ground for any distinction by the enemy between colored troops and white troops, that it should not lie in their mouths to say that we ourselves had made a distinction, and that therefore they were at liberty to consider them upon other footing than the regular soldiers of the United States." His concern would soon prove prophetic. But at a moment when war funding was once again in crisis, retroactive pay would add another $1 million or more to the already swollen deficit. Fessenden also pointed out that in the early days of the war many white regiments had enlisted when soldiers' pay was only $8 a month. If Negroes were to be paid retroactively, so must the whites: the government simply couldn't afford it.

Charles Sumner, who reciprocated Fessenden's personal dislike, found his argument repugnant. "Our country can ill afford to take the responsibility of refusing an act of justice to colored soldiers whom it has allowed to shed their blood in its cause," Sumner declared. The Senate, he added, had no moral right to postpone pay reform for a single day. Fessenden, tightly wound even on his best days, but now sleep-deprived and exhausted, snapped back sarcastically that "the honorable senator from Massachusetts has a fashion of deciding rather *ex cathedra,* it strikes me, upon what is just and what is unjust, and rather a fashion to leave us to infer that he thinks everybody who differs from him in opinion is disposed to do injustice."

Apart from his personal dislike for Sumner, for Fessenden every issue now boiled down to one merciless problem: how to pay for the war. Everything that deviated from that imperative was a distraction. The demand for more men and matériel was never-ending. Vessels sank, guns were lost, cannon wore out, soldiers had to be clothed and fed, mules and horses died and had to be replaced; tax collectors and provost marshals had to be hired, along with innumerable porters, messengers, and clerks for every burgeoning federal department. In the War Department alone, responses to the application for pensions by the maimed and widowed were running a year late for lack of clerks to process them. Money itself had to be paid for: the Philadelphia Mint was running out of nickel for coins, and new supplies were urgently needed. Budgetary predictions always fell short of the ballooning need. But as more and more greenbacks were pumped into circulation their value sank just as the critics of the currency bills had warned. Lamented Salmon Chase, "The injurious influences of oversupply have now been aided by fear of ill-success in military operations." The Bank Act had also left too many loopholes and failed to bring the money supply under control. Too many state banks were still issuing unsupported currency. Interest rates still swung wildly.

Meanwhile, unregulated speculation in gold threatened to undermine the entire economy. Trading was feverish. Premiums climbed inexorably from 52 percent in December 1863 to 75 percent in mid-April 1864, with no sign of slowing down. Two years earlier, the rate had stood at just 3 percent. Gold prices gyrated in reaction to rumors of victory and defeat as speculators bet for or against the government's greenbacks while battalions of prying clerks and secretaries in the pay of brokers dogged members of Congress for the latest war news. As greenbacks lost value, the price of the war soared, along with the cost of living for millions of ordinary Northerners.

The so-called "Gold Room," in a basement on William Street in New York, was the nexus of the frenzy: "a rat-pit in full blast," in the words of one observer, and "a swamp wherein human character quickly sank and never recovered," in those of another. There, from 10:30 a.m. to 3:00 p.m. frantic traders daily bet fortunes on success or failure of the Union war effort. The economic doldrums of 1861 were ancient history now. New York was awash in money, thanks to the war. Cotton bought in the Confederacy for twelve cents per pound and smuggled north was selling for $1.90 per pound in Manhattan. Investors reaped dizzying profits from trading in western land opened up for railroad construction and homesteading. And fabulous fortunes burgeoned virtually overnight for businessmen who secured contracts to supply the army. Much of this money eventually found its way to the Gold Room. It was estimated at the time that more than $15 million in gold changed hands there daily. A contemporary reported: "Men leaped upon chairs, waved their hands, or clenched their fists; shrieked, shouted; the bulls whistled 'Dixie,' and the bears sung 'John Brown'; the crowd swayed feverishly from door to door, and, as the fury mounted by white heat, and the tide of gold fluctuated up and down in rapid sequence, brokers seemed animated with the impulse of demons, hand-to-hand combats took place, and bystanders, peering through the smoke and dust, could liken the wild turmoil only to the revels of maniacs."

By mid-April, it took $188 in greenbacks to buy $100 in gold, and it looked as if things would only get worse. The Philadelphia financier Jay Cooke persuaded Chase that such rampant speculation had become a threat not just to the financial markets, but to the nation's political stability. New York, he reminded the treasury secretary, was a hotbed of Southern sentiment, and many of the plungers seemed bent on deliberately trying to ruin the government's credit. He convinced Chase that he could bring speculation under control by drawing $6 million or $7 million in federal gold from the subtreasury in New York and using it to buy up virtually all the $12 million to $18 million of greenbacks in the city, thus driving up their value. The two rendezvoused in New York and working in tandem began slowly selling off gold a few million dollars at a time over the course of several days. The strategy was a qualified success. They succeeded in bringing the premium down enough to cool the market, demonstrating that the government had the spine to bring order to the market and the willingness to ruin overleveraged speculators. But it was only a temporary respite.

Hardly had Chase returned from New York when monstrous news broke in the eastern papers. On April 12, eight hundred miles to the west, a hard-riding force of between 1,500 and 2,000 Confederate cavalry under Gen. Nathan Bedford Forrest, a prewar slave trader, surprised the garrison of Fort Pillow, forty miles north of Memphis. It was the climax of a daring raid that had taken Forrest's men deep inside Union lines as far north as Paducah, Kentucky, close enough to Illinois to stir panic beyond the Ohio River. The fort, a complex of earthworks and gun emplacements sprawling atop bluffs above the river, had been built by the Confederates and captured by the Union in 1862. Its river-facing defenses were formidable, but the handful of poorly situated field guns and howitzers that were meant to protect the landward side overlooked a maze of deep gulches that blocked the defenders' view. The garrison included a total of about 550 men from two black units, the Sixth U.S. Heavy Artillery and the Second

U.S. Light Artillery, and a white Unionist regiment, the 13th Tennessee Cavalry.

Forrest, whose reputation for ruthlessness preceded him, warned that he wouldn't be responsible for what happened to the defenders unless they surrendered immediately. Then, under the cover of a white flag, he infiltrated men through the gulches until they were immediately beneath the fort. The attack was ferocious, the defense chaotic. The broken land made it difficult, and soon impossible, for men from one part of the garrison to help those who were overrun. A sniper's bullet killed the fort's commander, and the white Tennesseans broke and fled. Most of the blacks resisted spiritedly until they were overwhelmed. The end was swift and horrific.

Forrest's men cried, "No quarter!" and "Black flag!"—that is, take no prisoners. Soldiers, whites as well as blacks, who tried to surrender were shot, hacked with sabers, and beaten to death with rifle butts. Wounded men were murdered where they lay. Several were burned to death in huts. Others were thrown into pits with the dead and buried alive. Fleeing men slid, fell, and jumped over the edge of the bluff. Many threw themselves into the river in an attempt to save themselves. Some drowned, but many others were picked off by Confederate riflemen firing at leisure from shore.

Confederates had murdered black Union soldiers before, but nothing approached the scale of butchery at Fort Pillow. News of the slaughter reached the North within hours by telegraph. Four days after the massacre, the Senate voted to immediately dispatch Ben Wade and one of his colleagues on the Joint Committee on the Conduct of the War, Rep. Daniel Gooch of Massachusetts, to interview eyewitnesses. At Cairo, Illinois, a shaken brigadier urged them to publish what they learned as quickly as possible before "bad men, who sympathize with the rebellion . . . *deny the facts.*" His concerns were not exaggerated. He handed Wade a clipping from that day's *Cairo Daily Democrat,* a Copperhead sheet, which claimed that no atrocities at all had occurred and scoffed at "extravagant stories" as government propaganda. From Cairo, Wade and Gooch continued south via Columbus, Kentucky, to Fort Pillow. The testimony they recorded still makes harrowing reading. They found bodies with gaping wounds, some bayoneted through the eyes, some with skulls broken through, others with their bowels ripped out. "We saw bodies still unburied of some sick men who had been fleeing from the hospital and beaten down and brutally murdered, and their bodies left where they had fallen. We could still see the faces, hands and feet of men, white and black, protruding out of the ground."

A white hotel keeper told them that he saw the Confederates trap about one hundred soldiers at the bottom of the bluffs along the river. When they begged to be allowed to surrender, "The rebels would reply, 'God damn you, why didn't you surrender before?' and shot them down like dogs." John Hogan, a Negro corporal, testified that he saw Forrest's men confront a Captain Carson, a white officer: "They asked him how he come to be there, and then asked if he belonged to a nigger regiment, and then they shot him." Several witnesses saw Lieutenant Akerstrom of the 13th Tennessee crucified against the side of a building that afterward was set on fire. Several black soldiers were also nailed to the floor of the same building. Others were lined up and shot while holding white handkerchiefs in their hands as tokens of surrender. A white lieutenant testified that he saw several black soldiers murdered as they lay wounded: "As they were crawling around, the secesh would step out and blow their brains out." Another white cavalryman, James Walls, testified, "I saw them make lots of niggers stand up, and then they shot them down like hogs." At least two women and three small black boys were shot and then beaten to death.

Woodford Cooksey, a white soldier who had been shot while lying unarmed on the ground, watched the Confederates murder three whites and seven blacks the morning after battle. "I saw one of them shoot a black fellow in the head with three buck shot and a musket ball," Cooksey said. "The man held up his head, and then the fellow took his pistol and fired that at his head. The black man still moved, and then the fellow took his saber and stuck it in the hole in the negro's head and jammed it way down, and said, 'Now, God damn you, die!' The Negro did not say anything, but he moved, and the fellow took his carbine and beat his head soft with it."

Forrest initially reported to his superiors that he had killed more than 450 of the enemy and suffered just twenty killed and sixty wounded from his own command. He wrote, "It is hoped that these facts will demonstrate to the Northern people that the Negro soldier cannot cope with Southerners." Of the 585 Union soldiers at the fort, at least 277 were killed, an astronomical death rate of 48 percent unmatched in any other battle of the war; of these, white soldiers were killed at a rate of 31 percent and blacks at a rate of 64 percent. Of the 269 black soldiers, 195 were killed, as well as an indeterminate number of black civilians. Although the Confederate authorities later tried to play down the barbarism of what Forrest had done, the worst was corroborated by a Confederate cavalryman, Achilles V. Clark, who wrote to his sisters: "The poor deluded negroes would run up to our men fall upon their knees with uplifted hands scream for mercy but they were ordered to their feet and then shot down. The white men fared but little better. Blood, human blood stood about in pools and brains could have been gathered up in any quantity."

The 128-page report that Wade penned in a feverish burst of anger on his return to Washington ranks among his most significant contributions to the entire war effort. Making the case that the rebels had clearly adopted a policy of systematic savagery against black troops, Wade wrote, "the testimony herewith submitted must convince even the most skeptical that it is the intention of the rebel authorities not to recognize the officers and men of our colored regiments as entitled to the treatment accorded by all civilized nations to prisoners of war." Distributed nationally in a print run of forty thousand copies, and widely cited in newspaper articles, the report helped build appreciation for the sacrifices of black volunteers and support for the vital legislation that would create civil rights for former slaves by awakening the Northern public to the unique risks that faced Negro volunteers, and more broadly to the barbarism that festered at the heart of racism. While the report was not sufficient by itself to transform Northern feelings toward blacks, it helped to create a constituency that would support the Radicals' drive toward general emancipation and eventually full civil rights.

Wade had barely finished the report when, on May 6, the entire Joint Committee traveled to Annapolis to take testimony from Union soldiers who had just been released from Richmond prison camps in an exchange with the rebels. What Wade saw appalled him all the more coming on the heels of the events at Fort Pillow. The former prisoners, many of them dying as a result of malnutrition, frostbite, and abuse, Wade wrote, bore "literally the appearance of living skeletons." So appalled were they by the men's condition that Wade and Rep. George W. Julian at one point "fled from the work" and found each other sobbing like children. The committee supplemented its report with a gallery of shocking photographs of men they had interviewed, some beyond saving by the army doctors who were treating them. "Your committee," Wade wrote, "are constrained to say that they can hardly avoid the conclusion, expressed by so many of our released soldiers, that the inhuman practices herein referred to reduce our soldiers in their power, by privation of food and clothing, and by exposure, to such a condition that those who may survive shall never recover so as to be able to render any effective service in the field." Such treatment, he added, was no less than the savagery visited upon black Union soldiers at Fort Pillow, "the result of a predetermined policy."

The Fort Pillow massacre demonstrated beyond any argument the savagery that would be visited upon blacks who defied the South's unforgiving strictures of race. It also underscored in blood the uncertain postwar fate of the South's nearly four million slaves, if Union victory succeeded in freeing them. A problem that had once seemed the preserve of ideologues now needed to somehow be solved, practically and permanently. For more than a year Congress had inconclusively debated what Reconstruction was to be. On what terms, and in what form, would seceded states be permitted to rejoin the Union? Should Reconstruction be punitive or forgiving? What role, if any, would government play? Who would decide? Congress? The president? Southern whites? How it was implemented would profoundly influence the lives not only of the freedmen, but also of many millions of Southern whites for whom the prospect of Negroes as anything but slaves was unimaginable.

A year earlier, with mingled disdain and anxiety the conservative Republican *New York Times* had anticipated the problems that the country would face if slaves were emancipated wholesale. "If the president supposes that millions of men, who never made a bargain in their lives, who were never consulted on any subject affecting their own interest, who never made provision for their own support, or had the slightest charge connected with the maintenance of wives or children, and who have worked all their lives under the pressure of force and fear, can pass suddenly to the condition of free men— recognizing at once all its responsibilities and performing all its duties—he must believe that the age of miracles is not yet passed." The *Times* added, betraying a widespread belief even in the North that Negroes would not work unless coerced, "If the Proclamation makes the slaves actually free, there will come the further duty of making them work." If they should choose to work, well and good. "But if they do not, they must be compelled to do it."

The problem of the freedmen had reached crisis proportions as hundreds of thousands of former slaves flooded into contraband camps from the Mississippi River Valley to the Carolinas to Maryland, clustering around military bases and at the edges of cities and towns wherever federal troops marched. Among the largest was a complete village established on the property of Robert E. Lee's family home, the future site of Arlington National Cemetery. For the most part, refugees huddled in threadbare tents and lean-tos, living on whatever scanty rations the army or civilian charities provided, hoping for work from the army. Many were sick and starving. Many also suffered from untreated gunshot wounds, received during their escape. They were people without rights and largely without prospects, vulnerable to abuse by civilians and racist soldiers, and to sudden reenslavement where the battle lines were fluid and the Confederates liable to reappear. Before the war, nearly all blacks were presumed to be slaves, and no one, North or South, imagined a relationship between the enslaved and the national government. Now there were hundreds of thousands, and the prospects of millions, whose increasingly visible presence demanded that a new place must somehow be made for them in the United States. In the Senate, Sumner proposed the creation of a new government agency— a "Freedmen's Bureau"—to ease the transition from slavery to freedom, an idea that steadily gained Republican support in the course of the session, but infuriated Democrats. Sneering at the "honey-tongued humanitarians of New England," "Sunset" Cox scoffed that such a "sweeping and revolutionary measure" would create a vast new arena for corruption while "no government farming system, no charitable black scheme, can wash out the color of the negro [or] change his inferior nature."

On December 8, Lincoln preempted the Radicals by issuing the "Proclamation of Amnesty and Reconstruction"—a notably charitable locution, "amnesty"—setting forth his plan for the eventual readmission of the seceded states to the Union. It declared that except for high-ranking political and military men, pardons would be granted to any rebel who took an oath of loyalty to the Constitution, and that all confiscated property would be restored to them, apart from slaves. It further stipulated that state governments could be reestablished once one-tenth of the number who had voted in the 1860 election had taken a loyalty oath, so long as the state agreed to recognize the permanent freedom of former slaves, in accordance with the Emancipation Proclamation.

Lincoln elaborated on this in his unusually prolix annual message, describing the amnesty offer as "a sufficiently liberal one, which accepts as sound whoever will make a sworn recantation of his former unsoundness." Almost apologetically, it seemed, he felt compelled to justify the proposal's requirement of a formal commitment to the Emancipation Proclamation in addition to a loyalty oath. The measures that had so far been taken against slavery were war measures and might legally be supposed to expire once the war had ended. But a moral commitment had been made to the thousands of black volunteers now in the Union service. In this, he agreed with the Radicals. To abandon them now would be to relinquish a lever of power, but also be a cruel breach of faith. He further promised that he would not attempt to retract or modify the Emancipation Proclamation or order the return to slavery of any person who had been freed by any act of Congress. Lincoln also offered recognition of the new state governments in Union-occupied Louisiana and Arkansas. The president's war policy rested on the premise that the Southern states had never actually left the Union, but rather had been captured by political pirates, so to speak, and deserved to be restored to their former place as smoothly as possible. Still, from the man who had announced not so long ago that he had no intention of tampering with slavery this was a remarkable evolution.

"Sunset" Cox scoffed, declaring of Lincoln, "He is a man whose mind has every angle but the right angle. In his nature, cunning contends with fanaticism." But conservative Republicans and some Democrats generally lauded the president. The New York Times approvingly commented, "The public mind, we have no doubt will accept it as another signal illustration of the practical wisdom of the president," while the populist New York Herald optimistically predicted that the proclamation would produce a "wonderful effect" on Lee's army, and that entire brigades would soon lay down their arms and march en masse to the federal lines.

The Radicals were another matter. Many of them were initially supportive. The president's secretary John Hay claimed that he saw delight on the faces of Chandler and Sumner, and that Horace Greeley exclaimed that Lincoln's plan was "devilish good!" But as the details of the president's policy sank in it became clear that he had completely cut Congress out of Reconstruction policy-making, created an opening for rebels to quickly reenter power, and left the possibility that many Negroes might still be left in slavery. A tiny number of voters could determine a state's fate—just 67,931 of South Carolina's 679,310 registered voters, for example, or 14,531 of Tennessee's 145,348. The Radicals' concerns were not ill-founded. Sen. Willard Saulsbury of Delaware, one of slavery's most forceful defenders in Congress, had said as much in the last session. Once restored Southern states were again free to govern themselves, he said, "they will not only reenslave every person you attempt to set free, but they will reenslave the whole race."

Resistance quickly built. Sumner and Thaddeus Stevens, independently of each other, had already laid out an alternative framework for Reconstruction under which the seceded states would be treated as conquered territories, essentially an empty space on the political map, whose soil should be divided up and resettled by Union soldiers, loyal poor whites, and black freedmen, and protected by the federal government until their reorganized societies were stable and safe from revanchist reprisals. (The New York Times accused Stevens, and implicitly Sumner, of being a de facto "secessionist" for asserting that the Confederate states were no longer in the Union, essentially granting the secessionists' argument that they *could* leave, a principle the government had denied for almost three years.) In these competing visions, the battle lines over Reconstruction had been drawn: they would dominate much of the most important remaining work of the Thirty-eighth Congress, and cast their shadow well beyond the war, dividing wartime allies, fissuring the Republican Party, and shaping postwar politics for years to come.

In the House of Representatives, in a series of brilliant speeches that he began on February 15, the newly elected Radical Henry Winter Davis of Maryland laid out the foundation of the Radicals' plan. A repentant former slave owner, the handsome and erudite Davis had quickly made a name for himself as one of the most eloquent, if rash, among the new crop of Radicals, and an unremitting gadfly to the president. He even claimed to believe that Lincoln was scheming to create a batch of new "pseudo" states in the South from among those under partial Union control so he could personally control their congressional delegations.

"We cannot stand still," Davis told the House. "We must go backward or we must go forward." If the old governments were reestablished "under the same aristocracy," how much longer could former slaves manage to retain their freedom? There would be nothing to protect them if they couldn't appeal to the right of habeas corpus or the courts. "Does the master resort to the court against the slave?" he asked. "No, he seizes him by the neck." Nothing less than a resolute declaration that slavery must be prohibited in every reconstructed state's constitution along with an explicit federal promise of judicial protection for freedmen could ensure the death of slavery.

Davis returned to the issue on March 22. "Our success will be the overthrow of *all* semblance of government in the rebel states," he said. No Southern state could be trusted with its own government for the foreseeable future. There was nowhere in the South a cadre of loyal patriots who were prepared to face down the rebels, much less to risk death for the republic. The so-called "loyal masses of the South" simply didn't exist. Under Lincoln's formula, there was nothing to prevent the rebel leaders from returning to power. In states where "the great mass of that population is devoted to the system of slave labor," the former rebels could never be trusted to abolish slavery. So, what then? The amendment to the Constitution that had been proposed—by James Ashley in the House and Sumner in the Senate—wasn't enough: weak as it was it had already failed in the House, and it would fall far short of winning ratification in enough states to become law, he predicted. Under his plan, Davis said, Congress itself would reorganize postwar state governments and "weed out" every law that thwarted republican government and the safety of freed blacks.

Radical as he was, Davis was no racial egalitarian, remarking to a Baltimore audience in 1864, "I am perfectly content that the negro shall be equal with [his enemies], but not with me or my friends." But he was at least intellectually honest. Proposals to erase the black population by deporting them were a foolish delusion, he told the House. No other countries wanted the United States's race problem. Even if taxpayers were willing to shoulder the cost, and there was no evidence that they were, deportation would lead to economic disruption in the United States. And who would fill the "enormous vacuum of labor swept away by this insane and unchristian philanthropy?" And why should American blacks be forced to move to "barbarous countries" anyway? And why would they consent to go? Look beyond the feverish passions and prejudices of the moment, he urged. "They have a right to remain here, and they will remain here to the latest recorded syllable of time." Davis's ideas, with input from Stevens and Ben Wade, would eventually coalesce in a deeply controversial bill that set more stringent conditions for the renewal of statehood than those offered by Lincoln, requiring a much higher percentage of voters to prove their loyalty, barring all former rebels from office, and explicitly guaranteeing the freedom of former slaves.

To counter Davis, "Sunset" Cox mustered all the overripe eloquence at his command to oppose the bill. In a speech that ranged capaciously across the histories of ancient Greece and Rome, seventeenth-century England and eighteenth-century France, he ventured to suggest that the dissolution of the Union might not be as terrible as people feared. Suppose the South did succeed in gaining its independence. Might not some kind of customs union bind the

sections loosely together, and might not that evolve "through common interests and kindness" into a "more intimate union" someday?
Was that really so terrible a prospect? Compare it to the vengeful
triumphalism embodied in Davis's bill. "If we pursue the South with
a licentious uncivic soldiery, gloating with anticipations of the plunder of private effects, or with the promises already held out of par-
celing out the lands of the South as the bounty which revenge pays
for pillage, thus whetting a tigerish appetite for a great festival of
blood and rapine, we may be sure that the special Nemesis which
Herodotus traced through the early eras of history, will haunt the
men who instigate and the men who execute such a fell and imbecile
policy." Never a man to rest upon one elaborate metaphor when several more might be heaped together, he added, citing among other
pitiless despoliations of wars' losers, the destruction of the Moors
of Andalusia, the slaughter of French royalists by revolutionaries,
the bloody British hunt for Scots dissenters, the "bloodshot eye of
maddened Poland," the persecution of the Irish, finally concluding,
"He who would destroy a part of his own country, as if it were alien,
has no more love for it than Saturn had for the children of his own
loins whom he devoured." Even for the orotund Cox this truly was a
show-stopping performance.

The military power of the Confederacy must be broken, Cox
allowed. (Though a relentless enemy of the administration, Cox
usually voted to fund the army, in contrast to more extreme Copperheads.) But after their defeat, he said, the South deserved to be
treated with paternal care. Despotic rule would only produce economic ruin and a promiscuous mixing of the races. The result of
*that,* he asserted, would be "half-breed bastards born of barbarism,
whose mothers have ceased to be slaves with the largest liberty to
be—worse!" He pleaded for the most generous terms of amnesty
for rebels. "Give forgiveness to the erring, hope to the desponding.
You cannot expel the poison of sedition by adding to its virulence."

His eloquence persuaded no one. The lines of battle were drawn
and unyielding. Later that day, May 4, Davis's bill passed decisively by
a vote of seventy-three to fifty-nine. Radical Reconstruction now had
a concrete strategy. But Reconstruction was of course predicated on
the assumption of complete Union victory.

That same day, 120,000 federal troops began marching south for what the president and every Republican in Congress hoped and prayed would be the last campaign of the war. After repeated disappointments, Northerners once again believed that the end was near. A celebrated, ever-victorious new general had come out of the West to lead the Army of the Potomac: Ulysses S. Grant. As proof of its confidence in him, Congress bestowed on him the rank of lieutenant general, unused since George Washington laid it down to return to civilian life.

# 17

# Majorities Must Rule

---

Can't you get a candidate for vice-president without
going down into a damned rebel province for one?

—REP. THADDEUS STEVENS

The Army of the Potomac didn't know quite what to make of
Ulysses Grant. Modest to a fault, he was the inverse of peacocks
like McClellan and Hooker, whose preening bombast belied their
mediocrity, while his quiet decisiveness would prove the antidote
to the hesitation that had characterized Meade's lackluster leadership ever since Gettysburg. It wasn't always thus. Until 1861, Grant
was a study in failed promise: graduation from West Point followed
by distinguished service in the Mexican War that petered out into
dreary years of garrison duty, rumors of alcoholism, and a succession of unrewarding and unrewarded civilian trades in the backwa-
ters of Missouri and Illinois. A Douglas Democrat in politics, he had
harbored mixed feelings about slavery. The Civil War rescued him
from obscurity, but unlike most it also rocketed him within months
from victory to victory, beginning with the seizure of enemy posts
on the Mississippi, the brilliant capture of Forts Henry and Donelson on the Tennessee and the Cumberland, the stunning recovery
from near-defeat at Shiloh, the triumph at Vicksburg, and the relief
of Chattanooga.

Promising to bring a new aggressive spirit to the so often defeated eastern army, he called up spare troops from as far away as New York and Boston, and stripped the defenses of Washington to restore the Army of the Potomac to more than 120,000 men, its greatest size since 1862. "We had to have hard fighting," Grant later wrote. "The two armies had been confronting each other so long, without any decisive result, that they hardly knew which could whip." He retained Meade as the army's nominal commander, although in practice the victor of Gettysburg served as something closer to a senior chief of staff for Grant, who planned the army's movements. In contrast to his predecessors, Grant saw the Army of the Potomac's overland campaign as but one piece, if the largest one, of a multi-pronged campaign to assault the Confederates simultaneously on every front. William T. Sherman, Grant's successor as commander of the Army of the Tennessee, would strike for Atlanta, the Confederacy's western manufacturing center and railroad hub. Gen. Nathaniel Banks would drive up the Red River into the heartland of Louisiana. A combined land and sea force would assault Mobile, the Confederacy's last major port on the Gulf of Mexico. Yet another army under Gen. David Hunter would campaign down the Shenandoah Valley. And while Grant himself marched south into Virginia in pursuit of Robert E. Lee, Gen. Benjamin Butler with another 36,000 men would swing inland from Chesapeake Bay to envelop Richmond from the south. Altogether, it was the most comprehensive and coordinated war plan that the Union had yet attempted, and its complexity a testament to the strategic sophistication of Grant's mind.

The Army of the Potomac in 1864 was no longer the battle-hungry and undisciplined mob that had stumbled into defeat at Bull Run three years earlier. It had been bloodied many times over since then. Most of the early volunteers were now dead or maimed, or had declined to reenlist after their three years were up. Although a steely patriotism, comradeship, and a determination to finish the job they had started all played their part, many of the veterans who still remained searched their souls for the strength to continue. One of them, Elwood Griest, a Pennsylvanian from Lancaster County, tried to explain to his wife how he coped with the pervasiveness of suffering and death. "I am more than ever convinced that life, strange and mysterious as it may seem to us, is but the sure and unerring workings of a grand machine, as much above our comprehension as the most complicated machinery of human invention is above the comprehension of brute creation. This being the case, we may go forward on life's journey without fear, confident that whatever may happen, we are but contributing to the grand result."

Along with veterans like Griest, tens of thousands of often unwilling draftees now filled the ranks. Even more were men who had been paid by affluent draftees to serve as hired substitutes. At the beginning of the war, bounties of $40 or $50 were common; by 1864, it often cost more than $1,000 to entice men to enlist. Thaddeus Stevens personally offered a bounty of $150 to every man in the first two companies from Lancaster County to volunteer for twelve months' service under the most recent Enrollment Act, plus a bonus of $50 for the first three companies whose officers pledged to abstain from liquor while in service. Apart from the standard $300 federal fee, many others were paid bounties by cities and towns, businesses and private donors such as Stevens, so that states could fill their draft quotas without resorting to politically risky mass conscription. Not surprisingly, many such men soon deserted and often reenlisted elsewhere to claim another bounty, and then absconded again: in one Connecticut regiment, 60 out of 210 recruits decamped within their first three days in camp. A satirical cartoon in *Harper's Weekly* that winter showed a broker leading a weedy-looking drunk into a barber shop, saying, "Look a-here—I want you to trim up this old chap with a flaxen wig and a light mustache, so as to make him look like twenty; and as I shall probably clear three hundred dollars on him, I sha'n't mind giving you a fifty for the job."

Once again, the Army of the Potomac crossed the desolation of northern Virginia, littered with abandoned fortifications, earthworks, old camps, rifle pits, burned bridges, wrecked railroad cars, ruined woodlands, and untilled fields. Even houses were scarce, having been torn apart for firewood by one army or another. On May 5, Grant collided with a Confederate army about half the size of his own near the old Chancellorsville battlefield, in the wasteland of scrub pine, briars, oak, swamps, and thickets known locally as the "Wilderness." Human skulls and bones left from the former battle were strewn everywhere, a forbidding sight for men about to go into battle. Maneuver was close to impossible. The narrow roads jumbled ranks and the dense woods wiped out the Union's advantage in artillery. For two days the armies grappled in bloody melees and fell in tangled heaps to devastating rifle fire from enemies hidden in the trees. Brushfires roasted hundreds of wounded alive, terrifying the living with their screams and the stink of burning flesh. The stalemate left more than seventeen thousand federals and eleven thousand Confederates killed, wounded, and captured. Several of Grant's senior officers advised him to retreat as every thwarted commander before him had done. He ignored them. He directed the army to skirt Lee's flank and keep marching south. Despite their wounds and their weariness, when the soldiers realized that Grant would not take them back to Washington, wild cheers echoed through the forest. Men swung their hats, flung up their arms, and cried, "On to Richmond!" with a gusto that they had not felt for many months.

On May 9, the two armies met again near Spotsylvania Court House, eight miles to the south. Grant hammered hard at the Confederate line but failed to break it. May 12 saw the longest sustained combat of the war, as for twenty-one hours straight soldiers battled only a few feet apart, standing atop the mingled dead and wounded three and four deep to poke their rifles over the breastworks, as the wounded writhed in agony beneath them. Wrote one federal soldier, "I saw one [man] completely trodden in the mud so as to look like part of it and yet he was breathing and gasping." Federal losses at Spotsylvania surpassed 18,000, the Confederates' somewhat less. Over just two weeks, the Army of the Potomac had been reduced by 36,000 men, more than a third of its number; the Confederates were diminished by about 24,000, a slightly greater proportion of their total. Stymied but undefeated, Grant once again sidestepped the enemy's position and pushed on south.

Northern newspapers barely mentioned the slaughter, instead emphasizing the skill of the generals and the bravery of the men. The *Lancaster Examiner* jauntily characterized Grant's slog as "a footrace to Richmond," and with a trumpeting boldface headline screamed— quite inaccurately—"Butler on the War Path! He is successful everywhere!" even as that hapless general succumbed to tactical paralysis. The soldiers, of course, knew the truth. The sheer bloodiness of the campaign traumatized even the most battle-hardened. Elwood Griest wrote to his wife, "What a ghastly spectacle do the dead present, torn and mutilated in every conceivable way their unburied corpses cover the country for miles and miles in every direction. I pray that I may be spared from seeing any more." And in a scribbled note to his parents, future Supreme Court Justice Oliver Wendell Holmes wrote, "It is still kill—kill—all the time," adding a few days later, "I tell you many a man has gone crazy since this campaign has begun from the terrible pressure on mind & body."

Only slowly did the magnitude of what was happening make itself felt in Washington. The atmosphere there became increasingly grim. "It is a tearful place here now," wrote Rep. James A. Garfield to his wife from Washington. "While the thousands of fresh troops go out to feed the great battle mills the crushed grain comes in." The wounded swamped field hospitals and piled up on train platforms and wharves. It got only worse. On June 3, in what Grant himself recognized as his worst mistake of the campaign, he ordered another frontal assault on Lee's lines at Cold Harbor, ten miles east of Richmond. Veterans knew it was suicidal and wrote their names on scraps of paper so that their bodies could be identified later. Grant lost six thousand men that morning, more than half of them in the first half-hour, but failed again to dent Lee's lines. When another assault was ordered that afternoon not a man stirred, refusing to commit suicide in what looked like a foregone massacre.

Grant realized that Cold Harbor was a watershed. Depleted, numb with exhaustion, shaken by trauma, and unwilling to attack dug-in Confederates, the Army of the Potomac was essentially fought-out. Since the beginning of the campaign, it had lost some 55,000 men, of whom more than 7,000 had been killed. A single division in the Second Corps had suffered the appalling loss of 72 percent of its strength since the campaign began. The Confederates had lost between 30,000 and 35,000, many of them irreplaceable.

Apart from Adm. David Farragut's dramatic seizure of Mobile— "Damn the torpedoes, full speed ahead," he famously cried as he ordered his warships into the heavily mined bay—all the other pieces of Grant's ambitious strategy had come to naught. Hunter had been driven ignominiously from the Shenandoah Valley. Butler had allowed himself to be bottled up by a much smaller enemy force outside Petersburg. Sherman was still maneuvering toward Atlanta. Banks had been thrown back in Louisiana. Grant had brought Lee to bay in the ring of fortified trenches around Richmond and Petersburg, but the Confederates still held their capital, and they were still willing to fight. Yet another year that had begun with high hopes and another celebrated general seemed to be sinking into torpid stalemate.

In Washington, as renewed public disillusionment with the war set in, tempers were on a hair-trigger. Zachariah Chandler, Ben Wade's rough-mannered Senate colleague from Michigan, was dining with friends at the National Hotel on Pennsylvania Avenue when he was overheard denouncing Copperheads by Rep. Daniel Voorhees of Indiana, who was sitting nearby. Voorhees rose, stepped closer to Chandler, and slapped him in the face. The two, both big men—Voorhees was known as "The Tall Sycamore of the Wabash"—then began wrestling across the dining room. When Chandler appeared to be getting the better of Voorhees, the Indianan's companion, a man named Hannigan, rushed to his aid. Seizing a pitcher of milk from a nearby table, he smashed it over Chandler's head, spraying milk over everyone nearby and leaving Chandler stunned. Hannigan then hit him again with a chair, at which point the men were finally separated, with great difficulty, by bystanders. It was a foretaste of the political campaign that was just getting under way.

As Grant's men were dying at Cold Harbor, Republican politicians and their War Democrat allies, amalgamated in what was officially being called the "National Union Party," were gathering in withering heat at the Front Street Theatre in Baltimore to renominate Abraham Lincoln. By June, his place on the ticket was assured. But it was not without controversy. As early as February, disaffected Radicals had begun searching for an alternative candidate. In a widely distributed letter, Sen. Samuel Pomeroy of Kansas asserted bluntly that Lincoln probably couldn't be reelected, and that even if he could he shouldn't be. And even if Lincoln managed to win a second term, his "addiction to milquetoast compromise" and halfway solutions would doubtless grow even more costly to "the cause of human liberty and the dignity and honor of the nation." Pomeroy was not alone. Another well-placed Washington Republican privately denounced to Ben Wade what he scathingly called Lincoln's "treatcherous imbecility," while John Hiestand, a Pennsylvania journalist close to Thaddeus Stevens, demanded, "are we to go through with this election and have four years more of procrastination and then die broken hearted, at having failed in our only chance, because we had a President who says he wants to make all free, but is too big a coward."

Alternative candidates were advanced: Benjamin Butler, a failure as a general but a deft politician who had thrown in his lot with the Radical cause; Grant himself, though no one knew his politics; John C. Frémont, the Republicans' 1856 standard-bearer; and above all Treasury Secretary Salmon P. Chase, an abolitionist of unimpeachable character, who had long angled for the nomination, and may have encouraged Pomeroy's circular in order to gauge public opinion. (Pomeroy had warmly praised Chase as a statesman who would "vindicate the honor of the Republic before the world.") Throughout the late winter, Chase's friends in Ohio worked to depress support for Lincoln, a party operative confided to Wade, who considered Lincoln weak but had not yet committed himself to a candidate. Chase also had the support of key newspaper publishers, including Horace Greeley, as well as several bankers and financiers, Jay Cooke the most prominent among them. But if the circular was meant to boost Chase's chances, it backfired by provoking Republican committees, newspapers, and state legislatures—including Ohio's—to hastily endorse the president. With Chase's star sinking, disaffected Radicals met in Cleveland at the end of May under the rubric of the "Radical Democracy Party" and nominated Frémont. Its platform scorchingly denounced "the imbecile and vacillating policy of the present administration, [and] its treachery to justice, freedom, and genuine democratic principles in its plan of reconstruction," and called for the immediate abolition of slavery and absolute equality of blacks and whites before the law. Apart from a handful of prominent figures such as Wendell Phillips and Elizabeth Cady Stanton, few of Frémont's supporters were nationally known, but it represented the sentiments of many more including, it was assumed, Ben

Wade. (At about the same time, a convention of spiritualists in New York presented a series of resolutions sent to it by "a concourse of departed spirits" denouncing the national government and calling for the nomination of a, presumably, flesh-and-blood peace candidate for the presidency.)

The instability of Lincoln's support was typified by the ambivalence of Rep. James Garfield, who shared Chase's antagonism to Lincoln and blamed the president's seeming lack of vigor on his supposed enslavement to the conservative Blair family, to whom he thought the president was "bound hand and foot." After the release of the Pomeroy Circular, however, like many restless Radicals, Garfield reluctantly began to resign himself to Lincoln's renomination, feeling that division in the party would fatally subvert the war effort. "He will probably be the man, though I think we could do better," he wrote to a friend in early March. In late April, his pessimism returned. By now he felt certain that although Lincoln would be renominated he would be defeated, and a Copperhead elected. He reflected gloomily, "I don't know a dozen men who believe it can be otherwise."

The crafters of the platform the Republicans adopted in Baltimore tried hard to satisfy the Radicals. It was firmly emancipationist: no compromise with the rebels, no terms of peace except unconditional surrender, and the "utter and complete extirpation [of slavery] from the soil of the American republic" by means of constitutional amendment. Clearly with the Fort Pillow massacre in mind, the platform also declared that the government owed every soldier "without regard to distinction of color" the full protection of the laws of war, and that any rebels who transgressed the "usages of civilized nations" must be appropriately punished. Not insignificantly, the platform also embodied the evolving business-friendly policies that were moving toward the center of Republican philosophy, committing the party to redemption of the public debt, support for the national credit, a "vigorous and just system of taxation," and the continuation of the new national currency. Lincoln, who did not attend the convention but monitored it closely from Washington, formally approved the platform on June 9. The seceded states, he wrote to the committee notifying him of his renomination, had been given notice that they could resume their allegiance "without the overthrow of their institution"—that is, slavery—but they had ignored that offer. Therefore, he said, with an eye to the Frémontites, a constitutional amendment ending slavery had become "a fitting and necessary conclusion to the final success of the Union cause." As dissatisfied as most of the congressional Radicals were with Lincoln, and as much as they might disagree with each other on the course that Reconstruction ought to take, they could at least, finally, take pride in the party's official embrace of abolition.

Having adopted a Radical platform, the convention now proceeded to make what would prove to be one of the most momentous political decisions of the war, the replacement of Vice President Hannibal Hamlin as Lincoln's running mate with former senator and wartime Tennessee governor Andrew Johnson, in a last-minute switch that would change the course of American history. Hamlin had every reason to assume that he would be renominated, as did probably most Republicans. For nearly four years, he had performed his duties with modesty and skill. Lincoln didn't much care for Hamlin personally, privately disparaging him as a boring "old mouser." But it was also said that he was Lincoln's best insurance against assassination, since the South knew that if he was killed it would face something much worse: a staunch abolitionist, who had long pushed the president forward on emancipation, and one of whose sons was among the first officers to volunteer to command a black regiment. Because Hamlin was wise in the ways of Washington, and close to the Radicals in Congress, Hamlin's former colleagues in the Senate, no one doubted that he was fully prepared to step into the presidency if he had to.

Hamlin had been assured by James G. Blaine, Lincoln's point man for Maine, that talk of replacing him was baseless. The events surrounding this still remain controversial. In later years, Lincoln's secretaries John Nicolay and John Hay asserted not entirely convincingly that the president had passively left the choice of his vice president up to the convention. (In a brief note to them, Lincoln indicated that he didn't wish to "interfere" in the choice of a vice president, but his choice of words made quite clear that he would not fight for Hamlin.) They also recalled a "general impression" that Lincoln thought it would be a good idea to select a War Democrat. However, Alexander McClure, a powerful Pennsylvania politician and editor who had been instrumental in Lincoln's nomination in 1860, later claimed that behind the scenes the president had "moved with masterly sagacity at every step in his efforts to nominate Johnson." Four years earlier, Lincoln had selected Hamlin largely to win support among abolitionists and in New England. Now, worried about reelection, McClure said, Lincoln wanted a man who could win over Democrats. It was smart, if ultimately tragically shortsighted, transactional politics.

Although not very well-liked, Johnson was by no means an eccentric choice. He enjoyed the support of Henry J. Raymond, the Union Party's chairman and editor of the *New York Times,* and his stern rule in Tennessee had earned him respect among the Radicals. Party spokesmen often quoted a now famous remark that he had made earlier that year, that "treason must be made odious." Sumner called him "that patriot Senator—faithful among the faithless." And in the words of one Tennessee delegate, Judge Horace Maynard, Johnson had "stood in the furnace of treason" without flinching. The only senator from a slave state to have remained loyal to the Union, he had reorganized Tennessee's government in what Lincoln hoped would serve as an eventual model for other Southern states that reentered the Union. In addition, according to McClure, should the election prove close, Lincoln believed that the electoral votes from newly reorganized states such as Louisiana and Arkansas led by conservative Unionists such as Johnson could ensure his victory.

In later years, Hamlin insisted that Lincoln really had wanted him all along but had been blindsided by an alleged "intrigue" masterminded by Sumner, who Hamlin had thought to be a personal friend. According to this scenario, which was supported by Blaine, Sumner was eager to see his rival Pitt Fessenden ousted from the Senate and believed that the most efficient way to do it would be to encourage a newly jobless Hamlin to run against him. To this Macchiavellian end, Sumner allegedly lobbied New England delegates on behalf of Sen. Daniel Dickinson of New York for vice president, a War Democrat known for his long silvery locks and his fondness for quoting the

Bible. (Some called him "Scripture Dick.") However, Secretary of State Seward, the most powerful Republican of all after the president, was determined to thwart Dickinson because his selection would mean that Seward would have to resign from his job since, according to the custom of the time, two men from the same state could not occupy senior executive offices simultaneously. Seward, therefore, threw his weight behind Johnson. Whatever the truth may have been, the trusting Hamlin was completely unaware of all these behind-the-scenes machinations.

When the roll was finally called in the congested hall, Lincoln was renominated almost without dissent, with the exception of Missouri's disaffected Radical delegation, which cast its twenty-two votes for Grant. When Hamlin's name was put into nomination, cries of "No! No!" rose above the tumult on the floor. A positive statement from the president would have ensured Hamlin's renomination: his silence was eloquent. According to McClure, Lincoln's agents arranged for a "complimentary" vote for Hamlin on the first ballot, so as not to humiliate him, although he received only 150 votes to Johnson's 200, and 120 for Dickinson. Sixty-one votes were scattered among other candidates. On the second ballot, Simon Cameron, who had put Hamlin's name in nomination, threw Pennsylvania's 55 votes to Johnson. Finally, even Hamlin's own state of Maine abandoned him. In the end, Johnson swamped him with nearly 500 votes to 17 for Hamlin, and 9 for Dickinson. Bands played, delegates cheered lustily for the new ticket, flags were waved, and instead of a lifelong abolitionist the party's choice would be one of the most Negrophobic men in high government office.

Johnson, who had owned slaves as recently as 1862, endorsed the platform's emancipation plank, and asserted his support for federal supremacy over the states. Falling on his sword for the ticket, Hamlin praised Johnson as an "incorruptible patriot" and "eminently fitted for the nomination." But not all Republicans were pleased with the choice. Some Radicals were apoplectic, among them Thaddeus Stevens, who detested Johnson as a scoundrel and a rank demagogue. Sensing the catastrophe that might be in store, he stalked the convention floor, muttering angrily, "Can't you get a candidate for vice president without going down into a damned rebel province for one?"

In the three weeks that remained before adjournment, a storm of bills blew through both houses of Congress. Measures that had been stalled up for months flooded onto the floor and were hastily dispatched: treaties with Indian tribes, approval for a canal from the Mississippi River to Lake Michigan, appropriations for surveying wagon roads in the Idaho Territory, repairs to the aqueduct that carried water to Washington, pensions for veterans of the War of 1812, testing submarine inventions for the Navy, paying lighthouse-keepers off the Maryland coast, and scores of other expenditures that had lain dormant beneath the spring's torturous debates over war and slavery.

In the House, Thaddeus Stevens, ignoring his worsening health, lashed members of his caucus forward to pass bills raising tariffs and taxes to pay for soldiers' ballooning bonuses. His stress was heightened further by the financial strain of rebuilding his forge and mill, left in ruins by Jubal Early's attack; the project dragged endlessly as more and more workmen were conscripted to replenish the dead and crippled of the spring campaign. Across the Capitol, Pitt Fessenden, also ragged with exhaustion, begged Republicans to stay in their seats no matter how tired they were, to "get through it," and stop insisting on perfection where it couldn't be gotten. His patience often frayed. "I have neither the strength nor the disposition to argue these things over and over again," he repeatedly snapped. To a colleague who urged him to read a constituent's letter of advice, he barked that he had no interest in "bushels" of suggestions from well-meaning ignoramuses who knew nothing whatever of the subject they presumed to advise the Senate on.

Not entirely unexpectedly, the constitutional amendment abolishing slavery went down to defeat in the House. Robert Mallory of Kentucky claimed shock that the "pigmies" who were pressing for the amendment would dare "to trifle with the Constitution," while Vallandigham ally George Pendleton of Ohio warned that the ratification of any such amendment "at bayonet point" would "destroy the last lingering hope, faint, small as it now is, that you will ever be able to restore this Union." The Radicals tried their best. "Let justice to all men be our aim," cried William D. Kelley, an evangelical abolitionist from Philadelphia. "I will trust the freed negroes to the care of God and our beneficent republican institutions." And Isaac Arnold, a Lincoln look-alike from Illinois, asserting that slavery was already at its last gasp—"It now reels and staggers toward its last death struggle"—fruitlessly called upon his colleagues to "strike the monster this last decisive blow." But they couldn't do it. An amendment to the Constitution needed a two-thirds majority to pass. It fell short of that goal by eleven votes, ninety-three to sixty-five, with twenty-three members declining to vote. Despite the celebrated bravery of black soldiers, despite the horrors of Fort Pillow, despite the heart-rending plight of the contrabands, despite the months of soaring abolitionist oratory, it seemed that slavery, battered and bruised as it was, would not yet die after all.

The Radicals fared better on recalibrating soldiers' pay without regard to race, voting to equalize all black soldiers' pay to January 1, 1864, and to the time of enlistment for all who had been free on April 19, 1861. (The distinction between free men and recent slaves caused friction in units comprising men in both categories until the colonel of the 54th Massachusetts invented what became wryly known as the "Quaker oath": advising soldiers to swear that they "owed no man unrequited labor on or before the 19th day of April, 1861," based on "God's higher law," which abolitionists had long maintained inherently nullified the ownership of men, a convenient locution that was soon delightedly copied by other black regiments.)

Sumner, in tandem with the Radical Ohio abolitionist James Ashley, who had introduced a similar measure in the House, also pressed hard for the establishment of a bureau dedicated to protecting the rights and safety of freedmen, and overseeing the distribution of land to them from plantations confiscated from rebels. He termed it a "transition measure" to "bridge over" the challenging passage from slavery to freedom, arguing that without such legislation Southern whites would soon impose a new regime of forced labor on them. In contrast to Ashley, however, whose version assigned the bureau to the War Department, Sumner's placed it under the Treasury Department, reasoning that Treasury was already responsible for the management of confiscated lands, which he wished to have handed over to the former slaves.

Democrats in both chambers excoriated the bill as a revolutionary measure that would turn the Treasury Department into a "fund for the Negro" and spawn a sump of corruption. "No government farming system, no charitable black scheme, can wash out the color of the negro, change his inferior nature, or save him from his inevitable fate," protested "Sunset" Cox, for it ought to be obvious to anyone that the Negro could never survive in freedom. In the Senate, Garrett Davis of Kentucky insisted that there was simply no constitutional basis for such a bureau, since that document had been made by and for white men alone: "The negro had nothing to do with it, no more than the Indian of the forest." In any case, charged the equally Negrophobic but more practical-minded James McDougall of California, the government could never administer the affairs of four million people: "It is a social as well as a mathematical absurdity."

In support of the bill, Zachariah Chandler declared that the proposed bureau represented just a first payment on the deep debt that Americans would owe Negroes for helping win the war for the Union. "I would use locomotives, I would use mules, I would use jackasses, I would use every single thing that God and nature had put in my hands to put down this rebellion," he roared—a steady roar being his characteristic mode of debate. "But first I would use the black element. I would let a loyal Negro vote. I would let him testify. I would let him fight. I consider a loyal Negro better than a secession traitor in either the North or South, and I will treat him better."

Although the bill passed overwhelmingly by a vote of twenty-one to nine, there was no time left to reconcile the Senate version with Ashley's in the rapidly dwindling hours of the session, leaving suspended not just the fate of the bureau but also that of the nearly four million slaves and freedmen whose uncertain and insecure future depended on what the Union chose to do with them when the war ended.

Two days later, with just three days left to the session, the Senate then returned to the highly fraught Wade-Davis bill, the flagship of the Radicals' legislative armada designed to seize the initiative for Congress on postwar Reconstruction. In its final form, the bill unequivocally required that the seceded states remain under military rule until 50 percent of the enrolled voters had taken the oath of allegiance; barred men who had held any military or civilian office under the rebel authorities, or who had borne arms against the United States from voting or holding office; stipulated that new state constitutions forbid all forms of involuntary servitude and extend the protection of state law to former slaves, including the crucial right to serve on juries. Finally, it imposed a fine of up to $1,500, a very substantial sum, and imprisonment up to twenty years for anyone attempting to return a person to servitude.

In defense of the bill, Ben Wade delivered one of his most powerful speeches of the war. The power to oversee Reconstruction, he declared, "belongs to us." It was absurd to suggest, as the president had, that just 10 percent of voters could guarantee a state a republican form of government. "Majorities must rule," he said, "and until majorities can be found loyal and trustworthy for state government, they must be governed by a stronger hand." Without that strong hand, the Slave Power would inevitably reassert itself over the rights of liberated slaves. He further warned that states must not be allowed to reenter the Union with precisely the same dangerous and corrupting "element"—that is, slavery—that had led them to secede in the first place. On July 2, hours before the gavel rang down on the session, Wade and Davis were vindicated by the bill's passage in the House by a comfortable majority of seventy-four to fifty-nine, but by just a single vote, seventeen to sixteen, in the Senate, the hair-thin margin offering a foretaste of the bitter divisiveness that Reconstruction policy would continue to engender long beyond the life of the Thirty-eighth Congress.


Once again, dynamic Republican majorities, especially in the Senate, had in almost every instance—with the notable exception of the putative Thirteenth Amendment—overwhelmed their enfeebled Democratic opposition. The war would go forward. Troops, black and white, would be found to keep fighting it, and money would be raised to pay them. A stronger and more assertive federal government continued to coalesce. And, though fear of freed slaves remained a potent force, the outlines of a new postwar America in which they might begin to claim the protection of government and the rights of free Americans had begun to emerge.

But the session wasn't quite done yet. All month, Thaddeus Stevens, debilitated by failing health, had labored heroically to manhandle the latest tax bill through the House. When it came to a vote in the early hours of July 3, however, it failed by a maddening three votes, fifty-four to fifty-seven. The evangelical William H. Wadsworth, a Kentucky Unionist, primly reminded his colleagues on a point of order that it was unlawful to work on the sabbath. Since the House had voted to adjourn on the 2nd, this would mean the tax bill's death. Then Schuyler Colfax, the exasperated Speaker, instantly silenced him, ruling that they were still in the "legislative day" of Saturday, and so it would remain until the House adjourned, whatever the hour. Clerks raced through the lounges to roust napping members until enough had been dragged or cajoled into the chamber for another vote, this time nudging the bill to victory by five votes, fifty-three to forty-eight. (Wadsworth, who presumably considered the casting of his ballot a form of work, declined to cast one.)

Then, finally, it was over. In parting, Elihu Washburne of Illinois rose to deliver a paean of thanks to the soldiers of the Union. Precisely a year to the day had passed, he said, since the armies of the North and South had grappled at Gettysburg. Yes, many men and much matériel had been lost since then. But federal arms were triumphant from Arkansas to Virginia. Sherman was just eighteen miles from Atlanta, "the great rebel heart of the Southwest." And Lee? Two months ago he had confronted the federal army on the Rapidan with "one hundred and thirty thousand of the best soldiers of the bogus confederacy." (This was a considerable exaggeration, but no one corrected him.) Two months later, Washburne went on, General Grant—"that child of victory"—had now "driven the desperate and maddened hordes of Lee through sixty miles of his intrenchments, outgeneraling him in every movement, and beating him in every battle. He now holds both Petersburg and Richmond by the throat." (This was another exaggeration.) The entire military situation never looked more promising, he claimed. "Returning to our seats on the 1st of December, as I hope we all may, I trust we shall see the rebellion crushed, peace restored, and the country regenerated and disenthralled."

# 18

# Bleeding, Bankrupt, and Dying Country

That is the point on which I doubt
the authority of Congress to act.

—ABRAHAM LINCOLN

Pitt Fessenden was impatient to return to Maine. The session had left him depleted, and he dreaded the onset of the steamy Washington summer. He had labored prodigiously to manage the tax bill, working day and night for months on end, arguing expertly for or against hundreds of amendments in sometimes excruciating detail— should the two types of leather used in the making of moccasins be taxed at different rates? Should taxes on fine-cut chewing tobacco be higher than those on cheap plug? Did a five-cent tax per head on slaughtered sheep make sense if swine were taxed at ten cents?— fending off the foolish, the picayune, and the self-interested, struggling to corral his fractious fellow senators with their multifarious competing special interests, pet industries, and regional jealousies. Fear for his remaining sons also weighed on him. In April, Frank had lost a leg in the failed Red River campaign, in Louisiana; having lost Sam two years earlier, he now worried that Frank would not survive. To William, in Maine, he wrote, "I can't hold out much longer, for I was never so near utter exhaustion."

On June 30, he was meeting with Treasury Secretary Chase at the Capitol when a messenger interrupted them. After speaking privately with him, Fessenden perplexedly asked Chase, "Have you resigned? I am called to the Senate and told that the President has sent in the nomination of your successor."

Chase's often contentious reign at Treasury climaxed with what amounted to a bureaucratic whimper. When the Treasury's highly regarded representative in New York, John Cisco, announced that he planned to resign, Chase breached protocol by appointing as his replacement a candidate who lacked the support of New York's senator Edwin D. Morgan. Although Lincoln sided with Morgan, Chase persisted. Cisco offered to remain in office to end the standoff, but Chase pompously told the president that he was so embarrassed that he felt duty-bound to offer his resignation. To his surprise, Lincoln accepted it. Chase's naked pursuit of the Republican presidential nomination had finally chilled what remained of Lincoln's goodwill; his management of the Treasury had also lengthened his list of enemies. To many, he seemed mentally burned out and politically exhausted, but vanity had made him blind, and he had clearly expected Lincoln to beg him to stay.

After the War Department, there was no more critical position in the cabinet than Treasury, all the more so at a time when the nation's precarious finances once again seemed in peril. Any change at the Treasury threatened to dangerously undermine public confidence. Led by Fessenden, the entire Senate Finance Committee trekked to the White House to plead with the president to reconsider his dismissal of Chase, but Lincoln was adamant. Chase's successor would face the herculean task of raising a hundred million dollars a month to keep the war going. Few men were qualified for the job, and even fewer wanted it. Lincoln's first choice, former governor David Tod of Ohio, immediately declined.

There was really only one man in Washington who was prepared to fill Chase's shoes: Fessenden himself. On the morning of July 2, Lincoln unilaterally and without consulting Fessenden sent his nomination to the Senate. Moments after dispatching the nomination to Capitol Hill, he learned that Fessenden happened to be in the anteroom waiting to see him. Still in the dark, Fessenden began discussing the vacancy and suggested the respected Indiana banker Hugh McCulloch. As Nicolay and Hay recalled it, Lincoln listened for a while with an amused smile and then told Fessenden that he had just sent his nomination to the Senate. Fessenden jumped to his feet, exclaiming, "You must withdraw it. I cannot accept." Replied Lincoln, "If you decline, you must do it in open day"—that is, publicly—"for I shall not recall the nomination."

He wrestled all day with his conscience and the pleas of his friends, who argued that he was perfectly fitted for the job: no one else, he knew as well as anyone, understood the intricacies of the nation's finances and also enjoyed the complete confidence of Congress, the business community, and the public. He was flooded with telegrams from chambers of commerce, businessmen, and bankers, and besieged by delegations of congressional Republicans and Democrats alike, as well as Chase himself, all urging him to accept. The press extolled him. Even the violently anti-Lincoln *New York World* dubbed him the fittest man in his party for the job. He was confirmed by his colleagues in the Senate in an executive session that lasted less than a minute.

The only person who objected was Fessenden himself. All he wanted was to go home to his garden and his nurturing cousin Lizzy. Ambitious as he was for influence, he had never seriously aspired to an office other than the one he already held. The Finance Committee required continuous and exhausting labor so debilitating, he wrote, that "preceding the close of the last session I found myself so worn down with fatigue that I was compelled to confine myself to the committee room except when my presence was absolutely necessary in the chamber to contest [legislation] emanating from my committee." Even if he had desired the job, he felt physically unable to discharge its duties. "In fact, I had no idea that I could continue in office for a month if I accepted. I thought that I could accept only at the cost of my own life." The next morning, he returned to the White House and handed Lincoln a letter declining the appointment. Lincoln replied that there was "no other man with whom the country could be satisfied," and that the moment called for every sacrifice, "even life itself." To this, Fessenden had no answer. "I became convinced that I could not decline but at the risk of danger to the country." He finally agreed to accept. "Everybody apprehended a financial crash as the result of my refusal." However, he made clear to Lincoln that he would only do so on a temporary basis and wished to return to the Senate as soon as federal finances were stabilized and public confidence restored.

Fessenden's appointment was greeted with joy in the financial community, overshadowing even the news that the notorious Confederate raider *Alabama* had at last been sunk by a federal warship off the French coast after wreaking havoc on Northern commercial shipping. "I cannot doubt but it will be hailed as a National blessing from a merciful God," rejoiced an ecstatic Albany, New York, banker when he heard news of Fessenden's appointment. He was one of many. Gold immediately dropped 20 points, and the price of pork $10 a barrel.

The Union's financial situation was once again dire. After a brief dip in early July, gold bounced up again to 270, which meant that $4,000 in gold would buy more than $10,000 worth of devalued government bonds. "Some of our staunchest friends say we had better give up the war than have such a state of things," an official at the U.S. Custom House in New York reported to Fessenden. Unionist financiers and businessmen warned that the currency collapse had to be brought quickly under control. Wrote one, "More depends on your success than on that of either Genl Grant or Sherman—errors of theirs may be corrected and defeats replaced with victory—but . . . you have no margin left for failures—success must attend your every move or ruin engulf us all." The national debt now stood at $1.75 billion, much of it in short-term paper. Spiraling inflation was disrupting commerce, destroying wages, and threatening social unrest, a prospect all too easy to imagine after the 1863 draft riots in New York. "Unless the direction given to the Treasury by Mr. Chase be changed, we shall have a season of revolutionary anarchy as the only alternative of starvation to the laboring classes. It is questionable whether success in the field, however decisive, can save us."

Meanwhile, a sequence of demoralizing events that July further sapped confidence in the administration. With the Army of the Potomac settling into a siege around Petersburg, Rep. Elihu Washburne of Illinois, Ulysses Grant's longtime patron, had confidently told the House of Representatives, "All the fight is whipped out of Lee, and he cowers in his defenses, not daring to come out and give battle." He was almost instantly proven wrong when a twenty-thousand-man Confederate army led by Jubal Early, one of Lee's most aggressive commanders, surged out of the Shenandoah Valley, hoping to free thousands of Confederate prisoners from camps in Maryland, threatening to capture either Washington or Baltimore, and sowing panic across the North. With Washington stripped of troops for Grant's campaign in Virginia, civilian clerks were given guns and hurried to the capital's outskirts, along with a collection of sailors, walking wounded, and camp cooks. On July 9, Early's army overwhelmed an outnumbered federal force at Monocacy Junction, less than fifty miles from Washington. On the 11th, Early's men could see the glint of the sun on the Capitol's dome as they marched through Silver Spring.

Their immediate objective was Fort Stevens, an earthen emplacement defended by two hundred men, just inside the Federal District's northern boundary. Early's men were too exhausted to press home their initial attack, and their chance of capturing the city evaporated overnight. In the dark, veteran troops hurriedly sent from the Army of the Potomac arrived and positioned themselves at Fort Stevens and other outworks. During the battle that followed, President Lincoln, who had driven out from the city in his carriage, climbed onto the fort's parapet to see the action. He only agreed to come down when bullets began snapping around him, endangering the soldiers nearby. (A persistent story, probably apocryphal, credited future Supreme Court justice Oliver Wendell Holmes with being the soldier who talked him down.) It was the only instance in American history when a sitting president came under fire in battle. Ben Wade and Gideon Welles arrived shortly afterward to find Lincoln sitting in the shade with his back against the parapet as cannon shot and bullets flew overhead. The bold Confederate thrust was parried. Early retreated to Virginia having achieved none of his objectives, except to underscore the capital's vulnerability, and the precariousness of the Union's plight: during his invasion the price of gold reached 285, its highest point during the war.

On July 30, yet another bloody humiliation befell the administration. With the Army of the Potomac settled into a static siege at Petersburg, the colonel of a regiment composed of Pennsylvania miners came up with a clever plan: they proposed to dig a five-hundred-foot horizontal shaft beneath a key Confederate bastion, pack it with tons of powder, and blow it sky-high. The initial phase of the plan worked brilliantly. "The world shook" and "a column of yellow earth spouted into the air" carrying with it some two hundred Confederate soldiers, cannon, cannonballs, and debris. The surviving Confederates remained paralyzed for an hour. Had the follow-up assault that was planned been carried out properly, it could have shattered the enemy line, broken the siege, and possibly even have transformed the course of the war. But it was horribly botched.

A division of fresh black troops had been specially trained for three weeks to rush through the broken line in the ensuing chaos. But at the last moment Meade and Grant swapped the black division for an unprepared white one led by an incompetent general who sat out the entire battle drunk in a bomb shelter behind the lines. It was a tragic decision that combined lingering doubt about black soldiers' competence with fear of political retribution from the Radicals on Capitol Hill if it seemed that blacks were being squandered as mere cannon fodder.

Initial reports claimed a breakthrough. But instead of rolling up the Confederate line as planned, the unguided federals poured into the thirty-foot-deep crater, and stayed there. Division after division was funneled into the same trap, eventually including the black division that had been meant to lead the attack. The Confederates recovered, ordered up reinforcements, surrounded the federals, and massacred them in what the *New York Tribune*'s reporter, an eyewitness, termed "a perfect slaughter pen." The black troops, in particular, were systematically murdered, including the wounded and many as they attempted to surrender. In all, nearly four thousand federal troops were lost. Wrote Grant afterward, "It was the saddest affair I have witnessed in the war."

Meanwhile, public horror at the spring casualty lists turned more and more Northerners against the war. Desertions climbed to 7,333 per month, a 40 percent increase over the previous year. Draft-dodging spread to formerly loyal strongholds in the upper Midwest,

New England, and upstate New York. "There is a grate meny deserters has been staying in the woods for a year one of the Copperheads has been suporting them with provisheons," a local Unionist
reported to Thaddeus Stevens from rural Luzerne County, Pennsylvania. Anti-administration newspapers urged open resistance. More
and more moderate Copperheads became willing to countenance
"violent remedies." Reports circulated of plots to blow up steamboats at their docks at Pittsburgh and Cincinnati, torch Northern
cities, spring Confederate prisoners from internment camps, seize
railroad lines, and spark a full-scale uprising in New York. Armed
Copperheads were seen openly drilling just two miles from the Ohio
state capital at Columbus. In Illinois, pro-Confederate bushwhack-
ers who burned property and threatened civilians were acquitted
by Copperhead juries. Brick Pomeroy, the extremist editor of the
La Crosse, Wisconsin, *Democrat* raged that if Lincoln were to be
reelected, "we trust that some bold hand will pierce his heart with
dagger point for the public good."

Once staunch Unionist voters were increasingly despondent.
Some Republicans started sounding like defeatist Democrats. The
Boston abolitionist Wendell Phillips blamed the war for grinding
working men down to the level of paupers and predicted that the
government would become a complete despotism if Lincoln were
to be reelected. Horace Greeley, who had spent most of the past
three years cheering on the troops and condemning generals for not
fighting hard enough, wrote to Lincoln in early July: "Our bleeding,
bankrupt almost dying country also longs for peace—shudders at
the prospect of fresh conscriptions, and further wholesale devasta-
tions, and of new rivers of human blood." Greeley even traveled to
Canada to meet self-proclaimed Confederate "emissaries" in Canada
in a melodramatic attempt to craft a freelance peace settlement,
an experiment that proved a gross embarrassment for the gullible
editor.

The war was now costing $3 million a day, taxes had once again
increased, and the draft was continuing to suck up sons, fathers, and
husbands for what promised to be a new season of bloodletting.
Many Republicans, and at times Lincoln himself, considered defeat
at the polls in November to be not just possible but virtually certain.

Even Republican stalwarts like Greeley and the New York power broker Thurlow Weed considered Lincoln's reelection an impossibility. At fifty-six, Lincoln looked like an old man. Every trace of the youthful, sinewy "rail-splitter" who had been elected to the presidency in 1860 had disappeared. His gaunt face had become the deeply furrowed, hollow-eyed mask that is familiar from Mathew Brady's wartime photographs. Physically he was breaking down. He had lost thirty pounds, his hands were shaking, and he barely slept. To many, returning him to office seemed little more than a guarantee of more futile bloodshed.

Radicals, in particular, felt that Lincoln was still too lukewarm in his support for emancipation and too dilatory in his pursuit of the war. In a letter to Wade, one Ohio abolitionist disgustedly wrote off Lincoln as "a man who has shamelessly, brazenly, besottedly ignored justice and humanity, at a time when they are qualities most needed in his position." For many in Congress, Lincoln's cavalier pocket veto of the Wade-Davis bill on the last day of the session was the final straw. It had been passed by both houses of Congress, and they fully expected him to sign it when it was placed on the desk where he sat in the Capitol, amid the tornado of last-minute bills. Zachariah Chandler was standing nearby. When he saw Lincoln put the Wade-Davis bill aside, he asked the president what he intended to do with it. Lincoln replied that he wasn't going to sign it. "If it is vetoed, it will damage us fearfully," Chandler protested. "The important point is that one prohibiting slavery in the reconstructed states." To this replied Lincoln, "That is the point on which I doubt the authority of Congress to act." Protested Chandler, "It is no more than you have done yourself."

"I conceive that I may in an emergency do things on military grounds which cannot be done constitutionally by Congress," Lincoln announced with finality. Staid though it might seem, the scene represented one of the most dramatic of the session: a gladiatorial collision between two of the branches of government, each claiming precedence over a policy that everyone knew would shape the postwar nation far into the future, and fix for years to come the precedence of Congress over the executive. A majority of Congress believed that they held the power to drive Reconstruction. Lincoln was just as certain that they did not, and that he did. Lincoln later defended his action by asserting, in effect, that he would pragmatically support any number of ways of restoring states. But in truth, he had already made clear in December that he was wedded to a far more conciliatory course of action than Congress, especially its Radical members, had in mind.

The president's refusal to sign the bill, Nicolay and Hay understatedly wrote, "caused a great effervescence" among the incensed members of Congress. Davis and Wade, in particular, were furious at seeing their labors of the last session come to nothing. On July 8, Lincoln then attempted to outflank the Radicals by issuing a unilateral proclamation. He reiterated his invitation to the seceded states to apply for reentry to the Union when they formed new governments with the support of 10 percent of voters, and he explicitly rejected the claim of Congress that it alone had the power to abolish slavery. That, he said, could and should only be done by means of a formal amendment to the Constitution. Having said that, he threw a sop to the Radicals, adding that he would not object to states that preferred the more stringent Reconstruction template advanced in the Wade-Davis bill. Thaddeus Stevens, for one, was utterly disgusted. To his friend Edward McPherson, he wrote, "What an infamous proclamation! How little of the rights of war and the law of nations our Prest. knows. But what are we to do? Condemn privately and applaud publicly!"

On August 5, Wade and Davis published a joint manifesto in the *New York Tribune* accusing the president of encroaching on the powers of Congress, and selfishly trying to reenfranchise disloyal Southern whites in order to buy their political loyalty. By preventing the Wade-Davis bill from becoming law, they charged, the president "holds the electoral votes of the rebel States at the dictation of his personal ambition." Lincoln must understand, they wrote, that their support—and implicitly that of other Radicals—was "of a cause and not of a man." The authority of Congress was paramount. "If he wishes our support he must confine himself to his executive duties—to obey and to execute, not to make the laws—to suppress by arms armed rebellion, and leave political reorganization to Congress." They urged the government's supporters to consider the obvious remedy for Lincoln's "usurpations," and "having found it, fearlessly execute it." They couldn't have been more clear: find another candidate for president.

Disaffected Radicals talked once again of replacing Lincoln with Butler, Chase, or Frémont. Butler made clear that he was not interested. Chase hinted that he wouldn't reject the nomination, but his star had waned after the Republican members of the Ohio legislature collectively declared their support for Lincoln. Frémont, the candidate of the Radical Democracy Party, was another story. A vain man, he still resented Lincoln for not naming him to a new command after he botched assignments in Missouri and the Shenandoah Valley. But a lingering charisma still clung to him from his exploration of the Far West in the 1840s, and his early embrace of abolitionism. He showed no inclination to withdraw.

Asserting as late as August that Lincoln had to be "gotten rid of," Henry Winter Davis, for one, continued agitating for an emergency Republican convention to dump Lincoln and come up with a new candidate. Davis, though bold and articulate, was a comparatively minor figure. Wade, however, was a lion of the Senate, a champion of freedom and aggressive war. He sincerely believed, as probably the great majority of Americans had since the founding of the republic, that Congress rather than the president was the central repository of government power. He had also long believed Lincoln to be wrongheaded and weak, and that the presidential Reconstruction plan left too much room for the revival of slavery. Although Wade had no objection to Andrew Johnson, whom he regarded as an uncompromising patriot, Lincoln's renomination had deeply dismayed him.

During the course of the war, Wade's stature had steadily grown. But in coauthoring the Wade-Davis Manifesto he had overreached. In the words of his biographer Hans L. Trefousse, the manifesto was "one of the most ill-tempered, ill-considered, foolhardy enterprises a politician could undertake in an election year." Gideon Welles felt personally disappointed in Wade, who, "though coarse and vulgar," he credited with a serious intellect and an abundance of patriotism. He considered Wade's behavior utterly inexplicable, unless he had himself "been bitten with the presidential fever," and was out to bring down the president in hope of replacing him.

Even many Republicans who hoped to see Lincoln removed were shocked at Wade's attack on the administration at a moment when the fate of the Union depended on Republican unity. The *National Anti-Slavery Standard* condemned the manifesto's "violence of language and bitterness of spirit," while the *New York Times,* the party's semiofficial mouthpiece, declared it "by far the most effective Copperhead campaign document thus far issued." Many Republicans who had long supported him never quite trusted him again. So stung was he by the criticism from his friends that he considered resigning but held back for fear, as one worried supporter put it, lest "some sleek conservative would slip in."

Fortunately for both Lincoln and Wade the manifesto's potential damage was at least partly mitigated by the news of Admiral Farragut's capture of Mobile, one of the few bright spots of the summer. Wade soon realized that he had gone too far and began to regret his impulsiveness. He could see as well as anyone that if the Republicans lost the election and the Democrats gained control everything he had worked for would come to nothing. While Republicans battled each other, Democratic propagandists hammered the administration without let-up. Day after day, the *La Crosse Daily Democrat* ran a front-page engraving of Lincoln urging readers to look on "the greatest widow maker God ever cursed mankind with," who had "filled the land with fear and mourning, caused a million of brave men to be sacrificed for nothing," forced numberless girls into prostitution in order to escape starvation, left "millions" of orphans, and condemned the rest of Americans "to groan, and toil, and sweat under the taxation his hell born administration has entailed upon the land."

Republican electoral prospects looked bleak. Fessenden, who remained loyal to the president, was extremely worried. Federal loans had lost their momentum and daily receipts steadily shrank. "I am at my wit's end, as well as at the bottom of my purse," he reflected grimly. "All will depend very much on the results of the elections. If we carry them the war is substantially over. If not, all is over with us." On August 22, *New York Times* editor Henry J. Raymond warned Lincoln that "the tide is setting strongly against us," and that if the election were held now the national ticket would certainly lose the swing states of Pennsylvania, Illinois, and New York, the last by at least fifty thousand votes. The dismal military situation was out of the party's hands, he admitted. But slavery was not. He proposed naming a commission to go to Richmond to offer the Confederacy peace on the sole condition of acknowledging the supremacy of the Constitution, in effect abandoning emancipation and the millions of still enslaved blacks. Raymond may have intended this mainly as a political feint, guessing that Jefferson Davis would reject the proposal out of hand, thereby undercutting Democratic claims that the Confederates were begging for just such a pledge. But it was a shocking proposal all the same, bordering on an open admission of defeat.

Lincoln himself expected to be defeated in November. The day after receiving Raymond's warning he wrote a two-sentence memo, sealed it, and without showing them the contents asked the members of his cabinet to sign the envelope. In it, he wrote: "This morning, as for some days past, it seems exceedingly probable that this Administration will not be reelected. Then it will be my duty to so cooperate with the President elect, as to save the Union between the election and the inauguration; as he will have secured his election on such ground that he can not save it afterwards." The next day, he sketched a reply to Raymond asking him to contact Jefferson Davis to propose a peace conference and the immediate end to hostilities, with "all remaining questions"—that is, slavery—to be left "for adjustment." Fortunately, by the time Raymond arrived at the White House a day later, Lincoln had changed his mind. He told the editor that sending a peace commission to Richmond would be worse than losing the election: "It would be ignominiously surrendering in advance." Lincoln's decision didn't change the harsh reality. His personal secretary John Nicolay wrote in his diary, "Everything is darkness and doubt and discouragement."

For the hundreds of thousands of contrabands, not to mention the millions who remained in slavery, the consequences of either a Union surrender or the administration's defeat at the polls in November would be tragic beyond imagining. Frederick Douglass feared with good reason that a Democratic president would void the Emancipation Proclamation. Slaves freed during the war would then have no standing in court, and bounty hunters would have free rein rounding up former slaves who had fled into Union lines. Douglass hoped, however, that he might persuade Lincoln to somehow free as many slaves as possible before the election. He wrote to the president urging that agents be sent deep into the Confederacy to organize slaves to escape while they still could, and to pilot them north to safety behind Union lines, essentially a retooling of the prewar Underground Railroad, this time under the auspices of the federal government. Lincoln never replied.

The Republicans' gloom that August was matched in intensity by the euphoria of the Democrats as they gathered for their convention in Chicago, confident that they would easily elect Lincoln's successor in November. For more than a year, Clement Vallandigham had restlessly marked time in Canada, reading history and political philosophy, "dipping a little into the ancient classics," riding and fishing, following events at home as best he could, and receiving a steady stream of political visitors, including at least several Confederate agents. In a letter to his brother James, he airily wrote, "I calmly dwell now in the present, awaiting the times which are to come." His days were not quite as languorous as he suggested. Earlier in the year he had been named the Grand Commander of the Sons of Liberty, a descendant of the proslavery Knights of the Golden Circle, which claimed 200,000 members and a network of "lodges" throughout the Midwest. Its Declaration of Principles included support for state sovereignty and slavery, which it termed "a just and humane servitude and tutelage to the superior race." Once Vallandigham's connection to it became known, he claimed that it was simply a mutual-aid society to protect Democrats against "outrages" perpetrated by Republicans.

However, a report by Judge Advocate General Joseph Holt based on confessions by turncoats and investigation by federal agents found that members were actively expected to resist the draft, discourage enlistment, provide intelligence to the enemy, recruit men to serve in the Confederate army, furnish the rebels with arms and ammunition, and support a Northwest Confederacy. Holt's report further

cited numerous plots to release Confederate prisoners from Northern internment camps, launch attacks on certain cities, assassinate
federal officers, ambush black soldiers, and provoke a general revolt
if Lincoln should be reelected. Without offering persuasive proof,
Holt asserted that the entire conspiracy was led by Vallandigham acting at the personal direction of Jefferson Davis. After Vallandigham's
death, his brother James conceded that the Sons of Liberty had in
fact harbored committed "disunionists" who supported Southern
independence and engaged in activities "which rendered them liable
to the charge of treason," though how much of this Clement Vallandigham was privy to isn't known.

Vallandigham had crossed back into the United States on the night
of June 14, disguised under a false beard and upswept mustache, with
a bed pillow stuffed beneath his coat to lend him "Falstaffian proportions." He anticipated an arrest as dramatic as the one the previous
year, even supposing that an entire regiment would be sent after him
once it was known that he had reentered the United States. Perhaps
to his disappointment, nothing happened. Stung by criticism from
civil libertarians over his arrest and highly publicized expulsion, the
administration simply ignored him. Although federal agents were
certainly well aware of his movements, he arrived without incident
at Hamilton, Ohio, to be greeted by a throng of supporters who
carried him on their shoulders to a dais. There by prearrangement
he was quickly nominated and elected to serve as a delegate to the
Democratic National Convention. ("He came unheralded from his
exile, and his sudden appearance was like an apparition from the
clouds," wrote one thrilled acolyte.) The speech he delivered demonstrated that exile had not diminished his passion. He declared that
his only crime, though his enemies called it treason, was his wor-
ship of the Constitution. He had come home in peace to vindicate
his rights as a citizen, he said. But, he added meaningfully, "Let no
man of the Democratic party begin any act of violence or disorder;
but let not shrink from any responsibility, however urgent, if forced
upon him."

In a revealing digression, he felt it necessary to address the allegations that he had become involved with a subversive organization,
which he didn't name. Lying, he flatly denied knowledge of any such

group, claiming that the charge was merely a fiction concocted by Republicans to smear Democrats by association. If there was any powerful "conspiracy" afoot, he said facetiously, it was the Democratic Party, and it was aimed at the defeat of the administration in November—through the ballot box. "And I am proud to be one of the conspirators."

In the weeks that followed, he traveled the North, reconnecting with allies, speaking at peace rallies, and campaigning tirelessly and for the most part successfully for the appointment of antiwar delegates to the party's convention. Strangely, amidst his travels, he failed to find time to visit his fatally ill mother in New Lisbon, Ohio, writing only, "That I cannot with safety start to see you in your present illness is the sorest of afflictions. This danger, too, will pass before long. But at present it may be too imminent to risk. Oh, how great is the denial that keeps me from you!" When she died, he sent just $100 for her funeral expenses.

19

# The People Decide

If traitors rule this land it is no place for me.

—SEN. ZACHARIAH CHANDLER

The Democratic convention opened on August 29 with a stream of rabble-rousing speakers who—sometimes struggling to be heard over the clangor and roar of railroad trains clattering past the hall—praised the South, denounced pro-war party members as "shoddy abolitionists in disguise," urged open resistance to the draft, an immediate end to the war, and repudiation of emancipation. "We are one and all for peace, and with this magic word upon our banner we shall sweep over the course, and roll into oblivion the black, negro-loving, negro-hugging worshipers of old Abe Lincoln," fulminated Isaiah Rynders, a thuggish Tammany stalwart who as a New York City official had helped hunt down fugitive slaves. Gov. Horatio Seymour of New York, the most prominent of the antiwar Democrats, declared to thunderous applause, "We demand no conditions for the restoration of our Union. We wish for fraternal relations with the people of the South." Others raged against "flat-nose, wooly-headed, cursed of God and damned-of-man descendants of Africa," and warned, to cheers, that if the voters did not put Lincoln out of power by means of the ballot "they will by the bullet."

Although some Democrats tried to promote former presidents

Millard Fillmore and Franklin Pierce or Horatio Seymour for their party's presidential nomination, a clear preference for George McClellan had taken shape. As the Washington Copperhead Charles Mason put it in his diary, "The majority of the party would prefer someone who was not engaged in the civil war at all. Such I am sure would be my preference, but among the warriors I prefer McClellan." His battlefield failures were less well understood than they later became, and many admired him for turning the disorganized volunteers into a professional army. That he enjoyed immense popularity with the soldiers, especially in the eastern armies, was taken for granted. Although born and raised in Philadelphia, he was personally repelled by Negroes, opposed interference with slavery and openly asserted his support for white supremacy.

Vallandigham was ubiquitous at the convention. He initially labored to deny the nomination to McClellan. He may initially have hoped to win the nomination for himself, or at least the vice presidential slot. Although he belonged to the relatively less extreme antiwar faction of the party—he didn't openly advocate armed rebellion and professed support for national reunion rather than secession—he had by now become the very personification of treason in the eyes of countless Northern voters. But it soon became clear that McClellan was the prohibitive choice of a majority of delegates. Lobbied hard by "Sunset" Cox and others, Vallandigham finally agreed, against his better judgment, to cast his vote for the general. As a gesture to the peace men, the convention placed Vallandigham's ally Rep. George Pendleton of Indiana on the ticket as the vice presidential candidate. (In May, Pendleton had suggested on the floor of the House that Ohioans might "appeal to the sword" if the federal government ever dared to overturn the state's law barring blacks from voting.) Vallandigham suspected, correctly, that McClellan was less than wholeheartedly committed to peace at any price, and urged him to ignore anyone who "in an evil hour may advise you to insinuate even a little war into your letter of acceptance. If anything implying war is presented, two hundred thousand men in the West will withhold their vote."

Vallandigham exerted more decisive influence over the committee that wrote the Democratic platform, and reportedly wrote key sections of it himself. The platform declared that "after four years of failure to restore the Union by the experiment of war . . . justice, humanity, liberty and the public welfare demand that immediate efforts be made for a cessation of hostilities, with a view to an ultimate convention of the States, or other peaceable means, to the end that at the earliest practicable moment peace may be restored on the basis of the Federal Union of the States." The "war failure" plank, as Republicans sarcastically called it, made no mention of resuming the war if an armistice and negotiations failed to lead to reunion. The platform further condemned the "subversion" of civil law by the military, arbitrary arrests, the "suppression of freedom of speech and the press," and made it clear that the Democrats were willing to reverse the administration's commitment to emancipation. Declared Democratic Party chairman August Belmont, speaking with the thick accent of his native Germany, Lincoln "thinks a proclamation worth more than peace. We think the blood of our people more precious than the edicts of the president."

In order to secure McClellan's nomination, the Peace Democrats had overlooked his actual views on the war, while McClellan ignored Vallandigham's peace plank. Hardly had the convention ended when McClellan fulfilled Vallandigham's fears. In his letter of acceptance, he indicated that he would not expect the Confederacy to accept emancipation as a condition of peace: "The Union is the one condition of peace. We ask no more." So far, so good. But he added that if peace negotiations failed he would hold the South responsible for the consequences, implying that he would be willing to continue the war. Although McClellan was revealing himself as, in effect, a War Democrat, it was highly unlikely that soldiers could be induced to shoulder their rifles again if they once laid them down, even temporarily. Writes historian Jennifer L. Weber, "For all the good their platform did McClellan and the Democratic party, the leadership might as well have tied the general into a sack filled with rocks and thrown him into Lake Michigan."

The most ardent Copperheads immediately began demanding a new convention and a new candidate. Vallandigham holed up in Dayton and at first refused to campaign for the ticket. Eventually he and his allies resentfully came around, having concluded that splitting the party would ruin their near-certain chance to win the election. He also reasoned that he would be able to exert direct influence on McClellan once he was elected. So in the end he swallowed his sense of betrayal, gritted his teeth, and returned to the campaign trail. The only alternative, after all, was four more years of the loathed Abraham Lincoln.

Neither Lincoln nor McClellan actively campaigned, relying almost entirely on surrogate speakers to articulate their parties' platforms. Although McClellan privately disdained the most extreme Copperheads, he was happy enough to have them campaign for him. It quickly became clear that he was a political novice. He had no political organization, rarely issued a statement, and made only two personal appearances. To one supporter, William Prime, he wrote from his home in Orange, New Jersey, "Don't send any politicians out here—I'll snub them if they come—confound them!" Asked by party operatives to visit the swing state of Pennsylvania, he loftily replied, "It would be better for me not to participate in person in the canvass."

McClellan's ineptitude aside, the Democrats compounded their campaign problems by their refusal to face the fact that what the Confederate leadership and doubtless a substantial majority of the white Southern public wanted was independence, not reunification. "Our people now look with contemptuous astonishment on those with whom they had been so recently associated," Jefferson Davis had told the Confederate Congress in 1861. "They shrink with revulsion from the bare idea of renewing such a connection." After three years of slaughter, Confederate determination had, if anything, only hardened. On October 4, 1864, at Columbia, South Carolina, Davis declared, "Let fresh victories crown our arms, and the peace party, if there be such at the North, can elect its candidate. But whether a peace candidate is elected or not, Yankee instinct will teach him that it is better to end the war and leave us to the enjoyment of our own rights." On the eve of the election, he reiterated in a speech to his Congress in Richmond that he would be willing to negotiate with the North only when it was "ready to abandon the war." But the Democrats seemed deaf to this.

Brushing aside their candidate's shortcomings, Democrats expected the soldier vote to deliver generous majorities in key states. However, the party's platform had woken soldiers to the fact that the Democrats were prepared to abandon the struggle for which they had fought and bled. They wanted the war to end, but they wanted to win it. By 1864, many of them had also changed their minds about emancipation. The vast majority now recognized it as an effective war measure that had caused many tens of thousands of blacks to abandon the Southern farms and factories that helped sustain the Confederate war effort, and had put more than a hundred thousand of them into federal uniform.

Moreover, the fog of pessimism that had clouded Northern feeling about the war unexpectedly lifted. Just days after the Democratic convention, William T. Sherman captured Atlanta following four months of brilliant maneuver across the mountains and valleys of northern Georgia. Then, beginning on September 19, Grant's equally aggressive young protégé Gen. Philip Sheridan began sweeping southward through the strategic Shenandoah Valley, destroying stocks of food, and nearly annihilating Jubal Early's army in the process. The Army of the Potomac remained bogged down at Petersburg, but the smell of real victory was finally in the air. The hard war that the congressional Radicals had demanded was finally military policy. The day after Atlanta's fall, Sherman wrote to Henry Halleck: "If the people raise a howl against my barbarity & cruelty, I will answer that War is War & not popularity seeking. If they want peace, they & their relations must stop war." Public opinion also began to turn: the Democrats' claim that the war had failed suddenly seemed unmoored from reality.

The Republicans' spirits rose still further when a few days later Zachariah Chandler delivered to the party a long-hoped-for political gift: an end to John C. Frémont's breakaway candidacy. In late August, Chandler—Ben Wade's closest ally, who maintained good relations with both the president and Frémont's circle—took it upon himself to heal the breach in the party by undertaking what turned into weeks of shuttle diplomacy. Chandler first traveled to Wade's home in Jefferson, Ohio, in an effort to persuade him to support the national ticket. Wade's price, he told his friend, was the ouster of the conservative postmaster general Montgomery Blair of Maryland.

Although a founder of the Republican Party and pivotal in mustering border state support for the administration in the early days of the war, Blair was an unabashed white supremacist and still hoped, however quixotically, for a peaceful reconciliation with the South. Radicals had long accused him, without much proof, of holding Lincoln back from decisive action on emancipation and firmer war measures. Chandler now returned to Washington to attempt to persuade Lincoln to accept Wade's quid pro quo. "You must see my whole heart is set upon success & I must win or leave this country," Chandler wrote to his wife. "If traitors rule this land it is no place for me."

The day after the Democratic convention, Chandler hurried to Philadelphia to enlist the support of leading Pennsylvania Republicans. From there, he returned to Washington, where he won over a number of prominent members of Congress and met with Lincoln, who agreed to drop Blair if Chandler could accomplish Frémont's withdrawal. He then hurried to New York City to make his case to the unreceptive Frémont, pursuing him to his vacation residence in Nahant, Massachusetts, telling him with all the force that the often overbearing Michigander could muster that unless he quit the race the Republicans would lose the election. Although he had no authority to do so, Chandler further hinted that Lincoln would reappoint him to high military command. For the next week, he told his wife, "I have been running a nightly express between here & New York." On September 17, Frémont at last announced that he would step aside. His letter announcing it, however, was the very epitome of a Parthian shot, insultingly declaring that Lincoln's administration "has been politically, militarily, and financially a failure, and that its necessary continuance is a cause of regret for the country." Chandler rushed back to Washington to remind the president of his commitment to remove Blair. Lincoln was furious at the tone of Frémont's letter and hardly in a mood to accommodate the bilious general, but in the end he stuck by his promise. Within days, both Ben Wade and the long recalcitrant Henry Winter Davis were actively campaigning for the Republican ticket.

In mid-October, Lincoln was presented with an unexpected opportunity to consolidate his grudging support among the Radicals. The chief justice of the Supreme Court, Roger Taney, who had served for twenty-eight years, died at the age of eighty-seven. Having stained his reputation with the Dred Scott decision, and then soiled it further in 1861 by his unilateral defense of secessionists in Maryland, he had for the last three years of his life essentially consigned himself, and the court, to near-irrelevance. Pithily remarked George Templeton Strong, "The Hon. old Roger B. Taney has earned the gratitude of his country by dying at last. Better late than never." Chase was the only replacement Lincoln seriously considered. The Radicals counted Chase as one of their number and lobbied hard for him, and his views on Reconstruction were well known. Moreover, his appointment to the court would both cement the ambitious Ohioan's not entirely dependable loyalty to the administration, and as a bonus further neutralize him politically.

Every American knew that the election would be a clear referendum on the war and emancipation, and that a Democratic victory would represent a virtual admission of Union defeat. Republican Party leaders regarded the political campaign ahead of them as more critical than any military campaign: if it failed, it would settle the war decisively, fatally, and forever. To the Republican state convention in Boston Benjamin Butler wrote, "This canvass differs from every other in this, that the life or death of the nation as a power on earth depends on the actions of the hour." To vote for McClellan, he said, was "a vote to forget our manhood, to abandon the doctrines of our fathers, to give up the hope of republican liberty forever, to check at once and forever the American Nation in its great missionary march of civilization, progress, and Christian freedom; to abandon the hopes of millions yet to be."

The Confederates, too, fully recognized all that was at stake. The South's limited resources were severely strained. Inflation was completely out of control. And, lacking the North's reserves of manpower, the army struggled with decreasing success to replace soldiers lost in battle. Provost marshals' gangs ruthlessly hunted down draft evaders, sometimes resorting to physical torture to force men into the ranks, including pacifist Quakers. The South's main armies still remained, and its leaders were confident of eventual victory. But

Confederate strategy now hinged on the belief that Northern war weariness would unseat Lincoln in November. Declared the Augusta *Daily Constitutionalist,* "The battlefields of 1864 will hold the polls of this momentous decision. If the tyrant at Washington be defeated, his infamous policy will be defeated with him."

With the North's prospects for battlefield victory brightening, the Democrats faced a more challenging political landscape than they had anticipated. Deprived of "war failure" as their salient issue, they relied heavily on demagoguery and venomous personal attacks to advance their campaign. Lincoln was savaged in the Democratic press as "a miserable trickster," "a low, cowardly buffoon," and "the NERO who fiddles at Washington in the light of the greatest conflagration that the world ever saw," and his administration denounced as "the rottenest, most stinking, ruin-working smallpox ever conceived by fiends or mortals." More than anything, however, the Democrats exploited racial fears, attacking abolitionism as "diabolism incarnate," and charging Republicans with gloating "with fiendish delight" at the prospect of poor white men "dragged from their houses and thrown into battle." When Gen. Nathaniel Banks ordered New Orleans public schools to admit blacks, Democrats shrilled that it was part of a systematic abolitionist plot to "mongrelize" the entire nation. Whispering campaigns alleged scandalously that Mary Lincoln had even taken "colored lady friends" out riding in her carriage. ("Whether this is true or not is not very important," Washington Copperhead Charles Mason wrote in his diary. "One thing is certain. The party in power is doing all it can to erase the line of separation between the two races. [But] they will never annihilate the instinctive repugnance that a higher power has ordained for wise purposes.")

Racist paranoia was further inflamed by a stream of brutal propaganda, most notably a seventy-two-page pamphlet titled "Miscegenation," a new coinage destined to permanently enter the nation's vocabulary. The pamphlet—later revealed as a Copperhead hoax—purported to be the work of an anonymous abolitionist who sought to prove the blessings of racial mixing. Packed with pseudoscientific jargon, it asserted that mixed races were far superior mentally, physically, and morally to "pure" ones, and that "of all the rich treasures of blood vouchsafed to us, that of the negro is the most precious." The "lowest people" on the scale of European civilization, the "brutal, ignorant, and barbarous" Irish, for example, could only be improved by mixing with Negroes, a provocation that could not be better calculated to antagonize one of the Democrats' bedrock voting blocs. "We must become a yellow-skinned, black-haired people," the pamphlet went on. The war, therefore, should be understood "as a war for the negro . . . looking, as its final fruit, to the blending of the white and black."

Some of the North's most famous abolitionists took "Miscegenation" at face value and publicly endorsed it, including Rev. Henry Ward Beecher, the Quaker Lucretia Mott, and the Boston orator Wendell Phillips. The pamphlet's "arguments" were quickly picked up by Copperhead newspapers and politicians as proof of a hidden Republican agenda. When a club in New York invited a few blacks to attend a social hour, the *World* mocked it as a "negro ball" where Republican officials spent the evening "miscegenating with the copper faces." The New York *Daily News* warned that the pamphlet proved that "a real, completely organized, living monster rears its horrible head in our midst," while others warned that if the abolitionists got their way white women were to be farmed out to "unbridled and unbroken-in Black Ourang-Outangs."

"Sunset" Cox, who may have helped engineer the hoax, read great swaths of "Miscegenation" into the *Congressional Globe*, thus ensuring that its shocking assertions would be carried into areas where the pamphlet itself could not be obtained. "No system," declared Cox, could be "so repugnant to the nature of our race," or would more certainly destroy both the white and black races alike, since as every "physiologist" knew the mulatto was doomed to sterility. "He does not recreate his kind; he is a monster." But such a dreadful outcome was precisely what the Republicans were bent on. "We have the negro at every moment and in every bill in Congress. All these things, in connection with the African policies of confiscation and emancipation in their various shapes for the past three years, culminating in this grand plunder scheme of a department for freedmen, ought to convince us that that party is moving steadily forward to perfect social equality of black and white, and can only end in this detestable doctrine of—Miscegenation!"

Even respectable conservatives were swayed, not all of them Democrats. "I, for one, have never had a particle of faith that a sudden, sweeping forcible emancipation could result in anything but mischief and misery for the black race, as well as the white," declared the Massachusetts Brahmin and prewar Whig champion Robert C. Winthrop, who threw his support to McClellan. "We are not for wading through seas of blood in order to reorganize the whole social structure of the South." Unalloyed racism was the last potent weapon of a party with nothing positive left to offer.

On the Republican side, most of the formerly disaffected Radicals threw themselves into the campaign with energy, if not always with enthusiasm. "Elect McClellan, and the Republic has ceased to exist," Thaddeus Stevens thundered to Lancaster voters. "On its ruins will spring up numerous petty empires, whose future condition will be one of perpetual wars and of grinding Slavery." Of Lincoln, he declared, "Let us forget that he ever erred, and support him with redoubled energy." Ben Wade stumped across Pennsylvania, Kentucky, and Ohio, including the Copperhead stronghold of Dayton, "dealing stalwart blows against the enemies of the country," as one exhilarated Republican put it. To Chandler he expressed confidence that the Republicans would prevail, and promised to work as hard as he could for the ticket. "I only wish we could do as well for a better man," he said, disparagingly. "But to save the nation I am doing all for him that I could possibly do for a better man, were it not for the country there would be a poetical justice in his being beaten by that stupid ass McClellan."

Even with the Radicals finally on board, Republican electoral prospects were far from assured. Gold continued its seemingly unending upward climb. The national debt now topped $2 billion, an increase of $300 million in just four months. Pitt Fessenden, now toiling rather unhappily as secretary of the Treasury, traveled personally to New York in an attempt to sell $10 million in government paper, but failed. He also considered sending Salmon Chase to Europe to flog bonds to bankers there, but decided that it would smack too much of desperation. Few Americans wanted to invest more money in what looked all too much like a lame-duck government, before the outcome of the election was known.

The state elections in October offered Republicans some encouragement. In Indiana, the epicenter of midwestern Copperhead activity, Gov. Oliver P. Morton was reelected by a 20,000-vote majority, along with four new Republican congressmen. In Ohio, the Unionist fusion ticket trounced the Democrats by 54,000 votes and flipped the state's congressional delegation from fourteen Democrats and five Republicans to seventeen Republicans and two Democrats; one of the losers was the Democrats' de facto floor leader in the House of Representatives, "Sunset" Cox. The Republicans also gained three House seats in Pennsylvania, where Thaddeus Stevens was reelected in a landslide. In addition, by a hair-thin majority, Maryland adopted a new constitution abolishing slavery—"Both fraud and force were most unblushingly exercised," claimed Copperhead Charles Mason— but Henry Winter Davis, who proved too extreme for the state's voters, lost his bid for reelection. The news from Lincoln's home state of Illinois was not reassuring, however. "Everything is at sixes and sevens; and no head or tail to anything," reported an anxious Elihu Washburne. "There is imminent danger of our losing the state."

As Election Day neared, there were persistent rumors of uprisings and sabotage, plots to assassinate Lincoln, schemes by disaffected officers to stage a coup if the election was close, and plans by pro-Confederate speculators to drive up the price of gold to generate turmoil among the working classes. Copperhead agitators were said to be ubiquitous, even in Stevens's district, where they tried to scare pacifist Dunkers and Mennonites by telling them that if Lincoln was reelected their sons would be dragged into the army by provost marshals.

Not all of this was fantasy. In Patoka, Indiana, Copperheads attempted to murder the local Unionist sheriff, and in western Pennsylvania a well-armed band of deserters and draft dodgers and Copperheads killed a colonel sent to arrest them. In mid-September, a Confederate team operating from Canada had failed in an attempt to seize a federal gunboat on Lake Erie and use it to liberate Confederate prisoners on nearby Johnson's Island. And in October, a band of raiders slipped across the Canadian border and robbed three banks in St. Albans, Vermont, stealing $220,000 and terrorizing the citizens. Meanwhile, the Republican press relentlessly shackled the Democrats to both Vallandigham and the Sons of Liberty. Vallandigham's protestations of innocence rang all the more hollow when it was revealed that the Sons of Liberty's Indiana state commander, Harrison Dodd, had received direct payments from the Confederate government and stockpiled hundreds of guns in his Indianapolis shop. Editorialized the *New York Tribune,* "The nation who votes for Vallandigham's candidate is a nation that has already perished." The Unionist *Cleveland Daily Leader* cried that if McClellan was elected he would drive 150,000 Negro soldiers out of the army and order a draft for 150,000 more white men to fill their places, and warned that "the conspiracies against the government will be revived unless the whole traitor crew are buried fathoms deep tomorrow."

Jumpy Copperheads feared violence, too. "A crisis is approaching," Charles Mason confided to his diary. "The result may be civil war at the north." Radical Republicans in New York were said to be preparing a coup in Albany if the state's Copperhead governor, Horatio Seymour, was reelected. In the Northwest, the Lincoln administration was rumored to be secretly arming Unionist toughs to use against Democrats who attempted to vote. Democrats also complained, with some justification, that Republicans were scheming to manipulate the soldier vote. For the first time in American history soldiers in the field were participating in a presidential election. Reliably Unionist regiments from states that did not allow absentee voting were furloughed, along with recuperating invalids from military hospitals, while agents from the Democratic-controlled state of New York arranging to collect soldiers' votes near Washington were allegedly arrested and thrown into the Old Capitol prison. Pro-administration officers were released to canvas for the Union Party, while anti-Lincoln officers already on furlough were abruptly recalled to duty. Of one such officer, a Colonel Moore of the 118th New York, his commander Benjamin Butler dryly wrote from the front lines in Virginia, "His present business is stumping the State of New York for McClellan. I think his present employment is as arduous as employment in the field would be, and he is much needed here."

In the complete absence of polling, no one knew what was going to happen on Election Day. McClellan was buoyantly optimistic. On October 27, he wrote to his advisor Samuel Barlow, "All is favorable in New York, & I hear that Penna people feel very jubilant." Lincoln, meanwhile, was steeling himself for defeat. Speaking to a crowd of well-wishers outside the White House, he reminded them that if the voters "should deliberately resolve to have immediate peace even at the loss of their country, and their liberty, I know not the power or right to resist them."

With fears of unrest peaking, five thousand trustworthy New England and New York troops under Butler's command were dispatched to New York City and stationed on commandeered tugs and ferries, ready to land on short notice. Gunboats covered Wall Street and the most restive neighborhoods. Guards were placed around armories. Shops dealing in weapons were put under surveillance. Warships were also sent up the Harlem River to cover the High Bridge aqueduct to prevent an attack on the city's water supply. Butler himself set up a sixty-wire telegraph center, connecting him to the War Department and every police station and polling place in the city.

On Election Day, determined voters in Manhattan waited anxiously in heavy rain for two hours or more to cast their votes, but the feared disruptions didn't take place. Soldiers at the front also felt the weight of the occasion. Wrote Wilbur Fiske of the Second Vermont, "Thousands of bits of paper are falling into ballot boxes today, all over the country. It is a little thing, and can be done very easily, but mighty consequences may hang on the result." In Washington, rain poured down. Wondering what his fate would be, Lincoln stoically waited with his secretary John Hay in the telegraph room at the War Department as telegrams trickled in. At midnight they dined on fried oysters. In the early hours of the morning the outcome began to take shape. Republicans had won by a majority of ten thousand votes in Philadelphia, and by four thousand in Boston. (Later, a friend commented, "The Almighty must have stuffed the ballot-boxes.") Even New York went for Lincoln. When all the ballots were counted, he had won 55 percent of the popular vote and carried all but three states—New Jersey, Delaware, and Kentucky—

and crushed McClellan by 212 electoral votes to 21, becoming the first president since Andrew Jackson in 1832 to be reelected, and the first Northerner to win a second term. In addition, the Democrats lost every governor's race in the free states except New Jersey, while the Republicans took control of most of the state legislatures. Most dramatic of all, Lincoln had won 78 percent of the soldiers' ballots. In Pennsylvania and several other states, it was the soldiers who gave him his margin of victory. The Union Party's victory in the House races was equally lopsided and diminished the Democratic contingent in the House from seventy-two seats to just thirty-eight.

"*Laus Deo!*"—Praise God! exclaimed George Templeton Strong. "The crisis has been past [*sic*], and the most momentous popular election ever held since ballots were invented has decided against treason and disunion." It showed to everyone—to war-weary Unionists, to defeatist Copperheads, to expectant Confederates, to the rest of the world—that the American people had ratified the war, and that they intended to stay the course. Never before had the United States waged a presidential contest in the middle of a war. If ever there was a moment when a state of emergency might have trumped democracy, it was 1864. Just the fact that the election took place at all was one of the nation's greatest wartime achievements.

George McClellan accepted his defeat with characteristic ill-grace. "For my country's sake, I deplore the result—but the people have decided with their eyes wide open and I feel that a great weight is removed from my mind," he peevishly told Samuel Barlow. For the Democrats, the election was a complete disaster and yet another personal humiliation for Clement Vallandigham and the entire peace movement. With even Cox defeated, though he would remain in his seat until the opening of the Thirty-ninth Congress in December 1865, the congressional Democrats were left leaderless and ill-equipped to contest the reemboldened Republicans when they returned to do battle over emancipation and Reconstruction in the next session of Congress.

On November 10, jubilant Republicans gathered in front of the White House to "serenade" the president. From a window over the north portico, while a secretary stood beside him lighting the pages of his speech with a candle, he declared, "The election was a necessity. We cannot have free government without elections; and if the rebellion could force us to forgo or postpone a national election, it might fairly claim to have already conquered and ruined us." Americans had proved, he said, "that a people's government can sustain a national election, in the midst of a great civil war. Until now it has not been known to the world that this was a possibility."

# 20

# Hurrah for Freedom!

*Emancipation is not enough.*

—SEN. CHARLES SUMNER

When the Thirty-eighth Congress resumed at the beginning of December, William T. Sherman was somewhere in Georgia, no one in Washington knew where, marching his sixty-thousand-man army toward the Atlantic. In mid-November, as martial bands played tunes that included the melancholy "When This Cruel War Is Over" and the rather less so "Oh, Jenny Come Tickle Me," he broke his telegraph links, sent his rolling stock north, and left Atlanta for Savannah, three hundred miles away. He promised to "make Georgia howl." His troops were all seasoned fighters, a rainbow of Yankeedom, hailing from Ohio and Illinois, Minnesota and Iowa, Indiana and Pennsylvania, New York and Connecticut, and even a unit of Unionist cavalry from the Alabama hill country. Stripped of all but essential baggage, they lived off the land, confiscating fodder and food, tearing up railroads, torching the plantations of rebel politicians, burning arsenals, mills, cotton gins, and warehouses. Wherever they marched, slaves poured off plantations and farms. "They flock to me old & young," wrote Sherman to his wife, Ellen. "They pray & shout—and mix up my name with Moses, & Simon."

Sherman's aims were strategic: to show that he could march a federal army with impunity through the heart of the Confederacy, and to demoralize its leadership by exposing their helplessness to stop him, a fact vividly illustrated when the entire Georgia state government fled the state capital, Milledgeville, at his approach. The scanty news that reached the North came from days-old Southern newspapers, which claimed that Georgians were rising en masse to the colors, that Sherman's army had been wiped out, or that they were starving and on the brink of surrender. In fact, Sherman's veterans easily brushed aside the feeble resistance that the Confederates put up. They bridged dozens of rivers and swamps, swept up tens of thousands of horses, mules, and livestock, millions of pounds of grain, and mountains of rations stockpiled for the Confederate armies. (The supposed savagery of the march is a myth: although considerable property was damaged, both sides *collectively* suffered only about three thousand military casualties, and very few civilians were killed.) None of this was yet known when the president's annual message reached Capitol Hill on December 4, where it was read aloud by the secretary of the Senate, J. W. Forney, and the clerk of the House, Edward McPherson.

In the tradition of such addresses, the president put a positive slant on everything he could. Although the national debt now stood at $1,740,690,489, the nation's financial system had proved resilient, and the number of new national banks was rapidly growing. (He might also have mentioned that thanks to improving Union fortunes on the battlefield and deft financial management by Pitt Fessenden, Thaddeus Stevens, and Jay Cooke, the gold rate was plummeting, and financial confidence in the government rebounding; by the day after Lincoln's address, the latest $40 million issue of five-year government securities had been disposed of.) More than one and a half million acres of western land had already been claimed under the Homestead Act. The Transcontinental Railroad now extended one hundred miles beyond Omaha and was continuing westward. Nevada had become a state, with its vast mineral wealth at the disposal of the Union. Louisiana and Arkansas now had organized loyal state governments, while Maryland had approved a free constitution. Despite the huge number of men under arms, hundreds of thousands more Americans had voted in the recent elections than had in

1860. Asserted Lincoln, "We are not exhausted or in the process of exhausting." In short, even amid the hardships of the past three and a half years the nation still thrived and prospered.

And then there was the war: it would and must continue, Lincoln said. "The insurgent leader"—Jefferson Davis—"would accept nothing short of severance of the Union, precisely what we will not and cannot give. Between him and us the issue is distinct, simple, and inflexible. It is an issue which can only be tried by war and decided by victory. If we yield, we are beaten." And, inescapably, there was slavery. Lincoln noted that in June the amendment abolishing slavery had fallen short in the House of Representatives for lack of a two-thirds majority. He now asked Congress to try again. The results of the election had vindicated the administration's policy, he said. The next Congress would surely pass the amendment even if this one did not. Would not sooner be better? To those who might doubt his commitment to emancipation, he asserted that he would not sacrifice principle for a premature peace. He would not modify or retract the Emancipation Proclamation, nor return to slavery any man or woman freed by the proclamation or by any act of Congress. This was an absolute condition of peace, and it was nonnegotiable.

Afterward Thaddeus Stevens lavished praise on the president. "I do not think I am extravagant when I say that it is the most important and best message that has been communicated to Congress for the last sixty years," he told his colleagues. "There never was a day since Abraham Lincoln was elected president that he stood so high, or deserved to stand so high in the estimation of the people as at this moment." This was remarkable praise indeed coming from the man who had for so long excoriated Lincoln for weak political leadership, indecisiveness as commander-in-chief, and inadequate support for abolition. Stevens and Lincoln were never close and often at odds with one another. But their paths were now converging. Stevens had come to believe that for all his shortcomings, Lincoln had at long last thrown his energy behind the greatest moral issue of their lifetimes. Sounding preacher-like—the evangelical mode was hardly a natural one for the freethinking Stevens—he ventured in language that seemed to echo Lincoln's own that a "righteous Providence" had brought the war upon Americans as punishment for their oppression of a "harmless race of men." More than the first-born of every household had been taken, he said, but "we still harden our hearts and refuse to let [that] people go." Fixing his eye on Democrats who had blocked the amendment, he said, "If we still harden our hearts and blood must still flow, may the ghosts of the slaughtered victims sit heavily upon the souls of those who cause it."

Although no member of Congress surpassed Stevens in passion for emancipation, he allowed the amendment to be piloted through the House by the younger, healthier, and less personally abrasive James Ashley of Ohio. An imposing, clean-shaven man of forty with a tumbling shock of dark curly hair, Ashley had risen, like Stevens and Lincoln, from next to nothing. Reared by an impoverished and overbearing father, an evangelical minister, he ran away from home at the age of twelve to work on flatboats plying the Ohio River. Despite a complete lack of early schooling, he learned the printing trade, edited a local newspaper, and eventually studied law before his election to Congress as a protégé of Ben Wade from the abolitionist bastion of Toledo, in 1859. (Politics there was a rough-and-tumble business: on one occasion he was hit in the face by a live goose thrown through an open window, and on another he dealt with a heckler by whacking him over the head with his cane.) He had loathed slavery as long as he could remember. All his life, he would remember a drover in Kentucky who refused to let his cattle drink from a stream in which Ashley's father was baptizing slaves. As a teenager, he ferried fugitive slaves north from Kentucky across the Ohio River at considerable personal risk, and he later became friendly with national antislavery figures including Sumner, Lucretia Mott, and the radical New York land magnate Gerrit Smith, who helped finance Ashley's career in politics. He was one of the few public figures who had dared to visit the imprisoned John Brown before his execution.

No one expected an easy victory for the amendment. The makeup of the House hadn't altered since June. But both the political and military landscapes had. The elections had devastated the Democrats, and left the Copperheads dead in the wreckage. In the next Congress, the Thirty-ninth, Republicans would enjoy a three-quarters majority with the power to push through any legislation they wanted. In addition, Lincoln was no longer the spent force that he had seemed to be the previous summer, when Wade and others had tried to push him off the Republican ticket. His crushing victory over McClellan was a personal triumph. And he once again had an abundance of patronage jobs to distribute or deny, tools that would prove their value in the battle that was now gathering over the amendment.

Away from the static siege lines at Petersburg, the North's military prospects had also brightened, further lifting public support for the government. On December 16, Gen. George Thomas—a native Virginian who had remained loyal to the Union—virtually annihilated the Confederates' last major western army at Nashville. Just days before that, Sherman's army had emerged in front of Savannah, captured the city, and compelled its defenders to flee. On December 22, Sherman telegraphed Lincoln: "I beg to present you as a Christmas-gift the city of Savannah, with one hundred and fifty heavy guns and plenty of ammunition, also about twenty-five thousand bales of cotton."

Although Ashley floor-managed the debate, Stevens, like a lode-star, remained at its center of gravity. On January 13, he hauled himself into the chamber to deliver one of his most heartfelt speeches, and one of the most moving of the entire debate. It had the ring of a valedictory, the words of an old man—at seventy-three, he was one of the chamber's oldest members—who sensed that his body would soon fail him completely. But he was also well aware that what was taking place represented the moral climax of his political life thus far. He began with a summary of his maturation as an antislavery man. "From my earliest youth I was taught to revere the Declaration of Independence and to revere its sublime principles," he said.

> As I advanced in life and became somewhat enabled to consult the writings of the great men of antiquity, I found in all their works which have survived the ravages of time and come down to the present generation, one unanimous denunciation of tranny and of slavery, and eulogy of liberty. Homer, Aschylus the great Greek tragedian, Cicero, Hesiod, Virgil, Tacitus, and Sallust, in immortal language, all denounced slavery as a thing which took

away half the man and degraded human beings, and sang paeans in the noblest strains to the goddess of liberty.

When, thirty years ago, I entered the legislature of the state which I now in part represent, I carried with me the same feeling and the same determination; for this feeling grew with my growth and strengthened with my strength, but I thank God it has not decayed with enfeebling age. When fifteen years ago, I was first honored with a seat in this body, it was dangerous to talk against this institution, a danger which gentlemen now here will never be able to appreciate. And yet, I did not hesitate, in the midst of bowie-knives and revolvers and howling demons upon the other side of the House, to stand here and denounce this infamous institution in language which possibly now, on looking at it, I might deem intemperate, but which I then deemed necessary to rouse the public attention and cast odium upon the worst institution on earth, one which is a disgrace to man and would be an annoyance to the infernal spirits.

Ingenious gentlemen argue, and many honest men will delude their consciences in voting in favor of still sustaining the institution [of slavery] on the ground that the Constitution does not allow an amendment on this point. They go on the ground that the subject of slavery has not been intrusted to us by the states, and that therefore it is reserved. Now, as the Constitution stands, that is true. But we are not now inquiring whether we have jurisdiction over slavery. We are inquiring whether the states have granted us the power of amendment. That is the subject—not the subject of slavery, not the subject of religion, not the subject of anything else—but have the states yielded to Congress the right to amend? If they have, then the whole question is answered. The power to amend the Constitution is unlimited. There is no subject on earth relating to government that you cannot touch. Nowhere in that original instrument did the states grant the right of legislating on the subject of religion; and yet the very first amendment that was made under this power refers to the subject of religion and the freedom of speech, showing the fallacy of the arguments of those who say that you can amend only the subjects granted to Congress.

Earlier, "Sunset" Cox had attempted to ensnare Stevens in a trap. Millions of Americans believed that the Confederate leadership was ready to negotiate for peace based on restoration of the pre-war Union, Cox said. All they needed was a conciliatory gesture—abandonment of the needlessly provocative amendment. Wouldn't Stevens be willing to give up his doctrine of Negro equality for the sake of the Union?

Startlingly, Stevens replied, "The gentleman will allow me to say that I never held to that doctrine of Negro equality."

"Then I understand the gentleman from Pennsylvania not to hold that all men are created equal?" responded the surprised Cox.

"Yes, sir," said Stevens, "but not equality in all things—simply before the laws, nothing else."

"I ask the gentleman to give up his idea of the equality of the black and white races before the law," Cox prodded.

To this, Stevens tersely answered, "I won't do it."

Stevens wouldn't allow himself to be drawn. Offered an opportunity to deliver one of his patented screeds on behalf of equality, which he very much did believe in, he ostentatiously declined. He was no one's fool, certainly not the transparent Cox's. He would say nothing to provoke his many enemies or to undermine the back-room negotiations that he knew were under way to cull votes from biddable Democrats. As skilled a politician as any man on Capitol Hill, he knew when to fight and when to give ground. No one held his forbearance against him; no one doubted what he really believed whether he spoke it aloud or not.

The amendment's opponents wielded long-familiar arguments whose potency had wilted since the Democrats' drubbing in November. Fernando Wood, who as New York City's pro-Southern mayor in 1861 had encouraged it to secede from the Union, denounced the amendment as "unwise, impolitic," and manifestly unconstitutional. George Pendleton, McClellan's erstwhile running mate, maintained that even if the Constitution permitted Congress to legislate on slavery—which he didn't believe it did—how could the states that were outside the Union ever be expected to abide by a measure that was passed only by the states that remained in it?

Cox, now a lame duck but still exerting considerable influence among Democrats, was more equivocal, revealing a subtle shift in his views, for listeners alert enough to catch it. The Democrats were now but few and weak, he admitted: "like stormy petrels tossing upon the angry waves of sectional agitation, we are at last overwhelmed in the flood of fanaticism." But the amendment would set a very dangerous precedent. If the status of Negroes could be altered in one way, couldn't it just as easily be changed in another? Couldn't the Constitution be amended even to give them the *vote*, in spite of the laws in many Northern states explicitly denying it to them? Couldn't states with "black laws," such as Illinois, Indiana, and his own Ohio, be forced to open their borders to black *immigration*? Couldn't state laws based on inequality be declared *void*? Worse yet, the laws that would have to be passed to carry out the amendment would fatally break down the walls that stood between the state and national governments. Slavery might be finished, he acknowledged. "The blows of war are breaking down its panting, exhausted body." But if it was already dead, then what was the point of this amendment, for which there was no earthly need?

So far, this kind of argument was to be expected from a man who had opposed almost every piece of antislavery legislation. But now something interesting happened. Cox said that as a Democrat loyal to the principles of Stephen A. Douglas, he had always believed that Congress had no power to either abolish or protect slavery—unless the Constitution itself were to be changed. "I said, 'Amend that instrument first if you would thus break down the incontestable rights of the State[s].'" He pointed out that in 1861 several amendments, such as the Crittenden compromise, had been proposed in order to protect slavery from "interference." Therefore, Southerners *themselves* had negated the argument that amendments bearing on slavery were inherently unconstitutional. He didn't like the proposed amendment: it would further consolidate federal power in ways which he as a "State-rights man" abhorred. But there was no question in his mind that Congress had the constitutional authority to enact it.

If the Confederates were open to a peaceful settlement, Cox said, the amendment was obviously an obstacle, as he had implied to Stevens. *However,* if they flatly rejected conciliation and continued to insist on independence, or if peace could somehow be restored by the abolition of slavery, he would be willing to cast his vote for it despite all his reservations. He didn't say so explicitly—he didn't need to, since everyone had already heard the rumors—but the Confederates were now said to be planning to arm slaves and give them freedom in return. "If they can let slavery go for independence," Cox said, surely "the Democracy can [let go of it] for the sake of the Union."

It was a convoluted speech. But it was possibly the single most important one delivered in the debate. Cox seemed to say that while he opposed the amendment he didn't quite rule out voting for it. Most significantly, he unequivocally granted the *right* of Congress to enact it. By doing so, he had provided prospective defectors with a principled rationale, or at least political cover, if they reversed their votes.

Nearly half the House members were lame ducks who had been beaten in the elections or were resigning. Most of them were Democrats and border state Unionists. Of these, the most important to Ashley were those who had voted against the amendment in June. If the amendment was to pass now many of them would somehow have to be convinced to reverse their earlier vote. The most pivotal of the lame ducks was Cox himself. Although over the years he had toggled opportunistically between the Democrats' war and peace factions, he had never toned down his extreme racism. But he was also as pure a political animal as there was in Congress. Since November, he had cast a cold eye on his party's diminished fortunes and had concluded that slavery was an albatross that had to be cut loose if the Democrats were to have any future in postwar America. In December, he met with Democratic power brokers in New York and told them so. "I was anxious, as a Democrat, and with a view to the upbuilding of the party I cherished, to drive this question from the political arena," he wrote.

Cox never did vote for the amendment. He later claimed that he was about to when he suddenly learned that a Confederate delegation was actually in Washington to talk peace. A flurry of frantic messaging ensued. Cox asked Ashley if the report was true. Ashley asked Lincoln's secretaries, who in turn queried Lincoln himself, who responded that no such commission was in the city.

Years afterward, George S. Boutwell, a Radical Republican from Massachusetts, wrote, "Such was the exigency for the passage of the resolution that the means were not subjected to any rigid rules of ethics." Whether much, or any, money changed hands remains unclear, though Democrats accused Secretary of State Seward of bribing defectors either to flip or to simply stay away when the roll was called.

What is clear, however, is that Lincoln, Seward, and their agents directly invested the executive power to an unparalleled degree in an effort to leverage votes. Lincoln personally assured Unionist and slave owner James S. Rollins that he could select the nominee for a federal judgeship in Missouri. George H. Yeaman, a slave-owning Kentuckian, who had once denounced abolitionism as "the Sunday rhetoric of a horde of canting, white-cravatted divines," was offered appointment as the minister to Denmark. Homer Nelson of Pough-keepsie, New York, was promised a job in the Treasury Department. Anson Herrick, also of New York, announced loftily that the amend-ment was an opportunity "for the Democracy to rid itself once and forever of the incubus of slavery," but was also promised a job as fed-eral revenue collector if he voted for it. Alexander Coffroth of Penn-sylvania declared, "If by my action today I dig my political grave, I will descend into it without a murmur"; however, he was embroiled in a bitter dispute over election returns and was apparently prom-ised that if he changed his vote the Republicans would allow his victory to be certified. Moses Odell of Brooklyn, a member of the Joint Committee on the Conduct of the War, and perhaps more sin-cere than most, declared that since it was obvious that the "peculiar institution" was dead, he was "in favor of giving it a constitutional burial." Andrew J. Rogers of New Jersey, a violent Negrophobe who had declared emancipation to be ruinous to the nation, skipped the vote altogether, apparently having been promised favorable treat-ment for a railroad deal in his state.

Ashley set the vote for January 31. At 3:30 p.m. silence fell over the chamber as the clerk began to call the roll. Despite Ashley's tireless head-counting, no one could be certain of the outcome. Everyone in sight seemed to be scribbling tallies on scraps of paper. One after another, lame ducks cast their ballots for the amendment to applause from Republicans and derisive hoots from Democrats: Archibald McAllister of Pennsylvania, Coffroth, James English of Connecticut, John Ganson of New York, Herrick, Wells Hutchins of Ohio, John Steele of New York . . . The chamber went silent again as the clerk counted up the votes, and then handed the totals to Speaker Colfax. The amendment, he declared, had passed by 119 to 56 with just three votes to spare, with eight Democrats absent.

Shouts exploded from the floor. "The tumult of joy that broke out was vast, thundering and uncontrollable," reported the *New York Tribune*. Members hurrahed in chorus with the deafening cheers of the gallery. Ladies waved their handkerchiefs. Men wept and flung their hats in the air. Waves of applause rolled back and forth across the chamber, as numberless voices cried, "Hurrah for freedom!" Frederick Douglass's son Charles, recently discharged from the Fifth Massachusetts Cavalry, who was in the visitors' gallery, reported, "Such rejoicing I never before witnessed, cannons firing, people hugging and shaking hands, white people I mean, flags flying all over the city." The next day's headlines in the *Tribune* screamed: "Freedom Triumphant. Commencement of a New Era. Death of Slavery."

But Cox had been right about the Confederate commissioners. There really was a delegation. Earlier in January, Lincoln had allowed Frank Blair Sr., a conservative founder of the Republican Party who was well-known to members of the Confederate government, to go to Richmond to unofficially put out a peace feeler to Jefferson Davis. Neither Lincoln nor Davis wanted to compromise, but nor did they want to be seen as failing to acknowledge any conciliatory overtures. Davis's three commissioners were en route to Washington when the amendment debate was coming to a climax, but they weren't actually "in the city." Lincoln and Ashley had dissembled, but they hadn't precisely lied. The commissioners—Confederate vice president Alexander Stephens, Assistant Secretary of War John Campbell, and former U.S. senator Robert Hunter, now president pro tem of the Senate in Richmond—remained on a federal steamboat at Hampton Roads, where they were kept waiting until after the vote on the amendment had been safely won.

On January 31, Lincoln directed Seward to meet with them, and then joined Seward himself on February 3. In the course of a four-hour conversation, they presented the Confederates with three conditions: complete restoration of national sovereignty in every state; no compromise on slavery; and no cease-fire before the disbanding of all rebel forces. In return, the commissioners offered no commitment and argued vaguely for "some other course" prior to any step toward reunion, a ploy that Lincoln and Seward knew would only lead to indefinite postponement and the diplomatic initiative left in the Confederates' hands. While later reports were contradictory, it appears that Lincoln at least hinted to the Confederates that once they rejoined the Union they might be able to vote down the just passed Thirteenth Amendment, and that he might even be willing to support compensated emancipation if the Southern states freed their slaves on their own.

Ben Wade was shocked when he learned that Lincoln and Seward had agreed to meet the Confederates on any terms at all. Was the North now "to kneel down at the throne of Mr. Davis and beg his pardon?" he thundered. Zachariah Chandler exclaimed that parleying for peace at this point was "foolish, unauthorized, *unholy,*" and grossly demeaned the president. Never having overcome their fundamental distrust of Lincoln, they feared that those, like themselves, who had driven the war policy for the past four years would now be sold out just when they were on the cusp of victory, while the peace-minded president would be politically co-opted by the Democrats. But Thaddeus Stevens, his new confidence in the president unabated, praised his "masterly style," "principle," and "sagacity," in effect offering him a lifeboat that kept his reputation afloat. Ironically, Jefferson Davis also came to Lincoln's aid. After the commissioners' return to Richmond, Davis had declared to a public assembly, "Sooner than we should be united again, I would be willing to yield up everything I have on earth; and if it were possible, I would yield up my life a thousand times rather than succumb." In short, the Confederates' gesture of "conciliation" was as much an exercise in Kabuki diplomacy as Lincoln's.

Passage of the amendment was only its first hurdle, of course. It would have to be ratified by three-fourths of the states before it became law. That posed another complex of concerns. In Ashley's view, all twenty-five Union states plus the three—Louisiana, Arkansas, and Tennessee—that had now nominally reentered the Union under Lincoln's 10 percent plan had the right to vote on the amendment; the eight states still in full rebellion could not. Under this scheme, the amendment would therefore be sent out to at least twenty-five and perhaps as many as twenty-eight states, and require ratification by between nineteen and twenty-one. Lincoln's position was quite different: he felt strongly that ratification by three-fourths of *all* the states, including the seceded ones, was imperative to ensure that the amendment remained irreversible in times to come.

Matters were made even more complicated because Congress had yet to solve the problem of readmitting Louisiana, whose nominal representatives and senators had been cooling their heels in Washington for months. Louisiana would presumably set the standard for every other state still in rebellion once they were qualified to be restored to the Union. This wasn't legislative nitpicking. The Radical Henry Winter Davis—himself a lame duck, having proved too radical for Maryland voters—warned that seating the Louisiana representatives based on Lincoln's 10 percent formula would set a fatal precedent. Every other reconstructed state would expect the same standard, so that when Congress next met, there could be "sixty-five Representatives from the states now in rebellion, and twenty-two senators, claiming admission." This was precisely what "Sunset" Cox and his more strategic allies were hoping for. Beneath their new openness to emancipation was a reckoning that readmitting the Southern states with little or no restriction on whom they elected would greatly improve the Democrats' chances to regain control of Congress.

The Radicals in Congress refused to seat Louisiana's delegation, asserting quite accurately that although the state's new constitution nominally abolished slavery, former slaves had merely been locked into a system of legal peonage instead. In hope of effecting a compromise, Ashley proposed seating Louisiana's congressmen in return for the immediate enfranchisement of the state's Negroes and a guarantee that the more stringent terms of the Wade-Davis bill would be followed in other reconstructed states. (The bill barred most rebels from voting or holding office and required the seceded states to remain under military rule until 50 percent of their enrolled voters had taken an oath of allegiance to the United States.) Lincoln refused to entertain black suffrage at this point, however, and Louisiana's military governor Gen. Nathaniel Banks predicted that whites would boycott any election in which blacks were allowed to vote. Ashley then proposed enfranchising just Negro war veterans. This inflamed Radicals who opposed any recognition of what they considered the state's fraudulent government.

Only months earlier few members of Congress dared to speak of the enfranchisement of freedmen. But this once forbidden subject was now moving rapidly toward the center of debate as a practical proposition. As Rep. James Garfield, one of the more forward-thinking of the Radicals, told an Ohio audience, "There ought to be no pariahs in a full-grown and civilized nation. Let us not commit ourselves to the absurd and senseless dogma that the color of the skin shall be the basis of suffrage, the talisman of liberty." It was also apparent by now that Lincoln's long-cherished belief that a vast silent majority of Unionists in the South would flock to the Republican Party was merely a fantasy, and equally clear that the only reliable Republican voting bloc in the Senate would be former slaves—if they were allowed to vote. Negroes were majorities in South Carolina and Mississippi, and large minorities in almost every other seceded state, pointed out Rep. William Kelley. He proposed that full citizenship immediately be conferred on *all* Negroes, and that suffrage be granted to all black soldiers and all blacks who were able to read the Constitution, a measure that, if adopted, would have an impact not only in the South. Free blacks were able to vote without restriction only in New England, and were still explicitly barred from it in most Northern states. Kelley openly admitted that he intended his proposal only as "an entering wedge" on the way to universal Negro suffrage. Republicans, he warned, ignored black enfranchisement at their political peril. If the rebels were speedily restored to full citizen-ship and regained control of their states, they would soon reduce the Negroes to serfdom, as they already had in Louisiana. "Though we find that we have buried the slavery question," he predicted, "our peace will be disturbed by the Negro question constantly, and [as] fearfully as it has been by the struggle between slavery and free labor."

Tempers ran high on every side of the debate. On January 20, Kel-ley and some friends were taking tea at Willard's Hotel, a block from the White House, when seventy-four-year-old A. P. Field, one of the frustrated Louisiana delegates, seated nearby and apparently very drunk, abruptly barked, "Why do you keep us out in the cold? Why don't you admit us?" Kelley tried to ignore him, but Field kept inter-rupting, and then, according to the *Congressional Globe,* "broke out with more violent and profane language." Finally he came at Kel-ley, shouting, "God damn you, sir," and demanding that he step out into the hall. Twenty minutes later Kelley emerged with his friends. Field immediately seized him by the collar, whirled him around, and exclaimed, "God damn you, you must give me satisfaction!" He then pulled a knife from his pocket, and stabbed Kelley in the hand. Kelley had hold of Field by his coat, and said, "Go away peaceably, you are too old a man for me to strike." Field tried again to stab Kelley, and when he was finally pulled away, he swore, "I will shoot him before he goes to bed." The next day, somewhat sobered, Field abjectly blamed his behavior on too much "ardent spirits." Several Radicals moved to bar him from entering the Capitol, but failed to win a majority on the floor. For many Northerners, however, Field's behavior epitomized the Southern propensity for personal violence, which they feared must lie in store for freed slaves and their white friends if they lacked the power to protect themselves after the war.

Ashley nevertheless persisted in seeking a pragmatic compromise. He proposed enfranchising all Negro men in states that did not yet have loyal governments, coupled to recognition of Louisiana, Arkan-sas, and Tennessee under the 10 percent plan, which required only that percentage of prewar voters in order to reestablish government in a seceded state. When that idea failed to gain traction, he offered yet another, which would guarantee the civil rights of Negroes and

restrict voting rights only to proven white Unionists and black veterans. But this too fizzled, leaving the federal government with no
coherent Reconstruction policy at all.


Meanwhile, Union-occupied areas of the rebel states were a crazy-
quilt of local initiatives. In the Mississippi Delta, land confiscated
from Jefferson Davis and his family had been turned over to freedmen to work communally with the assistance of self-governing local
councils. In the Sea Islands of South Carolina, Treasury agents were
responsible for land use, army officers for law and order, and Northern benevolent associations for education. In Louisiana, the army
enforced a system tailored to the interests of plantation owners,
including restrictive labor contracts, management by overseers, and
the prosecution for "vagrancy" of freedmen who left their place of
employment. Near-anarchy reigned across much of the South as the
war upset established economic arrangements and slaves fled their
plantations in droves. Impoverished though they were, displaced
freedmen everywhere aspired to own their own land, travel freely,
marry, and participate in political life. (Union-occupied South Carolina had sent Negro delegates to the Republican convention, and in
New Orleans freedmen had already organized to lobby for the vote.)
At the same time, in some areas, masses of freedom seekers impeded
military movements and drained the army's resources. The need for
a coherent overall policy was plain to see even in Washington, where
the population of contrabands had swelled from thirty to forty thousand between June 1864 and January 1865, most of them living in
extreme destitution.

Beyond the visible need, the larger conundrum of Reconstruction hinged on answering a host of questions that admitted of no
easy answers. What degree of freedom and power could freed slaves
be allowed to exercise? Were they capable of becoming citizens now
or ever? If left alone, could they take care of themselves? Or did the
government have a moral duty to care for them? Abolitionists themselves were divided. Many thought the Thirteenth Amendment was
the end in itself, including William Lloyd Garrison, who proposed
liquidating the American Anti-Slavery Society because he thought it

had nothing left to do. Others felt that emancipation was no more than a first step, among them James Garfield, who asked, "What is freedom? Is it the bare privilege of not being chained? If this is all, then freedom is a bitter mockery, a cruel delusion." All these doubts and conflicts coalesced around the establishment of the proposed Freedmen's Bureau, which had foundered in the last session of Congress.

As Sumner's enabling resolution put it, the bureau would oversee all civil activities relating to the nearly four million former slaves, and coordinate with the army "to secure to them and their posterity the blessings of liberty." It was a remarkably ambitious concept. For the first time, the federal government would undertake to oversee the affairs of individual men and women, expanding its authority into areas that antebellum Americans could hardly have dreamed possible: shouldering responsibility for their welfare, drawing up and approving private contracts, settling labor disputes, running schools, and licensing marriages. The bureau would also have the power to divide land confiscated from rebel owners into lots the freedmen could rent for three years, and then buy from the government, a critical tool in the effort to move freedmen toward self-sufficiency. There were few precedents. In some localities charities had aided in the settlement and assimilation of foreign immigrants, and the government had long provided food, clothing, and other supplies for Indians; this was generally stipulated as a treaty right between sovereigns. But nothing approached this scale.

Democrats and conservative Unionists opposed the establishment of such an agency in any form. During an earlier debate, one Democratic senator, Thomas Hendricks of Indiana, objected vociferously to what he claimed would be a veritable "second government" whose "despotism" would rival tsarist Russia and imperial Rome. Another, Willard Saulsbury of Delaware, had gasped rhetorically that such a bureau could, vampire-like, come to life only with "the blood of a murdered Constitution."

But the conservatives were just bystanders by this point. The real debate was taking place among the Radicals, reflecting a deep division between libertarians who believed that federal paternalism suffocated initiative, and those who believed that government had a moral duty to help the weakest members of society. Sen. Henry Lane of Indiana charged that the bureau was being justified with the same kind of argument that slave masters had always used to defend slavery: that Negroes were helpless without the guidance and control of white men. "As long as you hold them up they will never stand alone; but the very moment you make them free men and secure their rights in the courts of justice I believe they will be fully competent to take care of themselves," Lane said. Added Rep. James F. Wilson of Iowa, "The less restraint we put upon these freedmen the sooner we shall make men of them."

In the bureau's defense, William Kelley asserted that if former slaves weren't supported now when they needed it most, "we will doom them to vagrancy and pauperism, and throw upon another Congress, and perhaps upon another generation, the duty or the effort to reclaim those whose hopes we will have blasted, whose usefulness we will have destroyed." And in the Senate, Sumner declared, in ringing tones, "Emancipation is not enough. The freedmen for weary generations have fertilized these lands with their sweat. The time has come when they should enjoy the results of their labor." They could only do that if they were protected "from the tyranny of the dominant race." Only the federal government had the resources to do so, he argued; in an earlier phase of the debate, to underscore his point, he deployed a remarkable analogy that explicitly linked the future of ex-slaves with the larger Republican vision of an expanding postwar America. The national government, he said, "must interfere in this case precisely as in building the Pacific railroad."

Sumner had originally hoped for a full-fledged cabinet department devoted to the needs of the freedmen. In the final form that coalesced during the last hours of debate, the bureau was a much more modest confection. Despite its vast responsibilities, it was treated essentially as a temporary experiment, limited in duration to one year, and lodged beneath the umbrella of the War Department—the preference of most Radicals—and dependent on that department for its funding. In a politically expedient attempt to balance the bill's focus on blacks, white Southern Unionist refugees were at the last minute included in its mandate. A separate bill established a freedmen's bank with a view to encouraging savings and thrift.

The Radicals had the votes to pass both bills and they did, late in the night of March 3, just hours before Lincoln's inauguration. Although he knew that he would sway no one, Sen. Lazarus Powell of Kentucky, still a defender of slavery, delivered a final salvo, claiming that the bill would do nothing but create an army of parasitical bureaucrats—"broken-down politicians, dilapidated preachers, half-theologians, and half-worldlians"—and "send them upon these states as the locusts were sent upon Egypt." He added caustically, "Do you wish a bureau for every purpose? Do you intend that every interest of the people of the country shall be managed by bureaus in your War Office and other departments? This is a step in that direction." Such attacks would dog the Freedmen's Bureau throughout its short life, threatening its effectiveness and helping to set the terms by which activist government of any stripe would be judged in years to come.

A drenching rain soaked Washington that night, liquefying the streets, and making some so nearly impassable that army engineers half-seriously considered laying pontoons from the White House to Capitol Hill. Through the mist, the roof lights of the Capitol, where Congress remained in all-night session, cast an eerie but inspiring halo that highlighted the Stars and Stripes snapping in the wet wind. "Carpet-bagged and blanket-strapped" travelers come to town for the inauguration huddled in the Capitol for shelter as the senators and congressmen, swaying on their feet from exhaustion, hastily debated bills on last-minute army appropriations, Indian annuities, the Smithsonian Institution's trust fund, Minnesota land grants, and the like. The House wrapped up first. In his final words, Speaker Colfax of Indiana, invoking the new statue of the *Goddess of Liberty* atop the dome, who was soon to gaze down for the first time upon an inauguration, solemnly called upon members to remember, as the hour of battlefield victory neared, the "crushed and broken hearts in every hamlet," the "patriot graves in every churchyard, and the bones of brave men bleaching on every battlefield," fallen in the struggle "to prevent an alien flag from waving over the ashes of Washington."

At 9:00 a.m. the Senate was still at it even as workmen lugged settees into the chamber and muscled chairs between the senators' desks to accommodate the House members, governors, cabinet officers, Supreme Court justices, diplomats, agency heads, and their wives, mothers, and daughters who were already arriving for the ceremonies. Pugnacious Ben Wade was there, and Thaddeus Stevens risen from his sickbed, and "Fighting Joe" Hooker, and Adm. David Farragut, the hero of Mobile Bay, and Pitt Fessenden, finally shed of the burden of the now stabilized Treasury, from which he had resigned that very morning, having been once again reelected to the Senate by the Maine legislature, as he desired.

At noon, outgoing vice president Hannibal Hamlin, betraying no obvious regret at his departure from the great stage of government—his hope of reentering the Senate now dashed—said a few modest words of farewell. (He would later be named the federal collector of tariffs for the port of Boston, a well-paid sinecure, and a political graveyard.) Chief Justice Chase then administered the oath of office to incoming vice president Andrew Johnson, whose only half-coherent speech left more than a few Republicans wondering what kind of man was now one step away from the presidency. Already hungover from a late-night party, Johnson had complained of feeling "weak" and sent the Senate doorkeeper to bring him "a little stimulant" from the café outside the Senate chamber, and tossed off three full-to-the-brim tumblers of it in rapid succession. In what turned into a maudlin harangue, he boasted of his plebeian origins, woozily repeated himself, called out members of the cabinet but forgot some of their names, rudely ordered senators to remember that they were but "creatures of the American people," and then failed to properly swear in the new senators, so that a clerk had to finish the job. Taking up the Bible, Ben Butler sneered, Johnson then "slobbered the Holy Book with a drunken kiss." Lincoln was visibly embarrassed. Sumner hid his face in his hands. And Zachariah Chandler wrote to his wife, "I was never so mortified in my life, had I been able to find a hole I would have dropped through it out of sight."

Once Johnson had finally been quieted—Hamlin tugged on his coattails and told him to stop—the presidential procession began to form. As the sun broke through the clouds and the rain tapered off, Lincoln stepped out from among the columns of the Capitol's eastern portico and onto a wooden stand that had been erected there. Thousands cheered at the sight of him. Bands thumped. Splashes of color sparkled from the plumes of cadets and the gaudy uniforms of assembled fire companies. Sabers and bayonets gleamed. Negroes and whites, both soldiers and civilians, mingled freely together probably for the first time at a presidential inauguration.

Lincoln's brief address was majestic in its simplicity. He could have said anything at all, and he would have been cheered equally— praised the troops, celebrated the national spirit, reassured Southerners of the Union's good intentions. Instead, he chose to focus almost entirely on slavery. He recalled that four years earlier he had stood in the same place at a time when every American's thoughts were fixated anxiously on looming war. Slavery was the essential cause of the war, a fact that moderates like Lincoln rarely admitted in 1861. No one then, he said, had imagined the magnitude or duration of what was in store, and all Americans now prayed that the "mighty scourge" would soon come to an end. "Yet, if God wills that it continue, until all the wealth piled by the bond-man's two hundred and fifty years of unrequited toil shall be sunk, and until every drop of blood drawn with the lash, shall be paid by another drawn with the sword, so still it must be said 'the judgments of the Lord are true and righteous altogether.'" He ringingly concluded, in what would become perhaps his most famous words, "With malice toward none; with charity for all; with firmness in the right, as God gives us to see the right, let us strive on to finish the work we are in; to bind up the nation's wounds; to care for him who shall have borne the battle, and for his widow and his orphan, to do all which may achieve and cherish a just and a lasting peace among ourselves, and with all nations." Chief Justice Chase then administered to Lincoln the oath of office. When he had taken it, artillery let loose with a cannonade that reverberated through the marble halls of the Capitol.

It was soon obvious that the war would now last not a matter of months, but of just weeks, or even days. Sherman's army had captured Charleston, the seedbed of secession, on February 18. (Protected by federal bayonets, hundreds of freed men, women, and children would parade triumphantly through the streets carrying banners proclaiming, "We Know No Master But Ourselves," as thousands more wept by the curbsides as they passed.) Continuing his march northward, Sherman cut a swath through upcountry South Carolina, burning (or allowing to burn) much of the state capital, Columbia, and then driving on into North Carolina, where he administered a decisive defeat to Joseph Johnston's depleted Army of Tennessee at the battle of Bentonville, in mid-March.

When the fighting around Petersburg recommenced late that month, soldiers in the trenches dreaded a repetition of the slogging slaughter of the previous spring. For once, and at last, their worst fears were unfounded. The end came faster than anyone expected. On April 1, elements of the Fifth Corps ran into a force of rebels defending a strategic crossroads known as Five Forks. After an all-day battle, the Confederate lines collapsed, the federals poured around Lee's flank, the crucial South Side Railroad fell into Union hands, and the fate of Richmond was sealed.

On the night of April 2, Lee's battered army began evacuating the trenches they had occupied since the summer of 1864. The next day, federal soldiers cautiously felt their way through the Confederate minefields and breastworks to find them deserted. The advance soon turned into a wild rush as regiments raced each other to become the first to enter Richmond. Among them were the men of the 36th USCT—United States Colored Troops, as they were officially known—most of whom had been slaves just months before. "You've come at last!" shouted enslaved and free blacks at the sight of the arriving Yankees. Soldiers and slaves alike cheered, sang, wept, danced, and hugged. Meanwhile, smoke boiled through the streets from burning warehouses filled with cotton and tobacco. Shells exploding in torched Confederate arsenals rocked the entire city, in some neighborhoods with enough force to tear doors from their hinges and blow down tombstones. Nearly a thousand buildings went up in flames. In front of the Virginia statehouse, the drum corps of the 36th played a martial air called "Shouting the Battle Cry of Freedom." When Lincoln himself arrived to walk through the city the next day, enslaved men and women flung themselves to their knees, proclaiming him the Messiah.

All Washington seemed drunk with joy. One of Jay Cooke's agents was at the Treasury Department on April 3 when Ben Wade burst into the room with the news. "Ben was crazy with excitement, and before I had fired off the telegram to you, the whole department was in an uproar," he reported to Cooke. Secretary of War Stanton, also present, was ecstatic. "His skin would hardly hold him." When the news of Richmond's fall reached New York, vast spontaneous crowds cheered themselves hoarse and sang "John Brown's Body," Christian hymns, and "The Star-Spangled Banner" over and over. Strangers embraced. Men kissed each other, wept, retreated into doorways to dry their eyes, came back into the streets and began to weep again.

The rest was anticlimax. Lee's disintegrating army fled westward first in desperate hope of joining Johnston's forces in North Carolina. But Union troops raced them along the Appomattox River, harrying them at every step, countering their every attempt to slip the tightening federal noose, and sweeping up exhausted deserters by the thousand. Grant finally trapped what was left of the once mighty Army of Northern Virginia at the crossroads hamlet of Appomattox Court House. There, on April 9, Palm Sunday, after exchanging several face-saving messages with Ulysses Grant, Lee surrendered the ten thousand men he had left, a ghost of the army that had prevailed on so many battlefields of the war. Gen. George Meade, never a demonstrative man, galloped among his joyfully hallooing soldiers, waving his high-crowned hat and shouting, "Boys, your work is done. You can go home."

On April 11, Lincoln appeared on the balcony of the White House to speak to a large and boisterous crowd gathered below. He belittled the debate over Reconstruction policy that had roiled Congress. Were the seceded states still part of the Union or not? The question, he said, was no more than "a pernicious abstraction." The government's main task was now the practical one of bringing the Southern states back into their "proper practical relation" with the rest of the nation. No single "exclusive and inflexible" blueprint for Reconstruction should be applied to all the rebellious states, he said. However, support for the controversial new state government of Louisiana would validate the "hearts and nerve" of the white men who had voted for it and encourage them to "go further." Then he turned to the fraught question of enfranchising Negroes. He had come to believe that it would be appropriate to confer the vote on "the very intelligent and on those who serve our cause as soldiers." In any case, they would certainly achieve the franchise sooner by going along with the new Southern state governments than by challenging them. In essence, Lincoln was asking blacks to rely on the goodwill of white men, to postpone their demands for equality, and to trust that all would come right in the end if they would be but patient.

Anyone who hoped for a bold plan for Reconstruction was disappointed by the president's words. Wondered an editorialist for the *New York Times,* by no means a Radical mouthpiece, once whites were restored to their full rights wouldn't they take to abusing and oppressing the freed Negroes? "The government cannot without the worst dishonor permit the bondage of the black man to be continued in any form," the *Times* continued. "It is bound by every moral principle, as well as every prudential consideration, not to remit him to the tender mercies of any enemy." But of this Lincoln said not a word. It was the last statement he ever made on Reconstruction.

In the crowd that day there was at least one listener who was both unswayed by the president's promise of conciliation and revolted by his cautious gesture toward the enfranchisement of even a few black men. The only uniform this suave, stylishly dressed man had ever worn was, for just a matter of hours, that of a Virginia militiaman at the execution of John Brown. During the war he had aided the Confederate underground in Maryland and as a sometime spy in the capital. Lincoln had often enjoyed him on the stage, this furious, histrionic man who within days would leave his indelible mark on history, the popular actor John Wilkes Booth.

On April 14, a stirring event took place on the heap of rubble in Charleston harbor that was once Fort Sumter, four years to the day after the first shots of the Civil War were fired there. All morning, every kind of floating craft from steamships to homemade rafts ferried thousands of men, women, and children, white and black, to the fort from the docks in Charleston. The vast majority of the whites were visitors from the North who had come just for the day's events;

most of the blacks were locals, many of whom had been slaves only weeks or days before. There were hundreds of army and naval officers, members of Congress, at least one Supreme Court justice, and a multitude of abolitionists, including William Lloyd Garrison, who had he appeared in Charleston before the city fell to Sherman's army in February would have been lynched. The day was bright and breezy, the mood celebratory. The 54th Massachusetts Volunteers, the proud black heroes of the 1863 assault on Fort Wagner, served as an honor guard. From a stand wreathed with laurel boughs, the Reverend Henry Ward Beecher of New York's Plymouth Church delivered a formal oration that was intended as a gesture of friendship to the beaten South. But the highlight came when Gen. Robert Anderson, who had commanded Fort Sumter in 1861, stepped forth and took from a canvas bag the very flag that he had hauled down at the fort's surrender and preserved these four long years. "I thank God I have lived to see this day, to perform this perhaps the last act of duty to my country in this life," Anderson said. With the assistance of several younger soldiers, he then took hold of a halyard and pulled the old flag aloft to the tumultuous cheers of the crowd perched atop the mounds of debris. Anderson wept, everyone wept, as they sang "The Star-Spangled Banner," and hundreds of federal guns boomed triumphantly from the forts surrounding the harbor. There were a few scattered Confederate forces still in the field. Their surrender would soon come. But there was no more apt end to the war, at least symbolically, than the unfurling of the old flag over the shell-blasted ruin where the war had begun.

# Epilogue

By the gods, there will be no trouble
now in running the government!

—SEN. BENJAMIN F. WADE

In the early hours of April 16, Thaddeus Stevens was jolted awake at his home in Lancaster by a frenzied pounding on his door. A friend brought the terrible news that Lincoln had been murdered. Stevens's first thought was of the man who would take his place. His feelings about Lincoln were mixed, but he had no doubt about Andrew Johnson: he loathed him. He feared a disaster.

Stevens's dread made him an outlier. In the first weeks after Johnson's ascent to the presidency most congressional Radicals had high hopes for him. Ben Wade had served with him on the Joint Committee on the Conduct of the War and admired his hard-handed rule as the military governor of Tennessee. They remembered his declaration in 1861: "Were I the president of the United States, I would do as Thomas Jefferson did in 1806 with Aaron Burr: I would have [the secessionists] arrested; and if convicted within the meaning and scope of the Constitution, by the Eternal God I would execute them. Treason must be punished." It was a sentiment he had often reiterated. They now responded with enthusiasm. "Johnson, we have faith in you," Wade told him. "By the gods, there will be no trouble now in running the government!" And Charles Sumner reassuringly wrote to friends, "In the question of colored suffrage the President is with us." They misread their man.

Never a Radical, Johnson was canny enough to see that his political future must lie in forging an alliance between Democrats and disaffected Republicans. At the beginning of May, without consulting Congress, he recognized the conservative Unionist regime that had ruled a few townships of Virginia as that state's legitimate government. Three weeks later, he issued a unilateral proclamation offering amnesty to nearly all Southerners willing to take a loyalty oath—excluding only top leaders of the Confederacy and the wealthiest landowners—and he began appointing provisional governors for most of the seceded states. These proclamations instantly revived Southerners' hopes that they might be able to preserve slavery in some form. Across the South, men who only a few months earlier had loyally served the Confederacy were elected to state offices, while hurriedly organized state conventions adopted draconian black codes to quash the embryonic freedoms of the ex-slaves. Towns and cities passed ordinances barring blacks from carrying weapons, preaching, gathering in public, establishing businesses, owning houses, and moving about without written permission from their "employers."

From every corner of the South there were increasing reports of violence committed against both freed blacks and white Unionists. Negro schoolhouses were burned and teachers driven away in fear for their lives. Blacks who left plantations were beaten, flogged, and shot down on the roads. Former slaves who had run away during the war were prevented from recovering their wives and children. In many areas, bands of armed ex-Confederates roamed the countryside murdering freedmen and isolated Union soldiers with impunity. Without federal action, former general Carl Schurz reported after a fact-finding tour of the former Confederacy, the South would soon become a virtual slaughter pen for the black race. Stevens was beside himself. "I see our worthy president fancies himself a sovereign power," he bitterly wrote to Rep. William D. Kelley. "Yet what can we do?" Wade, still in Washington wrapping up the final reports of the Joint Committee on the Conduct of the War, finally realized how wrong he had been. He lamented, "We have lost the whole moral effect of our victories."

For most of the next four years the nation would be haunted by the effects of Lincoln's decision to accept the Tennessean as his running mate. Had Hannibal Hamlin become president instead, he would undoubtedly have prioritized the protection of former slaves and Southern Unionists, punished whites who defied federal law, and encouraged the evolution of a biracial society. Johnson's support for antislavery legislation was limited at best. He accepted the Thirteenth Amendment. With his support, by early December 1861 twenty-seven states—including eight former rebel ones, now under Reconstruction governments—had ratified it, making it law. But Johnson's fundamental views on race and reunion had more in common with reactionaries such as Garrett Davis and Lazarus Powell than with the likes of Wade and Stevens. His belief in white supremacy was unapologetic. He insultingly spurned a personal appeal for support from Frederick Douglass, whom he told that poor whites were the real victims of the slave system, which degraded the value of their labor.

When Sumner begged him to take action to protect the beleaguered freedmen, he responded sarcastically, "Mr. Sumner, do murders ever occur in Massachusetts?"

Sumner replied, "Unhappily yes, Mr. President."

"Do people ever knock each other down in Boston?"

"Unhappily yes, Mr. President, sometimes."

"Would you consent that Massachusetts should be excluded from the Union on this account?"

"No, Mr. President, surely not," Sumner said.

Johnson had made his point. After that, he ignored the rest of the Radicals as long as he could.

Stevens's valedictory mood in the waning weeks of the war proved premature. Despite his worsening physical infirmity, this new challenge infused him with a new vigor. First he tried diplomacy. "Can you not hold your hand and wait the action of Congress and in the meantime govern [the Southern states] by military rulers?" he suggested to Johnson. "Profuse pardoning will also embarrass Congress if they should wish to make the enemy pay the expenses of the war or a part of it." Johnson shrugged off his pleas.

Practical leadership of the congressional Radicals fell mainly to

Stevens and Wade, whose wartime leadership of, respectively, the House Ways and Means Committee and the Joint Committee on the Conduct of the War had earned them the respect of their colleagues as men of firm views as well as legislative realists. They maintained that Congress, not the president, possessed the constitutional authority to dictate the progress of Reconstruction, favored indefinite military rule in the South, and regarded the enfranchisement of former slaves not only as a moral imperative but also as a political necessity if the Republicans were to wield any power in the South. Their ultimate goal, as Stevens put it, was to reshape Southern society, to "strip a proud nobility of their bloated estates," and to reduce them to the level of ordinary citizens. Capitulation to the president was not on their agenda. Declared Wade, Radicals "are the men who go deeply down for principle and having fixed their eyes on a great principle are not to be detached by any of your higgling." Johnson, for his own part, would have been wise to make common cause with more moderate Republicans against the Radicals, but he was intransigent, sneering at his critics as virtual traitors hardly better than the Confederates.

For the next three years Congress and the ever more stubborn president waged ceaseless trench warfare. In December, in its first salvo from Capitol Hill, Congress created the high-powered Joint Committee on Reconstruction, co-chaired by Stevens and Pitt Fessenden, as a powerful tool to shape a legislative alternative to the president's policy. Until now, Fessenden had tried hard to avoid conflict with Johnson. But he was deeply offended by Johnson's all too apparent contempt for the will of Congress. "I could not rest," he declared on the floor of the Senate, if Congress were to yield to the president's "usurpation" of its clear constitutional power. If it did, "we should be yielding everything, we should have no power left, we should be less than children, we should hardly be entitled to call ourselves slaves."

Meanwhile, white terrorism continued to surge across the South. Dozens of black men, women, and children were lynched near Pine Bluff, Arkansas. White mobs sacked black neighborhoods in Memphis, murdering at least forty-six and destroying hundreds of homes, schools, and churches. In New Orleans, thirty-four blacks and three white Radicals were killed and more than one hundred wounded when rioting ex-Confederates attacked a constitutional convention that was to consider enfranchising Negroes. Anywhere, blacks might be murdered for the most trivial breaches of respect for whites, or for no cause at all. Everywhere, aspiring black leaders were singled out and assassinated. Nathan Bedford Forrest, the commander of the Confederate force that perpetrated the Fort Pillow massacre and a founder of the Ku Klux Klan, declared in Memphis, "There is not a Radical leader in this town but is a marked man, and if trouble should break out, none of them would be left alive." As atrocities multiplied, Stevens begged his colleagues to act. "While the South has been bleeding at every pore, Congress has done nothing to protect the loyal people there, white or black, either in their persons, in their liberty, or in their property," he pleaded. "We sit and move no hand, we sit by and raise no voice to effect what we declare to be the duty of Congress."

In early 1866, Congress enacted a raft of legislation in an attempt to seize the political initiative. Against Johnson's violent objections, it renewed the Freedmen's Bureau and passed the landmark Civil Rights Act, declaring former slaves to be citizens with the right to personal safety, to own and sell property, make contracts, sue in court, and empowering federal officers to prosecute any person who violated the act's provisions. When Johnson rejected both measures, Congress promptly overrode his vetoes, the first time in American history that this had ever happened.

In August, the report of the Joint Committee on Reconstruction, penned by Fessenden, excoriated the president's policy as a calamity. Action to prevent him from going any further was imperative, the report declared. Otherwise, "Treason, defeated in the field, has only to take possession of Congress and the cabinet." Embedded within the larger question of whether the president or Congress would control Reconstruction lay an exceedingly fraught problem, the report acknowledged: should freed slaves be allowed to vote. The Thirteenth Amendment had automatically negated the Constitution's three-fifths clause, which had granted slave states additional seats in the House of Representatives for 60 percent of the enumerated slaves in each state, but it left the practical matter of representation in limbo. Wrote Fessenden, "It did not seem just or proper that all the political advantages derived from their becoming free should be confined to their former masters, who had fought against the Union, withheld from themselves, who had always been loyal."

Although Fessenden lacked deep personal empathy with blacks, he wished to ensure that they were treated equally before the law, and he accepted that some degree of black suffrage was now close to inevitable. Unlike Stevens and Wade, however, he felt that universal black suffrage would work against Republican interests, because he assumed that the freedmen would passively vote as their former masters told them to. He also feared, with some reason, that even hinting that blacks might be allowed to vote in *Northern* states could be politically disastrous. Indeed, in recent months several Northern states had explicitly rejected ballot measures that would have enfranchised blacks.

When Congress reconvened in January, Fessenden and Stevens reported two alternative resolutions. One would apportion representation in Congress and direct taxes based on the total number of citizens in each state, and bar any form of discrimination by race. The second option would exclude from the count anyone who was denied the vote based on race, creed, or color. Significantly, both measures empowered Congress to guarantee for all citizens "the same political rights and privileges," and "equal protection in the enjoyment of life, liberty and property."

Their labors led ultimately to the Fourteenth Amendment. In its final form, it stated that all persons born in the United States were automatically citizens, and that no state had the authority to "deprive any person of life, liberty, or property, without due process of law," and that all citizens had a fundamental right to equal protection. The amendment further specified that while congressional representation would be based on the total number of persons in each state it would be reduced in proportion to the number of male inhabitants over twenty-one who were denied the right to vote. In practical terms, although it did not guarantee the vote to blacks, it created an incentive for Southern states to enfranchise blacks on their own, or else lose representatives. (The amendment also barred from high federal office anyone who had engaged in insurrection or given aid or comfort to the rebels, and, finally, repudiated any federal obligation to pay the Confederate debt.) Stevens would much have preferred the amendment to mandate universal suffrage, but he decided that it was the best he could get. On June 13, the amendment easily won approval by large margins in both houses of Congress over Johnson's opposition. Ratification was accomplished by July 1868, though not without bitter resentment in the ex-rebel states, which under a deliberately coercive federal law passed in March 1867 would not be permitted representation in Congress until they had approved it. (Hostility to the amendment was so strong even in some Northern states that two of them under Democratic control, Ohio and New Jersey, later rescinded their ratification and did not reratify it until 1973 and 2003 respectively.)

In the late winter and spring of 1867, Congress took further steps to wrench control of Reconstruction from the president's hands. On March 1, Senate Republicans selected Ben Wade as president pro-tem of the Senate, placing him—in accordance with the customs of the time, since there was no sitting vice president—next in line to the presidency. To protect the Radicals' best ally in the cabinet, Secretary of War Edwin Stanton, who oversaw the Freedmen's Bureau and the army of occupation, they had enacted a Tenure of Office bill, which required Senate confirmation of any removal of a cabinet officer by the president. On March 2, Johnson vetoed it; before the day was out, his veto was overridden by both houses. The same day, Congress passed the first Reconstruction Act, which divided the South into five military districts to supplant the civilian governments elected since the end of the war. It stipulated that states seeking readmission to the Union could do so only after they held elections for new constitutional conventions in which black voters participated, and empowered the commanders of each district to use military force in order to protect "all persons" and to "suppress insurrection, disorder, and violence." (There would eventually be two more Reconstruction Acts, tightening the rules for allowing ex-Confederates to vote, and explicitly declaring the civilian governments in the former Confederate states illegal and subject to the will of the district military commanders.) Johnson vetoed all of them and, just as predictably, Congress repassed them by commanding majorities.

The stage was set for the greatest political drama of the Reconstruction Era. Johnson next defied Congress and the Tenure of Office Act by firing Stanton and replacing the military commanders in the South with men loyal to himself. The Senate refused to accept Stanton's ouster and on January 13, 1868, it ordered Johnson to restore him to office. A week later, Johnson declared that he had again suspended Stanton, who refused to quit and barricaded himself in his office. At Stevens's direction, articles of impeachment were drawn up charging Johnson with violating the Tenure of Office Act, challenging the legitimacy of Congress, and other "high crimes and misdemeanors." The House then voted to impeach him by a margin of nearly three-to-one.

Emaciated and tinged with a deathlike pallor, on March 3, Stevens was carried to the Senate chamber on a chair borne by two muscular black men. He was accompanied by members of the House marching solemnly arm in arm. Facing Ben Wade where he sat in the presiding officer's chair, Stevens announced in a voice that was unexpectedly vigorous and stern, "We appear before you in the name of the House of Representatives and all the people of the United States. We do impeach the President of the United States for high crimes and misdemeanors."

For the first time, the Senate exercised its constitutional duty as a court of impeachment, with Chief Justice Chase presiding. The trial began on March 30 and continued for five weeks. Weakened from excruciating edema and numbed with morphine, Stevens left the prosecution to Benjamin Butler, now a member of the House from Massachusetts.

Wade's role was ambiguous, and his apparent conflict of interest made some members uncomfortable. In a postwar climate that was embracing national reconciliation over revenge, he was also increasingly out of step with the voters in Ohio. In the state elections the previous autumn, the Republicans had lost control of the legislature, turning Wade into a lame duck, since the Democrats would never reelect him once his present term ended in March 1869. Still a senator, however, he would serve as one of Johnson's judges, and as president pro tem he would become president if Johnson was removed. Some thought he should recuse himself, but he would not. The outcome was likely to be very close and the Radicals could not afford to lose his vote.

The trial reached its climax on May 16. The visitors' galleries were ablaze, the *New York Herald* reported, with female spectators flourishing "a great deal of showy silk, a fluttering of crystal and gold bedecked fans." Every senator who was ambulatory, and some who weren't, was somehow gotten into the chamber, Howard of Michigan leaning on the arms of friends, Grimes of Iowa transported in an invalid's chair. Thousands waited tensely in the Capitol's corridors and on the grounds outside beneath dull and cloudy skies. A reporter later remembered the strange, sweet odor of newly mown grass wafting eerily over the crowd.

The verdict came down to a single vote, that of Sen. Edmund G. Ross of Kansas, who had once been counted reliably among the Radicals. "Conviction had him to dinner last night; but Acquittal slept with him overnight," the *New York Times* wryly reported. (There were rumors, never proved, that he had been bribed by Johnson's friends.)

Thirty-six votes were necessary for conviction. The final tally was thirty-five to nineteen against the president. "The great Radical party has been thrown completely on its beam ends," crowed the pro-Johnson *New York Herald*.

Most prominent among the seven Republicans who voted to acquit was Pitt Fessenden. Had he voted to convict, not only could he have delivered the decisive vote, but he would likely also have swayed some of the other centrist Republicans who voted for acquittal. Although he had little regard for Johnson and had supported every measure taken to rein in his power, he didn't believe that he had committed the kind of "crimes" that justified impeachment. As one close observer remarked, "He preferred the individuality of conscientious conviction to the questionable subservience of party policy." Quite apart from principle, Fessenden was concerned that replacing Johnson with Wade would split the Republican Party, and would also lead to the appointment of Charles Sumner, his bane, as secretary of state.

Stevens was livid. As he was carried out of the chamber by his attendants he shouted to the crowd gathered in the halls, "The coun-

try is going to the devil!" Taken to Wade's room, he released a torrent of invective, roaring hopelessly, "It is the meanest case, before
the meanest tribunal, and on the meanest subject of human history."
Although the seven Republican defectors were called "deserters" by
some—it was a potent insult so soon after the war—the public's reaction was mostly one of relief that the crisis had passed.

Just days after the trial concluded the Republican convention at
Chicago, as expected, nominated Ulysses S. Grant as its candidate
for president. Wade had long been bruited as Grant's most probable
running mate. But he had offended too many people, frightened too
many conservatives, and presided over the fiasco of impeachment.
Some felt that his combative temperament was ill-suited to the presidency. Others resented his advocacy of equal rights for *Northern* as
well as Southern blacks, and still others were repelled by his support
for women's suffrage, then a position so far on the fringe of political
respectability that it was commonly denounced from pulpits to bar-
rooms as an offense against the natural order of society. He received
a solid plurality of votes on the first ballot, but his support quickly
eroded, and by the fourth he lost out to Schuyler Colfax of Indiana,
the Speaker of the House. Wade's political career was, in effect, over.

That November, Grant triumphed over the governor of New
York, Horatio Seymour, a former Copperhead, winning 214 electoral
votes to the Democrat's 80, and carrying twenty-six states, including six newly reconstructed ones in the South, where military rule
favored Republicans, and many whites remained disenfranchised. In
Pennsylvania, Thaddeus Stevens was renominated for another term
in the House of Representatives, and would doubtless have been
reelected again by a large margin. But that never happened.

The fizzling of impeachment left him depressed and fatalistic.
"My life has been a failure," he told his friend Alexander McClure.
"With all this great struggle of years in Washington, and the fear-
ful sacrifice of life and treasure, I see little hope for the Republic."
After the session adjourned he rarely left his Washington home on
B Street, where he was cared for by his intimate friend Lydia Smith.
Too weak to fend them off, he allowed two Methodist clergymen to
pray beside him, followed by a pair of nuns who baptized him as a

Catholic. Around midnight on the night of August 11 he whispered for ice, and died.

A troop of black Zouaves accompanied his remains to the Capitol Rotunda, where he lay in state. His coffin was then sent to Lancaster for burial. By prearrangement, he was interred in the only cemetery in town that was not racially segregated. On his stone were engraved these lines:

> I repose in this quiet and secluded spot,
> Not from any natural preference for solitude,
> But, finding other Cemeteries limited as to Race
> By Charter Rules,
> I have chosen this that I might illustrate
> In my death
> The Principles which I advocated
> Through a long life:
> EQUALITY OF MAN BEFORE HIS CREATOR

Among his bequests, in addition to a legacy for Lydia Smith, he left an endowment for children's literature for the public library in Peacham, Vermont, where he grew up and first discovered books, as well as a substantial sum to establish a school in Lancaster with the stipulation that it must be open to all children regardless of race. The school continues today as the Thaddeus Stevens College of Technology.

While commending Stevens's early recognition that emancipation must come, the *New York Times* rather sourly called him "the evil genius of the Republican party." McClure described him more aptly as a pioneer, always in advance of public sentiment: "Stevens was ever clearing the underbrush and preparing the soil, while Lincoln followed to sow the seeds that were to ripen in a regenerated Union." He was a freethinker in a pious age, impatient with orthodoxies, intolerant of racism and elitism of any kind. Perhaps no other man of his generation had a clearer vision of the more diverse and tolerant America that would begin to take shape in the twentieth century.

Less than a year after Stevens's death, in February 1869, Congress passed the Fifteenth Amendment, prohibiting states from denying any citizen's right to vote "on account of race, color, or previous condition of servitude." He would probably not have been satisfied with it because it did not guarantee freedmen the right to hold office or protect them from discriminatory voting laws. But always a realist, he would likely have supported it anyway as a major step toward full equality of the races.

Stevens feared with good reason that unrepentant Confederates would resort to every weapon in their Negrophobic armory, from repressive legislation to the pistol and the lynch rope, to prevent their former slaves from consolidating political or economic power. He had hoped to pass legislation to hand over vast plantation lands to freedmen. Had he succeeded, it might have provided Southern blacks with the means to become self-sustaining landowners. Even the tsar of Russia had given land to the freed serfs, he had argued. But in this, too, he was disappointed.

A sea change was taking place in Northern public opinion. Most Republicans regarded the Fifteenth Amendment less as the beginning of a new more enlightened age than as the climax of the long campaign to cleanse the country of the sin of slavery. They were increasingly tired of the whole subject, and more interested in sectional healing and recovery than in further moral crusades. Most of them were naively confident—or else in willful denial—insisting that suffrage was sufficient for freedmen to protect themselves. Few apart from aging Radicals like Ben Wade considered that the ex-Confederates might embark on a reign of terror so savage and so prolonged that it would turn the Reconstruction amendments into dead letters. "All apprehensions of the return of slavery are puerile and absurd," complacently opined the *New York Times*. "Nor is there any danger that the civil rights conferred upon the blacks will ever be taken away. We do not believe that the Southern whites have any such purpose or wish."

Pitt Fessenden was among them. Although he had no illusions about the depth of Southern racism, he failed to appreciate the freedmen's capacity to shape their own future or the urgency of ensuring their economic independence. Had he voted with the Radicals to oust Johnson, Reconstruction would have taken a different course. But he didn't seriously consider it. He preferred a politically neutered President Johnson to an all-too-potent President Wade.

When the Fortieth Congress ended its deliberations in the summer of 1869, Fessenden gratefully returned to Portland, with its cool breezes and invigorating sea air. But this year rest didn't come. The abdominal discomfort that had plagued him for years only got worse. On August 31, he retired to bed after a game of whist. In the middle of the night an attack of insupportable pain wrenched him awake. A doctor was summoned, morphine was administered. On September 8 he died from what was diagnosed as a ruptured intestine. He was sixty-two years old.

Although immensely respected by his peers, Fessenden was given to neither dramatic flair nor hyperbolic oratory. He was never really a Radical, although he aligned himself with them throughout the war. Nor was he a conventional abolitionist, though his weighty support was essential for the passage of wartime and postwar antislavery legislation. His greatest contribution to the Union's victory lay in his leadership of the Senate Finance Committee, which—in tandem with Stevens's House Ways and Means Committee—raised the money to sustain the war effort through crisis after crisis: near-bankruptcy, bursting budgets, unpopular taxation, currency reform, and spiraling inflation. Without his relentless pressure, the money to pay, feed, and clothe the army, to mount the cavalry, to cast the artillery, and to build the warships might never have been found. He left the federal government stronger than he found it, better fitted to lead the nation into a new era of economic dynamism that would continue far into the twentieth century, although the new financial system he helped create never worked out the way he optimistically predicted, as a harmonious community of interest between the banks, the government, and the public.

Despite Grant's election in 1868, the Democratic Party began to rebound that year, gaining twenty seats in the House of Representatives and many more in state legislatures. They gained another thirty-seven House seats in 1870, and eighty-nine in the election of 1874 to become the majority party in Congress for the first time since before the war. Disenchanted by the widespread corruption that was revealed during the Grant administration, even many prominent Republicans defected to the Democrats, including Lyman Trumbull, Salmon P. Chase, and Horace Greeley, who ran as the Liberal Republican candidate for president in 1872. Charles Sumner, though he never became a Democrat, declined to endorse Grant, shocking his longtime abolitionist friends.

One who would not share in the Democrats' revival was Clement Vallandigham, the party's angry face for so much of the war. "The accumulation of obloquy, persecution & wrong, heaped upon me, & [the] persistency which they are kept up, would assuredly crush any man of less nerve & fortitude than myself," he wrote with his customary self-regard. Although he remained active in Ohio politics and hoped for election to the U.S. Senate, his name remained permanently tainted by the odor of disloyalty. His own party fairly begged him to stay away from its 1868 convention. (He didn't.) He was still popular in Dayton, however, where he continued to practice law, winning nearly every criminal case he took on. In June 1871, he was defending a local rough named McGehan who was charged with shooting and killing one Tom Myers in a saloon brawl. In an attempt to show other lawyers how Myers could have accidentally shot himself, Vallandigham pulled his own cocked gun from his pants, not realizing it was loaded, and inadvertently shot himself in the stomach. He lingered for twelve hours and died in agony. He was fifty years old.

Had he lived in another era, or had different politics, Vallandigham might well have been celebrated for his wartime defense of civil liberties, if only for white men. (In 1918, Eugene Debs was heroized by American socialists when he was jailed for opposing the entry of the United States into World War I; fifty years after that, during the Vietnam War, protesters defied the draft using language not very much different from Vallandigham's.) But it is impossible to separate Vallandigham from his unalloyed, often vicious racism and reactionary politics. If he did not commit treason, he skirted perilously close to it. If he and his allies had had their way, the North would have abandoned the war and the racial revolution wrought by it would never have occurred. Unpalatable though many of his views are, and were to most of his contemporaries, he was nonetheless one of the great dissenters in American political history. His sympathetic biographer, Frank L. Klement, wrote of him, "Whereas Republicans equated dissent with treason, Vallandigham insisted upon practicing the same rights during the war that he exercised in times of peace." He was not the only member of Congress who feared the long-term consequences of unchecked authority. When Sen. William M. Stewart of Nevada asserted in March 1865 that but for the suspension of the writ of habeas corpus and "the strong arm of the war power there would be no country today," Lyman Trumbull, no friend to Vallandigham or what he stood for, warned that in war "we have a right when we meet the enemy to shoot him down. But because you have a right to use an army and navy in battering down the houses of Charleston, you have no right to use them to batter down the houses in Albany, New York, or Columbus, Ohio." Vallandigham's warnings about the misuse of arbitrary power have lost none of their pointedness in the twenty-first century.

In a mid-nineteenth-century world of monarchies and dictatorships, it was almost universally believed until the American Civil War that republics were fated to die from either external attack or internal collapse. The Union triumph proved such assumptions wrong and raised hopes for the ultimate triumph of democracy around the world. By freeing nearly four million enslaved Americans it also set the nation on the road toward fulfilling the original promise of the ideals enshrined in the Declaration of Independence. After the war, thousands of former slaves and free blacks were elected to public office, including Congress, while the work of the Freedmen's Bureau and of courageous volunteer teachers, both white and black, as well as the individual initiative of freed slaves laid the foundation, however fragile, for the modern black middle class in the South. That many of these gains were rolled back during the Jim Crow era does not mean that they weren't important. They established the expectations and the legal precedents for what the twentieth-century civil rights movement would more fully achieve.

The Union victory should also be understood not only in terms of what it achieved but also what it prevented. Confederate victory would have meant catastrophe for black Americans, including pogroms against former slaves who had taken up arms against their former masters and generations more of slavery for the rest. A victorious Confederacy would likely have attempted to carry its borders west to the Pacific Ocean, and south to Cuba and Central America, ambitions all advocated by proslavery expansionists as their version of Manifest Destiny. With secession established as a precedent, other portions of the United States might eventually have broken away as well. "The dream of national progress would dissipate forever," William H. Seward warned in 1861, foreseeing that unless the Union stood firm a congeries of small, weakened North American nations would proliferate, becoming enemies to one another and pawns for foreign powers. As Ohio senator John Sherman put it just after the Union's demoralizing defeat at First Bull Run, "If we divide into two sections now, soon we shall be divided into three, or four, or five. The East may be divided from the West, and Oregon and California may go off by themselves."

The consequences for the world of a weakened United States and a balkanized North America can only be imagined. Would a diminished United States have entered either World War I or World War II alongside the Allies, or have made as much difference even if it had? Would it ever have become a dominant global power? None of this is knowable, of course. But the Unionists of the 1860s were well aware of how much was at stake for future generations. In his annual message of December 1862, Lincoln said, "we cannot escape history. We of this Congress and this administration will be remembered in spite of ourselves. The fiery trial through which we pass will light us down, in honor or dishonor, to the latest generation. In *giving* freedom to the *slave*, we *assure* freedom to the *free*—honorable alike in what we give, and what we preserve. We shall nobly save, or meanly lose, the last best hope of earth."

Lincoln's address was directed to the members of Congress. He called for moral courage from the men of the House and Senate who sat listening to his words, and they responded. But as supremely eloquent as Lincoln was, they didn't need him to tell them what to do. The Republican members, and their allies among the Democrats, felt the weight of duty as much as soldiers did that of the Springfield rifles they carried onto a thousand battlefields. Victory cost at least 365,000 Union men their lives, and left another 290,000 Confederates dead. (Recent studies suggest that a total of 750,000 or more may have died.) But it could not have been achieved without the parallel political war that was fought on Capitol Hill.

The Thirty-seventh and Thirty-eighth Congresses must be reckoned among the most effective in American history, along with the First Congress, of 1789 to 1791, the New Deal Congresses of the 1930s, and the Great Society Congresses of the 1960s. The amount of legislation they enacted during the Civil War was prodigious in volume and transformative in its effects. That they accomplished as much as they did resulted in part from the fact that the eleven most backward-looking states had seceded, leaving the Republicans with commanding majorities throughout the war. Even so, it still took creative politics, legislative courage, and pragmatic accommodation to pass such controversial legislation as the suspension of habeas corpus, the freeing and arming of former slaves, the raising of the enormous sums of money needed to fight the war, the confiscation of rebel property, and radical banking and currency reform.

The effects of this were far-reaching. The Homestead Act transformed the prairie into farmland, helping to make the United States an agricultural superpower. The Pacific Railway Act bound the West Coast to the rest of the country and spurred the settlement of every corner of the West. Thanks to the Land-Grant College Act, new public universities modernized western farming and democratized higher education. The wartime financial measures created a permanent role for the federal government in the nation's financial affairs. There were, of course, unintended consequences, some of them grievous. Yoking the Republican Party to Wall Street paved the way for the corruption of the Gilded Age. For the native tribes that inhabited the Great Plains, homesteading was an unmitigated disaster, as reservations were removed entirely or radically reduced in size to make room for white settlers, leaving Indian communities fragmented and impoverished. And the failure of emancipation legislation to recognize the freedmen's need for capital and long-term protection meant that they would not have the independence to defend themselves against white reprisals. Yet, despite such serious shortcomings, the success of the Civil War Congresses was all the more remarkable for a party that had never held national power before, and that in 1861 was faced with managing a war that few Republicans expected to have to fight. That they rose to the challenge, and ultimately triumphed, was one of the greatest political achievements in American history.

After leaving office in 1869, Ben Wade returned to his modest frame home in Jefferson, Ohio, across the street from the tiny office where he had first learned the law from Joshua Giddings half a century before. He never returned to public office, although in 1872 he was spoken of as a possible vice presidential running mate for the controversial Victoria Woodhull, the first female presidential candidate in American history. Ever true to his egalitarian convictions, as a temporary government-appointed member of the board of directors of the Union Pacific Railroad, he traveled to California in 1869, where he publicly criticized the exploitation of Chinese laborers. The Republicans' flagging commitment to Reconstruction and their abandonment of Southern blacks left him with a deep sense of betrayal. "I feel that to have emancipated these people and then to leave them unprotected [was] a crime as infamous as to have reduced them to slavery once they were free," he reflected in April 1877. The following February, he fell ill with typhoid. On the night of March 1, 1878, he gasped that he could no longer speak. By the next morning, his once thunderous voice was stilled forever.

Wade was a driving engine of Republican war policy and inspired many men of lesser conviction to continue to stand fast behind the war effort when, repeatedly, it seemed doomed by failed generals and lost battles. He was also a guiding spirit of congressional Reconstruction, and in 1868 he came as close as any American ever did to becoming president without actually doing so. However, his most lasting monument exists in the thousands of pages of testimony gathered in the reports of the Joint Committee on the Conduct of the War. Its exhaustive investigations of four years of military tactics and strategy, and of such diverse issues as policy toward the contrabands, officers' attitudes toward emancipation, naval contracts, the quality of heavy ordnance, the treatment of prisoners, and the wanton massacre in 1864 of peaceful Cheyenne Indians by Colorado militia, all form an unparalleled record of the war effort in the words of those who fought it, recorded in real time, and sometimes even within sight of the enemy. Wade's relentless campaign against George McClellan helped rid the army of a commander who arguably did more than any other to hamper the war effort. And under his leadership, the committee helped to turn the war into a racial revolution by pushing for the recruitment of black troops and recognition of the rights of black Americans. Without its investigation, the Fort Pillow massacre—the worst war crime ever perpetrated on American soil outside the Indian wars—might well have been scrubbed from historical memory.

The *New York Times,* which had often railed against Wade's radicalism when he was alive, proclaimed him "the last of the Congressional Champions of Freedom." The *Washington Post* later wrote of him that as a senator he made his name "leading the bravest, shaming the timid, rebuking the treacherous, and giving himself no rest." It was a fitting epitaph not just for Wade, but for the whole generation of politically heroic Republicans who led Congress to victory in the Civil War.

# ACKNOWLEDGMENTS

Many people and institutions have contributed in ways great and small to making this book possible. I am particularly grateful to the staff of the Manuscript Division of the Library of Congress, who assisted my research on many occasions with their always superlative efficiency. Micah Messenheimer of the Prints and Photographs Division was of immense help in identifying collections of images, many of which appear in this book. Michelle A. Krowl, the library's expert on its Civil War holdings, pointed me toward several manuscript collections I would not otherwise have discovered.

United States Senate Historian Betty Koed and her staff shared their unmatched knowledge of the Senate, and offered much valuable research advice, as did former Senate Historians Donald A. Ritchie and Richard A. Baker. Mary Bauman cogently explained to me the daunting complexity of the Senate's quorum rules at the beginning of the Civil War. Amy E. Burton of the Senate Curator's Office graciously facilitated my access to images of the wartime Congress. Matt Wasniewski, the Historian of the House of Representatives, provided insights into numerous members of the House.

Many other libraries and archives also provided generous assistance. Among them, the Lancaster County Historical Society, now known as LancasterHistory, opened its doors to me; President and CEO Tom Ryan, Robin E. Sarratt, Heather Tennies, and Katie Fichtner generously made a place for me in their archives and library as I foraged for material on Thaddeus Stevens. LancasterHistory also helped to make my research possible through a research grant from the National Endowment for the Humanities.

Norma Waters of the Jefferson Historical Society, in Ohio, spent hours showing me its documents relating to Ben Wade. Nancy R. Horlacher of the Dayton Metro Library ferreted out a trove of material on Clement Vallandigham and his associates. Marieke Van Der Steenhoven and Caroline Mosely of Special Collections at Bowdoin College, in Maine, made my work in the papers of William Pitt Fessenden as frictionless as possible. My friend Carlin Holden of San Francisco kindly shared copies of the expressive wartime letters of her great-grandfather Harlan Page Paige; while Jillian Szaroleta, formerly of Florida State University, introduced me to the unpublished letters of William R. Sellon. Ross Hetrick, president of the Thaddeus Stevens Society, and Randy Harris of Lancaster, Pennsylvania, suggested many helpful lines of research.

I owe a special debt to Paul Finkelman, now the president of Gratz College. Although the idea for a political book about the waging of the war had been with me for a long time, it was ignited when Paul invited me to deliver a paper on the Joint Committee on the Conduct of the War at a symposium sponsored by the United States Capitol Historical Society, in 2012.

I also owe thanks to my editors at Knopf, George Andreou, who commissioned *Congress at War*, and Andrew Miller, who took it over in midstream, both of whom provided unflagging encouragement. My agent, Adam Eaglin, piloted my original proposal with his customary skill and judgment. My wife, Jean Parvin Bordewich, has been—as always—an incomparable sounding board for ideas, half-baked and otherwise, and a tireless source of good-humored tolerance for the selfish demands of the writerly life. This book would not exist without their contributions.

# NOTES

## ABBREVIATIONS

| | |
|---|---|
| AL: | Abraham Lincoln |
| BCL: | Bowdoin College Library |
| BFW: | Benjamin Franklin Wade |
| CG: | *Congressional Globe* (Sessions are indicated with a slash, e.g., 37/1 indicates the Thirty-seventh Congress, First Session, and so on) |
| CS: | Charles Sumner |
| DHS: | Dayton Historical Society |
| GBM: | George B. McClellan |
| GW: | Gideon Welles |
| HSP: | Historical Society of Pennsylvania |
| JC: | Jay Cooke |
| JCCW: | Joint Committee on the Conduct of the War |
| LH: | LancasterHistory (formerly Lancaster County Historical Society) |
| LOC: | Library of Congress |
| OHS: | Ohio Historical Society |
| SAD: | Stephen A. Douglas |
| SCHS: | South Carolina Historical Society |
| SPC: | Salmon P. Chase |
| TS: | Thaddeus Stevens |
| USG: | Ulysses S. Grant |
| UVT: | University of Vermont |
| WPF: | William Pitt Fessenden |
| WTS: | William T. Sherman |
| ZC: | Zachariah Chandler |

## PREFACE

xv  "Mr. Lincoln": Riddle, *Recollections of War-Times*, 2.
xvi  "Antagonism between": CG 37/Special, 1488.
xvi  "If you take": CG 37/2, 2049.

xvii "It was the members": Curry, *Blueprint for Modern America*, 9.

xviii "There is no place": Smith, *Life and Letters of James Abram Garfield*, Vol. 1, 363.

xix "Finding the coast": L. A. Alcott, spring 1861, Office of the U.S. Senate Historian, Civil War files.

xx "will be a monument": John Sherman to WTS, March 20, 1863, Thorndike, ed., *Sherman Letters*, 194.

xx "The past": Hartley, *Go-Between*, 1.

## I. A ROPE OF SAND

4 Secession fever was: *Charleston Mercury*, November 11 and 15, 1860, January 22, 1861; Ball Family Collection, SCHS; *The Liberator*, November 23, 1860; *Vincennes Western Sun*, December 8, 1860.

4 "The country has": CG 36/2, 1–7.

5 reports of lynchings: David Hamilton to BFW, December 22, 1860, Wade Papers, LOC; *Liberator*, September 28, 1860; CG 36/2, 99–104, 1354–56; Channing, *Crisis of Fear*, 30–41.

5 He waved away: CG 36/2, 1–7.

5 "a permanent and unchangeable": CG 36/2, 1393, 112–14.

6 South Carolina formally seceded: *Charleston Mercury*, December 25, 1860; Gilman Papers, SCHS; CG 36/2, 190; Loewen and Sebesta, eds., *Confederate and Neo-Confederate Reader*, 112–17.

7 "Old James Buchanan": Strong, *Diary*, 103.

7 "Is there any": D. Hamilton to BFW, December 22, 1860, Wade Papers, LOC.

7 "Are the president": Thomas Earl to BFW, December 28, 1860, Wade Papers, LOC.

7 "imitate [Andrew] Jackson": TS to SPC, February 3, 1861, Wade Papers, LOC.

7 "crawling on its knees": TS to Edward McPherson, Palmer Papers, LH.

8 "You own the cabinet": CG 36/2, 99ff.

8 the "new dogma": Republican Party Platform, May 17, 1860, at The American Presidency Project, www.presidency.ucsb.edu.

8 "For the first time": Green, *Freedom, Union and Power*, 60.

9 "Now that the black": Chesnut, *Diary from Dixie*, 1.

9 "God damn your": Stashower, *Hour of Peril*, 83.

9 "He is lank": Strong, *Diary*, 188.

9 "It is now apparent": E. M. Carpenter to BFW, December 26, 1860, Wade Papers, LOC.

9 man "who is taken up": CG 36/2, 1400.

9 "and they will soon": BFW to (unreadable), February 3, 1861, BFW Collection, OHS.

9 "coolly watch the": Green, *Freedom, Union and Power*, 66.

10 "You cannot whip": H. S. Julian to BFW, December 30, 1860, Wade Papers, LOC.

10 "The one flag": Eisenschiml and Newman, *American Iliad*, 11.

10 "I rejoiced at": CG 36/2, 1400.

11 A few independent: Daniel W. Crofts, "No Better Southern Man," *New York Times*, January 22, 2011.

11  was "hallucinating": James L. Vallandigham, *Life of Clement L. Vallandigham*, 147.

11  over his corpse: Klement, *Limits of Dissent*, 50.

11  a paradoxical figure: CG 36/2, 235–42; Klement, *Limits of Dissent*, 8–19, 29; James L. Vallandigham, *Life of Clement L. Vallandigham*, 14–15.

12  if Lincoln won: Klement, *Limits of Dissent*, 41.

12  he "never would": James L. Vallandigham, *Life of Clement L. Vallandigham*, 141.

12  "the saddest day": Ibid., 144.

12  took particular pride: CG 36/2, 490–92.

12  "low, simple, and democratic": James L. Vallandigham, *Life of Clement L. Vallandigham*, 150.

12  "We have an empire": Ibid., 147.

13  "When all possible": James L. Vallandigham, *Life of Clement L. Vallandigham*, 156; CG 37/3, 57–58.

13  "Star after star": CG 36/2, 235–42.

13  Only a radical: CG 36/2, 794–95.

13  "a sword for aggression": James L. Vallandigham, *Life of Clement L. Vallandigham*, 156.

14  Republicans were shocked: Green, *Freedom, Union and Power*, 74–76.

14  Worse yet came: Stahr, *Seward*, 74–76; CG 36/2, 341–44.

14  "Away with all": Green, *Freedom, Union and Power*, 78.

14  "Is it possible": D. D. Stewart to WPF, March 30, 1861, Fessenden Papers, LOC.

15  "Mr. Seward's course": TS to SPC, February 3, 1861, Palmer and Ochoa, eds., *Selected Papers of Thaddeus Stevens*, Vol. 1, 200.

15  "it fails to meet": Stahr, *Seward*, 226.

15  "gave the idea": Poore, *Perley's Reminiscences of Sixty Years in the National Metropolis*, Vol. 1, 539–40.

15  "Our position is": Loewen and Sebesta, eds., *Confederate and Neo-Confederate Reader*, 127–29.

16  "Remember that you": Martin, *The Great Parliamentary Battle and Farewell Addresses of the Southern Senators on the Eve of the Civil War*, 81.

16  North's "insulting" challenges: Ibid., 202.

16  "Your conquest": Ibid., 158–59.

16  "We want no negro": Ibid., 171.

16  "Good-bye, senators": Isaac Bassett diary, Office of the U.S. Senate Historian.

17  "like Heaven": Thayer, ed., *Life and Letters of John Hay*, Vol. 1, 14–15.

17  A less awed: *Atlantic Monthly*, July 1861.

17  Like a general: CG 36/2, 621–23.

18  "I have no hope": Ibid.

## 2. LET THE WAR COME

21  "a city of magnificent": Dickens, *American Notes*, 129.

21  "like some kind": Cooper, *Jefferson Davis, American*, 346.

21  "I am able": James L. Vallandigham, *Life of Clement L. Vallandigham*, 152.

21  Worrying rumors flew: Samuel Fessenden (Sr.) to WPF, January 10, 1861, Fessenden Papers, LOC; James L. Vallandigham, *Life of Clement L. Vallandigham*,

151; [first name unclear] Patterson to TS, January 8, 1861, Palmer Papers, LH; Strong, *Diary,* 87.

21  danger to the capital: Hendrickson, "Defending Washington," *Washington History.*

22  "Not only will": CG 36/2, 371.

22  In New York City: P. W. Dophley to JC, January 19, 1861, Cooke Papers, HSP; Hamilton Fish to WPF, December 11, 1860, Fessenden Papers, LOC.

22  "Depression today deeper": Strong, *Diary,* 76.

23  serving federal officers: CG 36/2, 1095ff.

23  wildly claiming: Loewen and Sebesta, eds., *Confederate and Neo-Confederate Reader,* 103.

23  "Had this old": Strong, *Diary,* 89.

24  "They are either": CG 36/2, 501.

24  "I hold most": Ibid.

24  Fessenden's was a voice: Brooks, *Washington in Lincoln's Time,* 26; Howard, *Civil War Echoes and Character Sketches,* 25–26; Jellison, *Fessenden of Maine,* 112–13.

24  "was like a chain": Poore, *Perley's Reminiscences of Sixty Years in the National Metropolis,* Vol. 1, 98.

24  "to be calm": CG 37/2, 1963.

26  "some suitable adjustment": Holzer, *Lincoln President-Elect,* 275.

26  "a tottering ashen ruin": Ibid., 276.

27  As the train: Stashower, *Hour of Peril,* 285–86.

27  "reached the Capital": Holzer, *Lincoln President-Elect,* 397.

27  But the compromisers: Green, *Freedom, Union and Power,* 72–73; Holzer, *Lincoln President-Elect,* 427–29; Oakes, *Freedom National,* 73–74.

28  As the last hours: CG 36/2, 1374–80; *New York Herald,* March 5, 1861.

28  Crittenden spoke: CG 36/2, 1374ff.

29  "rich in intellectual culture": CG 36/2, 1354.

30  "I do not propose": CG 36/2, 1366–77.

30  Abandoning the platform: CG 36/2, 1381–86.

30  "No more concessions": David Root to TS, January 31, 1861, Palmer and Ochoa, eds., *Selected Papers of Thaddeus Stevens,* Vol. 1, 197–98.

30  "Don't back an inch": Philip Wilcox to BFW, December 22, 1860, Wade Papers, LOC.

30  "I will never": CG 36/2, 1371–72.

30  Northern Democrats were: CG 36/2, 1390–91.

31  "a placebo": CG 36/2, 1388.

31  "The federal government": CG 36/2, 1399–1400, 1373ff; Howard, *Civil War Echoes and Character Sketches,* 22–23; Welch, *Texas Senator,* generally.

32  "bulldog obduracy": Brooks, *Washington in Lincoln's Time,* 26.

32  "looked at the contest": Poore, *Perley's Reminiscences of Sixty Years in the National Metropolis,* 100.

32  "I know no high": Trefousse, *Benjamin Franklin Wade,* 312.

32  "a mean God forsaken": Ibid., 311.

32  "The question will": CG 35/2, 1074.

32  "Men are not": Trefousse, *Benjamin Franklin Wade,* 312.

32  "a ridiculous old prejudice": Ibid., 285.

32  "Once you might": CG 37/2, 1919.

32  "the hopes of many": CG 36/2, 1393–96; *New York Times*, March 5, 1861, March 4, 1878.

34  Below the Capitol: *New York Herald*, March 5, 1861; *New York Times*, March 5, 1861.

35  "You will be shot": Stashower, *Hour of Peril*, 83.

35  "In taking final leave": CG 36/2, 1525–26; *New York Herald*, March 5, 1861; *New York Times*, March 5, 1861; Davis, "John C. Breckinridge," *Register of the Kentucky Historical Society*; Heck, "John C. Breckinridge in the Crisis of 1860–1861," *Journal of Southern History*.

36  "inflexible purpose": CG 36/2, 1525–26.

36  "judging from the": *New York Herald*, March 5, 1861.

36  "Fellow citizens, I": Ibid.


### 3. A WRETCHED HUMBUG

37  "I have no purpose": Fehrenbacher, *Abraham Lincoln: Speeches and Writings*, 215–24.

38  "a document of": *New York Times*, March 5, 1861.

38  "a monstrous compendium": Holzer, *Lincoln President-Elect*, 208, 460.

38  "with the forked tongue": CG 37/1, 57.

39  "vague generalities": *New York Herald*, March 7, 1861.

39  a "revolting declaration": Holzer, *Lincoln President-Elect*, 461.

39  "But I think": Strong, *Diary*, 106.

39  was "tolerably acquainted": John Rawlins to TS, April 15, 1861, Palmer Papers, LH.

40  "not totally blind": Joseph Ritner to TS, February 27, 1861, Palmer Papers, LH.

40  escape further "molestation": Theodore McGowan to TS, February 26, 1861, Palmer Papers, LH.

40  ignorant "of everything": Stahr, *Seward*, 272.

40  "ill-bred, ravenous crowd": Donald, *Lincoln*, 285.

41  "takes that business": Stahr, *Seward*, 258.

41  "no conception of": Ibid.

41  "disastrous, halting, and": CG 37/Special 1507–8, 1511.

41  "I want plain": Nelson Franklin to ZC, March 6, 1861, Chandler Papers, LOC.

42  "Without a little": Donald, *Lincoln*, 288.

42  "A wet buckskin": Israel Garrard to BFW, April 30, 1861, Wade Papers, LOC.

42  "All the powers": "Barrett and Todd" to BFW, March 7, 1861, Wade Papers, LOC.

42  Dominating the Senate's: CG 37/Special, 1437–39.

43  But his motives: Johannsen, *Stephen A. Douglas*, 845, 854–57.

43  "It is easy": CG 37/Special, 1439–42.

44  Fed up with: CG 37/Special, 1447–50.

44  "In my opinion": CG 37/Special, 1452.

45  impatient Republican Radicals: Donald, *Lincoln*, 386; Trefousse, *Thaddeus Stevens*, 143–44.

45  "I do not know": CG 37/Special, 1514.

46  With this, Douglas: CG 37/Special, 1452.

46  "He has no more": Ibid.

46  "The question is": CG 37/Special, 1457–60, 1471.

47  "It is evident": CG 37/Special, 1463.

47  "You fairly stripped": E. H. Thomas to WPF, March 17, 1861, Fessenden Papers, LOC.

47  "Seven states are": CG 37/Special, 1503.

48  "We do not attach": CG 37/Special, 1463.

48  "It is the duty": CG 37/Special, 1519.

48  A week earlier: Detzer, *Allegiance*, 226–31, 256–57.

49  Seward, still confident: Stahr, *Seward*, 271–72.

49  "If this must": Donald, *Lincoln*, 290.

49  No one in Charleston doubted: *Charleston Mercury*, December 12, 1860, February 15, 1861, and April 1, 4, 5, and 9, 1861.

50  Lincoln's long internal struggle: Donald, *Lincoln*, 285–92; Stahr, *Seward*, 258ff; *Charleston Mercury*, April 1 and 9, 1861.

50  The next afternoon: Doubleday, *Reminiscences of Forts Sumter and Moultrie in 1860–61*, 139–47, 157; *New York Times*, April 19 and 30, 1861; *Charleston Mercury*, April 13 and 15, and May 2, 1861.

50  "It is a demand": Crawford, *History of the Fall of Fort Sumter*, 422.

51  At 7:00 a.m.: *Dayton Daily Journal*, April 15, 1861; Doubleday, *Reminiscences of Forts Sumter and Moultrie in 1860–61*, 157–64; Chesnut, *Diary from Dixie*, 42.

51  "Some of the anxious": Chesnut, *Diary from Dixie*, 38.

51  The surrender almost: Crawford, *History of the Fall of Fort Sumter*, 442–46.


## 4. FORWARD TO RICHMOND!

53  Sumter changed everything: SPC to Alphonso Taft, April 28, 1861, Salmon P. Chase Collection, HSP; SPC to John A. Dix et al., April 23, 1861, Salmon P. Chase Collection, HSP; Donald, *Lincoln Reconsidered*, 140ff; Stahr, *Seward*, 284.

54  "It became necessary": Lincoln, "Message to Congress," May 26, 1861, in Basler, ed., *Collected Works of Abraham Lincoln*, Vol. 5, 241–42.

54  "fierce and jubilant": Thayer, *Life and Letters of John Hay*, Vol. 1, 2–22.

54  "No peace to": William Grandin to ZC, June 10, 1861, Chandler Papers, LOC.

54  "The traitors must:" E. B. Ward to BFW, April 29, 1861, Wade Papers, LOC.

54  "The time for": Speech in Cleveland, April 15, 1861, Wade Collection, OHS.

55  "It's all excitement": Pitt Cooke to JC, April 23, 1861, Cooke Papers, HSP.

55  "some of the colored": Horatio N. Rankin to H. B. Carrington, April 19, 1861, Governors' Papers, OHS.

55  "The Capital of": Johannsen, ed., *Letters of Stephen A. Douglas*, 509–10.

55  "dictatorship" and "usurpation": Medlar, *Gentleman and the Artist*, 148.

55  "not to vote": Ibid., 144.

55  The slave states: McPherson, *Tried by War*, 25; *New York Times*, April 18, 19, and 25, 1861; Loewen and Sebesta, eds., *Confederate and Neo-Confederate Reader*, 153–55.

56  "Some respectable gentleman": Medlar, *Gentleman and the Artist*, 51.

56  Waves of rumors: Wheeler Papers, LOC; Thayer, ed., *Life and Letters of John Hay*, Vol. 1, 11–12; *New York Times*, April 19, 24, and 27, 1861.

56  "I feel so oppressed": Diary of Charles Mason, April 27, 1861, Remey Family Papers, LOC.

57  "gaunt, tattered, uncombed": Thayer, ed., *Life and Letters of John Hay*, Vol. 1, 20–22.

57  "in belted and revolvered dignity": Ibid., 16–17.

57  "The heart of Maryland": *New York Times*, April 25, 1861.

57  On April 19: *New York Times*, April 21 and 25, 1861; CG 37/1, 44–45, 200–201; McGinty, *Body of John Merryman*, 47ff; McPherson, *Tried by War*, 45ff.

58  "unless they come": Wheeler Papers, LOC; Thayer, ed., *Life and Letters of John Hay*, Vol. 1, 11–12.

58  Outside Baltimore, pro-Southern: *New York Times*, May 30, 1861; McGinty, *Body of John Merriman*, 63ff.

58  "God damn them": McGinty, *Body of John Merryman*, 67.

58  labeling it "inexpedient": Ibid., 53; *New York Times*, April 29, 1861.

58  "Our men are not": McPherson, *Tried by War*, 26.

59  with his long legs outstretched: Thayer, ed., *Life and Letters of John Hay*, Vol. 1, 30–31.

59  Troops drilled morning: *New York Times*, April 19, 20, 24, and 27, 1861; Thayer, ed., *Life and Letters of John Hay*, Vol. 1, 20–21; Nicolay, *Our Capital on the Potomac*, 36–37; Wheeler Papers, LOC.

59  "a jolly, gay, set": Strausbaugh, *City of Sedition*, 182.

60  "Things are more": *The Senate's War*, pamphlet, Office of the U.S. Senate Historian.

60  "Never! Millions for": CG 37/1, 93, 98; Medlar, *Gentleman and the Artist*, 151–53.

61  "I want to hang": A.M. [last name unclear: Sattsy?] to Sherman, May 25, 1861, John Sherman Papers, LOC.

61  Another young soldier: Benjamin Hawkes to Sherman, May 24, 1861, John Sherman Papers, LOC.

61  When Congress reconvened: Russell, *My Diary North and South*, 144, 162.

61  "rather loose and ramshackle": Brooks, *Washington in Lincoln's Time*, 23; Myers, *Senator Henry Wilson and the Civil War*, 127–28; Howard, *Civil War Echoes and Character Sketches*, 30–31.

62  "to approve and confirm": CG 37/1, 2, 40, 47.

62  Former vice president: CG 37/1, 47–48; Davis, "John C. Breckinridge," *Register of the Kentucky Historical Society*; O'Connor, "John Cabell Breckinridge's Personal Secession," *Filson Club History Quarterly*.

63  Clement Vallandigham, brandishing: CG 37/1, 57–59.

64  Merryman and his band: McGinty, *Body of John Merryman*, 1–7, 69–70, 76–78, 154, 162–63.

64  "in the presence of": *New York Times*, June 2, 1861.

65  "too old and palsied": *New York Times*, May 30, 1861.

65  "In order to save": CG 37/1, 140.

65  "The whole of the laws": McGinty, *Body of John Merryman*, 100.

65 Merryman's arrest was: CG 37/1, 137–39; Blair, *With Malice Toward Some*, 44–45.
65 Vallandigham predicted that: CG 37/1, 60, 77, 97, 131.
66 "not an end but a means": CG 37/1, 141.
66 "Slavery offers itself": Thayer, ed., *Life and Letters of John Hay*, Vol. 1, 33.
67 "exterminated whites" ought: Ibid., 30–31.
67 "Rather than see": CG 37/1, 190.
67 "immediate and unconditional emancipation": CG 37/1, 142.
67 "The slow canker": CG 37/1, 119.
67 "run like cowards": ZC to Letitia Chandler, July 16, 1861, Chandler Papers, LOC.
67 "short, sharp blow": Cook, *Civil War Senator*, 133.
67 "The Nation's War Cry": Starr, *Bohemian Brigade*, 34–35.
68 "surround the scoundrels": ZC to Letitia Chandler, June 27, 1861, Chandler Papers, LOC.
68 "The average man": Riddle, *Life of Benjamin F. Wade*, 240.
68 "worse than the Turks": Russell, *My Diary North and South*, 148–50.
69 "The stern demand": Trefousse, *Benjamin Franklin Wade*, 148.
69 On July 16: *New York Tribune*, July 22 and 24, 1861; *Philadelphia Daily News*, July 7, 19, 22, 23, 24, and August 7, 1861; *Cincinnati Inquirer*, July 23, 1861; Riddle, *Life of Benjamin F. Wade*, 154–55; Riddle, *Recollections of War-Times*, 245–46; Russell, *My Diary North and South*, 161–73; Andrews, *The North Reports the Civil War*; Straussbaugh, *City of Sedition*, 188ff; *Report* of the JCCW/1863, Part 1, 38, 132.
69 "menacing tremolo": Howard, *Civil War Echoes and Character Sketches*, 53.
69 "That is splendid": Russell, *My Diary North and South*, 167.
70 "The canon balls": Elijah Brown to "Franky," July 26, 1861, Marshall, ed., *War of the People*, 38–39.
70 "We've whipped them": Russell, *My Diary North and South*, 167.
70 "I was run over": Elijah Brown to "Franky," Marshall, ed., *War of the People*, 38–39.
71 "We had to be rough": Letter from Albert J. Biddle, *Philadelphia Daily News*, August 7, 1861.
71 "Boys, we'll stop this": Riddle, *Life of Benjamin F. Wade*, 245.
71 "Whatever credit there was": Trefousse, *Benjamin Franklin Wade*, 151.
71 "That is not so": Nicolay, *Our Capital on the Potomac*, 372.
72 "these defeated soldiers": Whitman, *Prose Works*, 33.
72 All over Washington: *New York Tribune*, July 23 and 24, 1861; Whitman, *Prose Works*, 35.
72 "saw more sad countenances": Medlar, *Gentleman and the Artist*, 166.
72 "I have felt at times": Cook, *Civil War Senator*, 136.
73 "There you are, shoulder straps!": Whitman, *Prose Works*, 34.

## 5. THE CLINK OF COIN

74 "With men enough": J. W. Broads to ZC, July 25, 1861, Chandler Papers, LOC.
74 Wild stories of: *New York Tribune*, July 26, 27, and 28, 1861; *Philadelphia Daily*

News, July 26 and August 9, 1861; *Lancaster Evening Express,* July 31, 1861; Williams, "Benjamin F. Wade and the Atrocity Propaganda of the Civil War," *Ohio State Archaeological and Historical Quarterly.*

74 "We took it for": Sherman, *Memoirs,* 205.

75 "The Northern troops fight": *Lancaster Evening Express,* July 30, 1861.

75 "like streams of hot lava": *Philadelphia Daily News,* August 10, 1861.

75 "the clink of coin": Hall, ed., *Selections from the Works of Wendell Phillips,* 88.

75 "The augmentation of": SPC to TS, July 11, 1861, Palmer Papers, LH.

75 Chase, sounding a note: SPC to TS, July 10, 11, 16, and 18, 1861, Palmer Papers, LH; Simon Cameron to TS, July 11, 23, and 24, 1861, Palmer Papers, LH; TS to SPC, July 18, 1861, Palmer Papers, LH; Curry, *Blueprint for Modern America,* 149–50; Richardson, *The Greatest Nation of the Earth,* 31–38, 40–43; Spaulding, *History of the Legal Tender Paper Money Issued During the Great Rebellion,* 108.

76 "If you get one": CG 37/2, 2886.

76 "Committee of Mean Ways": CG 37/1, 459.

76 "no patience for humbug": Hatch, *Maine,* 372.

77 "a driver—bitter, quick": Riddle, *Recollections of War-Times,* 31–32.

77 "the great mogul": Unidentified Lancaster, Pennsylvania newspaper, December 1862, Palmer Papers, LH.

77 "The thought that it": Cook, *Civil War Senator,* 135.

77 "We come here": CG 37/1, 191.

77 "leaving all the jabber": Bogue, *Earnest Men,* 80.

77 They all knew: CG 37/1, 255, 314; SPC to TS, July 23, 1861, Palmer Papers, LH.

77 "It is unpleasant": CG 37/1, 247.

78 "The Northern people": *Daily Alta California,* August 8, 1861.

78 "By putting it off": CG 37/1, 250–51, 307.

78 "Why, sir": CG 37/1, 316.

78 The loan bill: CG 37/1, 60, 459, Appendix, 6, 60–61, 109–10, 128.

79 However, bankers and financiers: J. E. Williams to WPF, July 27, 1861, Fessenden Papers, LOC; James Gallatin to WPF, Fessenden Papers, LOC; SPC to "Gentlemen," May 17, 1861, Cooke Papers, HSP; Larson, *Jay Cooke,* 100–101, 110–12.

79 One of these agents: Larson, *Jay Cooke,* 98–100, 105–7; Taylor, *Philadelphia in the Civil War,* 220ff; Henry D. Moore to JC, July 23, 1861, Cooke Papers, HSP.

80 "His mantle has fallen": Larson, *Jay Cooke,* 105.

80 "a violent abolitionist": JC to Henry D. Cooke, May 15, 1861, Cooke Papers, HSP.

80 "Now is the time": Larson, *Jay Cooke,* 103.

80 "to keep on the right side": JC to Henry D. Cooke, April 8, 1861, Cooke Papers, HSP.

80 "manifest their love": Brands, *The Money Men,* 105.

81 "those natural advantages": Larson, *Jay Cooke,* 108.

81 "I have been at it": JC to Andrew G. Curtin, September 7, 1861, Cooke Papers, HSP.

81 "Every dollar subscribed": Unidentified Philadelphia newspaper, September 1861, Cooke Papers, HSP.

81  "I consider the central idea": Thayer, ed., *Life and Letters of John Hay*, Vol. 1, 30–31.
82  "any persons claiming": CG 37/1, 218–19.
82  "If traitors use": Ibid.
82  "Rather than see": CG 37/1, 190.
82  "Because a conspiracy": CG 37/1, 189.
83  "I am under no": Nolan, *Benjamin Franklin Butler*, 101.
83  "In the first place": *Report* of the JCCW/1863, Part 1, 226.
83  "When they come": Orville Browning to AL, April 30, 1861, Lincoln Papers, LOC.
84  "We see plenty of slaves": Harlan P. Paige to C.E.M., May 28, 1862, Paige Family Papers, UVT.
84  In New York State: Strong, *Diary*, 76.
84  "I want to see": CG 37/1, 190.
85  "Does war change": CG 37/1, 411–12.
85  "I thought the time": CG 37/1, 414–15.
86  elderly senator Jacob Collamer: CG 37/1, 374.
86  "Shall we be told": CG 37/1, 375.
86  "monstrous in a free society": CG 37/1, 342.
87  Unionist fears of subversion: BFW to ZC, October 8, 1861, Wade Papers, LOC; McGinty, *Body of John Merryman*, 155–56.
87  "the slimy track": *Lancaster Daily Express*, August 5, 1861.
87  "It is time!": Strausbaugh, *City of Sedition*, 197.
87  Fears were also spreading: *Philadelphia Daily News*, July 19 and 23, and August 10, 1861; *Lancaster Daily Express*, August 8 and 13, 1861; Gilbert L. Beeckman to ZC, August 2, 1861, Chandler Papers, LOC; Strausbaugh, *City of Sedition*, 198; Weber, *Copperheads*, 24–25.
87  A colorful but: Weber, *Copperheads*, 2–3.
87  "The whole Democratic party": CG 36/2, 1396.
88  "rant about hanging": Medlar, *Gentleman and the Artist*, 145.
88  He denounced the imminent: CG 37/1, 372, 376–77.
89  "Will the honorable": CG 37/1, 378.
89  "They would have hurled": Ibid.
89  "For me": Ibid.
90  "I believe the president": CG 37/1, 393.
90  "This extra session": *Philadelphia Daily News*, August 7, 1861.
91  Breckinridge told constituents: O'Connor, "John Cabell Breckinridge's Personal Secession," *Filson Club History Quarterly*.
91  "well-meaning baboon": GBM to Mary E. McClellan, October 11, 1861, in Sears, ed., *Civil War Papers of George B. McClellan*, 106.
91  "I confess to a prejudice": Sears, *George B. McClellan*, 116–117.
92  "the Napoleon of": *New York Herald*, July 15, 1861.
92  A Michigan officer: Anonymous to ZC, December 25, 1861, Chandler Papers, LOC.
92  "I find 'confusion'": Henry D. Cooke to JC, July 31, 1861, Cooke Papers, HSP.
92  "You might as well": *Report* of the JCCW/1863, Part 1, 143–44.
92  "You are obliged": CG 37/1, 52.

92  "You find men": CG 37/1, 239–40.

93  "There are about four hundred": George H. Randall to "Dear wife," November 8, 1861, in Marshall, *War of the People*, 50.

93  "by bargains and brandy": Starr, "Camp Dennison," *Bulletin of the Historical and Philosophical Society of Ohio.*

93  a Mexican War veteran: John Sherman to BFW, May 4, 1861, Wade Papers, LOC.

93  one of Wade's neighbors: N. J. Marble to BFW, August 19, 1861, Wade Papers, LOC.

94  young children "acquired habits": Wilson, *The Business of Civil War*, 14.

94  Everyone needed uniforms: *Philadelphia Daily News*, July 26, 1861; Strausbaugh, *City of Sedition*, 202–3.

94  a Lancaster newspaper complained: *Lancaster Evening Express*, August 1, 1861.

94  Vallandigham proposed hiring: CG 37/1, 85–87, 91, 100.

95  "It has been utterly": C. D. Ferguson to "captain," December 23, 1861, Wade Papers, LOC.

95  company of dissatisfied Michiganders: A. N. Norton et al. to George Stoneman, January 8, 1862, Chandler Papers, LOC.

95  "Confidence renewed!": *New York Tribune*, August 1, 1861.

95  "Presdt, Cabinet": GBM to Mary E. McClellan, July 27, 1861, in Sears, ed., *Civil War Papers of George B. McClellan*, 89.

95  "in full tog": *Lancaster Daily Express*, August 8, 1861.

95  "I can do it all": Thayer, ed., *Life and Letters of John Hay*, Vol. 1, 50.

## 6. THE MOLOCH OF SLAVERY

96  remarked Ben Wade: Sears, *George B. McClellan*, 119.

96  "I begin to despair": BFW to ZC, October 8, 1861, Wade Papers, LOC.

97  "a slight demonstration": *Report* of the JCCW/1863, Part 2, 252–53.

97  like "a pretty bird": Morgan, *A Little Short of Boats*, 139.

97  But brio wasn't enough: *Report* of the JCCW/1863, Part 2, 253ff; *New York Times*, October 30, November 5 and 26, 1861, and February 13, 1862; *Lancaster Daily Express*, October 22, 24, 25, and 28, 1861; *Philadelphia Daily News*, October 25, 1861; Murray and Hsieh, *Savage War*, 114–15; generally, Morgan, *A Little Short of Boats*.

98  "Is there any hope": Nelson Franklin to BFW, November 5, 1861, Wade Papers, LOC.

98  "All is gloom": BFW to Caroline Wade, October 25, 1861, Wade Papers, LOC.

98  "We are in a world": WPF to Elizabeth Warriner, January 4, 1862, Fessenden Papers, BCL.

98  "Everybody is grumbling": WPF to Elizabeth Warriner, February 15, 1862, Fessenden Papers, BCL.

99  "southern proclivities": Simeon Rush to BFW, December 28, 1861, Wade Papers, LOC.

99  Frémont, famed for: Harris, *Two Against Lincoln*, 140ff; Parrish, *Frank Blair*, 118–35; *Report* of the JCCW/1863, Part 3, 70.

99 Lincoln warned Frémont: Harris, *Two Against Lincoln,* 102, 145, 153; *Report* of the JCCW/1863, Part 3, 151–52.

99 "I wish to God": James Wade to Caroline Wade, February 3, 1862, Wade Papers, LOC.

99 Wade himself wrote: BFW to ZC, September 23, 1861, Chandler Papers, LOC.

100 McClellan fobbed them off: GBM to Mary E. McClellan, October 26, 1861, in Sears, ed., *Civil War Papers of George B. McClellan,* 112.

100 The "Jacobin Club": Thayer, ed., *Life and Letters of John Hay,* Vol. 1, 48.

100 "No country was ever": BFW to Caroline Wade, October 25, 1861, Wade Papers, LOC.

100 "I am convinced": WPF to Elizabeth Warriner, March 2, 1862, Fessenden Papers, BCL.

100 "a portent of evil": Thayer, ed., *Life and Letters of John Hay,* Vol. 1, 52.

100 "nothing yet done": *Report* of the JCCW/1863, Part 1, 129.

101 "There are many screws loose": Nelson Franklin to BFW, November 5, 1861, Wade Papers, LOC.

101 One of the boldest strokes: CG 37/2, 16; Tap, *Over Lincoln's Shoulder,* 21–24.

102 "The most striking": Julian, *Political Recollections,* 201–2.

102 "Yes, [Lincoln] is the commander-in-chief": CG 37/2, 1917.

103 Born to a laborer: Trefousse, *Benjamin Franklin Wade,* 17–23; Riddle, *Life of Benjamin F. Wade,* 25–28, 39–40, 57–59.

103 "shrewd but illiterate": Tap, *Over Lincoln's Shoulder,* 28.

103 "It is not military": *Report* of the JCCW/1863, Part 1, 207.

103 "the snakes are torpid": Ibid.

104 "it would be almost" Ibid., 148–49.

104 Samuel P. Heintzelman: Ibid., 117–18.

104 "I believe in letting": CG 37/2, 30.

104 Are we, he demanded: Ibid.

105 "the hotbed": CG 37/3, 325–26.

105 "There is something wrong": CG 37/1, 89–90.

105 "I am willing to carry": CG 37/1, 73.

105 Gen. Charles Stone: *Report* of the JCCW/1863, Part 2, 297–304, 385–90, 473ff, 499–500.

106 "The general feeling": Ibid., 300.

106 McClellan deflected attention: Ibid., 18.

106 "If I had any plans": *Report* of the JCCW/1863, Part 2, 266.

107 "Whereas slavery has caused": CG 37/1, 6.

107 In January, he went: CG 37/2, 439–41.

109 "Not only is this Moloch": J. H. Jordan to Henry Wilson, December 23, 1861, Wade Papers, LOC.

109 "A new order is upon us": *New York Herald,* April 4, 1862.

## 7. THE STRONG ARM OF GOVERNMENT

110 In early December: Davis, "Slavery and Emancipation in the Nation's Capital," *Prologue Magazine.*

111 Stevens argued that: CG 37/2, 439–41.

111 "the first practical triumph": CG 37/2, 1451.

112 "I do desire": CG 37/2, 1472–73.

112 Opposition to the bill: CG 37/2, 1339.

112 "will become a sore": CG 37/2, 1191–92.

113 "an entering wedge": CG 37/2, 1338–39.

113 an opening wedge: CG 37/2, 1473.

113 "How long would it be": CG 37/2, 1301–3.

114 Find a place for them: CG 37/2, 1632–34.

114 As a sweetener: *New York Herald*, April 18, 1862.

115 Garrett Davis argued: CG 37/2, 1337.

115 "It is the nation": *The Liberator*, May 16, 1862.

115 "All hail the day": *Christian Recorder*, April 26, 1862.

116 "I dislike slavery": CG 37/2, 2054.

116 The embarrassed Sheffield: Ibid.

116 "He is just the man": WPF to Elizabeth Warriner, January 19, 1862, Fessenden Papers, BCL.

117 "a dead failure": Sears, *George B. McClellan*, 168.

117 "sent a thrill of joy": D. Cadwell to BFW, February 20, 1862, Wade Papers, LOC.

117 So hopeful were congressional leaders: *New York Herald*, April 4, 1862.

117 "The army of the Union": *New York Times*, April 5, 1862.

117 As early as October: Taylor, *Philadelphia in the Civil War*, 222; Richardson, *Greatest Nation of the Earth*, 45–46, 70.

117 "I'm resigned to": Strong, *Diary*, 182.

117 Henry Cooke wrote repeatedly: Oberholtzer, *Jay Cooke*, 194.

118 "He is as much": James A. Briggs to BFW, February 13, 1862, Wade Papers, LOC.

118 "It is utterly": Oberholtzer, *Jay Cooke*, 169.

118 "One gentleman had": *Philadelphia Inquirer*, September 7, 1861.

118 "Their charge of money bags": *Philadelphia Inquirer*, September 13, 1861.

118 "They promise to shove": Henry D. Cooke to JC, March 27, 1862, Cooke Papers, HSP.

118 Chase hoped desperately: Chase, *Report of the Secretary of the Treasury*, 13–15, 18–21; Richardson, *Greatest Nation of the Earth*, 69–71, 75–78; Spaulding, *History of the Legal Tender Money Issued During the Great Rebellion*, 53–54.

119 "We will thus have to": CG 37/2, 2136.

119 "The idea of perpetual": Chase, *Report of the Secretary of the Treasury*, 13.

119 "more hours daily": CG 37/2, 1041.

120 "This bill is a measure": CG 37/2, 687–89.

120 "We want a currency": *Philadelphia Daily News*, August 5, 1861.

121 "The Ship of State": Spaulding, *History of the Legal Tender Money Issued During the Great Rebellion*, 53–54; CG 37/2, Appendix, 40–45.

121 "fetid trash" *New York Tribune*, May 17, 1862.

121 "Taking their cue": Richardson, *Greatest Nation of the Earth*, 72.

121 Only gold and silver: Spaulding, *History of the Legal Tender Money Issued During the Great Rebellion*, 60–62.

122    Gallatin, feverishly warned: James Gallatin to WPF, June 14, 1862, Fessenden Papers, LOC.

122    "This thing has tormented me": Richardson, *Greatest Nation of the Earth*, 81.

122    He had in mind: *Lancaster Evening Express*, August 1, 1861; Strausbaugh, *City of Sedition*, 202–3; "E.G.H." to Caroline Wade, November 5, 1861, Wade Papers, LOC.

122    "I would advocate": Spaulding, *History of the Legal Tender Money Issued During the Great Rebellion*, 104–6.

122    Never in the best: WPF to Elizabeth Warriner, January 4, 1862, Fessenden Papers, BCL.

123    "When a man feels": WPF to Elizabeth Warriner, February 1, 1862, Fessenden Papers, BCL.

123    Fessenden had "too much": TS to "Dear Sir," November 17, 1862, Palmer Papers, LH.

123    "a doleful sound": CG 37/2, 900.

123    "makes two classes": Ibid.

124    The bill was so "mutilated": Henry D. Cooke to JC, February 25, 1862, Cooke Papers, HSP.

124    "You should push": JC to Henry D. Cooke, March 5, 1862, Cooke Papers, HSP.

124    In November, Jay Cooke: SPC to JC, November 21, 1861, in Oberholtzer, *Jay Cooke*, 182.

124    The Cookes were: Henry D. Cooke to JC, March 1, 1862, Cooke Papers, HSP.

124    "the business matters": JC to SPC, March 6, 1862, Cooke Papers, HSP.

124    Chase, Jay reminded Henry: JC to Henry D. Cooke, March 4, 1862, Cooke Papers, HSP.

125    "Waterloo of the war": *New York Herald*, April 3, 1862.

126    "We are on the eve": Henry D. Cooke to JC, February 27, 1862, Cooke Papers, HSP.

126    "It was as if": Hawthorne, "Chiefly About War Matters," *Atlantic Monthly*, July 1862.

126    "Everybody feels annoyed": WPF to Samuel Fessenden Sr., March 29, 1862, Fessenden Papers, BCL.

126    "utterly unfit": WPF to Elizabeth Warriner, March 1, 1862, Fessenden Papers, BCL.

127    "The greatest expedition": Stiles, *Custer's Trials*, 40.

127    "The moment for action": Proclamation, March 14, 1862, in Sears, ed., *Civil War Papers of George B. McClellan*, 211.


## 8. BENEFICENT REFORM, HOTHOUSE CAPITALISM

128    "Proslavery men seem": CG 37/2, 1919.

128    He had toiled: WPF to Elizabeth Warriner, April 25, 1862, Fessenden Papers, BCL.

128    As the costs of war mounted: CG 37/2, 103, 1194–97, 1576–77, 2423–28.

128    "We are ready": George S. Ward to WPF, January 23, 1862, Fessenden Papers, LOC.

128  "Is the tax": CG 37/2, 1576.

129  the bill spread "its fingers": CG 37/2, 1194.

129  Republicans "must have forgotten": CG 37/2, 1361.

129  "When this vast system": CG 37/2, 1227.

130  one is "called out": *New York Herald,* April 2, 1862.

130  "The country is waiting": CG 37/2, 2227–28.

130  "My hair has gone": WPF to Elizabeth Warriner, May 10, 1862, Fessenden Papers, BCL.

130  colleagues' "confounded" demands: Ibid.

131  The centerpiece of: CG 37/2, 910.

131  "one of the most": White, *"It's Your Misfortune and None of My Own,"* 143.

131  "a man of safe and steady": Riddle, *Life of Benjamin F. Wade,* 31.

131  Grow orotundly declared: CG 37/2, 909–10, 1031–35.

132  senator Louis Wigfall protested: CG 36/1, 1293ff.

132  proslavery Unionists in Congress: CG 37/2, 1030ff, 1916, 1937ff.

132  California representative Timothy Phelps: CG 37/1, 83; CG 37/2, 1590 ff.

133  Thaddeus Stevens, an ardent: CG 37/2, 1591–93.

133  Build the railroad now: CG 37/2, 1949–1950.

134  "hothouse capitalism": White, *Railroaded,* 17.

134  "one of the most stupendous": CG 37/2, 1728.

134  "Everything that conspires": CG 37/2, 2807–9.

134  On May 5, Wade: CG 37/2, 1935, 2248–2249, 2275–77.

134  It would provide: Ron, "Summoning the State," *Journal of American History;* Cross, *Justin Morrill,* 81–85.

135  "the tastes of": Cross, *Justin Morrill,* 1ff.

135  "We have schools": CG 35/1, 1692–97.

135  a "monstrous" measure: CG 35/2, 256.

135  allow Congress to "fasten": Ron, "Summoning the State"; CG 35/1 716, 719.

136  Wright startled his colleagues: CG 37/2, 2441.

136  "The great agricultural interests": Dean, *An Agrarian Republic,* 92–93.

136  "to its pristine vigor": Ibid.

137  "It is claimed": CG 37/2, 1591–93.

137  "The confiscation bill": WPF to William Fessenden, May 23, 1862, Fessenden Papers, BCL.

138  "Most of them must": *Philadelphia Daily News,* July 19, 1861.

138  "John Brown raid": CG 37/2, 2795.

138  Saulsbury of Delaware warned: CG 37/2, 1923.

138  "We are to punish": CG 37/2, 2240–43.

139  Wade boomed, "We might": CG 37/2, 1917–18.

139  warned against magnifying: Ibid.

139  "If no other means": CG 37/2, 439–41.

139  The bill that finally emerged: *Statutes at Large,* Vol. 12, 589–92; Oakes, *Freedom National,* 234–37.

139  "a slavery saving machine": J. Eastman Johnson to ZC, July 15, 1862, Chandler Papers, LOC.

140  "The question has given": WPF to Samuel Fessenden Sr., March 29, 1862, Fessenden Papers, BCL.

140 "If you would save": Samuel Fessenden Sr. to WPF, May 9, 1862, Fessenden Papers, BCL.

140 Although Fessenden frequently: CG 37/2, 1963, 2202–3.

140 "If I could cut": WPF to Elizabeth Warriner, June 1, 1862, Fessenden Papers, BCL.

140 "a mere milk-and-water concern": CG 37/2, 1957.

140 "I am in favor": CG 37/2, 2202–3.

140 Wade thundered: Ibid.

141 "I should like": Ibid.

141 Wade grumbled that: Ibid.

142 McClellan continued to insist: GBM to Winfield Scott, April 11, 1862, in Sears, ed., *Civil War Papers of George B. McClellan,* 236–37; GBM to Edwin Stanton, April 27, 1862, in Sears, ed., *Papers of George B. McClellan,* 247–48; Uriah H. Painter to the JCCW, July 10, 1862, in *Report* of the JCCW / 1863, Part 1, 283ff; CG 37/2, 1972.

142 "And once more": AL to GBM, April 9, 1862, in *Report* of the JCCW / 1863, Part 1, 322.

142 "I am confident": GBM to AL, April 20, 1862, in Sears, ed., *Civil War Papers of George B. McClellan,* 244–45.

142 "I will finish": GBM to Mary E. McClellan, May 10, 1862, in Sears, ed., *Civil War Papers of George B. McClellan,* 262–63.

142 "The little Napoleon": Thayer, ed., *Life and Letters of John Hay,* Vol. 1, 57.

142 "They are concentrating": GBM to Mary E. McClellan, May 10, 1862, in Sears, ed., *Civil War Papers of George B. McClellan,* 262–63.

### 9. TAX IS PATRIOTIC

144 a "perfect republic": Foner, "Thaddeus Stevens and the Imperfect Republic," *Pennsylvania History.*

145 Some argued that: CG 37/2, 2240–43.

145 Charles Sumner, who: CG 37/2, 1473.

145 "I would plant": CG 37/2, 3125–27.

145 Fessenden, reflecting the views: CG 37/2, 1473.

145 Even as Congress argued: Oakes, *Freedom National,* 213ff.

146 Then, in May 1862, Hunter: General Orders, No. 11, May 9, 1862, Wade Papers, LOC.

146 "By one stroke": J. Elwell to BFW, May 10, 1862, Wade Papers, LOC.

146 "bloodthirsty Jacobins": *New York Herald,* April 2, 1862.

146 "No regiment of": David Hunter to Edwin M. Stanton, June 23, 1862, in CG 37/2, 3122.

146 "No commanding general": Oakes, *Freedom National,* 215.

146 "I reserve to myself": Ibid., 216.

147 Zachariah Chandler was: Isaac Bassett diary, Office of the U.S. Senate Historian.

147–48 Samuel C. Pomeroy of Kansas: CG 37/2, 2396.

148 Ira Harris of New York: CG 37/2, 2401.

148 Edgar Cowan of Pennsylvania: CG 37/2, 2469.

148  "This would be consolidation": CG 37/2, 2399.

148  Sumner set off: CG 37/2, 2401–2.

148  "It is the business": CG 37/2, 2403.

148  "Upon every occasion": CG 37/2, 2428.

149  "I am tired and sick": CG 37/2, 2467.

149  "If we do not intend": CG 37/2, 2463.

149  "Tax is patriotic": *Lancaster Daily Inquirer,* July 7, 1862.

149  "one of the necessities": *New York Herald,* September 1, 1862.

149  the country's first income tax: CG 37/2, 2486; Richardson, *The Greatest Nation of the Earth,* 121–22; Curry, *Blueprint for Modern America,* 177–80.

149  "resort to every possible": CG 37/1, 320.

150  "The public business requires": CG 37/2, 2450–51.

151  "As early as April, John Sherman": Ibid.

151  "I acknowledge its defects": CG 37/2, 2606–8.

151  "a stupendous system": *New York Herald,* July 18, 1862.

152  "If we bleed": Cross, *Justin Morrill,* 67.

152  The immensely detailed bill: CG 37/2, 2936–37, 2978–86, 3050–54, 3168–77; Curry, *Blueprint for Modern America,* 161–62.

152  Addressing the House: CG 37/2, 2338.

153  "We invite immigrants": Ibid.

153  "In morals and": CG 37/2, 2339.

154  Even taken together: CG 37/2, 2606–8, 2766–68, 3071–79, 3182; Richardson, *Greatest Nation of the Earth,* 82–83.

154  "No man, not even": CG 37/2, 2766.

154  Lee, McClellan wrote: GBM to AL, April 20, 1862, Sears, ed., *Civil War Papers of George B. McClellan,* 244.

155  "We will have Richmond": GBM to Mary E. McClellan, June 2, 1862, Sears, ed., *Civil War Papers of George B. McClellan,* 286.

155  "Had I twenty thousand": GBM to Edwin M. Stanton, June 27, 1862, Sears, ed., *Civil War Papers of George B. McClellan,* 321.

155  "If I save this Army": GBM to Stanton, June 28, 1862, Sears, ed., *Civil War Papers of George B. McClellan,* 322.

155  Self-pitying and demoralized: GBM to Mary E. McClellan, July 13, 1862, Sears, ed., *Civil War Papers of George B. McClellan,* 354; *Report* of the JCCW/1863, Part 1, 435–36.

156  "I have not yielded": GBM to AL, July 2, 1862, Sears, ed., *Civil War Papers of George B. McClellan,* 329.

156  "Fearing failure": Keegan, *American Civil War,* 151.

156  He confessed that: GBM to Mary E. McClellan, July 10, 1862, Sears, ed., *Civil War Papers of George B. McClellan,* 349.

156  "One hundred and fifty-eight thousand": CG 37/2, 3390–92.

157  They explicitly authorized the president: CG 37/2, 3198ff.

157  "Is it any worse": CG 37/2, 1141.

158  "knowing his depraved nature": CG 37/2, 3125–27.

158  "rising by degrees": Poore, *Perley's Reminiscences of Sixty Years in the National Metropolis,* Vol. 2, 101.

158  "Why, then, object": CG 37/2, 3125–27.

158 "to elevate the miserable": CG 37/2, 3198–99.
158 "Neither confiscation of": GBM to AL, July 7, 1862, Sears, ed., *Civil War Papers of George B. McClellan,* 344–45.
159 "the cruelest imposition": Oberholtzer, *Jay Cooke,* 197.
159 "wholesale murder": *New York Herald,* July 18, 1862.
159 "That criminal": CG 37/2, 3390–92.
159 "It is a question": CG 37/2, 3198–99.
159 "The severest justice": CG 37/2, 3406.
159 "Is it better": CG 37/2, 3376.
159–60 "The navigator is sometimes": CG 37/2, 3406.
160 About midnight: Isaac Bassett diary, Office of the U.S. Senate Historian.
161 "These and similar propositions": *New York Herald,* July 18, 1862.
161 "May we not be": CG 37/2, 1404.

## 10. THE SLAVES MUST BE WITH US

162 Sam, always impulsive: Cook, *Civil War Senator,* 98; WPF to William Fessenden, February 25, 1862, Fessenden Papers, BCL.
162 "Choice must be made": WPF to Samuel Fessenden Jr., January 1, 1862, Fessenden Papers, BCL.
163 "I have witnessed": Samuel Fessenden Jr. to WPF, June 15, 1862, Fessenden Papers, BCL.
163 "This is the crisis": *New York Herald,* July 15, 1862.
163 In early July 1862, he boasted: *Report* of the JCCW/1863, Part 1, 282.
163 "We have come": *New York Herald,* July 15, 1862.
163 "We expect marching orders": Samuel Fessenden Jr. to WPF, August 22, 1862, Fessenden Papers, BCL.
164 "Your army is the center": WPF to Samuel Fessenden Jr., August 24, 1862, Fessenden Papers, BCL.
164 "I have a very strong idea": GBM to Mary E. McClellan, August 10, 1862, Sears, ed., *Civil War Papers of George B. McClellan,* 389.
164 "It seems Pope": WPF to Frank Fessenden, August 31, 1862, Fessenden Papers, BCL.
164 rebels were "badly used up": *Report* of the JCCW/1863, Part 1, 466.
165 And among the wounded: Telegram to WPF, September 1, 1862, Fessenden Papers, BCL.
165 "For the loss of": WPF to John C. Hodson, September 13, 1862, Fessenden Papers, BCL.
165 "Are imbecility and treason": ZC to Peter H. Watson, September 10, 1862, Chandler Papers, LOC.
165 "Unquestionably, he has acted": Thayer, ed., *Life and Letters of John Hay,* Vol. 1, 65.
166 "McClellan claimed baselessly": GBM to Henry W. Halleck, November 29, 1862, in *Report* to the JCCW/1863, Part 1, 509.
166 "The spectacle yesterday": GBM to Mary E. McClellan, September 18, 1862, Sears, ed., *Civil War Papers of George B. McClellan,* 482.
167 "I was silent": Cook, *Civil War Senator,* 153.

167   He had, he said, "made a covenant": Welles, *Diary*, Vol. 1, 143–45.

167   Lincoln, who personally preferred: Ibid., 150–52.

168   "The slaves must be": Ibid., 143–45.

168   "There has been no": *New York Times*, September 23, 1862.

168   "Hurrah for Old Abe": BFW to George W. Julian, September 29, 1862, in Trefousse, *Benjamin Franklin Wade*, 187.

168   "Thank God I live": *New York Herald*, October 9, 1862.

168   "Harsh experience has destroyed": *New York Times*, September 27, 1862.

168   A Circleville, Ohio, paper: Weber, *Copperheads*, 63–64.

168   "in a furious hatred": *New York Herald*, December 31, 1862.

169   "inaugurating servile war": GBM to William H. Aspinwall, September 26, 1862, Sears, ed., *Civil War Papers of George B. McClellan*, 482.

169   "on this pontoon": *The Liberator*, October 3, 1862.

169   "a few old fogies": Thayer, ed., *Life and Letters of John Hay*, Vol. 1, 67.

169   Thaddeus Stevens was skeptical: *Lancaster Examiner*, September 10, 1862.

169   "Abolition—*yes!*": Ibid.

169   "It is better for them": Diary of Charles Mason, May 31, 1862, Remey Family Papers, LOC.

170   shouting "down with the": Weber, *Copperheads*, 57.

170   "The bones of our dead": *New York Herald*, July 15, 1862.

170   Reaction and counterreaction: Weber, *Copperheads*, 52–54; Towne, *Surveillance and Spies in the Civil War*, 40, 46–48; Barr Spangler to TS, September 25, 1862, Stevens Papers, LH.

170   Two days after issuing: McPherson, *Tried by War*, 132.

171   "We must denounce": Weber, *Copperheads*, 66.

171   With the initiation of: CG 37/1, 332–35; Neely, *Fate of Liberty*, 55; diary of Charles Mason, March 30, 1862, Remey Family Papers, LOC.

171   The threat of subversion: *Philadelphia Daily News*, July 23, 1861; *New York Herald*, April 2 and August 31, 1862; *Dayton Daily Empire*, November 8, 10, and 25, and December 15, 1862; CG 37/3, 27; Towne, *Surveillance and Spies in the Civil War*, 20; Neely, *Fate of Liberty*, 56–62; Klement, *Limits of Dissent*, 109.

171   that he "wouldn't wipe": Neely, *Fate of Liberty*, 64.

172   "Where has the right": CG 37/1, 446; James L. Vallandigham, *Life of Clement L. Vallandigham*, 203.

172   Vallandigham believed: Vallandigham, *Record of Hon. C. L. Vallandigham on Abolition, the Union and the Civil War*, 126.

172   the "blackest traitor": L. A. Pierce to ZC, December 6, 1861, Chandler Papers, LOC.

172   "There are thousands": J. H. Brotherton to BFW, May 11, 1862, Wade Papers, LOC.

173   "Today they who are": Vallandigham, *Record of Hon. C. L. Vallandigham on Abolition, the Union and the Civil War*, 122ff.

173   the "Almighty African": Ibid., 129.

173   "within whose marble walls": Ibid., 130.

173   In speech after speech: Ibid., 146–51.

174   "I am weary": James L. Vallandigham, *Life of Clement L. Vallandigham*, 213; Klement, *Limits of Dissent*, 74–76.

174 Fearing his assassination: James L. Vallandigham, *Life of Clement L. Vallandigham,* 212ff.

174 "It is appointed": Ibid., 214–15.

175 The *New York Tribune* predicted: *New York Tribune,* November 4, 1862.

175 Democrats railed against: H. S. Bundy to WPF, May 20, 1862, Wade Papers, LOC.

175 Everywhere, "runaway negroes": *Dayton Daily Empire,* October 13, 1862.

175 Horatio Seymour declared": *Dayton Daily Empire,* October 1, 1862.

175 "lusty black fiends": *Dayton Daily Empire,* October 4, 1862.

175 By early October: Diary of Charles Mason, October 6 and 16, 1862, Remey Family Papers, LOC.

175 "While it ruled": *Dayton Daily Empire,* October 9, 1862.

175 "Today the shackles": *Dayton Daily Empire,* October 18, 1862.

175–76 "The war has gone far enough": *New York Times,* November 10 and 11, 1862.

176 "Total rout": Strong, *Diary,* November 5, 1862.

176 "a political revolution": Vallandigham, *Record of Hon. C. L. Vallandigham on Abolition, the Union and the Civil War,* 155.

176 "The folly of the president": WPF to James W. Grimes, October 19, 1862, Fessenden Papers, BCL.

176 "the most pestilent abolitionist": Trefousse, *Thaddeus Stevens,* 126–27.

176 "That arch-traitor": Klement, *Limits of Dissent,* 113.

177 Even the churches: Vallandigham, *Record of Hon. C. L. Vallandigham on Abolition, the Union and the Civil War,* 163.

177 he "has obtained the greatest": *Dayton Daily Empire,* October 16, 1862.


## 11. FOLLY, STUPIDITY, AND WEAKNESS

178 He suffered from: WPF to Elizabeth Warriner, November 30, 1962, Fessenden Papers, BCL.

178 Although his spirits: Morris Ketchum to WPF, December 18, 1862, Fessenden Papers, BCL.

178 "Folly, stupidity": WPF to William Fessenden, December 4, 1862, Fessenden Papers, BCL.

178 "The country has little": WPF to Elizabeth Warriner, December 7, 1862, Fessenden Papers, BCL.

179 Congress reassembled in a city: *The Senate's War,* pamphlet, Office of the U.S. Senate Historian; Nicolay, *Our Capital on the Potomac,* 376–77; Lowry, *Tourist Guide to Civil War Washington DC,* 89ff; Barber, "Alexandria in the Civil War," master's thesis, Virginia Polytechnic Institute; Hawthorne, "Chiefly About War Matters," *Atlantic Monthly,* July 1862; diary of Charles Mason, June 14 and 22, 1862, Remey Family Papers, LOC; Benjamin B. French to TS, March 2, 1863, Palmer Papers, LH.

180 "like a giant fungus-growth": Nicolay, *Our Capital on the Potomac,* 373.

180 Across the Potomac: Barber, "Alexandria in the Civil War"; Buckman, DeButts, and Fox, "The Journal of Chalkley Gillingham," pamphlet; Blaine, *Twenty Years of Congress from Lincoln to Garfield,* 34–36.

180 "I am fearing": WPF to Elizabeth Warriner, December 11, 1862, Fessenden Papers, BCL.

180 Burnside, in the words: Poore, *Life and Public Services of Ambrose E. Burnside*, 112.

181 "Poor Burn feels dreadfully": GBM to Mary E. McClellan, November 7, 1862, Sears, ed., *Civil War Papers of George B. McClellan*, 520.

181 There were rumblings: Sears, *Lincoln's Lieutenants*, 435.

181 Burnside assumed command: *Report* of the JCCW/1863, Part 1, 643–46, 650–52; Woodbury, *Major General Ambrose E. Burnside and the Ninth Army Corps*, 215–33.

182 "The grape and canister": Sears, *Lincoln's Lieutenants*, 460.

182 "terrible fighting and slaughter": WPF to Elizabeth Warriner, December 13, 1862, Fessenden Papers, BCL.

182 A few days later: WPF to Samuel Fessenden Sr., December 20, 1862, Fessenden Papers, BCL.

182 "the grand squeegee": Harlan Page Paige to "Brothers and Sisters," December 15, 1862, Paige Family Papers, UVT.

182 "The widow's wail": *Dayton Daily Empire,* December 15, 1862.

183 "Many loyal citizens": Joseph P. Ropes to WPF, January 12, 1863, Fessenden Papers, BCL.

183 "He may have faults": WPF to James Grimes, October 19, 1862, Fessenden Papers, BCL.

184 "Here was an army": *Report* of the JCCW/1863, Part 1, 677.

184 Meade testified that: Ibid., 691–93, 698–99, 705.

185 Joseph "Fighting Joe": Ibid., 667–69, 672.

185 "I knew nothing": Ibid., 661–62.

185 "No, I did not": Ibid., 709–10.

186 In testimony later published: Ibid., 716ff.

186 Newton said that: Ibid., 733–38.

187 "you will not be surprised": Carl Schurz to AL, January 24, 1863, Lincoln Papers, LOC.

187 "blundering and imbecility": James W. White to BFW, December 27, 1862, Wade Papers, LOC.

187 Treasury Secretary Chase estimated: CG 37/3, 21–25.

187 Capitalists feared runaway inflation: Reuben W. Howes to WPF, December 6, 1862, Fessenden Papers, LOC; Morris Ketchum to WPF, December 18, 1862, January 15, February 2 and 7, 1863, Fessenden Papers, LOC; CG 37/3, 25–27.

188 "It is next to impossible": SPC to TS, December 23, 1862, Palmer Papers, LH.

188 a malign "back-stairs influence": Francis Fessenden, *Life and Public Services of William Pitt Fessenden*, 237; Trefousse, *Benjamin Franklin Wade*, 190–93.

188 On the evening of December 16: Francis Fessenden, *Life and Public Services of William Pitt Fessenden*, 233–34, 239, 242; Donald, *Charles Sumner*, Part 2, 89; Stahr, *Seward*, 354ff.

189 a situation that "does not now exist": Francis Fessenden, *Life and Public Services of William Pitt Fessenden*, 233–34.

189   Nine senators led: Ibid., 240–44, 247–49.

190   Lincoln, however, was determined: Welles, *Diary,* Vol. 1, 199–200.

190   Chase, who caved: Donald, *Charles Sumner,* Part 2, 94.

190   the senators once again accused: Welles, *Diary,* Vol. 1, 195–97.

190   "his boldest move": Cook, *Civil War Senator,* 156.

191   Lincoln's "long arm and fingers": Welles, *Diary,* Vol. 1, 201.

191   "Seward comforts him": Ibid., 205.

191   "productive of good": WPF to Samuel Fessenden Sr., December 20, 1862, Fessenden Papers, BCL.

192   "The country demands": WPF to William Fessenden, December 21, 1862, Fessenden Papers, BCL.

192   "Our great trouble": WPF to Samuel Fessenden Sr., December 20, 1862, Fessenden Papers, BCL.

192   Democrats continued to attack: CG 37/3, 95.

192   "How much longer": *Dayton Daily Empire,* January 6, 1863.

192   With Christmas approaching: *Dayton Daily Empire,* December 22, 1862.

193   twenty-four guillotines: *Dayton Daily Empire,* December 12, 1862.

193   "I am alive": CLV to John A. Walters, December 5, 1862, in Arthur, "The 'Copperhead' Vallandigham," master's thesis, West Chester University of Pennsylvania.

193   "Vallandigham is one of": December 1862 (date unclear), *Dayton Daily Empire.*

193   One of his proposals: CG 37/3, 21, 165; *Dayton Daily Empire,* December 11, 1862.

193   "But the people did not": CG 37/3, 53–55.


## 12. MEN, AND MORE MEN.

195   Such policies, charged Frederick Douglass: *Douglass' Monthly,* August 1862.

195   "If I could save": *Christian Recorder,* September 6, 1862.

195   William Lloyd Garrison disgustedly: *The Liberator,* December 26, 1862.

195   Lincoln called upon Congress: CG 37/3, 1–5.

196   There were those who doubted: Oakes, *Freedom National,* 342.

197   "fit and necessary war measure": *New York Times,* January 3, 1863.

197   "Whatever may be": Ibid.

197   In Boston, a racially mixed crowd: *Liberator,* January 16, 1863.

197   At Cooper Union: *Douglass' Monthly,* February 1863.

197   "Dat's me—I'm free": Ibid.

197   "Three Million Slaves": Mayer, *All on Fire,* 547.

198   The anti-abolitionist *New York Herald*: *New York Herald,* July 16, 1862.

198   "It was . . . the skeleton": Oakes, *Freedom National,* 342.

198   "The change in": *Douglass' Monthly,* March 1863.

198   Governor James F. Robinson urged: *New York Times,* January 1, 1863.

198   "Why not issue": CG 37/3, 233–34.

198   "In this war": *Dayton Daily Empire,* January 5, 1863.

199   Vallandigham declared: CG 37/3, 53–59.

200   "I have always been a step ahead": CG 37/3, 240–44.

200  "under our absolute power": CG 37/3, 50.

201  "It seems to me as if": CG 37/3, 244.

201  "honest, sober, industrious" men: Benjamin B. French to TS, February 2, 1863, Palmer Papers, LH.

201  Stevens doubted that: CG 37/3, Appendix, 79ff.

201  Desertion had become epidemic: Geary, *We Need Men*, 51–53; Levi Reist to TS, December 15, 1862, Palmer Papers, LH.

202  "Horse-jockeys and negro traders": CG 37/3, 1443.

202  Boston alone: *New York Herald*, July 14, 1862.

202  "like the destroying angel": Vallandigham, *Record of Hon. C. L. Vallandigham on Abolition, the Union and the Civil War*, 212.

203  Alarmed Democrats warned: CG 37/3, 684, Appendix, 75.

203  Henry May, a Maryland Unionist: CG 37/3, Appendix, 73–75.

203  "by the decree of Providence": Ibid., 72.

203  "The arming of the Negroes": CG 37/3, 243, 282, 557.

203  Gov. Samuel J. Kirkwood of Iowa: Brodie, *Thaddeus Stevens*, 161.

203  Racism, he implied: CG 37/3, Appendix, 79ff.

204  The bill also established: *Statutes at Large*, Vol. 12, 1863, 731.

205  these "strange, ominous" words: Vallandigham, *Record of Hon. C. L. Vallandigham on Abolition, the Union and the Civil War*, 215–26.

206  Demanded Sen. James Bayard: CG 37/3, 26.

206  "illegal, cruel, and unjust": CG 37/3, 184.

206  Grant, he said: CG 37/3, 245.

206  "no man in the Senate": CG 37/3, 246.

207  "We cannot afford": CG 37/3, 31.

207  "Detestable as are the motives": *Douglass' Monthly*, March 1863.

207  In December, Stevens: CG 37/3, 14.

207  Senate Democrats charged: CG 37/3, 71–72.

207  More emotionally, Lazarus Powell: CG 37/3, 68.

208  "The placidity of his mind": "Biographical Sketch of Hon. Lazarus W. Powell," pamphlet.

208  "I have gone and demanded": CG 37/3, 33–35.

208  "I hear a long, low howl": CG 37/3, 68–69.

209  Worrying letters came at him: Morris Ketchum to WPF, January 13 and 27, 1863, Fessenden Papers, BCL; B. H. Hulton to WPF, January 31, 1863, Fessenden Papers, LOC.

209  The country's chaotic currency: CG 37/2, 3072ff; CG 37/3, 841; Jellison, *Fessenden of Maine*, 165.

209  "We might as well do without": D. Wilder Jr. to WPF, January 6, 1862, Fessenden Papers, LOC.

209  The National Bank Act: CG 37/3, 843–44.

210  The prospect of paper money: CG 37/3, 21–27, 824–25.

210  Garrett Davis of Kentucky sarcastically: CG 37/3, 879.

210  Jacob Collamer of Vermont, who: CG 37/3, 869–70.

211  "we are obliged": CG 37/3, 931.

211  There was backroom speculation: Francis Fessenden, *Life and Public Services of William Pitt Fessenden*, 229.

211 "Every man knows it": CG 37/3, 825.

211 What *was* lacking: CG 37/3, 842–45.

### 13. RESISTANCE, CONSPIRACY, AND MARTYRDOM

214 As always happened at the end: CG 37/3, 1483–86, 1495, 1512, 1523, 1552.

215 "We can make them": CG 37/3, 1441.

215 "There is a point": CG 37/3, 1465.

216 "Let this bill pass": CG 37/3, 1460–64.

216 Powell, Wall, and their allies: CG 37/3, 1470ff.

216 The filibuster continued: CG 37/3, 1476–77.

219 "the most laborious": CG 37/3, 1581.

219 "With all its faults": Cook, *Civil War Senator*, 159.

220 "If the rebellion": Francis Fessenden, *Life and Public Services of William Pitt Fessenden*, 254.

220 an artillery captain offering: A. J. Chapman to BFW, March 10, 1863, Wade Papers, LOC.

220 "as we are unfortunately": Henry W. Owen to BFW, March 10, 1863, Wade Papers, LOC.

220 "Upon the 'conduct of' ": *Report* of the JCCW/1863, Part 1, 3.

221 "There was treason": Ibid., 61–62.

221 "Had that army fulfilled": Ibid., 3–4.

222 "Ask the soldiers": Harlan P. Paige to "A.H.P.," November 28, 1862, Paige Family Papers, UVT.

222 "Give us little Mack": Harlan P. Paige to "A.H.P.," December 18, 1862, Paige Family Papers, UVT.

222 "Every energy of the government": *Report* of the JCCW/1863, Part 1, 5.

223 "McClellan is as dead as a herring": ZC to Letitia Chandler, January 22, 1863, Chandler Papers, LOC.

223 In January 1862, for instance: *Report* of the JCCW/1863, Part 1, 77.

223 "Let no officers": Ibid., 61.

224 "Lost, lost, all is lost!": Welles, *Diary*, Vol. 1, 203.

224 "reign of terror": Vallandigham, *Record of Hon. C. L. Vallandigham on Abolition, the Union and the Civil War*, 233.

225 "a faithful sentinel": Ibid., 238.

225 "He has passed": *Dayton Daily Empire*, March 14, 1863.

225 well-organized Copperhead conspiracy:"The Great Conspiracy," anonymous pamphlet; "Copperhead Conspiracy in the North-West," anonymous pamphlet; *Indiana State Sentinel*, February 16, 1863; Sherman, "Vallandigham's Record Reviewed," pamphlet; CG 37/3, Appendix, 79ff.

225 Indiana governor Oliver P. Morton: Towne, *Surveillance and Spies in the Civil War*, 47.

225 By mid-1863, violent resistance: "Copperhead Conspiracy," pamphlet; Towne, *Surveillance and Spies in the Civil War*, 53, 75–77, 94, 99–100.

226 "It was a secesh paper": Roseboom, "Southern Ohio and the Union in 1863," *Mississippi Valley Historical Review*.

226 Burnside's brief was twofold: *War of the Rebellion*, Series 2, Vol. 5, 480, 556;

*Dayton Daily Empire,* May 1, 1863; James L. Vallandigham, *Life of Clement L. Vallandigham,* 241; Woodbury, *Major General Ambrose E. Burnside and the Ninth Army Corps,* 265ff.

226 he stridently denounced: James L. Vallandigham, *Life of Clement L. Vallandigham,* 233, 253, 263–64; Porter, *Ohio Politics During the Civil War Period,* 161ff.

227 Three days later: James L. Vallandigham, *Life of Clement L. Vallandigham,* 255ff; *Dayton Daily Empire,* May 5, 1863; "M" to Friend Lane, in Shankman, "Vallandigham's Arrest and the 1863 Dayton Riot," *Ohio History Journal.*

227 "You have now broken": James L. Vallandigham, *Life of Clement L. Vallandigham,* 257.

227 "Unless their eyes": "M" to "Dear Beacon," in Shankman, "Vallandigham's Arrest and the 1863 Dayton Riot," *Ohio History Journal.*

228 "A Dastardly Outrage!!": *Dayton Daily Empire,* May 5, 1863.

228 Only with difficulty: James L. Vallandigham, *Life of Clement L. Vallandigham,* 255–59; *The Crisis,* May 13, 1863; "M" to Friend Lane, in Shankman, "Vallandigham's Arrest and the 1863 Dayton Riot," *Ohio History Journal.*

228 "I am here in a military bastille": James L. Vallandigham, *Life of Clement L. Vallandigham,* 260.

228 charged with "declaring disloyal sentiments": *War of the Rebellion,* Series 2, Vol. 5, 633–46.

228 The trial, such as it was: James L. Vallandigham, *Life of Clement L. Vallandigham,* 266, 269–72; *The Crisis,* May 13, 1863.

229 "When the life of the Republic": "Decision of Judge Leavitt of Ohio, in the Vallandigham Habeas Corpus Case," pamphlet.

229 "monstrous in theory": Porter, *Ohio Politics During the Civil War Period,* 169.

230 "aimed at the rights": "The Truth from an Honest Man: The Letter of the President," pamphlet.

230 Horatio Seymour further charged: James L. Vallandigham, *Life of Clement L. Vallandigham,* 290.

230 "The proceedings were arbitrary": Welles, *Diary,* Vol. 1, 321.

230 Abraham Lincoln maintained: "The Truth from an Honest Man," pamphlet.

230 Earlier in May: *War of the Rebellion,* Series 2, Vol. 5, 548.

230 "not of my own will": James L. Vallandigham, *Life of Clement L. Vallandigham,* 297.

230–31 In another letter: CLV to Horatio Seymour, May 21, 1863, Vallandigham Collection, OHS.

231 "They were hours of": James L. Vallandigham, *Life of Clement L. Vallandigham,* 300–301.

231 Bragg ceremoniously congratulated: Braxton Bragg to CLV, May 26, 1863, Vallandigham Collection, OHS.

231 "It is plain to my understanding": Robert E. Lee to Jefferson Davis, June 25, 1863, Dowdey, ed., *Wartime Papers of Robert E. Lee,* 530.

231 His plight was finally solved: Braxton Bragg to Samuel Cooper, June 1, 1863; CLV to Bragg, May 31, 1863; Davis to Bragg, June 2, 1863, all in Vallandigham Collection, OHS; Weber, *Copperheads,* 99.

233 The nomination, he declared: James L. Vallandigham, *Life of Clement L.*

*Vallandigham,* 319–21; Klement, "Vallandigham as an Exile in Canada, 1863–1864," *Ohio History.*

### 14. DIRE WARNINGS

235  "We must all expect to suffer": TS to Simon Stevens, July 6, 1863, Palmer and Ochoa, eds., *Selected Papers of Thaddeus Stevens,* Vol. 1, 400.

235  "He is considered rather": Welles, *Diary,* Vol. 1, 349.

235  "Behind the front line": Sears, *Lincoln's Lieutenants,* 575.

236  "Arms, heads, blankets": Ibid.

236  "We had them within": Thayer, ed., *Life and Letters of John Hay,* Vol. 1, 85–86.

236  Gideon Welles concurred: Welles, *Diary,* Vol. 1, 369–70.

236  "The woman-floggers": Strong, *Diary,* 328.

237  The worst disturbances by far: *New York Times,* July 15, 16, and 17, 1863; Strong, *Diary,* 334–46; Schecter, *Devil's Own Work,* especially 250–52.

237  cursing the draft and: *New York Times,* July 15, 1863.

237  When the children: Egerton, *Thunder at the Gates,* 118.

237  "If a quarter [of what] one": Strong, *Diary,* 336.

238  "Nigger recruiting prospers": Ibid., 347.

238  Negrophobic politicians issued: CG 37/3, 1445–46; *Dayton Daily Empire,* October 13, 1863.

238  "The paper [Emancipation] proclamation": Speech by Frederick Douglass, October 13, 1853; *Douglass' Monthly,* March 1863.

238  a Cleveland editor invited: Egerton, *Thunder at the Gates,* 4; McPherson, *Negro's Civil War,* 183; Oakes, *Freedom National,* 383–88; Grant, *Memoirs and Selected Letters,* 1031.

239  "We hab done wid": "Song of the First of Arkansas," broadside.

239  Even before black regiments: CG 37/3, 1445–46.

239  "We took no prisoners": Silkenat, "I Surrender!," *Civil War Monitor.*

240  "I never more wish to": McPherson, *Negro's Civil War,* 190.

240  Among the dead: Egerton, *Thunder at the Gates,* 119.

240  "I wont trust": WTS to JS, April 26, 1863, Simpson and Berlin, eds., *Sherman's Civil War,* 459–63.

240  Their performance converted Ulysses Grant: Grant, *Memoirs and Selected Letters,* 1030–32.

241  "You say you will not": AL to James C. Conkling, August 26, 1863, Fehrenbacher, *Abraham Lincoln: Speeches and Writings,* 495–99.

241  Vallandigham presided over: CLV to Manton Marble, August 8, 1863, Vallandigham Collection, OHS; Klement, "Vallandigham as an Exile in Canada, 1863–1864," *Ohio History; Dayton Daily Empire,* August 21, 1863.

242  Pro-Vallandigham parades: *Dayton Daily Empire,* August 25 and September 18, 1863.

242  Predicted a local newspaper: *Wellsville Patriot,* in James L. Vallandigham, *Life of Clement L. Vallandigham,* 332.

242  "We are coming, Abraham Lincoln": "The Vallandigham Songbook," pamphlet.

243 "delusional," he laughingly wrote: CLV to Manton Marble, August 13, 1863, Vallandigham Collection, OHS.

243 "If we fail this fall": CLV to Manton Marble, October 4, 1863, Vallandigham Collection, OHS.

243 "a brave, honest, persecuted man": "Speech of Mr. Pugh to 50,000 Voters Who Nominated Vallandigham," pamphlet.

243 "stricken down by": *Dayton Daily Empire*, October 13, 1863.

243 As the campaign progressed: Porter, *Ohio Politics During the Civil War Period*, 181ff.

243 "*Slavery to God was*": Morse, "An Argument on the Ethical Position of Slavery in the Social System and Its Relation to the Politics of the Day," pamphlet.

244 Ohio's two senators, Ben Wade: Porter, *Ohio Politics During the Civil War Period*, 119–20; "State Convention of War Democrats," anonymous pamphlet.

244 "convicted traitor": Sherman, "Vallandigham's Record Reviewed," pamphlet.

244 "It is your purpose": Anonymous to BFW, October 5, 1863, Wade Papers, LOC.

244 "I am a Radical": Trefousse, *Benjamin Franklin Wade*, 206.

244 just two days before the election: Towne, *Surveillance and Spies in the Civil War*, 123.

245 "Disenfranchise them": WTS to JS, April 3, 1863, Simpson and Berlin, eds., *Sherman's Civil War*, 437ff.

245 "We will open up Polls": Lucius Wood to "Parents & Sister," October 11, 1863, Wood Papers, Dayton Metro Library.

245 "There arose a shout": Smith, *Life and Letters of James Abram Garfield*, Vol. 1, 374.

245 "Well—the gubernatorial contest": *Dayton Daily Empire*, October 14, 1863.

245 "The tail of the national Copperhead": Strong, *Diary*, 364.

245 Ohio Democrats blamed: James L. Vallandigham, *Life of Clement L. Vallandigham*, 333; *Dayton Daily Empire*, October 12, 1863; GBM to Charles J. Biddle, October 12, 1863, Sears, ed., *Civil War Papers of George B. McClellan*, 558–59.

245 "Somewhere I don't know where": Julius Wood to "Parents & Sister," October 17, 1863, Wood Papers, Dayton Metro Library.

246 One told his local newspaper: Roseboom, "Southern Ohio and the Union in 1863," *Mississippi Valley Historical Review*.

246 "that old arch instigator": Lucius Wood to "Parents & Sister," September 17, 1863, Wood Papers, Dayton Metro Library.

246 "As to the future": James L. Vallandigham, *Life of Clement L. Vallandigham*, 335–36.

246 "It is a bad year": CLV to Samuel S. Cox, October 28, 1863, Vallandigham Collection, OHS.

246 reports of unrest and violence: Towne, *Surveillance and Spies in the Civil War*, 101–10.

247 One of the dead: Thaddeus Stevens Jr. to TS, September 28, 1863, Palmer Papers, LH.

247 Fortunately, victory was snatched: Grant, *Memoirs and Selected Letters,* 413–14; Chernow, *Grant,* 306, 323–24.

248 "General Meade's budding laurels": *Chicago Tribune,* December 8, 1863.

## 15. AN EVENT WITHOUT PARALLEL

249 Shortly after noon: CG 38/1, 365–67; "The Senate's War," pamphlet.

249 "I can think of nothing": Henry L. Dawes to Electra Dawes, December 8, 1863, Dawes Papers, LOC.

250 Tennessee Unionist Emerson Etheridge: CG 38/1, 4–11; Belz, "The Etheridge Conspiracy of 1863," *Journal of Southern History;* Foley, *Ballot Battles,* 106–7; Lindsey, *"Sunset" Cox,* 80–81; *Buffalo Evening Courier,* November 11, 1863.

250 "the pit which these": *New York World,* December 8, 1863.

251 "If Mr. Etheridge undertakes": Burlingame, ed., *With Lincoln in the White House,* 120–21.

251 Their credentials, announced Etheridge: CG 38/1, 4–5; Dennett, ed., *Lincoln and the Civil War in the Diaries and Letters of John Hay,* 130–31.

251 "a high-handed outrage": *Chicago Tribune,* December 8, 1863.

251 became "exceedingly obsequious": Ibid.

252 He would soon emerge as de facto: Lindsey, *"Sunset" Cox,* 80–81.

252 In the last session: CG 37/3, 95–97.

252 "Emerson ain't worth": Belz, "The Etheridge Conspiracy," *Journal of Southern History.*

253 "When the border States": CG 38/1, 762.

253 "Grim, savage, sarcastic": Trefousse, *Thaddeus Stevens,* 137.

254 "sweeping at him with": Benedict, *Compromise of Principle,* 42.

254 "I took the ground": William McKee to TS, January 26, 1864, Palmer Papers, LH.

254 "The nigger is done with": *New York Herald,* February 3, 1864.

255 "We cannot save the institution": CG 38/1, 1461–65; Harris, *Lincoln and the Border States,* 205–6.

255 On January 7, in reply: CG 38/1, 133.

255 On January 14: CG 38/1, 719–23, 1325.

256 "clean the statute books": CG 38/1, 1482.

256 "a poetical turn of thought": Russell, *My Diary North and South,* 145.

256 "He had no genius for": Benedict, *A Compromise of Principle,* 37–38.

257 "egotistical, susceptible to flattery": Welles, *Diary,* Vol. 1, 502.

257 "Only a few years ago": CS to Duchess of Argyll, February 8, 1864, Palmer, ed., *Selected Letters of Charles Sumner,* Vol. 2, 224.

257 "The way seems open": CS to William E. Gladstone, January 1, 1864, Palmer, ed., *Selected Letters of Charles Sumner,* Vol. 2, 218.

257 At his behest: CG 38/1, 536.

257 They came, he trumpeted: Ibid.

257 Sumner followed up: Donald, *Charles Sumner,* Part 2, 148–49.

258 Sumner pumped out: CG 38/1, 554, 1175; Donald, *Charles Sumner,* 153.

258 complained Garrett Davis: CG 38/1, 2757, 3184.

258  still "straight as an arrow": Roske, *His Own Counsel,* 81.

258  one of the most distinguished: Ibid., 1ff, 25–26.

258  There could be no question: CG 38/1, 1313ff.

259  Garrett Davis spat out: CG 38/1, 1364.

259  Another proposed: CG 38/1, 1370.

260  A third proposed: CG 38/1, 1475.

260  "the most handsome senator": Roske, *His Own Counsel,* 97; *The Liberator,* February 6, 1863; *New York Herald,* January 31, 1863.

260  Saulsbury raked the Republicans: CG 38/1, 1364–67.

261  Sumner weighed in: CG 38/1, 1479–81.

261  "'a tale told by an idiot'": CG 38/1, 1484.

262  Jowly, nearly blind: Harris, *Two Against Lincoln,* 9, 17, 26–27, 38.

262  "To manumit at once": CG 38/1, 1419–24.

## 16. NO QUARTER!

265  "Everyone says that": CG 38/1, 3449.

265  General Alfred Terry: CG 38/1, 565.

265  "It was the first time": Coffin, *Reminiscences,* 637.

265  "We want the best": WTS to Henry W. Halleck, September 4, 1864, Simpson and Berlin, eds., *Sherman's Civil War,* 700.

265  "If negroes are to fight": WTS to Edwin M. Stanton, October 25, 1864, Simpson and Berlin, eds., *Sherman's Civil War,* 740–41.

266  It had at first been supposed: CG 38/1, 564–65.

266  a "gross injustice": CG 38/1, 634.

266  Fessenden insisted that: CG 38/1, 869–70.

267  "Our country can ill afford": CG 38/1, 563.

267  "the honorable senator from Massachusetts": CG 38/1, 870.

267  The demand for more men: CG 38/1, 335–36; P. H. Watson to TS, January 27, 1864, Palmer Papers, LH; James Pollock to TS, March 18, 1864, Palmer Papers, LH.

268  "The injurious influences": SPC to TS, June 29, 1864, Palmer Papers, LH.

268  Meanwhile, unregulated speculation: Shuckers, *Life and Public Services of Salmon Portland Chase,* 356–57; Bolles, *Financial History of the United States from 1861 to 1885,* 141; Burrows and Wallace, *Gotham,* 900; diary of Charles Mason, November 30, 1863, Remey Family Papers, LOC; J. W. McMillen to TS, January 16, 1864, Palmer Papers, LH.

268  "a rat-pit in full blast": Medbery, *Men and Mysteries of Wall Street,* 244.

268  "a swamp wherein": Bolles, *Financial History of the United States from 1861 to 1885,* 143.

268  It was estimated: Henry G. Stebbins to TS, February 15, 1865, Palmer Papers, LH; Burrows and Wallace, *Gotham,* 899–901.

268  "Men leaped upon chairs": Medbery, *Men and Mysteries of Wall Street,* 241.

269  By mid-April: Larson, *Jay Cooke,* 155–57; Shuckers, *Life and Public Services of Salmon Portland Chase,* 357–60; McKay, *The Civil War and New York City,* 244.

270    Forrest's men cried, "No quarter!": *Report* of the JCCW/1864, Part 1, 21, 14; *New York Times*, April 16, 1864; *New York Herald*, April 16, 1864; CG 38/1, 1662–63; Edwin M. Stanton to "Officers commanding at Cairo," April 18, 1864, Wade Papers, LOC.

270    a shaken brigadier: M. Brayman to BFW, June 19, 1864, Wade Papers, LOC.

270    "extravagant stories": *Cairo Daily Democrat*, June 19, 1864.

271    "We saw bodies": *Report* of the JCCW/1864, Part 1, 5.

271    "The rebels would reply": Ibid., 94.

271    Several witnesses saw: Ibid., 31, 91, 107.

271    several black soldiers: Ibid., 105–10, 121–23.

271    "As they were crawling": Ibid., 39.

271    Another white cavalryman: Ibid., 34.

271    "I saw one of them": Ibid., 37.

271    "It is hoped that": Tap, *Fort Pillow Massacre*, 62.

272    "The poor deluded negroes": Achilles V. Clark to "Judith and Henrietta," Sheehan-Dean, ed., *The Civil War*, 42–44.

272    Wade wrote, "the testimony herewith": *Report* of the JCCW/1864, Part 1, 2–4.

273    "literally the appearance": *Report* of the JCCW 1864/Part II, 1–2.

273    "fled from the work": Julian, *Political Recollections*, 239.

273    "Your committee," Wade wrote: *Report* of the JCCW/1864, Part II, 3.

273–74    "If the president supposes": *New York Times*, January 3, 1863.

274    The problem of the freedmen: Manning, *Troubled Refuge*, 107, 162–63, 213–15.

274–75    "honey-tongued humanitarians": CG 38/1, 709.

275    On December 8, Lincoln: "Proclamation of Amnesty and Reconstruction," www.freedmen.umd.edu/pracamn.htm.

275    Lincoln elaborated on this: CG 38/1, Appendix, 3ff.

276    "Sunset" Cox scoffed: Cox, *Eight Years in Congress*, 376.

276    "The public mind": *New York Times*, December 10, 1863.

276    a "wonderful effect": *New York Herald*, December 8, 1863.

276    John Hay claimed: Dennett, ed., *Lincoln and the Civil War in the Diaries and Letters of John Hay*, 131–32.

276    "they will not only reenslave": CG 37/2, 1926.

276    Resistance quickly built: CG 38/1, 184, 266, 316–19; Trefousse, *Benjamin Franklin Wade*, 138–39; *New York Times*, February 6, 1864; Sumner, "Our Domestic Relations," *Atlantic Monthly*.

276    a de facto "secessionist": *New York Times*, February 6, 1864.

277    A repentant former slave owner: Harris, *Lincoln and the Border States*, 283, 288–89.

277    "We cannot stand still": CG 38/1, Appendix, 44–46.

277    "Our success will be": CG 38/1, 83–85.

278    "I am perfectly content": Harris, *Lincoln and the Border States*, 288.

278    the "enormous vacuum": CG 38/1, Appendix, 44–46.

278    To counter Davis: Cox, *Eight Years in Congress*, 383–87.

279    "half-breed bastards born": Ibid., 390–91.

### 17. MAJORITIES MUST RULE

282  "We had to have hard fighting": Grant, *Memoirs and Selected Letters*, 512.

282  In contrast to his predecessors: USG to WTS, April 4, 1864, Sheehan-Dean, ed., *The Civil War*, 21.

282  "I am more than ever": Elwood Griest to "Dear Wife," April 13, 1864, Griest Papers, LH.

283  unwilling draftees now filled the ranks: Geary, *We Need Men*, 125–26, 132–33.

283  "Look a-here": Ibid., 123.

283  On May 5: Grant, *Memoirs and Selected Letters*, 512ff; Sears, *Lincoln's Lieutenants*, 620ff; USG to Henry W. Halleck, May 7, 1864, Grant, *Memoirs and Selected Letters*, 1053; "Journal of Theodore Lyman," Sheehan-Dean, ed., *The Civil War*, 68–89; Charles Brewster to Martha and Mary Brewster, May 11, 1864, Sheehan-Dean, ed., *The Civil War*, 113ff.

284  "On to Richmond!": Horace Porter, from *Campaigning with Grant*, Sheehan-Dean, ed., *The Civil War*, 100–101.

284  "I saw one [man] completely": Charles Brewster to Martha and Mary Brewster, May 11, 1864, Sheehan-Dean, ed., *The Civil War*, 118.

284  "a footrace to Richmond": *Lancaster Examiner*, May 7, 1864.

284  "Butler on the War Path!": *Lancaster Examiner*, May 14, 1864.

285  "What a ghastly spectacle": Elwood Griest to "Dear Wife," May 1, 1864, Griest Papers, LH.

285  "It is still kill": Howe, ed., *Touched with Fire*, 137.

285  "I tell you many a man": Oliver Wendell Holmes to "Dear Parents," June 24, 1864, Howe, ed., *Touched with Fire*, 150.

285  "It is a tearful place": Smith, *Life and Letters of James Abram Garfield*, Vol. 1, 370.

285  Veterans knew it was suicidal: Grant, *Memoirs and Selected Letters*, 579–88; Frank Wilkeson, from *Recollections*, in Sheehan-Dean, ed., *The Civil War*, 178ff.

286  Zachariah Chandler . . . was dining: Stampp, *Indiana Politics During the Civil War*, 211; *Lancaster Examiner*, June 4, 1864.

286  In a widely distributed letter: "Pomeroy Circular," broadside.

287  "treatcherous imbecility": Adam Gurowski to BFW, January 14, 1864, Wade Papers, LOC.

287  John Hiestand, a Pennsylvania journalist: John Hiestand to TS, May 29, 1864, Palmer and Ochoa, eds., *Selected Papers of Thaddeus Stevens*, Vol. 1, 480–81.

287  Pomeroy had warmly praised: "Pomeroy Circular," broadside.

287  Chase's friends in Ohio: S. S. Osborn to BFW, February 8, 1864, Wade Papers, LOC; Benjamin F. Butler to J. K. Herbert, Marshall, ed., *Private and Official Correspondence of Gen. Benjamin F. Butler During the Period of the Civil War*, Vol. 4, 292.

287  "the imbecile and vacillating policy": Nicolay and Hay, *Abraham Lincoln*, Vol. 9, 30–31.

288  "a concourse of departed spirits": *Lancaster Examiner*, June 4, 1864.

288  "bound hand and foot": Smith, *Life and Letters of James Abram Garfield*, Vol. 1, 377.

288  "He will probably be": James A. Garfield to Harmon Austin, March 4, 1864, in ibid., 376.

288  "I don't know a dozen": James A. Garfield to "Rhodes," April 28, 1864, in ibid., 376.

288  The crafters of the platform the Republicans adopted: Basler, ed., *Collected Works of Abraham Lincoln*, Vol. 7, 380–82.

289  Hamlin had every reason to assume: McClure, *Abraham Lincoln and Men of War-Times*, 115ff; Blaine, *Twenty Years of Congress from Lincoln to Garfield*, 517ff; Charles Eugene Hamlin, *Life and Times of Hannibal Hamlin*, 461ff; Hunt, *Hannibal Hamlin of Maine*, 151ff, 173; Flood, *1864*, 131ff.

289  a boring "old mouser": "Addresses delivered . . . in commemoration of the lives and public services of James M. Ashley and Alpheus Felch," January 10, 1897, at www.lib.umich.edu.

289  In a brief note: AL to John G. Nicolay and John Hay, June 6, 1864, Basler, ed., *Collected Works of Abraham Lincoln*, Vol. 7, 376.

290  However, Alexander McClure: McClure, *Abraham Lincoln and Men of War-Times*, 121.

290  "treason must be made odious": *Lancaster Examiner*, June 18, 1864.

290  "that patriot Senator": *Atlantic Monthly*, October 1863.

290  Johnson had "stood in the furnace": Charles Eugene Hamlin, *Life and Times of Hannibal Hamlin*, 476.

290  In later years, Hamlin: Ibid., 461–67.

290  According to this scenario: Blaine, *Twenty Years of Congress from Lincoln to Garfield*, 521.

291  According to McClure: McClure, *Abraham Lincoln and Men of War-Times*, 123; Flood, *1864*, 141–42.

291  "incorruptible patriot": *Lancaster Examiner*, June 18, 1864.

291  "Can't you get a candidate": McClure, *Abraham Lincoln and Men of War-Times*, 282.

292  a storm of bills blew: CG 38/1, 3533–36.

292  Pitt Fessenden . . . begged: CG 38/1, 2740–41.

292  "I have neither": CG 38/1, 2758.

292  the "pigmies" who: CG 38/1, 2981.

292  "at bayonet point": CG 38/1, 2992.

293  "I will trust the freed": CG 38/1, 2985.

293  "It now reels and staggers": CG 38/1, 2988.

293  The Radicals fared better: CG 38/1, 3078, 3104; Egerton, *Thunder at the Gates*, 202–9, 237–38; McPherson, *Negro's Civil War*, 197ff.

293  He termed it a "transition": CG 38/1, 3300–3302.

294  Democrats in both chambers: CG 38/1, 3346ff.

294  "No government farming system": CG 38/1, 709.

294  "The negro had nothing": CG 38/1, 3342.

294  "It is a social": CG 38/1, 3349.

294  "I would use locomotives": Ibid.

295  In defense of the bill: Ibid.

296   the exasperated Speaker: CG 38/1, 3531–32.
296   In parting, Elihu Washburne: CG 38/1, 3534–35.

## 18. BLEEDING, BANKRUPT, AND DYING COUNTRY

298   "I can't hold out": Jellison, *Fessenden of Maine,* 180.
299   "Have you resigned?": Ibid.
299   Chase's often contentious reign: Nicolay and Hay, *Abraham Lincoln,* Vol. 9, 92–97.
299   As Nicolay and Hay recalled it: Ibid., 99–102.
300   Even the violently: Jellison, *Fessenden of Maine,* 183.
300   The Finance Committee required: WPF to Joseph Tremayne? (name unclear), December 17, 1864, Fessenden Papers, BCL.
301   "I cannot doubt": Thomas W. Elliot to WPF, July 1, 1864, Fessenden Papers, BCL.
301   "Some of our staunchest friends": B. F. Mudgett to WPF, July 7, 1864, Fessenden Papers, BCL.
301   Wrote one, "More depends": E. M. Moffett to WPF, July 9, 1864, Fessenden Papers, BCL.
301   "Unless the direction": (name unreadable) to WPF, July 21, 1864, Fessenden Papers, BCL.
302   "All the fight is whipped": CG 38/1, 3534.
302   Ben Wade and Gideon Welles: Welles, *Diary,* Vol. 2, 74–75; Sears, *Lincoln's Lieutenants,* 721–22.
302   On July 30: *Report* of the JCCW/1865, 1–12, 30–31ff, 105ff; Sears, *Lincoln's Lieutenants,* 726–31.
303   "The world shook": *Cleveland Daily Leader,* August 1, 1864.
303   "a perfect slaughter pen": *New York Tribune,* August 2, 1864.
303   "It was the saddest affair": USG to Henry W. Halleck, August 1, 1864, in Grant, *Memoirs and Selected Letters,* 1063.
304   "There is a grate meny": Jameson Harvey to TS, June 30, 1864, Palmer Papers, LH.
304   More and more moderate Copperheads: Diary of Charles Mason, January 25, 1864, Remey Family Papers, LOC.
304   Reports circulated of: Weber, *Copperheads,* 128ff, 165–66; J. H. Potter to BFW, August 4, 1864, Wade Papers, LOC.
304   "we trust that some bold": Weber, *Copperheads,* 159.
304   Wendell Phillips blamed: Nicolay and Hay, *Abraham Lincoln,* Vol. 9, 35, 37.
304   Horace Greeley, who had spent: Horace Greeley to AL, July 7, 1864, Basler, ed., *Collected Works of Abraham Lincoln,* Vol. 7, 435.
304   The war was now costing: McClure, *Abraham Lincoln and Men of War-Times,* 117, 124.
305   In a letter to Wade: Orson S. Murray to BFW, September 6, 1864, Wade Papers, LOC.
305   Lincoln replied that: Nicolay and Hay, *Abraham Lincoln,* Vol. 9, 105ff; Long, *The Jewel of Liberty,* 183ff.

306 "caused a great effervescence": Nicolay and Hay, *Abraham Lincoln*, Vol. 9, 105ff.

306 He reiterated: "Proclamation Concerning Reconstruction," July 8, 1864, Basler, ed., *Collected Works of Abraham Lincoln*, Vol. 7, 433–34.

306 "What an infamous proclamation!": TS to Edward McPherson, July 10, 1864, Palmer and Ochoa, eds., *Selected Papers of Thaddeus Stevens*, Vol. 1, 500.

306 On August 5, Wade and Davis: *New York Tribune*, August 5, 1864; Nicolay and Hay, *Abraham Lincoln*, Vol. 9, 125–27.

307 Disaffected Radicals talked: Nicolay and Hay, *Abraham Lincoln*, Vol. 9, 56.

307 Lincoln had to be "gotten rid of": Henry Winter Davis to ZC, August 24, 1864, Chandler Papers, LOC.

307 Wade, however, was a lion: Trefousse, *Benjamin Franklin Wade*, 224ff.

307 the manifesto was "one of": Ibid., 224.

307 "though coarse and vulgar": Welles, *Diary*, Vol. 2, 95.

308 the manifesto's "violence of language": *National Anti-Slavery Standard*, August 13, 1864.

308 "by far the most effective": *New York Times*, August 13, 1864.

308 "some sleek conservative": A. Taylor to BFW, September 8, 1864, Wade Papers, LOC.

308 "the greatest widow maker": *La Crosse Daily Democrat*, August 15 and 24, 1864.

308 "I am at my wit's end": Jellison, *Fessenden of Maine*, 186.

309 "the tide is setting strongly": Henry J. Raymond to AL, August 22, 1864, Lincoln Papers, LOC.

309 "This morning, as for some days": "Blind Memorandum," August 23, 1864, www.housedivided.dickinson.edu.

309 "all remaining questions": AL to Henry J. Raymond, August 24, 1864, Basler, ed., *Collected Works of Abraham Lincoln*, Vol. 7, 518.

309 "It would be ignominiously surrendering": Nicolay and Hay, *Abraham Lincoln*, Vol. 9, 221.

309 "Everything is darkness": John Nicolay to John Hay, August 25, 1864, Burlingame, *With Lincoln in the White House*, 152.

310 He wrote to the president: Frederick Douglass to AL, August 29, 1864, Holzer, *Dear Mr. Lincoln*, 268–70.

310 "dipping a little into": Weber, *Copperheads*, 128.

310 "I calmly dwell now": James L. Vallandigham, *Life of Clement L. Vallandigham*, 346.

310 Its Declaration of Principles: Klement, "Vallandigham as an Exile in Canada, 1863–1864," *Ohio History;* Holt, "The Great Conspiracy," anonymous pamphlet; Weber, *Copperheads*, 115.

311 After Vallandigham's death: James L. Vallandigham, *Life of Clement L. Vallandigham*, 370–75.

311 "Falstaffian proportions": Ibid., 352.

311 "He came unheralded": Klement, "Vallandigham as an Exile in Canada, 1863–1864," *Ohio History.*

312 If there was any powerful "conspiracy": James L. Vallandigham, *Life of Clement L. Vallandigham*, 360.

312 "That I cannot with safety start": CLV to "Mother," July 7, 1864, Vallandigham Collection, OHS.

## 19. THE PEOPLE DECIDE

313 "shoddy abolitionists in disguise": "The Real Chicago Platform as Expounded by the Democratic Orators at Chicago," broadside.

314 "The majority of the party": Mason diary, February 21, 1864, Remey Family Papers, LOC.

314 Although born and raised in Philadelphia: Sears, *George B. McClellan*, 116–17.

314 Vallandigham was ubiquitous: Zornow, "Clement L. Vallandigham and the Democratic Party in 1864," *Bulletin of the Historical and Philosophical Society of Ohio*, January 1961.

314 Vallandigham suspected, correctly: Ibid.

315 The platform declared: Ibid.

315 Lincoln "thinks a proclamation": "The Real Chicago Platform as Expounded by the Democratic Orators at Chicago," broadside.

315 "The Union is the one condition": GBM to Democratic Nominating Committee, September 8, 1864, Sears, ed., *Civil War Papers of George B. McClellan*, 595–96.

315 "For all the good": Weber, *Copperheads*, 170.

315 The most ardent Copperheads: James L. Vallandigham, *Life of Clement L. Vallandigham*, 366–77; Zornow, "Clement L. Vallandigham and the Democratic Party in 1864," *Bulletin of the Historical and Philosophical Society of Ohio*.

316 "Don't send any politicians": GBM to William C. Prime, August 10, 1864, Sears, ed., *Civil War Papers of George B. McClellan*, 586.

316 "It would be better for me": GBM to Charles Mason, October 3, 1864, Sears, ed., *Civil War Papers of George B. McClellan*, 609.

316 "Our people now look": Cooper, ed., *Jefferson Davis: The Essential Writings*, 219–23.

316 "Let fresh victories crown": Ibid., 351.

316 On the eve of the election: Ibid., 355–56.

317 "If the people raise a howl": WTS to Henry W. Halleck, September 4, 1864, Simpson and Berlin, eds., *Sherman's Civil War*, 697.

318 "You must see my whole heart": ZC to Letitia Chandler, August 27, 1864, Chandler Papers, LOC.

318 "I have been running": ZC to Letitia Chandler, September 24, 1864, Chandler Papers, LOC.

318 Frémont at last announced: Trefousse, "Zachariah Chandler and the Withdrawal of Frémont in 1864," *Lincoln Herald*.

318 Lincoln's administration "has been": Welles, *Diary*, Vol. 2, 156.

319 "The Hon. old Roger B. Taney": Strong, *Diary*, 519.

319 "This canvass differs": Benjamin F. Butler to William Clafflin, October 30, 1864, Marshall, ed., *Private and Official Correspondence of Gen. Benjamin F. Butler During the Period of the Civil War*, Vol. 5, 301.

320 "The battlefields of 1864": Long, *Jewel of Liberty*, 196.

320 "a miserable trickster": *Lancaster Intelligencer*, September 8, 1864.

320  "the NERO who fiddles": *Lancaster Intelligencer,* September 1, 1864.

320  "the rottenest, most stinking": Weber, *Copperheads,* 142.

320  "diabolism incarnate": *Lancaster Intelligencer,* July 14, 1864.

320  Whispering campaigns alleged"; Charles Mason diary, January 4, 1864, Remey Family Papers, LOC.

320  a seventy-two-page pamphlet: "Miscegenation: The Theory of the Blending of the Races, Applied to the American White Man and Negro," pamphlet.

321  Some of the North's most famous: Long, *Jewel of Liberty,* 158.

321  a "negro ball": Wood, *Black Scare,* 72.

321  "a real, completely organized": Ibid., 61.

321  "unbridled and unbroken-in": Ibid., 64.

321  "No system," declared Cox: CG 38 / 1, 708–13.

322  "I, for one, have never": Sears, ed., *Civil War Papers of George B. McClellan,* 616.

322  "Elect McClellan, and": Palmer and Ochoa, eds., *Selected Papers of Thaddeus Stevens,* Vol. 1, 500–502; *Lancaster Examiner,* September 14, 1864.

322  "Let us forget that": *Lancaster Examiner,* October 24, 1864.

322  "dealing stalwart blows": G. Volney Dorsey to BFW, September 13, 1864, Wade Papers, LOC.

322  "I only wish we could do": BFW to ZC, October 2, 1864, Chandler Papers, LOC.

323  "Both fraud and force": Diary of Charles Mason, November 2, 1864, Remey Family Papers, LOC.

323  "Everything is at sixes": Nicolay and Hay, *Abraham Lincoln,* Vol. 9, 372.

323  scare pacifist Dunkers and Mennonites: John Naille to TS, October 14, 1864, Palmer Papers, LH.

323  Not all of this was fantasy: *New York Herald,* November 7, 1864; Weber, *Copperheads,* 193ff.

324  Meanwhile, the Republican press: Zornow, "Clement L. Vallandigham and the Democratic Party in 1864," *Bulletin of the Historical and Philosophical Society of Ohio;* James L. Vallandigham, *Life of Clement L. Vallandigham,* 385.

324  "The nation who votes": *New York Tribune,* October 3, 1864.

324  "the conspiracies against the government": *Cleveland Daily Leader,* November 7, 1864.

324  "A crisis is approaching": Diary of Charles Mason, October 2, 1864, Remey Family Papers, LOC.

324  Radical Republicans in New York: C. E. Frost to Benjamin F. Butler, November 6, 1864, Marshall, ed., *Private and Official Correspondence of Benjamin F. Butler,* Vol. 5, 320.

324  while agents from the Democratic-controlled: Diary of Charles Mason, November 2, 1864, Remey Family Papers, LOC.

324  "His present business": Benjamin F. Butler to Edwin M. Stanton, October 22, 1864, Marshall, ed., *Private and Official Correspondence of Benjamin F. Butler,* Vol. 5, 277.

325  "All is favorable": GBM to Samuel L. M. Barlow, October 27, 1864, Sears, ed., *Civil War Papers of George B. McClellan,* 617.

325  if the voters "should deliberately": *New York Times,* October 20, 1864.

325   With fears of unrest peaking: Marshall, ed., *Private and Official Correspondence of Benjamin F. Butler*, Vol. 5, 315–20, 327–33.

325   "Thousands of bits of paper": Waugh, *Reelecting Lincoln*, 348.

325   "The Almighty must have stuffed": Thayer, ed., *Life and Letters of John Hay*, Vol. 1, 238–42; Nicolay and Hay, *Abraham Lincoln*, Vol. 9, 376–77.

326   *"Laus Deo!"*: Strong, *Diary*, November 9, 1864, 511.

326   "For my country's sake": GBM to Samuel L. M. Barlow, November 10, 1864, November 10, 1864, Sears, ed., *Civil War Papers of George B. McClellan*, 618.

326   "The election was a necessity": Basler, ed., *Collected Works of Abraham Lincoln*, Vol. 8, 100–101.

## 20. HURRAH FOR FREEDOM!

328   as martial bands played: WTS to Henry W. Halleck and to George H. Thomas, both November 11, 1864, Simpson and Berlin, eds., *Sherman's Civil War*, 757–58.

328   "make Georgia howl": WTS to USG, October 9, 1864, Simpson and Berlin, eds., *Sherman's Civil War*, 731.

328   "They flock to me": WTS to Ellen E. Sherman, December 25, 1864, Simpson and Berlin, eds., *Sherman's Civil War*, 778.

329   the president put a positive slant: CG 38/2, 1ff.

330   "I do not think I am extravagant": CG 38/2, 124.

331   An imposing, clean-shaven man: Horowitz, *Great Impeacher*, 2ff, 41; "Addresses Delivered in the Unitarian Church, Ann Arbor, Michigan, January 10, 1897," pamphlet.

332   "I beg to present you": WTS to AL, December 22, 1864, Sherman, *Memoirs*, 711.

332   "From my earliest youth": Palmer and Ochoa, eds., *Selected Papers of Thaddeus Stevens*, Vol. 1, 520ff.

334   Earlier, "Sunset" Cox had attempted: CG 38/2, 125.

334   "unwise, impolitic," and manifestly unconstitutional: CG 38/2, 194–95.

334   George Pendleton, McClellan's erstwhile: CG 38/2, 223.

335   "like stormy petrels": CG 38/2, 238–42.

336   The most pivotal of the lame ducks: Cox, *Eight Years in Congress*, 397–98; Lindsey, *"Sunset" Cox*, 93–95; Richards, *Who Freed the Slaves?*, 118–19, 187ff; CG 38/2, 2995.

336   "I was anxious": Cox, *Eight Years*, 397–98.

337   "Such was the exigency": Boutwell, *Reminiscences of Sixty Years in Public Affairs*, Vol. 2, 36.

337   What is clear, however: CG 38/2, 151–53, 170–74, 258–60, 524–25, 531; Burlingame, *With Lincoln in the White House*, 171; Richards, *Who Freed the Slaves?*, 205–11.

338   "The tumult of joy": *New York Tribune*, February 1, 2, and 3, 1865; *New York Times*, January 31, 1865; *New York Herald*, February 1, 1865; *Lancaster Intelligencer*, February 8, 1865.

338   "Such rejoicing I never before": Blight, *Frederick Douglass*, 454.

338 "Freedom Triumphant": *New York Tribune,* February 1, 1865.

339 On January 31, Lincoln directed: CG 38/2, 729–30; Welles, *Diary,* Vol. 2, 235–36; Stahr, *Seward,* 421–26; Burlingame, *With Lincoln in the White House,* 172–73.

339 Ben Wade was shocked: George, *Zachariah Chandler,* 120.

339 "foolish, unauthorized, *unholy*": Ibid.

339 But Thaddeus Stevens: CG 38/2, 733–34.

340 Lincoln's position was quite different: Richards, *Who Freed the Slaves?,* 218–19, 227.

340 The Radical Henry Winter Davis: CG 38/2, 969–70.

340 The Radicals in Congress: Horowitz, *Great Impeacher,* 106ff.

341 "There ought to be no pariahs": Garfield, *Works,* Vol. 1, 86.

341 pointed out Rep. William Kelley: CG 38/3, 282–90.

342 "Why do you keep us": CG 38/2, 971.

343 Union-occupied areas of the rebel states were: CG 38/2, 988; Bickers, "The Power to Do What Manifestly Must Be Done," *Roger Williams University Law Review;* Foner, *Reconstruction,* 62–64, 70–74; *Lancaster Intelligencer,* January 25, 1865.

344 "What is freedom?": Garfield, *Works,* Vol. 1, 86.

344 As Sumner's enabling resolution put it: CG 38/2, 79, 563.

344 a veritable "second government": CG 38/1, 3346, 760.

344 "the blood of a murdered Constitution": CG 38/1, 2969.

345 "As long as you hold them up": CG 38/2, 985.

345 "The less restraint we put": CG 38/2, 689.

345 In the bureau's defense: CG 38/2, 692–93.

345 "Emancipation is not": CG 38/2, 961–62.

345 Only the federal government had the resources: CG 38/1, 2798–99.

346 "broken-down politicians, dilapidated preachers": CG 38/2, 1307–8.

346 A drenching rain soaked: *New York Tribune,* March 6, 1865; *Washington Evening Star,* March 4, 1865.

346 In his final words: CG 38/2, 1424.

347 Already hungover: Isaac Bassett Diary, Office of the U.S. Senate Historian; Charles Eugene Hamlin, *Life and Times of Hannibal Hamlin,* 497–98.

347 In what turned into a maudlin: CG 38/2, 1394–95.

347 Johnson then "slobbered": George, *Zachariah Chandler,* 124; generally, Welles, *Diary,* Vol. 2, 252; *New York World,* March 7, 1865; Trefousse, *Andrew Johnson,* 189–190.

347 "I was never so mortified": quoted in Trefousse, *Andrew Johnson,* 190.

348 He recalled that four years earlier: CG 38/2, 1424.

348 "We Know No Master": *New York Times,* March 30, 1865; *New York Tribune,* April 4, 1865.

349 On the night of April 2: Furgurson, *Ashes of Glory,* 331–32, 339; *Philadelphia Press,* April 4 and 6, 1865, in Sheehan-Dean, ed., *The Civil War,* 656–57.

350 "Ben was crazy": Oberholtzer, *Jay Cooke,* Vol. 1, 527.

350 vast spontaneous crowds cheered: Strong, *Diary,* April 3, 1865, 574–75; *New York Times,* April 4, 1865.

350 "Boys, your work is done": Sears, *Lincoln's Lieutenants,* 756.

350  On April 11, Lincoln appeared: *New York Tribune*, April 12, 1865.

351  "The government cannot": *New York Tribune*, April 13, 1865.

351  On April 14: Blair and Kytle, *Civil War Monitor* 8 (Winter 2018); *New York Times*, April 18, 1865.

352  "I thank God": *New York Times*, April 18, 1865.


### EPILOGUE

353  In the early hours: Trefousse, *Thaddeus Stevens*, 159.

353  "Treason must be punished": CG 39/1, 932.

353  "Johnson, we have faith in you": Julian, *Political Recollections*, 257.

354  "In the question of colored": Donald, *Charles Sumner*, Vol. 2, 222.

354  At the beginning of May: Schurz, *Report on Condition of the South 1865*, 6ff, 28ff, 68–69, 77, 162ff; Fessenden, *Report of the Joint Committee on Reconstruction*, 7ff.

354  "I see our worthy president": TS to William D. Kelley, May 30, 1865, Palmer and Ochoa, eds., *Selected Papers of Thaddeus Stevens*, Vol. 2, 6.

354  "We have lost the whole moral effect": BFW to CS, July 29, 1866, Trefousse, *Benjamin Franklin Wade*, 257.

355  He insultingly spurned: Blight, *Frederick Douglass*, 474–75.

355  When Sumner begged him: Donald, *Charles Sumner*, Vol. 2, 238.

355  "Can you not hold your hand": TS to Andrew Johnson, July 6, 1865, Palmer and Ochoa, eds., *Selected Papers of Thaddeus Stevens*, Vol. 2, 7.

356  Their ultimate goal, as Stevens put it: CG 39/1, 1309.

356  Radicals "are the men who": CG 38/2, 158ff.

356  "I could not rest": CG 39/1, 986.

356  Meanwhile, white terrorism: Foner, *Reconstruction*, 119–21, 262–63, 343.

357  "There is not a Radical leader": Hurst, *Nathan Bedford Forrest*, 314.

357  "While the South has been": CG 39/1, 1213–14.

357  "Treason, defeated in the field": Fessenden, *Report of the Joint Committee on Reconstruction*, 7ff.

358  Unlike Stevens and Wade: CG 39/1, 705–8; Cook, *Civil War Senator*, 215–18.

358  Their labors led ultimately: CG 39/1, 3148–49; Trefousse, *Thaddeus Stevens*, 185–86.

359  The same day, Congress passed: Trefousse, *Thaddeus Stevens*, 207–8, 226–27.

360  At Stevens's direction, articles: CG 40/2, 1336ff, 1382ff, 1399–1401.

360  Emaciated and tinged: *New York Times*, February 26, 1868.

361  "a great deal of showy silk": *New York Herald*, May 17, 1868.

361  A reporter later remembered: *New York Times*, May 17, 1868.

361  "Conviction had him to dinner": Ibid.

361  "The great Radical party has been": *New York Herald*, May 17, 1868.

361  Most prominent among the seven Republicans: Cook, *Civil War Senator*, 232–34.

361  Stevens was livid: *New York Times*, May 17, 1868; *New York Tribune*, May 16, 1868; Trefousse, *Thaddeus Stevens*, 230.

362  "It is the meanest case": McClure, *Abraham Lincoln and Men of War-Times*, 285.

362   Others resented his advocacy: Trefousse, *Benjamin Franklin Wade*, 285ff.

362   "My life has been a failure": McClure, *Abraham Lincoln and Men of War-Times*, 286.

363   "the evil genius of": *New York Times*, August 13, 1868.

363   "Stevens was ever clearing": McClure, *Abraham Lincoln and Men of War-Times*, 279ff.

364   Even the tsar of Russia had given: *New York Herald*, March 20, 1867.

364   "All apprehensions of the return": *New York Times*, November 8, 1867.

365   On August 31, he retired: Cook, *Civil War Senator*, 244.

366   "The accumulation of obloquy": CLV to James W. Wall, November 26, 1865, Vallandigham Collection, OHS.

366   In June 1871, he was defending: James L. Vallandigham, *Life of Clement L. Vallandigham*, 516–17, 524–30.

366   In 1918, Eugene Debs: Lepore, "The Fireman," *The New Yorker*, February 18, 2019.

367   "Whereas Republicans equated dissent": Klement, *Limits of Dissent*, 321.

367   "the strong arm": CG 38/2, 1372

367   "we have a right": Ibid., 1373.

368   "The dream of national progress": CG 36/2, 341–44.

368   "If we divide into two sections": CG 37/1, 262.

368   Lincoln said, "we cannot escape history": CG 37/3 Appendix, 1ff.

370   Ever true to his egalitarian convictions: Trefousse, *Benjamin Franklin Wade*, 313–15.

370   "I feel that to have emancipated": BFW to Uriah H. Painter, April 9, 1877, in *New York Times*, March 4, 1878.

371   "the last of the Congressional Champions": *New York Times*, March 3, 1878.

371   "leading the bravest": *Washington Post*, March 4, 1878.

# BIBLIOGRAPHY

## BOOKS

Ambrosius, Lloyd E. *A Crisis of Republicanism: American Politics During the Civil War Era*. Lincoln: University of Nebraska Press, 1990.

Ames, Mary Clemmer. *Ten Years in Washington: Life and Scenes in the National Capital as a Woman Sees Them*. Hartford, CT: A. D. Worthington & Co., 1874.

Andrews, J. Cutler. *The North Reports the Civil War*. Pittsburgh: University of Pittsburgh Press, 1955.

Ayers, Edward L. *The Thin Light of Freedom: The Civil War and Emancipation in the Heart of America*. New York: W. W. Norton, 2017.

Barron, David J. *Waging War: The Clash Between Presidents and Congress, 1776 to ISIS*: New York: Simon & Schuster, 2016.

Basler, Roy B., ed. *The Collected Works of Abraham Lincoln*. New Brunswick, NJ: Rutgers University Press, 1953.

Beale, Howard K. *Diary of Gideon Welles*, Vols. 1 and 2. New York: W. W. Norton, 1960.

Benedict, Michael Les. *A Compromise of Principle: Congressional Republicans and Reconstruction, 1863–1869*. New York: W. W. Norton, 1974.

Bernstein, Iver. *The New York City Draft Riots: The Significance for American Society and Politics in the Age of the Civil War*. New York: Oxford University Press, 1990.

Blaine, James G. *Twenty Years of Congress from Lincoln to Garfield*. Norwich, CT: Henry Bill Publishing Co., 1884.

Blair, William A. *With Malice Toward Some: Treason and Loyalty in the Civil War Era*. Chapel Hill: University of North Carolina Press, 2014.

Blight, David W. *Frederick Douglass: Prophet of Freedom*. New York: Simon & Schuster, 2018.

Bogue, Allan G. *The Congressman's Civil War*. New York: Cambridge University Press, 1989.

———. *The Earnest Men: Republicans of the Civil War Senate*. Ithaca, NY: Cornell University Press, 1981.

———. "Some Dimensions of Power in the Thirty-Seventh Senate," in *The Dimensions of Quantitative Research in American History*. Edited by William

Aydedotte, Allan G. Bogue, and Robert W. Fogel. Princeton, NJ: Princeton University Press, 1972.

Bolles, Albert S. *The Financial History of the United States from 1861 to 1885.* New York: Appleton & Co., 1886.

Boutwell, George S. *Reminiscences of Sixty Years in Public Affairs,* Vol. 2. New York: McClure Phillips Co., 1902.

Boykin, Edward. *Congress and the Civil War.* New York: McBride, 1955.

Brands, H. W. *The Money Men: Capitalism, Democracy, and the Hundred Years' War over the American Dollar.* New York: W. W. Norton, 2006.

Brodie, Fawn M. *Thaddeus Stevens: Scourge of the South.* New York: W. W. Norton, 1966.

Brooks, Noah. *Washington in Lincoln's Time.* New York: Century Co., 1895.

Burlingame, Michael, ed. *Lincoln Observed: The Civil War Dispatches of Noah Brooks.* Baltimore: Johns Hopkins University Press, 1998.

———, ed. *With Lincoln in the White House: Letters, Memoranda, and Other Writings of John G. Nicolay, 1860–1865.* Carbondale: Southern Illinois University Press, 2000.

Burrows, Edwin G., and Mike Wallace. *Gotham: A History of New York City to 1898.* New York: Oxford University Press, 1999.

Channing, Steven A. *Crisis of Fear: Secession in South Carolina.* New York: W. W. Norton, 1974.

Chase, Salmon P. *Report of the Secretary of the Treasury on the State of the Finances for the Year Ending June 30, 1861.* Washington, D.C.: Government Printing Office, 1861.

Chernow, Ron. *Grant.* New York: Penguin, 2017.

Chesnut, Mary Boykin. *A Diary from Dixie.* New York: D. Appleton & Co., 1906.

Coffin, Levi. *Reminiscences.* Cincinnati: Western Tract Society, 1879.

Cook, Robert J. *Civil War Senator: William Pitt Fessenden and the Fight to Save the American Republic.* Baton Rouge: Louisiana State University Press, 2011.

Cooper, William J., Jr. *Jefferson Davis, American.* New York: Vintage, 2001.

———, ed. *Jefferson Davis: The Essential Writings.* New York: Modern Library, 2003.

Cox, Samuel S. *Eight Years in Congress.* New York: D. Appleton & Co., 1865.

Crawford, Samuel W. *The History of the Fall of Fort Sumter: Being an Inside History of the Affairs in South Carolina and Washington, 1860–61.* New York: Jenkins & McCowan, 1887.

Cross, Coy F. *Justin Morrill: Father of the Land-Grant Colleges.* East Lansing: Michigan State University Press, 1999.

Curry, Leonard P. *Blueprint for Modern America: Nonmilitary Legislation of the First Civil War Congress.* Nashville: Vanderbilt University Press, 1968.

Davis, Burke. *Sherman's March.* New York: Vintage, 1988.

Dean, Adam Wesley. *An Agrarian Republic: Farming, Antislavery Politics, and Nature Parks in the Civil War Era.* Chapel Hill: University of North Carolina Press, 2015.

Dennett, Tyler, ed. *Lincoln and the Civil War in the Diaries and Letters of John Hay.* New York: Dodd, Mead & Co., 1939.

Detzer, David. *Allegiance: Fort Sumter, Charleston, and the Beginning of the Civil War.* New York: Harcourt, 2001.

Dickens, Charles. *American Notes*. New York: Penguin, 2000.

Donald, David H. *Lincoln*. New York: Touchstone, 1995.

———. *Lincoln Reconsidered*. New York: Vintage, 2001.

———. *Charles Sumner*. New York: Da Capo, 1996.

Doubleday, Abner. *Reminiscences of Forts Sumter and Moultrie in 1860–61*. New York: Harper & Bros., 1876.

Dowdey, Clifford, ed. *The Wartime Papers of Robert E. Lee*. Boston: Little, Brown, 1961.

Edwards, Richard, Jacob K. Firefeld, and Rebecca S. Wingo. *Homesteading the Plains: Toward a New History*. Lincoln: University of Nebraska Press, 2017.

Egerton, Douglas R. *Thunder at the Gates: The Black Civil War Regiments That Redeemed America*. New York: Basic Books, 2016.

———. *Year of Meteors: Stephen A. Douglas, Abraham Lincoln, and the Election That Brought on the Civil War*. New York: Bloomsbury, 2010.

Eisenschiml, Otto, and Ralph Newman. *The American Iliad*. New York: Bobbs-Merrill, 1947.

Escott, Paul D. *Lincoln's Dilemma: Blair, Sumner, and the Republican Struggle over Racism and Equality in the Civil War Era*. Charlottesville: University of Virginia Press, 2014.

Fehrenbacher, Don E., ed. *Abraham Lincoln: Speeches, Letters, Miscellaneous Writings, Presidential Messages and Proclamations*. New York: Library of America, 1989.

Fessenden, Francis. *The Life and Public Services of William Pitt Fessenden*. Boston: Houghton Mifflin, 1907.

Fessenden, William P. *Report of the Joint Committee on Reconstruction*. Washington, D.C.: Government Printing Office, 1866.

Finkelman, Paul, and Donald R. Kennon, eds. *Congress and the People's Contest: The Conduct of the Civil War*. Athens: Ohio University Press, 2018.

Flood, Charles Bracelen. *1864: Lincoln at the Gates of History*. New York: Simon & Schuster, 2009.

Foley, Edward F. *Ballot Battles: The History of Disputed Elections in the United States*. New York: Oxford University Press, 2016.

Foner, Eric. *Reconstruction: America's Unfinished Revolution, 1863–1877*. New York: Harper & Row, 1988.

Freidel, Frank, ed. *Union Pamphlets of the Civil War, 1861–1865*, Vols. 1 and 2. Cambridge, MA: Harvard University Press, 1967.

Furgurson, Ernest B. *Ashes of Glory: Richmond at War*. New York: Vintage, 1996.

———. *Freedom Rising: Washington in the Civil War*. New York: Vintage, 2004.

Garfield, James A. *The Works of James A. Garfield*, Vol. 1. Boston: James R. Osgood & Co., 1882.

Geary, James W. *We Need Men: The Union Draft in the Civil War*. DeKalb: Northern Illinois University Press, 1991.

George, Mary Karl. *Zachariah Chandler: A Political Biography*. East Lansing: Michigan State University Press, 1969.

Goodheart, Adam. *1861: The Civil War Awakening*. New York: Alfred A. Knopf, 2011.

Grant, Ulysses S. *Memoirs and Selected Letters*. Edited by Mary Drake McFeely and William S. McFeely. New York: Library of America, 1990.

Green, Michael S. *Freedom, Union and Power: Lincoln and His Party During the Civil War*. New York: Fordham University Press, 2004.

Grimsted, David. *American Mobbing, 1828–1861*. New York: Oxford University Press, 1998.

Guelzo, Allen C. *Fateful Awakening: A New History of the Civil War and Reconstruction*. New York: Oxford University Press, 2012.

Gugliotta, Guy. *The United States Capitol and the Coming of the Civil War*. New York: Hill & Wang, 2012.

Hall, A. D., ed. *Selections from the Works of Wendell Phillips*. Boston: Arthur D. Hall, 1902.

Hamlin, Charles Eugene. *The Life and Times of Hannibal Hamlin*. Cambridge, MA: The Riverside Press, 1899.

Harris, William C. *Lincoln and the Border States*. Lawrence: University Press of Kansas, 2011.

———. *Two Against Lincoln: Reverdy Johnson and Horatio Seymour, Champions of the Loyal Opposition*. Lawrence: University Press of Kansas, 2017.

Harrold, Stanley. *Lincoln and the Abolitionists*. Carbondale: Southern Illinois University Press, 2018.

Hartley, L. P. *The Go-Between*. New York: NYRB Classics, 2011.

Hatch, Louis Clinton. *Maine: A History*, Vol. 1. New York: The American Historical Society, 1919.

Holzer, Harold. *Lincoln and the Power of the Press: The War for Public Opinion*. New York: Simon & Schuster, 2014.

———. *Lincoln President-Elect: Abraham Lincoln and the Great Secession Winter, 1860–1861*. New York: Simon & Schuster, 2008.

———. ed. *Dear Mr. Lincoln: Letters to the President*. Reading, MA: Addison-Wesley, 1993.

Horowitz, Robert F. *The Great Impeacher: A Political Biography of James M. Ashley*. New York: Brooklyn College Press, 1979.

Howard, Hamilton Gay. *Civil War Echoes and Character Sketches*. Washington, D.C.: Howard Publishing Co., 1907.

Howe, Mark De Wolfe, ed. *Touched with Fire: Civil War Letters and Diary of Oliver Wendell Holmes, Jr.* New York: Fordham University Press, 2000.

Hubbell, John T., and James W. Geary, eds. *Biographical Dictionary of the Union: Northern Leaders of the Civil War*. Westport, CT: Greenwood Press, 1995.

Hunt, Harry Draper. *Hannibal Hamlin of Maine*. Syracuse, NY: Syracuse University Press, 1969.

Hurst, Jack. *Nathan Bedford Forrest: A Biography*. New York: Vintage, 1993.

Ilisevich, Robert D. *Galusha Grow: The People's Candidate*. Pittsburgh: University of Pittsburgh Press, 1988.

Jellison, Charles A. *Fessenden of Maine: Civil War Senator*. Syracuse, NY: Syracuse University Press, 1962.

Johannsen, Robert W. *Stephen A. Douglas*. Urbana: University of Illinois Press, 1997.

———, ed. *The Letters of Stephen A. Douglas*. Urbana: University of Illinois Press, 1961.

Julian, George Washington. *Political Recollections, 1840 to 1872*. Chicago: Johnson, McClurg & Co., 1884.

————. *Speeches on Political Questions.* Boston: Hurd & Houghton, 1872.

Keegan, John. *The American Civil War: A Military History.* New York: Vintage, 2009.

Klement, Frank L. *The Copperheads in the Middle West.* Chicago: University of Chicago Press, 1960.

————. *The Limits of Dissent: Clement L. Vallandigham and the Civil War.* New York: Fordham University Press, 1998.

Larson, Henrietta M. *Jay Cooke, Private Banker.* Cambridge, MA: Harvard University Press, 1936.

Lawson, Melinda. *Patriot Fires: Forging a New Nationalism in the Civil War North.* Lawrence: University Press of Kansas, 2002.

Leech, Margaret. *Reveille in Washington, 1860–1865.* New York: Harper & Bros., 1941.

Lindsey, David. *"Sunset" Cox: Irrepressible Democrat.* Detroit: Wayne State University Press, 1959.

Loewen, James W., and Edward H. Sebesta, eds. *The Confederate and Neo-Confederate Reader.* Jackson: University of Mississippi Press, 2010.

Long, David E. *The Jewel of Liberty: Abraham Lincoln's Re-election and the End of Slavery.* Mechanicsburg, PA: Stackpole, 2008.

Lowry, Thomas Power. *A Tourist Guide to Civil War Washington, DC.* Portland, OR: Idle Winter Press, 2017.

Mach, Thomas S. *"Gentleman George" Hunt Pendleton: Party Politics and Ideological Identity in Nineteenth-Century America.* Kent, OH: Kent State University Press, 2007.

Mahony, Dennis A. *The Four Acts of Despotism.* New York: Van Evrie, Horton & Co., 1863.

Manning, Chandra. *Troubled Refuge: Struggling for Freedom in the Civil War.* New York: Vintage, 2017.

Marshall, Jeffrey D., ed. *A War of the People: Vermont Civil War Letters.* Hanover, NH: University Press of New England, 1999.

Marshall, Jessie Ames, ed. *Private and Official Correspondence of Gen. Benjamin F. Butler During the Period of the Civil War.* Norwood, MA: Plimpton Press, 1917.

Marshall, John A. *American Bastille: A History of Illegal Arrests and Imprisonment of American Citizens During the Late Civil War.* Philadelphia: Thomas W. Hartley, 1871.

Martin, Thomas Ricaud. *The Great Parliamentary Battle and Farewell Addresses of the Southern Senators on the Eve of the Civil War.* New York: Neale Publishing Company, 1905.

Marvel, William. *Lincoln's Autocrat: The Life of Edwin Stanton.* Chapel Hill: University of North Carolina Press, 2015.

Matsui, John H. *The First Republican Army: The Army of Virginia and the Radicalization of the Civil War.* Charlottesville: University of Virginia Press, 2016.

Mayer, Henry. *All on Fire: William Lloyd Garrison and the Abolition of Slavery.* New York: St. Martin's, 1998.

McClure, Alexander K. *Abraham Lincoln and Men of War-Times.* Lincoln: University of Nebraska Press, 1996.

McGinty, Brian. *The Body of John Merryman: Abraham Lincoln and the Suspension of Habeas Corpus.* Cambridge, MA: Harvard University Press, 2011.

McKay, Ernest A. *The Civil War and New York City*. Syracuse, NY: Syracuse University Press, 1990.

McPherson, James M. *Tried by War: Abraham Lincoln as Commander in Chief*. New York: Penguin, 2009.

———. *The Negro's Civil War: How American Blacks Felt and Acted During the War for the Union*. New York: Vintage, 2003.

Medbery, James K. *Men and Mysteries of Wall Street*. Boston: Fields, Osgood & Co., 1870.

Medlar, Carole Rauch. *The Gentleman and the Artist: A Journal of D. L. Medlar, September 1, 1859–April 30, 1862*. Dayton, OH: Dayton Metro Library, 2007.

Meyer, Howard N., ed. *The Magnificent Activist: The Writings of Thomas Wentworth Higginson*. New York: Da Capo, 2000.

Morgan, James A., III. *A Little Short of Boats: The Battles of Ball's Bluff & Edwards Ferry*. New York: Savas Beatie, 2011.

Murray, Williamson, and Wayne Wei-Siang Hsieh. *A Savage War: A Military History of the Civil War*. Princeton, NJ: Princeton University Press, 2016.

Myers, John L. *Senator Henry Wilson and the Civil War*. Lanham, MD: University Press of America, 2008.

Neely, Mark E., Jr. *The Fate of Liberty: Abraham Lincoln and Civil Liberties*. New York: Oxford University Press, 1991.

———. *Lincoln and the Democrats: The Politics of Opposition in the Civil War*. New York: Cambridge University Press, 2017.

Nicolay, Helen. *Our Capital on the Potomac*. New York: The Century Co., 1924.

Nicolay, John G., and John Hay. *Abraham Lincoln: A History*. New York: The Century Co., 1914.

Niven, John, ed. *The Salmon P. Chase Papers*, Vols. 3 and 4. Kent, OH: Kent State University Press, 1996.

Nolan, Dick. *Benjamin Franklin Butler: The Damnedest Yankee*. Novato, CA: Presidio Press, 1991.

Nye, Russell B. *Fettered Freedom: Civil Liberties and the Slavery Controversy*. East Lansing: Michigan State College Press, 1949.

Oakes, James. *Freedom National: The Destruction of Slavery in the United States, 1861–1865*. New York: W. W. Norton, 2014.

Oberholtzer, Ellis Paxson. *Jay Cooke: Financier of the Civil War*, Vol. 1. Philadelphia: George W. Jacobs & Co., 1907.

Palmer, Beverly Wilson, ed. *The Selected Letters of Charles Sumner*, Vol. 2. Boston: Northeastern University Press, 1990.

———, and Holly Byers Ochoa, eds. *The Selected Papers of Thaddeus Stevens*, Vols. 1 and 2. Pittsburgh: University of Pittsburgh Press, 1997.

Parrish, William E. *Frank Blair: Lincoln's Conservative*. Columbia: University of Missouri Press, 1998.

Pierce, Edward Lillie, and Charles Sumner. *Memoir and Letters of Charles Sumner*, Vol. 4. Memphis: General Books, 2012.

Poore, Ben Perley. *The Life and Public Services of Ambrose E. Burnside*. Providence, RI: J. A. and R. A. Reid, 1882.

———. *Perley's Reminiscences of Sixty Years in the National Metropolis*, Vols. 1 and 2. Philadelphia: Hubbard Bros., 1886.

Porter, George H. *Ohio Politics During the Civil War Period*. New York: Columbia University Press, 1911.

Potts, William D. *Freemen's Guide to the Polls: And a Solemn Appeal to American Patriots*. New York: 1864.

Randall, James G. *Constitutional Problems Under Lincoln*. New York: D. Appleton & Co., 1926.

Rawley, James A. *The Politics of Union: Northern Politics During the Civil War*. Lincoln: University of Nebraska Press, 1971.

Richards, Leonard L. *Who Freed the Slaves?: The Fight over the Thirteenth Amendment*. Chicago: University of Chicago Press, 2015.

Richardson, Heather Cox. *The Greatest Nation of the Earth: Republican Economic Policies During the Civil War*. Cambridge, MA: Harvard University Press, 1997.

Riddle, Albert Gallatin. *The Life of Benjamin F. Wade*. Cleveland: William W. Williams, 1887.

————. *Recollections of War-Times*. New York: G. P. Putnam's Sons, 1895.

Roske, Ralph J. *His Own Counsel: The Life and Times of Lyman Trumbull*. Reno: University of Nevada Press, 1979.

Russell, William H. *My Diary North and South*. New York: Harper & Bros., 1863.

Schecter, Barnet. *The Devil's Own Work: The Civil War Draft Riots and the Fight to Reconstruct America*. New York: Walker, 2005.

Schurz, Carl. *Report on Condition of the South 1865*. New York: Arno Press, 1969.

Sears, Stephen W. *George B. McClellan: The Young Napoleon*. New York: Da Capo, 1999.

————. *Lincoln's Lieutenants: The High Command of the Army of the Potomac*. New York: Houghton Mifflin Harcourt, 2017.

————, ed. *The Civil War Papers of George B. McClellan: Selected Correspondence, 1860–1865*. New York: Ticknor & Fields, 1989.

Sheehan-Dean, Aaron, ed. *The Civil War: The Final Year Told by Those Who Lived It*. New York: Library of America, 2014.

Sherman, John. *Recollections of Forty Years in the House, Senate and Cabinet*, Vol. 1. Chicago: The Werner Company, 1895.

Sherman, William T. *Memoirs*. New York: Library of America, 1990.

Shuckers, Jacob W. *The Life and Public Services of Salmon Portland Chase*. New York: D. Appleton & Co., 1874.

Silbey, Joel H. *A Respectable Minority: The Democratic Party in the Civil War Era, 1860–1868*. New York: W. W. Norton, 1977.

Simpson, Brooks D., and Jean V. Berlin, eds. *Sherman's Civil War: Selected Correspondence of William T. Sherman, 1860–1865*. Chapel Hill: University of North Carolina Press, 1999.

Smith, Henry Nash. *Virgin Land: The American West as Symbol and Myth*. Cambridge, MA: Harvard University Press, 1950.

Smith, Theodore Clarke. *The Life and Letters of James Abram Garfield*, Vol. 1. New Haven, CT: Yale University Press, 1925.

Spaulding, Elbridge Gerry. *History of the Legal Tender Paper Money Issued During the Great Rebellion*. Buffalo, NY: Express Printing Co., 1869.

Stahr, Walter. *Seward: Lincoln's Indispensable Man*. New York: Simon & Schuster, 2012.

————. *Stanton: Lincoln's War Secretary.* New York: Simon & Schuster, 2017.

Stampp, Kenneth M. *Indiana Politics during the Civil War.* Indianapolis: Indiana Historical Bureau, 1949.

Starr, Louis M. *Bohemian Brigade: Civil War Newsmen in Action.* Madison: University of Wisconsin Press, 1987.

Stashower, Daniel. *The Hour of Peril: The Secret Plot to Murder Lincoln before the Civil War.* New York: Minotaur, 2013.

*Statutes at Large, Treaties and Proclamations of the United States of America,* Vol. 12. Thirty-seventh Congress, www.loc.gov/law/help/statutes-at-large.

Stevens, Thaddeus, et al. *Report of the Joint Committee on Reconstruction.* Washington, D.C.: Government Printing Office, 1866.

Stewart, David O. *Impeached: The Trial of Andrew Johnson and the Fight for Lincoln's Legacy.* New York: Simon & Schuster, 2009.

Stiles, T. J. *Custer's Trials: A Life on the Frontier of a New America.* New York: Vintage, 2015.

Stormont, Gilbert, ed. *Hight's History of the 58th Indiana Volunteer Regiment.* Princeton, IN: Press of the Clarion, 1895.

Strausbaugh, John. *City of Sedition: The History of New York City during the Civil War.* New York: Twelve, 2016.

Strong, George Templeton. *The Diary of George Templeton Strong: The Civil War, 1860–1865.* New York: Macmillan, 1952.

Tap, Bruce. *The Fort Pillow Massacre: North, South and the Status of African-Americans in the Civil War.* New York: Routledge, 2014.

————. *Over Lincoln's Shoulder: The Committee on the Conduct of the War.* Lawrence: University Press of Kansas, 1998.

Taylor, Frank H. *Philadelphia in the Civil War, 1861–1865.* Philadelphia: City of Philadelphia, 1913.

Thayer, William Roscoe, ed. *The Life and Letters of John Hay,* Vol. 1. Boston: Houghton Mifflin, 1915.

Thorndike, Rachel Sherman, ed. *The Sherman Letters: 50 Years of American History.* New York: Charles Scribner's Sons, 1894.

Towne, Stephen E. *Surveillance and Spies in the Civil War: Exposing Confederate Conspiracies in America's Heartland.* Athens: Ohio University Press, 2015.

Trefousse, Hans L. *Benjamin Franklin Wade: Radical Republican from Ohio.* New York: Twayne, 1963.

————. *Thaddeus Stevens: Nineteenth-Century Egalitarian.* Chapel Hill: University of North Carolina Press, 1997.

————. *Andrew Johnson.* New York: W. W. Norton & Co., 1989.

Vallandigham, Clement L. *The Record of Hon. C. L. Vallandigham on Abolition, the Union and the Civil War.* Cincinnati: J. Walter & Co., 1863.

Vallandigham, James L. *A Life of Clement L. Vallandigham.* Baltimore: Turnbull Bros., 1872.

Wade, Benjamin F., et al. *Report of the Joint Committee on the Conduct of the War,* Parts 1, 2, and 3. Washington, D.C.: Government Printing Office, 1863.

————, et al. *Fort Pillow Massacre: Report of the Joint Committee on the Conduct of the War.* Washington, D.C.: Government Printing Office, 1864.

———, et al. *Returned Prisoners: Report of the Joint Committee on the Conduct of the War.* Washington, D.C.: Government Printing Office, 1864.

———, et al. *Report of the Joint Committee on the Conduct of the War, at the Second Session of the Thirty-eighth Congress.* Washington, D.C.: Government Printing Office, 1865.

———, et al. *Supplemental Report of the Joint Committee on the Conduct othe War.* Washington, D.C.: Government Printing Office, 1866.

Wakelyn, Jon L., ed. *Southern Pamphlets on Secession, November 1860–April 1861.* Chapel Hill: University of North Carolina Press, 1996.

*The War othe Rebellion: A Compilation othe Official Records of the Union and Confederate Armies.* Washington, D.C.: Government Printing Office, 1880–1901.

Waugh, John C. *Reelecting Lincoln.* New York: Da Capo, 2001.

Weber, Jennifer L. *Copperheads: The Rise and Fall of Lincoln's Opponents in the North.* New York: Oxford University Press, 2006.

Weber, Thomas. *The Northern Railroads in the Civil War, 1861–1865.* Bloomington: Indiana University Press, 1952.

Weisberger, Bernard A. *Reporters for the Union.* Boston: Little, Brown, 1953.

Welch, June Rayfield. *The Texas Senator.* Dallas: G.L.A. Press, 1978.

Welles, Gideon. *Diary of Gideon Welles, Secretary of the Navy under Lincoln and Johnson,* Vols. 1 and 2. Boston: Houghton Mifflin Co., 1911.

White, Richard. *"It's Your Misfortune and None of My Own": A New History of the American West.* Norman: University of Oklahoma Press, 1991.

———. *Railroaded: The Transcontinentals and the Making of Modern America.* New York: W. W. Norton, 2011.

Whiting, William. *War Powers of the President; Military Arrests in Time of War; Return of Rebellious States.* Boston: John L. Shorey, 1864.

Whitman, Walt. *Prose Works.* Philadelphia: David McKay, 1892.

Wilson, Mark R. *The Business of Civil War: Military Mobilization and the State, 1861–1865.* Baltimore: Johns Hopkins University Press, 2006.

Winkle, Kenneth J. *Lincoln's Citadel: The Civil War in Washington, DC.* New York: W. W. Norton, 2013.

Wood, Forrest G. *Black Scare: The Racist Response to Emancipation and Reconstruction.* Berkeley: University of California Press, 1970.

Woodbury, Augustus. *Major General Ambrose E. Burnside and the Ninth Army Corps.* Providence, RI: Sidney S. Rider & Bros., 1867.

## ARTICLES, PAMPHLETS, BROADSIDES, THESES, AND OTHER SOURCES

Abzug, Robert H. "The Copperheads: Historical Approaches to Civil War Dissent in the Midwest." *Indiana Magazine of History* 66 (March 1970).

"Addresses delivered in the Unitarian church, Ann Arbor, Michigan, January 10, 1897, at service in commemoration of the lives and public services of Hon. James M. Ashley and Hon. Alpheus Felch." Anonymous pamphlet. University of Michigan University Library digital collections, www.lib.umich.edu.

Arthur, Roger William. "The 'Copperhead' Vallandigham: Civil War, Civil Rights, and the Constitutional Conundrum." Master's thesis, West Chester University of Pennsylvania, 2003.

Baker, Jean H. "A Loyal Opposition: Northern Democrats in the Thirty-seventh Congress." *Civil War History* 25 (June 1979).

Barber, James B. "Alexandria in the Civil War." Master's thesis, Virginia Polytechnic Institute, 1977. Library of George Washington's Mount Vernon.

Becker, Carl M. "Disloyalty and the Dayton Public Schools." *Civil War History* 1 (March 1965).

Belz, Herman. "The Etheridge Conspiracy of 1863: A Projected Conservative Coup." *Journal of Southern History* 36 (November 1970).

Bickers, John M. "The Power to Do What Manifestly Must Be Done: Congress, the Freedmen's Bureau, and Constitutional Imagination." *Roger Williams University Law Review* 12 (Fall 2006).

"Biographical Sketch of Hon. Lazarus W. Powell, Governor of the State of Kentucky and a Senator in Congress." Anonymous pamphlet. Frankfort: Kentucky Yeoman Office, 1868.

Blair, Montgomery. "On the Revolutionary Schemes of the Ultra Abolitionists." Pamphlet, 1863.

Buckman, Christine, Christy DeButts, and Tom Fox. "The Journal of Chalkley Gillingham: Friend in the Midst of Civil War." Pamphlet. Publication of the Alexandria Monthly Friends Meeting (undated). Library of George Washington's Mount Vernon.

"Copperhead Conspiracy in the North-West: An Expose of the Treasonable Order of the 'Sons of Liberty.'" Anonymous pamphlet. New York: Union Congressional Committee, 1864.

Crofts, David W. "No Better Southern Man." *New York Times,* "Opinionator," January 22, 2011.

Davis, Damani. "Slavery and Emancipation in the Nation's Capital." *Prologue Magazine* 42 (Spring 2010).

Davis, William C. "John C. Breckinridge." *The Register of the Kentucky Historical Society* 85 (Summer 1987).

"Decision of Judge Leavitt of Ohio, in the Vallandigham Habeas Corpus Case." Anonymous pamphlet. Philadelphia, 1863.

Foner, Eric. "Thaddeus Stevens and the Imperfect Republic." *Pennsylvania History* 60 (April 1993).

"The Great Conspiracy." Anonymous pamphlet. Albany: Weed, Parsons & Co., 1864.

Hawthorne, Nathaniel. "Chiefly About War Matters." *Atlantic Monthly,* July 1862.

Heck, Frank H. "John C. Breckinridge in the Crisis of 1860–1861." *The Journal of Southern History* 21, no. 3 (August 1955).

Heiges, George L. "1860—The Year Before the War." Pamphlet. Lancaster: Lancaster County Historical Society, 1961.

Hendrickson, Ed. "Defending Washington: The District of Columbia Militia, 1861." *Washington History* 23 (2011).

Klement, Frank L. "Vallandigham as an Exile in Canada 1863–1864." *Ohio History* 74 (Summer 1965).

Landis, Charles I. "Thaddeus Stevens: A Letter Written to the *Daily New Era*, Lancaster, PA." Pamphlet. Lancaster, PA: New Era Press, 1916.

Lepore, Jill. "The Fireman." *The New Yorker*, February 18, 2019.

Lord, W. C. "Young Louis Wigfall: South Carolina Politician and Duelist." *The South Carolina Historical Magazine* 59 (April 1958).

Marvel, William. "Soldiers of Misfortune." *Civil War Monitor* 8 (Summer 2018).

"Miscegenation: The Theory of the Blending of the Races, Applied to the American White Man and Negro." Anonymous pamphlet. New York: H. Dexter, Hamilton & Co., 1864.

Morse, Samuel F. B. "An Argument on the Ethical Position of Slavery in the Social System and Its Relation to the Politics of the Day." Pamphlet. New York: Papers from the Society for the Diffusion of Political Knowledge, 1863.

Neely, Mark E., Jr. "The Lincoln Administration and Arbitrary Arrests: A Reconsideration." *The Journal of the Abraham Lincoln Association* 5 (1983).

O'Connor, John R. "John Cabell Breckinridge's Personal Secession: A Rhetorical Insight." *The Filson Club History Quarterly* 43 (October 1969).

"Pomeroy Circular." Broadside. New York: Union Lincoln Association, February 20, 1864.

Presidential "Proclamation of Amnesty and Reconstruction." December 8, 1863, www.freedmen.umd.edu/pracamn.htm.

Randall, James G. "The Indemnity Act of 1863: A Study in the War-Time Immunity of Government Officers." *Michigan Law Review* 20 (April 1922).

"The Real Chicago Platform as Expounded by the Democratic Orators at Chicago." Broadside, 1864.

"Resolutions Introduced to the Legislature of the State of Connecticut by Hon. Wm. W. Eaton." Anonymous pamphlet. Hartford: Young Men's National Democratic Association, 1863.

Roberts, Blair, and Kytle, Ethan F. "When the Abolitionists Went to Charleston." *Civil War Monitor* 8 (Winter 2018).

Ron, Ariel. "Summoning the State: Northern Farmers and the Transformation of American Politics in the Mid-nineteenth Century." *Journal of American History* 103 (September 2016).

Roseboom, Eugene H. "Southern Ohio and the Union in 1863." *Mississippi Valley Historical Review* 39 (June 1952).

Sellery, George Clarke. "Lincoln's Suspension of *Habeas Corpus* as Viewed by Congress." Diss., University of Wisconsin, 1907.

"The Senate's War." Anonymous pamphlet. Benjamin F. Wade File, Office of the U.S. Senate Historian.

Shankman, Arnold. "Vallandigham's Arrest and the 1863 Dayton Riot: Two Letters." *Ohio History Journal* 79 (Spring 1970).

———. "Vallandigham's Supporters." Typescript. Vallandigham Collection, Dayton Metro Library.

Silkenat, David. "I Surrender!" *Civil War Monitor* (Fall 2017).

Smock, Raymond. "Search for the Political Legacy of Thaddeus Stevens." *Pennsylvania History* 60 (April 1993).

"Song of the First of Arkansas." Broadside. Supervisory Committee for Recruiting Colored Regiments, 1864.

"Speech of Mr. Pugh to 50,000 Voters Who Nominated Vallandigham." Anonymous pamphlet. Papers from the Society for the Diffusion of Political Knowledge, no. 9. Vallandigham Collection, OHS.

Starr, Stephen Z. "Camp Dennison, 1861–1865." *Bulletin of the Historical and Philosophical Society of Ohio* 19 (July 1961).

"State Convention of War Democrats." [Ohio], 1863. Anonymous pamphlet.

Sumner, Charles. "Our Domestic Relations: Or, How to Treat the Rebel States." *Atlantic Monthly,* October 1863.

Taylor, Alan. "The Virtue of an Educated Voter." *The American Scholar,* September 2016.

Thompson, David K. "'Like a Cord Through the Whole Country': Union Bonds and Financial Mobilization for Victory." *Journal of the Civil War Era* 6 (September 2016).

Trefousse, Hans L. "Zachariah Chandler and the Withdrawal of Fremont in 1864." *Lincoln Herald* 70 (Winter 1968).

"The Truth from an Honest Man: The Letter of the President." Anonymous pamphlet. Philadelphia: King & Baird, 1863.

"The Use of the Term 'Copperhead' During the Civil War." *Mississippi Valley Historical Review* 25 (June 1938).

"The Vallandigham Song Book." Anonymous pamphlet. Columbus, OH: J. Walter & Co., 1863.

Vallandigham, Clement L. "Address to the Democrats of Ohio." Pamphlet. Vallandigham Collection, OHS.

"Vallandigham's Record Reviewed: A Political Traitor Unmasked. Speech by Hon. John Sherman." Pamphlet. Vallandigham Collection, Dayton Metro Library.

Williams, Harry. "The Attack upon West Point During the Civil War." *Mississippi Valley Historical Review* 25 (June 1938).

———. "Benjamin F. Wade and the Atrocity Propaganda of the Civil War." *The Ohio State Archaeological and Historical Quarterly* 48 (January 1939).

Zietlow, Rebecca E. "James Ashley's Thirteenth Amendment." *Columbia Law Review* 112 (November 2012).

Zornow, William Frank. "Clement L. Vallandigham and the Democratic Party in 1864." *Bulletin of the Historical and Philosophical Society of Ohio* (January 1961).

## MANUSCRIPT COLLECTIONS

Ball Family Collection, SCHS

Zachariah Chandler Papers, LOC

Salmon P. Chase Collection, HSP

Jay Cooke Papers, HSP

Henry L. Dawes Papers, LOC

William Dennison Papers, OHS

William P. Fessenden Papers, LOC

Fessenden Papers, BCL

Gilman Papers, SCHS

Governors' Papers, OHS

Elwood Griest Papers, LH

William Kelley Papers, HSP
Abraham Lincoln Papers, LOC
Paige Family Papers, Silver Special Collections Library, UVT
Beverly W. Palmer Papers, LH
Remey Family Papers, LOC
Theodore Roosevelt Papers, LOC
Thaddeus Stevens Papers, LH
Trenholm Papers, SCHS
Vallandigham Collection, DHS
Vallandigham Collection, OHS
Benjamin F. Wade Papers, LOC
Benjamin Wade Collection, OHS
H. Pinckney Walker Papers, SCHS
John H. Wheeler Papers, LOC
Wood Papers, Dayton Metro Library

## NEWSPAPERS

*Buffalo Evening Courier and Republic*
*Charleston Mercury*
*Chicago Tribune*
*The Christian Recorder*
*Cincinnati Daily Gazette*
*Cincinnati Inquirer*
*Cleveland Daily Leader*
*The Crisis*
*Daily Alta California*
*Daily News of Philadelphia*
*Dayton Daily Empire*
*Douglass' Monthly*
*La Crosse Daily Democrat*
*Lancaster Daily Evening Express*
*Lancaster Daily Express*
*Lancaster Examiner and Herald*
*Lancaster Intelligencer*
*National Anti-Slavery Standard*
*New York Herald*
*New York Times*
*New York Tribune*
*New York World*
*Philadelphia Press*
*Washington Evening Star*
*Washington Post*

# INDEX

abolitionism, abolitionists, xvii, 6, 12,
  14, 15, 18, 23, 32, 39, 66–67, 77, 80,
  91, 101, 110, 139, 145, 156, 157, 188,
  198, 287
  constitutional amendment
    abolishing slavery, see Thirteenth
    Amendment
  Declaration of Independence
    and, 15
  Frémont and, 99
  fugitive slaves and, 83
  Lincoln and, 39, 147, 195–96
  Republican Party's official embrace
    of, 289
  Vallandigham on, 173–74
  see also emancipation
Adams, Charles Francis, 14, 41
Adams, John, xviii
Adams, John Quincy, 14
African Americans, 254
  "black laws" and black codes, 84,
    335, 354
  citizenship for, 341, 343
  Civil Rights Act and, 357
  civil rights movement and, 368
  deportation proposals for, 84, 113–14,
    140, 167–68, 196, 278
  elected to public office, 367
  freedmen, 111, 113–14, 273–75, 277,
    293, 343, 354, 355, 370
  Freedmen's Bureau for, 274–75,
    293–94, 344–46, 357, 359, 367
  integration of, 84

Jim Crow era and, 367
miscegenation hoax and, 320–21
postwar violence against, 354
rights for, 103, 154, 272, 342–43, 357,
  364
slaves, see slaves
suffrage for, 84, 335, 341–43, 350–51,
  356–59
African American soldiers, xv, xvii, 67,
  86, 139–40, 157–58, 167, 188, 203–4,
  214–15, 219, 238–41, 254–56, 265–67,
  275, 293, 317, 324, 349, 352, 369, 371
  Confederacy's view as slaves in
    rebellion, 239
  in Crater battle, 303
  draft and, 239
  at Fort Pillow, 270–73, 293
  Grant on, 240–41
  Lincoln on, 241
  pay for, 255–56, 266–67, 293
  racism and, 84–85, 169–70, 203, 238,
    240, 241, 254, 265–66, 272
  Sherman on, 240, 265–66
  Stevens on, 158, 203–4
  suffrage for, 341
Agriculture, Department of, 130–31,
  135–37
Alabama, 4
Alabama, CSS, 301
American Anti-Slavery Society, 343–44
American Colonization Society, 114
Anderson, Robert, 7, 10, 41, 48–52, 352
Andrew, John, 105–6, 203

A NOTE ON THE TYPE

This book was set in Monotype Dante, a typeface designed
by Giovanni Mardersteig (1892–1977). Modeled on the Aldine
type used for Pietro Cardinal Bembo's treatise De Aetna in
1495, Dante is a modern interpretation of the venerable face.

Composed by North Market Street Graphics,
Lancaster, Pennsylvania

Printed and bound by Berryville Graphics,
Berryville, Virginia

Designed by Anna B. Knighton